MAYHEM AND MURDER: NARRATIVE AND MORAL PROBLEMS IN THE DETECTIVE STORY

The detective story centres on unravelling two questions: whodunit? and who is guilty? In *Mayhem and Murder*, Heta Pyrhönen examines how these questions organize and pattern the genre's formal and thematic structures. Beginning with a semiotic reading of the detective as both code-breaker and sign-reader, Pyrhönen's theoretical analysis then situates the reader and the detective in parallel worlds – both use the detective genre's typical motifs in solving the crime, but do not employ the same narrative interpretations to do so. This difference is examined with the help of the familiar game analogy: while the fictional world of the criminal functions as the detective's antagonist, readers see both the detective and the criminal as the fictional masks behind which their own adversary, the author, is hiding. The reading of detective stories as complex interpretative games reveals how the genre engages the reader's formal imagination and moral judgment.

Discussing a range of detective stories from works by Conan Doyle and Chesterton to Borges and Rendell, and drawing on the work of major critics – including Dennis Porter, Umberto Eco, John T. Irwin, and Slavoj Žižek – Pyrhönen offers a unique, sophisticated, and engagingly lucid analysis of a complex genre.

HETA PYRHÖNEN is Associate Professor, Department of Comparative Literature, University of Helsinki.

D0911679

HETA PYRHÖNEN

Mayhem and Murder: Narrative and Moral Problems in the Detective Story

UNIVERSITY OF TORONTO PRESS
Toronto Buffalo London

© University of Toronto Press Incorporated 1999
Toronto Buffalo London
Printed in Canada

ISBN 0-8020-4489-1 (cloth)
ISBN 0-8020-8267-X (paper)

Printed on acid-free paper

Toronto Studies in Semiotics
Editors: Marcel Danesi, Umberto Eco, Paul Perron, and Thomas A. Sebeok

Canadian Cataloguing in Publication Data

Pyrhonen, Heta
    Mayhem and murder : narrative and moral problems in the detective story

(Toronto studies in semiotics)
Includes bibliographical references and index.
ISBN 0-8020-4489-1 (bound)   ISBN 0-8020-8267-X (pbk.)

1. Detective and mystery stories – History and criticism.   2. Semiotics and
literature.   I. Title.   II. Series

PN3448.D4P973 1999   809.3'872'014   C99-930697-9

University of Toronto Press acknowledges the financial assistance to its
publishing program of the Canada Council for the Arts and the Ontario
Arts Council.

University of Toronto Press acknowledges the financial support for its
publishing activities of the Government of Canada through the Book
Publishing Industry Development Program (BPIDP).
Canadä

Contents

Acknowledgments

From its beginning, the writing of this study has been a transatlantic project. I am greatly indebted to Linda Hutcheon (University of Toronto) for helping me in many ways over the years and for making Toronto feel like a second home. Her careful reading of this work has certainly improved it; the lively and charming manner in which she expresses her comments makes working with her a great pleasure. I am equally indebted to Patricia Merivale (University of British Columbia), whose expertise in both the low and high forms of detective fiction far surpasses mine. Her critical comments, spiced with her wonderful sense of humour, have greatly helped me clarify my own thoughts. In the final stage of revision I benefited from the perceptive suggestions of Susan Elizabeth Sweeney (Holy Cross College) concerning a number of contextual and organizational issues.

This study was largely written while I was a member of the School of Literary and Textual Theory. I wish to express my gratitude to Pekka Tammi (University of Tampere) and Hannu Riikonen (University of Helsinki) for their productive feedback on various drafts. I would also like to thank Michael Holquist (Yale University) for his insightful comments on chapter 2 and warm encouragement; Sheldon Brivic (Temple University) for drawing my attention to the difference between irony and cynicism; and Peter J. Rabinowitz (Hamilton College) for his useful suggestions for improving the whole manuscript. I am grateful to Patricia Eberle (University of Toronto) for the time she set aside to talk about this project with me and to Professor Emeritus Aarne Kinnunen for the interest he took in its progress. I appreciate the kind help Teemu Ikonen offered on various psychoanalytical issues. Warm thanks also go to Dr Mark Shackleton (University of Helsinki), who streamlined my English, and to Ron Schoeffel, Barb Porter, and Margaret Allen at the University of Toronto Press for their editorial expertise.

I gratefully acknowledge the financial aid of the Emil Aaltmen Foundation and the School of Literary and Textual Theory during the writing of this study.

I dedicate this study to my spouse, Markku Ollikainen, who has tirelessly listened to me talk about mayhem and murder. From someone who does not particularly like detective stories this certainly is an expression of love, and one which I value above all.

MAYHEM AND MURDER

Introduction

Have you ever caught yourself reading? You know, you are sitting in a chair engrossed in a good book, enjoying the story and the author's prose-style, and then suddenly, it's as if you have an out-of-the-body experience and you catch sight of yourself as you really are: not trading wisecracks with Philip Marlowe, or struggling with Moriarty atop the Reichenbach Falls, but as someone sitting alone in a room, with a book open on your lap. (Kerr 1995, 177)

In Philip Kerr's *A Philosophical Investigation* (1995), a serial killer keeps a journal of his murders. He poses this question about reading to the reader he imagines one day perusing his diary. He regards reading as a self-reflexíve activity that not only transports readers into a fictional world but also makes them aware of reading itself. For him, this 'rare ability to step in or out of the picture' (177) distinguishes reading. His choice of examples is interesting, for the detective-story authors he refers to – Arthur Conan Doyle and Raymond Chandler – are often cited to support the opposite view of readers as passive consumers of the genre. Thus, for example, Dennis Porter's excellent book *The Pursuit of Crime: Art and Ideology in Detective Fiction* (1981) defines the detective story as a textual 'machine for producing thrills' (108) that evokes in readers pleasurable bodily sensations which they experience as an agreeable state of excitement, associated with either fear or anxiety, and its release (109). Porter analyses the various strategies detective fiction employs in order to promote pleasure, arguing that the pleasure largely derives from the fact that reading is made not only easy and readily intelligible but also inoffensive as regards social and moral values.

The genre's readability is grounded in a relationship of complicity between authors and readers that resembles a game played according to a set of rules (ibid., 85). The 'fundamental formal rule' in this set, Porter maintains, is embodied in the familiar question 'Whodunit?' and the investigation it provokes, which structures the whole detective narrative. This action sequence encompasses all others, as it opens with the mystery of crime and closes with its solution. The question of 'whodunit' also patterns reading by transforming it into the search for an answer, as the reader, desirous of knowing the outcome, gathers and discards clues (ibid., 86). But Porter's formulation of the 'fundamental formal rule' is incomplete, for in detective fiction the reconstruction of the past includes the analysis of the causal network, made up of human interaction, that leads to crime. As answering the question of 'whodunit' involves putting together a coherent explanation of what happened, this narrative invariably touches on questions of guilt and responsibility. The detective's solving of the crime thus has a marked moral dimension, engaging the reader in moral evaluation as well. Hence there are, in actual fact, *two* generic questions that orient and structure each and any detective narrative: the question 'Whodunit?' is paired with the question 'Who is guilty?'

While Porter's approach conforms to and reinforces standard notions about the typical reading strategies of popular fiction, it disregards the way the genre itself represents reading. The genre repeatedly emphasizes the complexity and difficulty, verging on the impossibility, of unravelling a crime. A character in *A Philosophical Investigation* expresses this idea by pointing out that 'whereas the commission of crime is natural, the task of the detective, like that of the philosopher, is counter-natural, involving the critical analysis of various presuppositions and beliefs, and the questioning of certain assumptions and perceptions. For example, you will seek to test an alibi just as I will aim to test a proposition. It's the same thing, and it involves a quest for clarity ... there exists the common intention of wresting form away from the god of Muddle' (184). This stress on difficulty and complexity suggests another kind of pleasure which Porter downplays: the pleasure of ratiocination and mental agility.

In this book, I take as my starting point the 'fundamental formal rule' of detective fiction, that is, the structuring force of the two (instead of one) generic questions 'Whodunit?' and 'Who is guilty?' The question that I study is this: How do these two generic questions organize and pattern the detective narrative? The terms 'organization' and 'patterning' refer to those formal *and* thematic structures that these two generic questions typically generate. My topic thus partly converges with Porter's, for he too scrutinizes in detail the genre's formal structures in order to theorize about pleasurable reading, though the context of my examination diverges from his. This difference arises from our respective attitudes towards the sort of self-reflexive musings about the genre's various narrative conventions, and the activities of writing and reading it, exemplified in the two excerpts from Kerr's book. Such deliberations are very typical of the genre. Porter considers them as so many familiar devices strengthening the generic reading contract and facilitating consumption (see his chapter 4). I will, in contrast, interpret them as 'self-focusing appeals' (Eco 1990, 54–5) to the reader to ponder the formal and thematic issues raised by the genre. In effect, I argue that they add a self-conscious dimension to reading.

In order to focus my discussion, I concentrate on the detective: the agent who makes the formal and thematic patterning force of the two generic questions available. Detectives have this function because their work is oriented by the attempt to identify the criminal and to assign guilt. As characters who provide answers to the mystery of crime posed at the beginning, detectives are portrayed in the genre as textually embedded *model readers* whose readerly and interpretive activities mirror the reader's own activity. Therefore, studying the organizing and patterning force of the two generic questions means, in this study, analysing the investigative process of the detective. Given this character's status as a model reader, such an examination will inevitably lead to an analysis of how the representation of the detective's reading affects the reader's own reading process.

The detective's function as a model reader emerges once we realize that the enmity between criminals and detectives largely consists of a series of entangled writing and reading 'contests' triggered by a crime. Indeed, we may say that the detective narrative is about writing and deciphering plots (Hühn 1987). Detective-fiction criminals are artists who 'write' their stories of crime in such a way that the stories are partly hidden, partly distorted, and entirely misleading. By manipulating the clues to a crime, the criminals attempt to convey a sense of a coherent, yet false, sequence of events which is at odds with what really is the case. Thus they 'author' at least two stories about the crime: the authentic one and the false one(s). By making things 'strange,' crime endows the fictional world with a rich potentiality of unsuspected meanings, transforming the world of the novel into a conglomeration of potential signs (ibid., 454). Since the detective must decipher the limits of the criminal's text, the set of signs constituting it, and the code in which this text is written, his or her activities are the same as those of a reader. While 'reading' the clues to a crime, detectives present these activities in such a manner that they, too, 'author' a text – the story of detection – the purpose of which is to uncover the criminal and substitute for the criminal's text their own version of the events (ibid., 457).

The analogue between detectives and readers becomes apparent when we think of the genre's structures of narration. Usually, neither the stories of crime written by criminals nor the texts of detection written by detectives are directly attainable by readers of detective fiction. Instead, the stories are narrated by uncomprehending 'Watson' figures and narrators who deliberately keep back crucial pieces of information. Readers encounter the same situation as detectives do: an enigmatic signifying surface whose meaning they attempt to find out by reading. Detective-story authors have a double status: they are both deceivers and undeceivers, for they have tied the knot so that they may also stage an investigation which unties it. Hence, in certain ways authors are analogous to criminals and readers to detectives, for one is responsible for the problem, seeking not to get caught, while the other is desirous of the solution, pursuing it through the text (Bennett 1979, 238). Authors use various strategies when omitting important information at strategic points in the plot: devices of fragmenting information and presenting it in an ambiguous manner, techniques of highlighting insignificant-seeming details and using the detective to safeguard the solution to the mystery. Author, detective, and text thus all play a dual role: ostensibly their purpose is to enlighten readers; in fact, much of the time all three aim at delaying their understanding (ibid., 239).

This notion of the detective as a model reader suggests that readers imaginatively adopt the detective's role: they 'play detective' in order to reflect on what they themselves do as they read detective stories. What sets my study apart from previous ones is that I consistently try to explore this idea of readers inserting themselves into the detective's role, for my intention is to show that by 'playing detective' creatively, we gain insight into hitherto undetected aspects of the genre. Therefore, throughout this study I analyse in great detail what various fictional detectives do while solving crimes, elucidating the various steps of their reasoning and the stages of their actions more explicitly than they themselves – or even their authors – do. Obviously, it is not the 'personality' of detectives that interests me in such role playing, but their working methods. Or, to quote Kerr's serial killer, who himself quotes Sherlock Holmes: 'Crime is common. Logic is rare ... Therefore it is upon the logic rather than upon the crime you should dwell' (1995, 309). 'Playing detective' will help us pin down the 'logic' that helps to disentangle the structuring functions of the two generic questions, offering readers an instructive parallel about what they themselves do.

'No one who is [reading detective] fiction properly,' Porter argues, 'is a professor of literature when he reads, if being a professor means practising detachment' (1981, 230). Others concede that such an academic reading strategy is possible, but claim that it nevertheless remains alien to the genre's nature as popular entertainment (Calinescu 1993; Irwin 1994; Kermode 1983; Rabinowitz 1987; Tani 1984), while still others maintain that the genre always embeds two kinds of model readers; one who reads semantically and the other who reads semiotically (Eco 1979 and 1990; Champigny 1977; Sayers 1988a and 1988b). While my aim is certainly not to construct the 'proper' strategy for reading detective fiction, I will, instead, propose *a* way of reading it which pays heed to the genre's various self-reflexive promptings. Such a foregrounding has in fact a long history in the academic study of this genre, which has a solid tradition of examining the investigation of a crime as a portrayal of the detective story itself as a *self-reflexive textual enigma*.[1] Indeed, many academics have made detective fiction into a semi-allegorical and thematic exploration of *narrative poetics*, demonstrating how it self-consciously mirrors its own form and implies a commentary not only on its own narrativity but also on narrativity in general. Hence, these readers read detective stories as metaliterary stories devoted to their own principles of construction and, by extension, as representations of the basic principles of the art of the novel (e.g., Brooks 1984; Hodgson 1992; Prince 1980; Shklovsky 1990; Steele 1981–2).

Of course, Porter, too, treats the detective story as a 'laboratory' of a more general phenomenon within narrativity by turning it into the paradigm of readability and intelligibility. Yet he never makes the claim which those who study the genre as a self-reflexive textual enigma would make: that the detective narrative is *about* readability and intelligibility and that the genre invites its readers to perceive and ponder the mechanisms that generate the kind of reading Porter discusses. The difference between these approaches draws attention to the fact that detective-story criticism includes two broad conceptualizations of reading the genre: a 'lowbrow' explanation accounting for its appeal to a mass readership, and a 'highbrow' explanation accounting for its appeal to a distinctly academic audience. This dichotomy reproduces, at the level of reading, the typical detective-story distinction between mind and body. With its focus on the emotional side of reading, the lowbrow conceptualization emphasizes suspense, excitement, anxiety, and fear, as well as the effects that those emotions have on the body. In contrast, by concentrating on the various self-reflexive elements, the highbrow explanation offers a 'cerebral' version of reading, which stresses mental agility requiring attention, intelligence, inferential thought, and inventiveness.

S.E. Sweeney's 'Locked Rooms: Detective Fiction, Narrative Theory, and Self-Reflexivity' (1990) usefully demonstrates how the detective story may be read as a textual enigma which emphasizes basic principles of narrative. As the consequences of a crime are revealed well before the events that led up to it become known, plot is structured backwards: it establishes a linear, chronological sequence of events which will eventually explain its own initial baffling situation. This effect depends on a narrative presentation in which the story of the investigation embeds the story of a crime that supposedly has taken place prior to the beginning of the investigation. The story of the investigation is itself, in turn, often embedded in a story told, for example, by a 'Watson' figure, highlighting the fictitious writing of the text itself. Located at different narrative levels, the hierarchical organization of these three stories creates the sense of time, of anteriority and posteriority. The reader's desire to find out 'whodunit' combined with the suspension of the answer act together as the structuring force of plot. The ambiguously fragmented presence of the crime story causes detective and reader to decode and order clues and events in the light of the questions they are both trying to answer. The 'writing' of a narrative explanation highlights interpretation as the means of doing so, for the story of the crime is never fully present in the text. As the end of the plot coincides with the solution to the crime, explaining the initial mystery, the trajectory of the plot imparts a strong sense of completion and closure. By thus emphasizing narrative sequence, suspense, and closure; by making the hierarchical organization of narrative levels visible; and by reflecting reading, writing, and interpretation, the detective story, Sweeney argues, 'represents narrativity in its purest form' (3).

This neatly self-reflexive hierarchical organization of all the various narrative components and levels of the detective story has, as Sweeney points out, the effect of geometric architecture, which is mirrored in such traditional detective-story settings as the locked room and the labyrinth. I would like to set the particularization of my research task in this architectural context[2] by taking up Porter's objection to the academic cerebral strategy of reading detective fiction. This approach tends to emphasize rationality and order as the primary appeal of the genre, with special notice accorded to the creation of narrative order and cohesion.

Porter draws attention to the fact that the approach regards the detective narrative as a system existing in space. 'Such an attitude,' he writes, 'is an expression of the tendency to deduce from a book's existence as a physical object the conclusion that the novel it contains is itself an artifact available, like a building, for visual inspection' (229). Hence, the explanation of a work's meaning includes its *spatialization*. Porter finds fault with such an approach, because he thinks it fails to do justice to the process of the involved and affective working through that reading which the genre always entails (228–9). I think he is wrong in claiming that the book's existence as a physical object leads to its spatialization; instead, the very narrative structure of the genre creates this effect. Slavoj Žižek (1991) points out that what unites the detective narrative with the modern(ist) novel is their similar focus on the impossibility of telling a story in a linear, consistent way, of rendering the 'realistic' continuity of events. Both replace realistic narration by a diversity of literary techniques breaking up the 'organic' historical totality of narrative. The detective narrative thereby becomes a genre devoted to the effort of telling a coherent, sequentially ordered 'real story' (48–9). And what is typical of modern(ist) literature, Joseph Frank (1963) argues, is its move in the direction of *spatial form*: the self-reflexive organization of the work so that its disparate ideas and emotions are unified into a complex presented spatially in a moment of time (8–9). Such a technique 'undermine[s] the inherent consecutiveness of language, frustrating the reader's normal expectation of a sequence and forcing him to perceive the elements of the [work] as juxtaposed in space rather than in time' (10). When we are dealing with narrative fiction, this technique pertains most obviously to *plot* as a design that, in Frank's phrase, creates 'an indigenous kind of unity that overarches and shapes the constraints of pure temporal linearity.' In this view, plots construct relations of meaning that are detached from pure succession (Frank 1991, 91).[3]

Frank Kermode (1967) and Peter Brooks (1984) regard plot as a basic structure of understanding with whose help human beings give shape to and pattern their temporal existence. Plot structures pure temporal duration and locates within such a structure the meaning of human life. Brooks defines plot as an organizing and 'intentional' structure (in the sense of forward-moving and end-oriented) that locates the reader as if on a map or a graph by means of its shape-giving coordinates (11–12). And the detective-story plot is what Kermode calls a 'concordant structure' (6), for it patterns the narrated material in such a manner that the reader is able to grasp the *relations* of its beginning, middle, and end through time. The detective-story plot effects a narrative transformation of the situation obtaining in the beginning; this transformation takes place through its protracted middle and culminates in the ending, which, by closing off the narrative, enables the reader to perceive, and to confer meaning on, the totality the plot constructs. As the detective-story plot moves readers forward, it also makes them continually project a diagram of the totality it will eventually constitute. In Brooks's phrase, it is thus based on the 'anticipation of retrospection' (23).

If spatial form of narrative fiction alludes to the 'figures of design' (Brooks 1984, 4) plots make, then it is worthwhile to examine how the detective-story plot portrays the relationship between *fabula*, or *story* (the set of narrated situations and events in their chronological sequence; the basic story material), and *sjuzet*, or *discourse* (the set of narrated situations and events in the order of their presentation to the receiver) (Prince 1987, 30, 87). Tzvetan Todorov (1977) explains that the detective-story plot weds *story*, which largely coincides with the story of the crime, to *discourse*, which corresponds to the story of the investigation, according to a set pattern. Located in the past, the story of the crime exists only in the form of clues in the present in which the story of the investigation unfolds, the primary function of the investigation being the reconstruction of this first story.[4] Because authors leave out important information at strategic points of the plot, as well as fragmenting and presenting in an ambiguous manner the information they do supply, detectives must continually order clues and decode the events in the light of the two generic questions they are trying to answer. It is this constant rearranging of the causal and temporal relationships among narrative fragments (clues) that explains the 'spatiality' of the detective narrative. In order to understand what happened and why, detectives and readers have to fit the narrative fragments into a framework which unites them into a meaningful totality. They must thus identify the *plot pattern* that orders the disparate pieces, lending them unity and coherence. Indeed, the genre is based on the belief that a system of multiple connections between the apparently random fragments can be reconstructed. Therefore, although in their narrative presentation these fragments follow each other in time, their meaning does not depend on this temporal relationship. Instead of assigning reference individually to separate fragments, detectives and readers must keep these pieces in mind until, by reflexive reference, they can link these pieces with one another and with a whole which infuses them with significance. They thus progress through the investigation connecting fragments spatially, gradually becoming aware of the pattern of relationships among them. This intricate inter-dependence between parts and the totality they form represents, in Frank's phrase, 'an "intemporal" organization of temporality' (1991, 92) that is perceived in a moment of time.

With this specification of the detective narrative's spatial form, the idea of examining the structuring force of its two generic questions acquires new meaning. Set in this context, the genre exhibits a tension between the causal–chronological sequentiality of the investigation and the spatiality of the crime story this investigation aims to re-establish. Analysing the detective's and the reader's mutual effort to find answers to the two generic questions means analysing this very tension. Understanding the crime is impossible without understanding the causal and chronological relationships obtaining between various narrative fragments, but these relationships can be comprehended only as a complex pattern. Conse-quently, reading clues becomes a continual fluctuation between moving forward and halting this movement in order to reflect upon the frag-ments one has gathered, their mutual relationships, and the totality they form together. Or, reading is directed by the 'anticipation of retrospec-tion,' the attempt to grasp the totality that still remains hidden from view. It resembles the testing of a hypothesis, as detectives and readers first place a crime against a rudimentary explanatory pattern and then either reject it or correct, adjust, and elaborate it as they acquire more informa-tion. Thus, when criticism emphasizes that it is only in the end that detective narratives constitute themselves into wholes, it downplays the fact that that whole is reached through an ongoing *process of figuration*, of continually fitting narrative fragments against various narrative patterns and assessing the explanatory reach of such patterns.

Conceiving of detection as a process of figuration brings out yet an-other sense in which the tension between sequentiality and spatiality functions in the genre. Brooks points out that a completed plot always results from *plotting*, which arises from the characters' conflicting desires and interests. Frequently what organizes plot is a scheme or machination, whose purpose is to achieve a goal which breaks the legalities of the fictional world (Brooks 1984, 12). Moreover, often criminals remain active throughout the investigation, so that detectives must cope with the chang-ing tactics of the quarry. The genre represents an attempt to predict the likely course of the criminal's actions, a task that requires detectives to have the capacity to plot, to put themselves into the criminal's position in order to reflect on how that other person thinks and acts. Such imagina-tive identification enables detectives to play criminals in order to find out not only why and how a crime could have taken place but also what possible moves the opponent may, in the future, make in certain specific circumstances. This approach is based on the detectives' understanding of 'criminal psychology,' that is, of the wants and needs driving people to commit crimes, as well as of the goals of criminal action. This 'psychology' is of a kind in which investigators themselves partake, for sharing the conscious and unconscious desires behind crimes makes crime solving possible in the first place. Imaginative identification necessitates that the detective reflect on the overall design underlying the criminal's plotting. Often such a design emerges when the detective goes over the same ground that has previously been covered by the criminal.

Matei Calinescu (1993, 27) and Marie-Laure Ryan (1991, 201) point out that spatial concepts in discussing literature have heuristic value by directing attention to the compositional structure and the architectonics of a work. Ryan explains that, as structures such as plot are spatial configurations of elements, they are most efficiently represented in a visual model. She adds that graphic representations of plot simulate the mental processing of a text, capturing the way readers store plots in their memories (201). What makes detective fiction special is the self-reflexive foregrounding of its spatial aspects in the form of various *geometrical patterns* which have a metaphoric visual shape. For one thing, the organization of the detective-story plot demonstrates such patterning. We traditionally think of plot as a line, and this 'image of the line tends always to imply the norm of a single continuous unified structure determined by one external organizing principle. This principle holds the whole line together, gives it its law, controls its progressive extension, curving or straight, with some *arché*, *telos*, or ground' (J.H. Miller 1992, 18). Brooks evokes this same idea in his analysis of Conan Doyle's 'The Musgrave Ritual' in which Holmes physically traces out the criminal's movements on the lawn in order to arrive at the solution. This repetition draws up the line on which the clues hang: the interpretive thread of plot. It supplies a figurative analogue for the shape of this line, which here has a geometrical design (1984, 23–7). Stephano Tani (1984) reminds us that often such designs have an even more specific shape: the *mirror*, the *labyrinth*, and the *map* supply both formal and thematic figurations of the detective-story plot's significance. Each relates time to the development of the detection process. The detective maps the labyrinth (the mystery, the murder) by trying to cut through the distorted view of the past available in the present (the mirror). As finders of solutions, detectives are 'map-makers' who grapple with the flow of the present, which, by moving farther away from the time of murder, changes and distorts the image of that past (47–50).

The specificity of detective fiction shows in the fact that the formal designs of its completed plots result from social interaction that itself may be organized in various geometrical patterns. In other words, the genre invites its reader to use narrative form to make sense of various recurring thematic questions, in particular moral issues, that arise from this social interaction. The antagonistic opposition between detective and criminal leads to *doubling* between them, which is frequently highlighted by the mirror motif, suggesting that this is a dyadic bond. Such set roles as victim, criminal, and detective insert themselves into the three positional slots of the *triangle*, showing what their interrelationships are like in the social situation in which the investigation takes place; the *quadrangle* as a figure in which two triangles reflect each other describes interactional patterns resulting from the doubling of one of the basic roles (as, for example, a situation with a victim, a detective, and two criminals). What attests further to the significance of the genre's spatial organization is that the examination of these geometrical patterns has a long history in detective-story criticism (Lacan 1988; Derrida 1988; Johnson 1988; Irwin 1994; Muller and Richardson, eds, 1988; Tani 1984). I make extensive use of these designs in analysing the genre's formal and thematic patterns.

Frank argues that when readers scrutinize a narrative spatially, they have to apply a *rereading* strategy to it, as a knowledge of the whole is essential to understanding any of its parts. In such rereading, readers follow what Matei Calinescu (1993) calls a 'retrospective logic,' which consists of their attempt to pattern the work under perusal, achieving a synchronic-spatial view of it and seeing it as a whole, as a structure (19, 21). Thus, what characterizes rereading is the heightened attention it demands of the reader; Calinescu, taking his cue from Roland Barthes, defines it as an 'active, productive, ultimately playful [activity] ... involv[ing] the reader in the pleasure of (mentally) writing or rewriting the text' (46). Thanks to the applicability of geometrical patterning to the detective story, rereading in this sense is appropriate to it, for the reader must construct an overall sense of the plot's design. The genre is not, however, usually thought to invite the sustained attention of rereading; yet there is a tradition of analysing it within this paradigm. For while rereading may refer to the repetition of a previous act of reading with the aim of rediscovering it from a different vantage point, it may also allude to a reader's decision to treat a text as an example of its kind, so that reading includes a constant comparison between this particular text and similar texts held in the reader's memory (139). John G. Cawelti (1976) points out that, as the detective-story genre relies on variations on generic structures, it calls for the reader's continual aesthetic evaluation of an author's performance (8–20). Such an evaluation reinforces the notion of reading as a process of continuous hypothesis building and revising, as readers, on the basis of their generic knowledge, make forecasts of a given narrative's development and outcome. Hence, rereading detective fiction may be thought to combine our effort as readers to grasp the geometrical patterning of a work and the intertextually comparative approach it encourages us to adopt. These are the two senses in which I understand a rereading strategy to apply to detective fiction.

Calinescu maintains that rereading entails a basically *ludic* attitude to the text that is being read. Texts that call for rereading frequently invite or challenge readers to play a game with them while reading. The notion of the detective narrative as a game is, of course, a critical commonplace. As early as the 1920s, critics and novelists formulated various humorous, even parodic, rules that the author had to heed in order to 'play fair,' supposedly giving the reader a chance to solve the case. In 1928 the two best-known sets of rules for playing the game of literary detection were first published: Ronald Knox's 'A Detective-Story Decalogue' (1946) and S.S. Van Dine's 'Twenty Rules for Writing Detective Stories' (1946). According to these rules, for a detective story to be recognized as one there must be a detective, a victim, and a criminal (who must be one of the major characters, but not the detective; a rule much breached in recent detective fiction). The crime, committed for some personal reason, has to be solved by rational means, all clues being plainly offered to the reader. This game puts a premium on plot, with 'every major episode subsequent to the opening crime proceed[ing] from the duel between sleuth and criminal' (Haycraft 1974, 236). Yet, as Howard Haycraft points out, these rules were never followed in any strict sense (ibid., 225–6).

Given the conventional nature of this game analogy, it is worthwhile to ponder whether it still has some use as an analytical tool. Obviously, it is impossible to set down the precise rules for playing games with detective fiction. Similarly, guessing 'whodunit' is only a small part of such a game. What is at stake is something far more nebulous: the author's and reader's mutual familiarity with generic conventions, which the author manipulates to the best of his or her ability, and on whose basis the reader tries to conceive how exactly the author has constructed his or her narrative. We may describe this relationship as interaction based on the strategic behaviour of both players. This interaction has its parallel in the fictional world. As was already noted, the presence of, and interdependent relationship between, author and reader at each narrative level is the hallmark of the genre. The criminal authors the story of crime, which the detective reads; the criminal, in order to escape detection, is forced to try to read the detective's reading; the detective writes the story of the investigation which is narrated, for example, by a less-talented friend, who, while the investigation proceeds, vainly attempts to decipher the detective's reading. In effect, each agent acts in the dual role of writer and reader. Moreover, in order to function as a reader, each has to project the image of the opponent, the author.

Similarly, because detective-story authors keep back crucial pieces of information from their readers, as they have enigmas and secrets to safeguard, they must project the image of their readers while writing, anticipating their readers' response. In turn, readers, desirous of forming a sense of narrative patterning and of the plot's outcome, imagine the author, trying to conceive of the various strategies the opponent uses to retain the upper hand. Indeed, Calinescu argues that one of the most challenging aspects of playing a literary game is *imagining* or *inventing the author* (154). While usually the detective's projection of the criminal author and the correctness of his or her reading is eventually verified by the criminal's capture, the invention of the author remains, for readers of detective narratives, a *hypothetical and self-projected* construct. Imagining an author involves both conflict and collaboration on the part of readers. Conflict results from our efforts to insert ourselves into the textual role(s) the author has prepared for us; the confrontation with the otherness of another's way of thinking and writing engenders tension, which is, however, alleviated by collaboration, our willingness to respect the textually embedded guidelines for actualizing the fictional world and the author-reader interaction. The purpose – and the reward – of our projection of the author is, Calinescu argues, full participation in the creation of a tradition, a purpose which underlines the creativity of rereading as playing a game (154–6).

I use this metaphoric game analogy in order to study the geometrical patterns resulting from a rereading strategy as applied to detective fiction. This approach is grounded in the fact that the antagonistic pursuit in the fictional world serves as a model for the reader's relationship with the author. Because the investigation of crime within the fictional world represents a complex process of discovery and understanding, it has this linking function. Criminals and detectives as well as authors and readers are all engaged in processes of mental agility requiring attention, intelligence, inferential thought, and inventiveness. The game metaphor also allows me to discuss the levels of the detective story. One is what Calinescu calls a *game of make-believe* (127, 164) between detectives and criminals, transporting readers into fictional worlds and making them participate in the experiences of fictive people; the other I designate the *author-reader game*,[5] which treats the narrative as 'a calculated, rule-governed, self-reflexive playful artifact' (127). Instead of treating these games as two different types, I discuss them as two phases of the same game: readers can first become immersed in the fictional events, and can then step back, becoming absorbed in a second-level reflection of the text.[6]

The two 'game-levels' tie up nicely with Brooks's distinctions between plotting, plot, and narrative transmission. The antagonism in the fictional world tangibly brings into play plotting; and as plotting proceeds, as readers we can, along with the detective, begin to pattern the logic it follows, until we are able to form a sense of its overall organization and, hence, of the plot's design. And if, as Brooks argues, the motivation of plotting is inherently connected to the desire to narrate (1984, 216), then we can reflect on the ways in which the antagonism between detective and criminal transposes itself into our interaction with the author. Playing the detective-story game becomes, thus, the fitting together of two levels of figuration in order to conceive the system regulating an author's work.

In order to examine the detective's (and reader's) solving of a crime as a process of figuration, I first concentrate on the detective's attempt to construct a sense of what the crime is about by imaginatively identifying with the criminal. I am particularly interested in tracing the various uses to which the detective's doubling of the criminal is put in the genre. I then consider issues that the fragmentation and ambiguous presentation of narrative material raise. Conceiving of reading as a fluctuation between narrative sequentiality and figurative spatiality draws attention to the strategies detectives apply in order to construct the story of the crime as well as to the various stages this process goes through. In brief outline, this process involves, first, deciding what objects and character traits, for example, to treat as clues, and then narrativizing these clues by trying out ways of linking them with one another and by looking for a narrative pattern that would show how the fragments fit into a totality. I specifically elucidate the strategies – the 'logic' employed – that detectives as model readers use. While this focus spotlights the slow process of narrative reconstruction, it does not explain what procedures, in turn, enable the narrative fragments to be connected into a *coherent* totality. By studying these procedures, we may discern how authors guarantee that the solution fits the enigma of their own making, thereby producing elegantly streamlined narratives.

Perhaps the most surprising oversight by the academic tradition on which I ground my study concerns its forgetfulness of the fact that narrativity also covers thematic aspects. By definition, it includes 'conflict[s] consisting of discrete, specific, and positive situations and events, and meaningful in terms of a human(ized) project and world' (Prince 1987, 64). By depicting death, murder, and violence, Roger Caillois argues, the genre breaks its strictly formal ambitions, attracting readers with traditional 'novelistic' concerns (1983, 12).What is particularly interesting about the investigation is the fact that detectives' attempts to identify the criminal invariably lead to a consideration of guilt and moral responsibility. They cannot conclusively determine 'whodunit' unless they are able to assess how moral responsibility is to be allotted among the suspects. Criticism has overlooked the fact that the reading of clues also turns moral evaluation into a semiotic endeavour, for detectives have to ferret out the guilty person by reading. The genre represents the investigation as a two-pronged activity that involves naming the culprit by determining who is guilty of transgressing the law.

In considering the investigation of guilt, I shift the focus to the semiotics of reading and evaluating the moral issues typical of the genre. Again, the genre represents this process as one of figuration, for neither detectives nor readers can form hypotheses, let alone come to a decision, about the criminal without forming an overall 'picture' of the context in which the (supposed) crime has happened. This evaluative task suggests that the question of 'whodunit' coincides with the question of who is guilty. The focus lies on motive, the evaluation of who had sufficient cause to harm the victim. To complicate the question of motive and to hide the perpetrator among a group of suspects, the genre shows that many characters have grounds to want to harm the victim. Both investigators and readers have to go beyond general considerations of motive to analyse differences between motives in order to distinguish the one that fits a specific crime. But such elaboration may, in turn, complicate the question of guilt. As many agents have a feasible motive and seem guilty, investigators must compare acts, motives, and kinds of guilt to decide which agent is *responsible* for what particular aspect of the crime and what consequences this responsibility has. Critics discussing the genre's moral dimension are quick to point out that its handling is first and foremost literary, so that whatever issues are raised are subordinated to generic conventions, such as having a 'most likely suspect,' which raises doubts in the reader's mind, for this position seldom provides a narratively interesting solution.[7] Another convention is the rule of fair play, whose purpose is, by presenting all clues to readers, to give them a fair chance of arriving at the solution before the detective does.

Much of the complexity in moral evaluation in detective stories arises from the difference between two sets of criteria: the *judicial* and the *moral* codes, respectively. The law decrees certain deeds wrong and hence punishable, but it may overlook a number of acts which may be central in assessing the factors behind detective-story crimes. Examining crime in the light of these codes brings into view a fundamental distinction between legal and moral responsibility. Similarly, agents may be either legally or morally guilty. These two types of responsibility and guilt can overlap, but they need not: a morally wrong deed is not necessarily legally wrong, and vice versa. Slander, for example, is an actionable deed, but the sly insinuation of injurious things about a person remains 'only' morally wrong. The question 'Whodunit?' is *not* identical with the question 'Who is guilty?,' because criminal investigation shows guilt to be a more universal phenomenon than crime.

In detective stories, moral evaluation includes balancing the judicial code against the moral code in order to arrive at a just decision about the distribution of responsibility and guilt. After all, the moral code is the more fundamental one of the two; ideally, the judicial code instantiates its principles. The law, however, may remain mute as regards certain key moral issues, or contain oversights and loopholes. The law itself may be unjust, or it may be interpreted unfairly. The fictional community assigns the right of investigation to detectives, because it needs a pronouncement of how guilt is to be allotted, and because it is not in a position to acquire this understanding by itself.[8] By so doing it transfers responsibility to these functionaries, for it has to trust them to be familiar with the law, understand the morals subtending communal life, know how to apply both codes, and how to balance the codes against one another in a situation of contradiction.[9] For this reason, many critics argue that the detective represents the guardian of the legal and/or moral boundaries of the fictional society (Auden 1988; Chesterton 1946; Nicolson 1946; Sayers 1988b; as regards the hard-boiled detective, see Cawelti 1976; Chandler 1946; Margolies 1982; Parker 1984; Slotkin 1988). In their view, the detective gives voice to the moral principles by which a fictional society abides – or ought to abide. But another interpretation is feasible, as Caillois argues, describing the detective as an aesthete, if not an anarchist, by no means a protector of morality and still less of law (1984).

The most fruitful way to conceive the detective's function seems to lie in the middle, as is best demonstrated by private investigators, who are placed between official purveyors of justice and those who violate that justice. As detectives, they stand for law and order which, in principle, they must follow to stay in business. To do their job, however, they must often resort to illegal methods, for which reason, among others, their professional skills resemble the skills of criminals. In the private investigator the legal and moral codes of law enforcement intersect with those of the criminal order, making it possible for an author to stress either pole. (This description holds for the representatives of the police, as well.) Therefore, from the reader's perspective, the investigation is just as much a probing into and a revelation of an investigator's moral principles as it is a scrutiny of the suspects and their social context. This means that the final arbitration of moral issues always belongs to authors and readers.

This description of the basics of moral consideration has implicitly built on, but also elaborated, W.H. Auden's influential essay 'The Guilty Vicarage' (1988). Auden draws attention to the communal nature of crime and its consequences in detective-story worlds, arguing that the mystery of crime is best interpreted in terms of the 'dialectic of innocence and guilt' (16). This dialectic plays itself out through primary character roles and the fictional world: setting, crime, victim, criminal, suspects, and detective (the police and private and amateur investigators). What sets this dialectic into motion is plot, both initiating and sustaining the interplay of these components. As this interplay among these components is found in any detective narrative regardless of subgeneric variations, it is useful in analysing the genre. Thanks to its generality, it forms what might be called the *minima moralia*, supplying the basic ingredients for thinking about the 'dialectic of innocence and guilt' in the genre.

Examining the ordering force of the generic questions reveals that any moral reflection is inflected through the formal structures of the genre, which thus set the terms and boundaries for such reflection. Frank points out that a narrative's spatial organization affects its thematics as well, for the juxtaposition of syntactically unrelated narrative fragments with each other means that significance is not determined by narrative sequence (1991, 67). By treating the detective's reading as eventually producing an evaluation and assignment of guilt, we can study how this process also functions as one of patterning and figuration. Answering the question about guilt and responsibility entails, as I will show, drawing a 'picture' of the interpersonal relations among the suspects, which throws light on a fictional community's moral state. Following Martha Nussbaum (1990, ch. 1), I refer to such a 'picture,' produced through the detective's reading and bounded by generic conventions, as a *view of life*. The detective's status as moral evaluator suggests that the author's handling of the detective is the reader's means of accessing this view. The detective thus functions as one among other generic conventions shaping the formation of a view of life. This view calls on us to ponder the room for manoeuvre generic practices allow for the author's discussion of moral issues and the effects these practices have on our reading experience. Given that the detective's evaluation includes the drawing of moral distinctions, its results may be organized in various patterns. By scrutinizing such patterns, we gain insight into the moral differentiations underlying the genre's and a particular author's view of life.

Clearly, anyone studying the organizing force of the two generic questions cannot do so without drawing extensively on the impressive body of work by narratologists and semioticians. I draw on this work in analysing the genre's narrative patterns; moreover, I use the loose combination of reader-response study and narratology in scrutinizing the creation of coherence through thematization. In order to discuss aspects such as the detective's identification with the criminal and the reader's identification with the author, as well as narrative transmission, I turn to various psychoanalytical critics, most notably, Peter Brooks, Slavoj Žižek, and John T. Irwin. In analysing the genre's geometrical patterns, I draw extensively on Irwin's magisterial book *The Mystery to a Solution: Poe, Borges, and the Analytical Detective Story* (1994). In examining how the detective's and the reader's semiotic reading turns into an exploration of moral values, I turn to two like-minded theorists of the link between ethics and narrative: Wayne C. Booth and Martha C. Nussbaum. My choice is motivated by the fact that both supply straightforward, easily applicable guidelines for studying this link. Moreover, the suspicion each shows towards popular literature as a worthwhile object of ethical study provokes me to try what they most likely would not.

In speaking of detective fiction, I use this term as a generic one, as does Porter, who defines it as a narrative 'whose principal action concerns the attempt by a specialist investigator to solve a crime and to bring a criminal to justice, whether the crime involved be a single murder or the endeavor to destroy a civilization' (5). A 'specialist investigator,' however, need not refer to a professional crime-solver. Moreover, this genre by no means consists of a group of homologous texts. There is, for example, no single archetypal plot, but a number of plot schemata and a range of plot conventions. Traditionally, at least four broad variants are identified as constituting the subgenres of detective fiction: *classical detective fiction, hard-boiled detective stories, the (police) procedural, and the metaphysical detective story.* Taking stock of these variants is necessary, for each treats crime and detection in different ways: within the relational system of the genre, they emphasize shared formal and thematic elements in differing ways. Certain features hold a dominant position in one variant but a subordinate position in others.[10] The following description of the subgenres of detective fiction identifies both the features which these variants share, and those which differentiate them – through narrower determinations – from one another. Such features as patterns of plot, modes of narration, basic character roles, settings, and the author-reader relationship serve as the criteria with whose help distinctions can be made.

The *classical detective story* (the *whodunit*) presents crime as a mystery to be solved. Typically, plot moves from the introduction of crime to the presentation of clues and the interrogation of suspects, culminating in the announcement of the criminal's identity and proof of the solution. Thus the story of the investigation uncovers the story of the crime. Ideally, the solution produces insight, that is, the perception of the interlocking pattern governing the author's setting and the solution of the enigma. The fragmented and ambiguous handling of clues safeguards the sense of mystery, inviting active reader participation in playful rivalry with the author. Our chances of beating the author mostly lie in our familiarity with generic conventions and literary-cultural knowledge. The setting is an (upper)-middle-class milieu, in which private detectives and policemen are interlocked in (friendly) rivalry; if the detective is a member of the police, he or she is usually an educated person with a middle-class family background. The 'whodunit' traditionally represents crime as an irruption into a basically harmonious world, so that the function of the investigation is to restore this harmony.

In the *hard-boiled detective story*, the story of the crime recedes in importance, giving place to the story of the investigation, with a focus on what will happen next. The mystery motivation may be preserved, but it need not be; instead, structures of adventure and the chase keep the focus on investigative action. The crime to be solved becomes increasingly amorphous and keeps spreading in new directions. The plot begins with the introduction of a problem, and leads to a series of interrogations and confrontations during which this problem acquires new dimensions. Much of the action deals with the investigator's attempts to fathom what exactly he or she is to solve, climaxing in a situation demanding a personal, usually a moral, decision about the criminal's fate. Given that the setting is one of corruption and urban moral decay, the investigator's motives, strategies of action, and moral judgment acquire key significance. Thus the plot makes the reader probe not only crime but also the figure of the investigator. By creating suspense about the outcome of the investigator's actions, this subgenre evokes a more emotional form of reader participation than does the 'whodunit.' The typical investigator is a socially marginalized private detective or a police(wo)man whose investigation throws light on the extreme poles of society: the very rich and the poorest poor. As many crimes spring from confrontations among professional criminals, the underworld, too, is explored.

The *police procedural* may optionally keep certain facts concealed from readers; often, however, we know from the start who the criminal is, while the police do not, so that the question is whether the police can solve the crime. The plot typically moves between the investigation and the criminal's planning and committing of crimes, thus creating suspense. It traces the slow process of police investigation, highlighting the technical and specialized skills this investigation demands: the result often resembles a crime documentary. Of interest also are the relations among the various investigators and their attitudes towards the criminals. Procedurals usually take place in urban settings.

In the *metaphysical detective story* (also called the *antidetective story*, the *postmodern detective story*, and the *analytic detective story*) the very ideas of mystery and crime are placed under scrutiny, especially the possibility of creating enigmas through narrative and linguistic means. Whether there is a crime and an investigation does not really matter; the interest lies in the metatextual and metanarrative processes of creating and sustaining a sense of them. This subgenre celebrates the text itself as a mystery to be solved. The plot manipulates temporal and causal relations without establishing the ground from which to organize the pieces narrated into a coherent whole. It parodies the notion of solution as closure, either by supplying inconclusive solutions or by refusing to provide one. It uses the conventions and settings of the three mainstream variants in order to textualize reality, drawing attention to its constructed nature. Through these measures it calls on the reader to act as the co-creator of the text, for our reading and interpretation are the major, often even the only, means of lending coherence to the narrative. The intention is to make us examine more closely these acts and generic conventions. Moreover, as Patricia Merivale and S.E. Sweeney point out, '[m]etaphysical detective stories – composed in equal parts of parody, paradox, epistemological allegory (nothing can be known with any certainty), and insoluble mystery – self-consciously question the very nature of reality' (1999, 4).

I principally discuss the mainstream, popular, mass-marketed detective story, focusing primarily on the classical and hard-boiled variants of the genre. I also, to some extent, discuss the police procedural. Although the metaphysical detective story represents a related form, its conventions, as many critics demonstrate, differ markedly from those of the mainstream type (Calinescu 1993; Holquist 1971; Irwin 1994; Merivale 1968, 1997a, and 1997b; Merivale and Sweeney, eds, and Merivale and Sweeney [intro.], 1999; Spanos 1972; Tani 1984). Kevin Dettmar condenses this divergence by pointing out that the metaphysical detective story invites the reader to read 'like a detective a tale which cautions *against* reading like a detective' (1990, 156; my italics). Therefore, while I can refer to it only in passing, I must point out that the application of the semiotic rereading strategy brings the mainstream detective story somewhat closer to the metaphysical one, because the latter explicitly assumes that the reader will adopt such a strategy. To make the discussion more manageable and the choice of examples easier, I discuss only books from the British and American traditions of the genre, which have always been and continue to be the most significant, the British tradition often being associated with the 'whodunit,' whereas the American legacy is connected with the hard-boiled detective story. My examples are from the earliest phases of the genre (E.A. Poe, Arthur Conan Doyle, G.K. Chesterton), its 'Golden Era' (Christie), the period of the emergence of the hard-boiled narrative (Dashiell Hammett, Chandler, Ross Macdonald, Mickey Spillane), and the contemporary scene (Caleb Carr, Colin Dexter, Michael Dibdin, Laurie King, Ruth Rendell). Most authors discussed are internationally recognized practitioners of the genre with large sales figures; all the earlier writers are among the classics of the genre; most of the books are best sellers; and many of the authors (Dexter, Dibdin, King, Rendell) have been awarded prizes (Edgars or Golden Daggers) from the British and American Crime Writers' Associations. Such selections as these are thus characteristic of the mainstream detective story.

In the first three chapters of this study, I concentrate on the question 'Whodunit?' as involving the tactics and stages of putting together a coherent solution to the crime, while the subsequent four chapters scrutinize the traditional 'novelistic' concerns of narrativity by considering the nize the traditional 'novelistic' concerns of narrativity by considering the various ways in which questions of moral evaluation engage the reader. The particular issues with which I deal are as follows:

Given that the detective and the criminal represent the two fundamental terms of the conflict which characterizes the genre, this positional constellation turns these two characters into each other's doubles. In detective stories, doubling entails the detective's imaginative and affective adoption of the criminal's perspective and situation. Detectives intentionally place themselves in the criminal's position, trying to conceive how this other person thinks and acts, in order to catch him or her. Imaginative identification introduces tension into the narrative, for it requires investigators to become the quarry they are after; identification may lead to understanding and empathy with the criminal, though detectives cannot allow that to hinder them from pursuing their primary goal of capture. As a recurrent generic narrative pattern, doubling thus spotlights the nature of the detective's relationship with the criminal as an issue to be considered. I analyse this bond in terms of self-reflection, for our capacity to identify with someone else is grounded in our relationship to ourselves. Our only first-hand experience of psychic otherness is the experience of that difference which constitutes personal identity: the self's original otherness to itself, which enables us to think of ourselves both as ourselves and as someone else. I consider how the detective's relationship with him- or herself carries over to his or her relationship with the criminal, for the detective's flexibility in mentally assuming various roles seems to correlate with success in pinning down the criminal. Frequently the patterning effect that doubling has on plotting and the plot is further enhanced through the motif of the mirror. In fact, the mirror image supplies a well-known metaphorical description of self-reflection, for by providing an antithetical image of the person in front of a mirror, this image makes tangible the notion of an internal sameness and difference enabling and sustaining it. I examine not only how detectives use this motif as an aid in imaginative identification but also how the motif organizes the whole narrative.

The process of projecting the opponent's profile transposes itself to the reader's relationship with the author, for, in order to set the crime problem, authors think like criminals, while in solving this very same problem, they think like detectives. They thus split, as John T. Irwin (1994) points out, into two, setting their internal halves to chase each other: criminal and detective are their own two masks (386–7). If, as readers, we take up the challenge of attempting to determine 'whodunit,' we must also try to insert ourselves into the roles of criminal and detective. By examining the two key players and the author's use of them to safeguard the enigma, I analyse our projection of our opponent, the author, whose plotting has produced a given detective narrative. I approach this 'exercise in duality' by linking it with the question of *narrative transmission*. Brooks argues that narratives invariably express a concern for transmitting whatever is focal in them to readers. Narrative is a way of informing, teaching, warning, impressing, and even contaminating readers. Reading thus places the reader in a situation of exchange, asking for something in return for what reading supplies (1984, 216–21). I am interested in analysing the ways in which the representation of the detective's relationship to the criminal conditions narrative transmission from authors to readers. What roles do authors envisage for readers, and how can readers use this representation as a clue to those roles that authors have reserved for them?

The basic similarity between academic disciplines and detective fiction has fascinated academics (Freeman 1946; Nicolson 1946; Porter 1981, ch. 12; Eco and Sebeok, eds, 1983; Stowe 1983); the analogy is also well known in the detective-story genre itself, for detectives often boast of applying an analytic or scientific method to the unravelling of crimes. Detective fiction represents the fulfilling of this epistemological task as a complex process. Detectives observe people and things, gather information, and interpret clues, formulating conjectures about the course of past events. The investigation involves observation, inference, the construction of hypotheses, and the testing and validation of hypotheses, phases which also form the backbone of scientific inquiry. Consequently, the contributors to *The Sign of Three: Dupin, Holmes, Peirce* (1983), edited by Umberto Eco and Thomas Sebeok, argue that theories of scientific inquiry provide an adequate metatheory for analysing the detection process. They suggest that it be studied in the context of what the American philosopher C.S. Peirce calls *abduction*, a mode of inference explaining how observations and data lead to the formation of conjectures, as well as accounting for the general principles conjectural thinking follows. They point out that science and everyday life share this process, as both involve situations in which interpreters start from facts (or what they tentatively take to be facts) without, at the outset, having any particular explanation in view. They treat these facts as resulting from a certain sequence of events or a state of things, but it remains unknown what brought this result about. As only the result is known, they have to reason backwards, from the result to its cause. They thus search for a known law or rule which, when applied, would bring a certain outcome of which the specific instance at hand is an example. The process involves fitting facts against the background of the rules and patterns that classify and define those facts.

Unlike scientific inquiry, however, detective fiction explicitly savours the *narrative* nature of the explanatory process. After all, in this genre, reaching a solution means the ability to put together a more or less coherently and plausibly emplotted account of past events: the solution equals narrative. Therefore, my focus on abduction differs from the one in *The Sign of Three*, for I study it as an integral means of constructing a narrative explanation, throwing light on the inferential movement fictional detectives – and readers in general – employ in making clues yield narrative elements. I analyse this activity as one which demonstrates that putting together an emplotted explanation involves a complex inferential movement in which clues are made to suggest separate plot units by ascribing them to various classifying headings; these headings are then linked together by projecting them against an overarching plot pattern. This pattern defines which individual plot components are included as relevant ones; but the pattern itself is also governed by the specific nature of these separate units. Each gives the other meaning.

Critics argue that the ending of the detective story has a special nature, for, as the mystery was defined as the text's meaning, the solution to the crime resolves things conclusively, leaving nothing to be desired (Hühn 1987, Porter 1981, Sweeney 1990). This notion of completeness includes logic and, especially, coherence, because the ending reveals any possible fallacies in the detective's reasoning. The convention which has a detective first construct a wrong explanation, and then, after a lapse of time, come up with the correct one underlines this fit between problem and solution. It is worth juxtaposing this notion of the ending with a fictional detective's musings on her own narrative activity. In *A Philosophical Investigation*, detective Jake Jakowicz observes that 'there were times when connections eluded her, when she could connect "nothing with nothing," when something could not be known. And there it remained only to make things fit. To fit. No detective much liked the verb. It smacked of corruption and of malpractice, of suppressing some connections and highlighting others. It was much too active. Too premeditated' (194). While the notion of the solution as a complete resolution captures the generic ideal, detective Jakowicz spells out what the practice is actually like. Although the premeditated circularity of the author's task may suggest that the solutions connect perfectly with the problems he or she has concocted, this match is always the result of a lot of 'fitting,' privileging some connections over others.

I analyse this circularity as the author's invitation to readers to consider how a narratively coherent solution to a crime is generated through the interpretation of clues. By drawing on the work of such critics as Claude Bremond and Alexander Zholkovski, I examine this question in terms of *thematization* as the means of creating the sense that the solution flows directly from the reading of the clues, so that it seems not only coherent but also logical. This notion of thematization, understood as the interpretation of a text in the light of a specific theme or cluster of themes, enables me to consider the fitting of the solution to the problem as a figuration serving as a *mise-en-abyme*, a miniature reflecting device, of the formal and aesthetic *design* of the whole plot. This approach suggests, in turn, that authors use detectives for what may be called self-reflexive architectural ends, for a detective's thematization makes visible the general patterning not only of the emplotted solution but frequently also of the whole plot of a book. Thus, I take the challenge authors issue to readers to include the exercise of *formal imagination*, testing whether readers can conceive the way in which a detective's strategies of uniting plot elements with one another and creating coherence among these elements produce global aesthetic designs of plot. In so doing, I treat the detective's reading as a process of figuration which includes the sketching, in imagination, of the 'picture' of a plot's design, whether it be described in terms of a locked room, a maze, or a puzzle.

For all the emphasis in criticism on characters and their interaction in a social milieu, no one has so far examined how exactly the evaluative process takes place. Consequently, how authors invite readers to assess guilt also remains virtually unexplored. I envisage this process as one of reading guilt, referring to those aspects of the investigation involving the observation, explanation, and evaluation of numerous, diffuse clues as potential signs of a character's participation in crime. This focus directs the reader's attention to the detective as someone who reads other people and the community in order to arrive at a pronouncement of guilt and responsibility. I show that this process is closely connected with forming a sense of character in terms of *ethos*, that is, moral makeup, requiring the assignment and appraisal of personal qualities and patterns of action. As the means of performing this task are placed under the reader's scrutiny, they provoke further questions about ethos by making us think about the author's ethos as well as about our own. I discuss these issues in terms suggested by Wayne C. Booth in his *The Company We Keep: An Ethics of*

Fiction (1988). Booth's approach includes the analysis of what happens to our ethos as we read detective fiction.

The portrayal of the determination of guilt is governed by various generic rules and conventions. This fact calls for a reversal of focus, making the particular generic framework the starting point, so that it becomes possible to examine the effects it has on the author's practice. A key convention accords the detective a special status, because he or she both enacts and expresses a moral interpretation of communal life. By analysing the range of options generic conventions give the author in depicting the detective, I ponder how he or she invites the reader to form a sense of what Martha Nussbaum calls *a view of life*, a representation of life 'as' something or other. In Nussbaum's view, such representations have moral value, because they make readers think about how characters work out moral dilemmas in specific, practical situations. She emphasizes that such views always result from the selection of genre, narrative strategies, plot formulae, style, and vocabulary, setting up, in the reader, certain activities and transactions, and precluding others (1990, ch. 1). By examining the generic conventions themselves, I explore the boundaries of the author's relationship to the reader, especially as they control the formation of the views of life the genre puts forth. Finally, the *minima moralia* as the interaction, sustained by plot, among the generic roles of victim, criminal, detective, and suspects suggests that the geometrical patterns are inscribed into the genre's typical manner of representing views of life. I conclude my study by showing how the reader can use the geometrical patternings of moral distinctions to form a sense of the whole 'anatomy' of good and evil subtending a particular author's view of life. I use as my examples the two best-known practitioners of the 'whodunit' and the hard-boiled detective story – Agatha Christie and Raymond Chandler – to demonstrate how their geometrical patterning of the relationships among generic roles enables the reader to draw a full-fledged picture of the moral underpinnings of their respective worlds.

INVESTIGATING 'WHODUNIT'

1

Projecting the Criminal

In Edgar Allan Poe's 'The Purloined Letter' (1994b) C. Auguste Dupin, by using a schoolboy's reply about his success at a guessing game as an example, explains the method of effecting a *'thorough* identification' and the 'admeasurement of the astuteness of opponents' as follows: 'When I wish to find out how wise, or how stupid, or how good, or how wicked is any one, or what are his thoughts at the moment, I fashion the expression of my face, as accurately as possible, in accordance with the expression of his, and then wait to see what thoughts or sentiments arise in my mind or heart, as if to match or correspond with the expression' (347). Dupin identifies with the criminal, using an *I-am-you* approach,[1] which entails the imaginative and affective adoption of the other's perspective and situation. He produces an image of the opponent's mind by treating his own mind as other to itself and probing into its reactions. He intentionally opposes his mind to itself as a means of conceiving *somebody else's* mind. He stands, as it were, face to face with a self-generated picture of the criminal. Imaginative identification is thus based on the detective's *doubling* of the criminal: the projected picture looks at him as the *mirror image* looks at us when we look into a mirror.

Doubling involves *splitting*, a fact which the human body demonstrates. Its bilateral asymmetry makes its two halves mirror images of each other. A split marking the line of their separation runs vertically down the exact middle of the body. This vertical axis is traversed by a horizontal axis constituting the halves as opposites: right and left. The right side is thought to dominate the left, as, for example, notions of handedness show. The mirror image doubles this constitutive asymmetry, but by *reversing* it so that right is reflected as left and left as right: it is our *antithetical* double. In imaginative identification the mirror image serves as a metaphor of self-reflection (Irwin 1994, 5–7, 24–5), which involves the idea of the self folding back on itself along a 'hinge' that differentiates its 'parts.' This split forms an asymmetry between them, a bipolar tension between a subject, or the reflecting self, that faces an object, or the self under observation. The splitting and doubling of the self is framed and held together by the self's recognition that its objectified mirror image, although reversed and hence other, reflects, nevertheless, a picture of its own self. This identification involves the recognition of the act of reflection.[2] The I-am-you approach is thus based on the only immediate experience we have of psychic otherness, that is, the self's original otherness to itself, that difference which constitutes personal identity (ibid., 25). As the criminal externally duplicates an internal division in the detective's self, but with the binary polarity of that division reversed, doubling is a structure of four halves problematically balanced across the inner/outer limit of the self rather than a structure of two separate, opposing wholes (ibid., 5). And if the self's inner split is coded, for example, in moral terms, then the good ('master') side of the detective usually dominates his or her bad ('slave') side, whereas in the internal makeup of the criminal, the bad side dominates the good one.[3]

Ever since Poe, doubling between detective and criminal has become a recurrent pattern in the genre. Their positional constellation makes them each other's 'doubles' if only because they represent the two fundamental terms of the conflict which characterizes the genre. Often this structural antagonism is enhanced by linking it with the motif of the double, which, in Lubomír Doležel's definition, is generated 'when the alternative embodiments (X and X^1) of one and the same individual exist in one and the same fictional world'; that is when 'an individual characterized by personal identity appears in two alternative manifestations, usually as two fictional characters' (1995, 95–6).[4] This motif explicitly demonstrates that the criminal externally doubles an internally split detective, producing a pattern Stefano Tani characterizes as the 'game of opposites reluctantly restrained in the same persona' (1984, 7).

In this chapter I examine the different facets of imaginative identification in the mainstream detective story by analysing how it works in three examples. Although Irwin appears to believe that the detectives' doubling of the opponents' thought processes so as to anticipate their next move and end up one jump ahead of them is a standard element only in the metaphysical detective story (5), I demonstrate that the I-am-you approach plays an important role in the popular variant as well. Given that the relationship between the doubled characters can range from perfect similarity to absolute contrast (Doležel, 98), I have chosen one example from each end of the spectrum and one from its middle in order to demonstrate the continuum the application of this approach constructs between the detecting 'I' and the criminal 'you.' Using Mickey Spillane's *Kiss Me, Deadly* (1953) as my first example, I begin with what Tani calls the 'mortally vampiresque' (9) tradition in which detectives destroy the double in whom they either cannot or will not recognize themselves. I then discuss Caleb Carr's *The Alienist* (1994) as an example that grounds doubling primarily on the structural positions the antagonists occupy. I close by discussing the 'playfully vampiresque' variant (Tani, 9) which acknowledges the criminal as the detective's double and uses crime solving as the means of exorcizing one half of the inwardly split detective. G.K. Chesterton's *The Secret of Father Brown* (1981c) supplies the third example.[5] As the analysis shows, the treatment of doubling in these narratives has the same thematic effect as in the metaphysical detective story, for each uses it as a means of dealing with questions of self-reflection. Therefore, I follow the example set by Irwin – and, before him, by Jacques Lacan in particular – in paying special attention to the various ways in which these stories include the notion of mirroring, whether it be as concrete mirrors or as the acts of seeing and looking or, conversely, being seen and looked at. Simultaneously, this analysis demonstrates how we can visually map the structures of the detective-story plot with the help of mirror imagery.

The special nature of detective fiction is that writing it involves doubling, requiring authors, as it were, to split into two: they are like criminals in concocting the crime problem, whereas they are like detectives in unravelling these mysteries of their own making. Neither role is primary, for while they are devising the crime, they simultaneously have to 'think through' its solution (Bennett 1979, 236–9). Authors must take up both roles in their imaginations: criminal and detective are two of their own masks (Irwin, 386–7). But this description pertains to readers as well, for in order to engage in the battle of wits with authors, we, too, have to be able to think like both fictional antagonists. We thus use the game between criminal and detective as a clue to the game authors are playing with us. Given that authors and readers can never textually meet one another, Irwin reminds us, their meeting can take place only indirectly through their fictive encounter. Consequently, authors and readers square off as specular doubles, each intending to outwit a self-projected image of the other (386).

Reading the game within the fictional world as a *mise-en-abyme* of the higher-level game places under scrutiny the way in which the detective's imaginative identification with the criminal carries over to the reader's relationship with the author. Such a self-reflexive structure consisting of the frame and the content it frames, Peter Brooks argues, always dramatizes reading as a *transferential interaction* by highlighting the presence of a narrator (author) and a narratee (reader) and the interlocutionary relations thus established. Framing makes readers pay attention to the motives of narration. What does the narrator want from his or her audience? This question, in turn, invites us to think about our own participation in reading. What consequences does reading have? What is one supposed to do with the tale read? (Brooks 1984, 216–21). In discussing the three examples of Spillane, Carr, and Chesterton I consider how the representation of imaginative identification in the fictional world affects narrative transmission from the author to the reader. If the drama within the framed story is about self-reflection, then it is worth examining the extent to which narrative transmission reflects upon its own conditions in these sample narratives.

I Am Not You: The Inbuilt Repulsion of Opposites

The hard-boiled novels of Mickey Spillane emphasize the unredeemable depravity of the world portrayed. With the priority on vengeance and violence, hatred is the basis of the detective's bonding with the criminal, resulting in an aesthetic of repugnance and death. His work is written in a highly emotional register, which is best illustrated by the narrator's attacks on the Mafia, Communists, women, and minorities of all types. Narration serves both as a vehement, gleeful attack on the vices of modern civilization and as a reinforcement of the shared values of the envisaged audience (white, heterosexual, working-class and lower-middle-class men). I discuss Hammer's projection of the criminal in *Kiss Me, Deadly* (1953) as an example of Spillane's work, paying attention to the function of the mirror motif in this process, and relating it to the author's game with the reader. As this book includes a similar thematic structure of looking and seeing as Poe's proto-metaphysical short story 'The Purloined Letter,'[6] a comparison of these two texts fruitfully structures its analysis. What makes this thematics particularly intriguing in Spillane's novel is that the criminal succeeds in hiding right under Hammer's gaze until the very end, and, even after his realization of her (as it turns out) guilt, he never really sees her for what she is. As is typical of the hard-boiled subgenre, the detective's blindness relates to the relations between the sexes; therefore, I differentiate between Hammer's projection of male criminals and the female culprit.

Kiss Me, Deadly starts *in medias res* when Berga Torn stops Hammer's car, begging him to help her flee her pursuers. Her enemies manage to catch them; they kill her and frame him. In order to highlight the thematic structure of looking and seeing, we can designate the opening as the first scene. The motif of the 'transfer of guilt' (Žižek 1991, 74) triggers the events: to prove his own innocence, Hammer has to find out 'whodunit.' Berga Torn was to testify against Carl Evello, a wealthy businessman whose Mafia connections the police want to prove. Hammer's undercover investigation pits him against members of the Mafia, so that, at regular intervals, confrontations and killings take place. He tracks down Berga Torn's roommate, Lily Carver; to protect her, he hides her in his own home. Eventually, Hammer finds out that the case is about the theft of a package of drugs, stolen by Berga Torn and a Mafia courier. By torturing her, the Mafia had tried to make her reveal where the drugs are hidden. The situation leads to a fight over leadership within the Mafia, as its individual members would like to have sole possession of the drugs. Hammer eventually traces this struggle to Dr Soberin. Hammer kills him, only to find himself challenged by Lily Carver, who turns out to be Soberin's aide. She shoots Hammer in the arm; he kills her by setting her on fire. *Kiss Me, Deadly* is structurally symmetrical, for its ending circles back to its beginning: it opens with Hammer's encounter with Berga Torn, dressed in nothing but a raincoat, and closes with his destruction of Lily Carver, clad in nothing but a bathrobe. We can thus designate the final scene as the transformed repetition of the first one. (The transformation derives from the fact that, in the final scene, the culprit holds the position the victim had in the opening.)

In hard-boiled detective stories, the ineffectuality and corruption of the law-enforcing agency and the system of justice compel the private eye to perform the job that normally belongs to them: the unmasking and punishment of the wrongdoer. The mistrust of these systems signals the investigator's general scepticism about society's capacity to ensure order. What makes Spillane special is that he is a hard-boiled writer who has turned this mistrust into *paranoia*, thereby bringing the subgenre closer to *conspiracy fiction*. On the basis of Žižek's Lacanian definition of paranoia (1991, 18) as the subject's belief in the existence of a hidden manipulator behind the symbolic order[7] (the 'Other of the Other'), the reader can recognize Hammer's mental makeup right from the beginning. When the criminals take him back to his car, he understands their tactics: 'Very clever of them. If anybody passed they'd see a car in trouble with warn-ing signals properly placed and the driver obviously gone into town for help. Nobody would stop to investigate' (13). Hammer ascribes the ingenuity of his adversaries to their ability to manipulate the symbolic order for their own sinister purposes. This realization opens up his eyes to the true state of reality: 'It was a forced awakening that hurts ... *Then suddenly there's an immediate sharpness to the awakening as you realize that it hadn't been a bad dream after all, but something alive and terrifying instead*' (14; italics in the original). The 'terror' is the fact that the symbolic order has been corroded from the inside, for criminals have managed to infiltrate it. Its thorough deceptiveness leads Hammer to believe in the existence of a hidden master – and a hidden order – *behind* the symbolic order holding the reins.[8] Thus, only two agents see the fake nature of the symbolic order: he himself and the Mafia orchestrating the game of deception.

Following Lacan's analysis of 'The Purloined Letter,' we can analyse the opening as a triad constituted by a series of glances. The first is the glance that sees nothing: that of the police, the FBI, and the system of justice. The second, 'a glance which sees that the first sees nothing and deludes itself as to the secrecy of what it hides,' is the Mafia's. 'The third sees that the first two glances leave what should be hidden exposed to whomever would seize it': that is, Hammer's (Lacan 1988, 32). Thanks to his place outside the two mutually reflecting glances, the detective has the analytical upper hand. Spillane, however, recodes the characteristics that are typically associated with this position. While Dupin, for exam-ple, sets his rational side aside in order to open himself up for a moment to the irrationality of the criminal, Hammer, dominated by irrationality, only temporarily listens to his rational side. His paranoia explains this reversal. Given the simplicity of men's motives and goals in Spillane's world, projecting an image of another man poses no difficulty, as Ham-mer's observation attests: 'I thought about it while I lay there, trying to figure the mind of one little guy who thought he could beat the Mafia out of a fortune and pretty soon I was reading his thoughts as if they were my own' (117). It is the audacity the Mafia shows in infiltrating the symbolic order which calls for Hammer's investment in irrationality, for these ferocious criminals can be defeated only by a doubly ferocious detective who pushes this trait to a degree unknown to the opponent. Fostering hatred and rage allows him to surpass his adversaries in fierceness and wickedness: 'they're bad, but they know me and I'm worse' (59) he brags, boasting that '[t]hey were just like the rest; crumbs who knew how to play a one-sided game, but when they were playing somebody who could be twice as silent, twice as dirty and twice as quick they broke in the middle and started begging' (60). The nurture of these 'slave' qualities reaches the point where even stupidity is prized over cleverness: 'In a way it paid to be stupid as long as you overdid it' (147).

Hammer thus needs only to think of himself in fathoming his male opponents, defeating them because their minds are so much alike. Given that the game he plays is about revenge and survival, it culminates in physical combat where the opponents are literally interlocked: Hammer beats and strangles his enemies, and even tears their eyes out (80–1; 115; 145). The physicality of these encounters effects the closure of the gap between the antagonists, assimilating them in the moment of death: 'The blood trickled down out his nose and ears when I stood over him, a bright red that seemed to match the fire burning in my lungs' (120). The basis for such bonding derives from instinct, for men are aggressive by nature in Spillane's world. The narrator reinforces this association by describing himself and others in animal terms.[9] What distinguishes men from animals, however, is that human nature includes moral sense: this natural human order also gives society its primitive morality. The specific 'twist' of hard-boiled conspiracy fiction is that the detective's paranoia justifies his violence and wickedness. Žižek points out that the paranoiac correctly perceives the constructedness of the symbolic order, but errs in his belief in a hidden agent who is responsible for this deception (1991, 81). Hammer goes one better, however, for he believes that, before the criminal invasion took place, the ruling order really did match the natural state of things. He thus fails to grasp the fact that the social fabric is always symbolically constructed. This misconception is his justification: his violence and wickedness serve the natural order, and hence serve the natural 'good,' while the criminals use violence and wickedness – as well as rationality – for the furtherance of evil. The inversion of the usual hierarchy has an instrumental function in the upkeep of the natural order for the benefit of the ordinary man. Thus, within the fictional world, Hammer nevertheless represents the characteristics associated with the male detective: mind, rationality, and good.

Because of these male attributes, the detective cannot identify the female criminal until it is almost too late. The disclosure of Lily Carver's guilt comes in the last scene of the narrative, and even then it does not result from Hammer's projection of her, but from the facts of the case. If this scene repeats the opening, in what way is the thematic structure of looking and seeing inscribed in it?

As in 'The Purloined Letter,' repetition effects a shift in the positions of the players, restructuring their relationships. The Mafia is ignorant of Lily Carver's role in the power struggle; moreover, it does not know that she has the key to the locker with the purloined drugs (given into her safekeeping by Hammer himself). Thus, now the first glance which sees nothing is the Mafia's. Hammer, in turn, sees the blindness of the Mafia, but is oblivious himself to the fact that the criminal woman sees and partakes in the situation, manipulating it to her advantage. Consequently, the second glance is the detective's, while the third belongs to the criminal. What this means is, of course, that the criminal has gained the analytical upper hand over the detective. Two issues in particular concern us in this shift: what accounts for the detective's blindness, and what does his destruction of the criminal woman signify?

The answers have to do with the protagonist's self-concept as expressed by his self-image, which can be elaborated with the help of the mirror motif. It is useful to begin with Hammer's relationship to Velda, his fiancée-cum-secretary. He describes her by stating that '[s]he was everything you needed just when you needed it, a bundle of woman whose emotions could be hard or soft or terrifying, but whatever they were it was what you wanted' (27). In another connection he refers to their mutual rapport, for her feelings match his (53–4). Velda reinforces his self-image by reflecting him back to himself in exactly the way he wants. In her eyes, he sees himself as the epitome of masculinity and, hence, of authority.[10] Hammer is taken in by Lily Carver's[11] performance as a damsel in distress because her pliancy suggests her submission. Yet, although occasionally her expressions agree with his moods – '[h]er eyes went soft, reflected the hurt in mine' (127) – he cannot 'read' them, for there is 'something too big in her eyes' (102), 'reflecting some emotion nobody in the world would be able to put his finger on' (129). Inevitably, his blindness seems to stem directly from his paranoia.

Discussing imaginative identification as the ability to 'look awry,' Žižek (1991) argues that it is made possible, so to speak, by a shot of paranoia. Looking awry means spotting the ill-fitting element at the scene of the crime, that clue whose significance the detective cannot explain by resorting to the symbolic order (i.e., the 'something too big' in Lily's eyes). Looking awry is analogous to the paranoiac's lack of belief in the efficacy of this order, for the detective realizes not only its contractual nature but also the concomitant possibility of manipulating it. Wandering outside the normal point of view, he tries to place himself in a position from which the incongruous element would seem meaningful. This new vantage point stakes out another subject position than the detective's. If we relate this shift in perspective to the mirror image, it is as if the detective switched places with his reflection: the image represents the reflecting subject, while the detective is himself the reflected object. The sense of paranoia in imaginative identification comes from this awareness of the instability of the subject positions on which the symbolic order is founded (ibid., 11–12, 114, 125–6).

Hammer recognizes in the criminal woman the ill-fitting element, but fails to decipher it, for he cannot identify himself projectively with her. If the very idea of conceiving himself as another is incomprehensible to him, then this means that his capacity of self-reflection is considerably restricted, if not totally lacking. Self-reflection involves differentiation and objectification: the subject can take itself as its object of thought, recognizing its simultaneous sameness with, and difference from, itself. In imaginative identification one projects onto the external world this internal condition. Being able to think of himself only as himself but not as the reflected other, Hammer can neither recognize nor understand anything that diverges from his self-concept. Consequently, Hammer is Dupin's veritable antithesis, comprehending neither symbolization nor self-reflection.

In order to hide the purloined letter, Minister D— disguises it by refolding it and rewriting its address in 'a diminutive female hand.' Lacan draws attention to the fact that its possession feminizes D—. What is significant is that disguise – imitation – is associated with femininity, for Hammer's rigidity derives from his conviction that the source of the nationwide deception is the inversion of the proper distribution of gender-coded qualities. The natural order sets up hierarchies of dominance and submission between the sexes; as long as they stay intact, nature and morality remain uncorrupted. Ideally, in each species, females are subordinate to males, who find out through contest and combat which of them has the authority and strength to lead society. Society's corrupt macro structures reflect the unnatural inversions of sexual relationships. What should be dominated by traditional masculine characteristics is overtaken by traditional feminine ones, and vice versa. The Mafia is a case in point: although it consists of men, as an organization it has the female identity of the Medusa (133). Similarly, the crime-infested city is described as a man-eating, sardonically laughing female monster (33, 82). The 'Other of the Other,' the true concealed manipulator behind the scenes, is not the Mafia but the criminal woman. Hammer's inability to think like the female criminal thus correlates with the typical detective-story distinction between the masculine mind and the feminine body.

The female criminal inverts her conventional constitution by subordinating her body to her mind, gaining sexual and emotional dominance over the detective. As her aim is to destroy him, yielding to her seduction would mean his death. Therefore, as Cawelti notes, the investigation resembles a ritual testing of the detective's self-control and self-mastery (1976, 153–4). His prolonged failure to realize her true identity is caused by the emasculating effect of her tactics, for the sexual cravings of his body eclipse his mind. Losing touch with his masculinity, he is in danger of becoming feminized.

The reassertion of the detective's masculinity leads to the climax Cawelti has aptly designated as 'violence as orgasm' (185). *Kiss Me, Deadly* culminates in a scene in which Lily Carver first strips before Hammer, revealing her badly burned body, and then threatens to kill him; but before doing so, she wants him to kiss her. Again, his feelings of repulsion are expressed in terms of looking and seeing: '*There was no skin, just a disgusting mass of twisted, puckered flesh from her knees to her neck making a picture of gruesome freakishness that made you want to shut your eyes against it*' (152; italics in the original). Her mangled body proves the criminal conspiracy against the natural order: its 'freakishness' stands for utter moral depravity. Epistemology and morality intertwine in Spillane's world, for in order to remain a 'natural' and hence a 'moral' man, Hammer must always think 'straight.' To think like the criminal woman would pervert his mind, making him lose touch with masculinity. He gains control of himself and of the situation by setting her on fire:

The smile never left [Lily's] mouth and before it was on me I thumbed the lighter and in the moment of time before the scream blossoms into the wild cry of terror, she was a mass of flame tumbling on the floor with the blue flames of alcohol turning the white of her hair into black char and her body convulsing under the agony of it. The flames were teeth that ate, ripping and tearing, into scars of other flames and her voice the shrill sound of death on the loose.
    I looked, looked away. (152)

This defeat of the female other represents not only a triumph over the femininity the male desires, argues Tim Dayton, but it is also a triumph over that 'desire lodged within his own untrustworthy flesh, over his own embodiment' (1993, 100). In Spillane's book, however, the protagonist never understands that the physical encounter between him and the female criminal folds back into his encounter with himself. Instead of looking awry, he looks at her and then looks away, shutting his eyes against the elements he neither recognizes in himself nor is capable of assimilating. Such repulsion and hatred lead to the rejection of the qualities the criminal 'you' represents. The private 'I' can merge with 'you' only in the all-consuming fire of violence, a perverse parody of the sexual act, ensuring that all that remains of 'you' is a scarred memory of near escape.

The ending brings out a significant difference between Spillane and Poe which is best articulated by the transfer-of-guilt motif initiating Hammer's adventure. The Mafia frames him, thus placing him in the position of the guilty one; unable to identify with and analyse this dual identity of criminal and detective, he fails. The transfer-of-guilt motif spotlights the Oedipal configuration underlying the genre, illustrating that the I-am-you method includes identifying with a murderous desire (if not with a desire for murder) as the means of finding out the criminal. Such a desire is, of course, familiar from psychoanalytical theories about the development and stabilization of individual self-consciousness. Indeed, by associating the Queen's letter with a substitute phallus she herself does not have, Lacan reads Poe's story, in particular its triangular structure, as a dramatization of the Oedipal stage dealing with the sexual differentiation of the subject. Barbara Johnson explains that at issue is neither the phallus as such (anatomical difference) nor its imaginary loss (castration), but the subject's acceptance of it as the sign that marks sexuality as *difference*, which, in turn, enables symbolization and self-reflection (1988, 243–5). Given that Hammer perceives women only as mirrors of himself, one might characterize his reaction to the criminal woman as that of a voyeur whose gaze is fixated on the sexual difference she represents. His destruction of her indicates, however, that he refuses to acknowledge it as difference, which further explicates his incapacity for self-reflection. Spillane's book is thus, thanks to its strongly anti-Oedipal nature, the antithesis of 'The Purloined Letter.'[12]

The protagonist's mental inflexibility raises the question of its effects on the author's game with the reader, for the reader's role includes the acceptance of the private 'I' as that point from which the unfamiliarity represented by crime is probed. The hermeneutic task of reading, interpretation, and explanation not only makes this position familiar to the reader, but also singles it out as a representation of narrative transmission, for detectives, after all, decipher the messages criminals send to them. Again, a comparison of *Kiss Me, Deadly* with 'The Purloined Letter' demonstrates how this representation transposes itself into the author-reader game.

Irwin draws attention to the fact that Poe makes this game one of *reading*, a 'form in which the emotional energy generated by the reader's effort to interpret the text ... flow[s] directly into the main character's activity of solving the mystery ... the reader [is] asked to interpret the author's intentions by participating in the detective's attempt to interpret the criminal's' (414). By contrast, Spillane's author-reader game is shaped by Hammer's inability to imitate. When, in reading *Kiss Me, Deadly*, our reader's 'I' merges with the private 'I,' we find ourselves placed in a position in which 'I' is, tautologically, 'I,' but definitely not the criminal 'you' represented by the treacherous woman. Should flesh-and-blood readers – women, members of racial or sexual minorities, for example – reject this textually embedded role, they find themselves figured in the text as the criminal 'you.' Constituted by the text as 'you,' they realize they cannot take up the position reserved for the private 'I,' leading to an inverse tautology in which 'you' are 'you,' but 'you' are certainly not 'I.' This textual repulsion mechanism also gives the author the means to prevent the properties that the investigator and the criminal represent from getting mixed with one another at this higher-level game.

This rigid separation of 'I' from 'you' reveals the basic rule of Spillane's author-reader game by profoundly affecting the interpretive room for manoeuvre it leaves to the reader. The ending of 'The Purloined Letter' shows Dupin succumbing to his rage at the Minister, whereby he slides into the position formerly occupied by his opponent. This shift, in turn, signals that Dupin's own previous position, associated with the analytical upper hand, is now open for the reader to take. This gesture shows that Poe's author-reader game self-reflexively acknowledges that narrative transmission includes a reciprocity inviting interpretation. The author expects the narrative to take hold on readers, so that their reading becomes their own articulation of the author's message. Left open to the intervention of readers, the author not only accepts but also encourages the otherness they bring into the encounter. The contrast with Spillane could not be greater, for in his book the ending destroys the character occupying the analytic position, which amounts effectively to saying that *to be analytical is to be deviant*. By closing down the position of analysis, Spillane tries to discourage and hinder our reinterpretation of his text. Because analysis is envisaged as deviance, our rearticulation of the narrative in any other terms than those identified by the narrator-protagonist would amount to a destruction of the game the author has designed. We are not expected to carry over the game initiated by Hammer to our game with the author, but to accept the ending of the book as definitive.

Moreover, Spillane, too, includes a structure of self-inclusion like Poe's by naming his narrative *Kiss Me, Deadly*. Referring to the criminal's final seductive appeal to the protagonist ('You're going to die now ... but first you can do it. Deadly ... deadly ... kiss me' [152]), the title draws further attention to the fact that imitating the protagonist leads to the destruction of all difference. Thereby the author guarantees that his game with the reader never challenges our mental faculties by anything new, but remains within the circuit of the dully same. And that surely best explains Hammer's epithet 'deadly.'

You Are My Construction

Besides achieving the primary goal of capture, in many detective stories investigators knowingly use the I-am-you approach as a means of analysing the criminal's role(s) in order to increase their knowledge of how idiosyncratic behaviour can be modelled and made accessible to further elaboration and use. The personal advantages for the investigators are heightened professional skills as well as a feeling of victoriousness. At least initially, their approach distances and objectifies the criminal, for this person is viewed through different lenses. The reader's fascination consists of the gradual buildup from random data to a fully formed picture of the culprit. This is typical of police procedurals, which overwhelm investigators – and readers – with a wealth of detail, creating the sense of a crime documentary. (Their length shows the importance of establishing through detail the sense of process; the Bantam paperback edition [1994] of Caleb Carr's *The Alienist*, for example, has 597 pages.) Readers are at every step privy to the conjectures detectives make, thereby becoming silent participants. Playing this game involves knowledge of popular psychology, psychopathology, and various crime-detection techniques, which today include, for example, computer technology.

Caleb Carr's best seller, *The Alienist*, takes place in New York, in the year 1896.[13] A serial killer murders transvestite boy-prostitutes. Dr Lazlo Kreizler, a controversial alienist (criminal psychologist), heads the investigation team of members of the police force, a journalist, and his protégés. The events are set in the era noted for the birth of psychopathology, forensic medicine, and various technological procedures, which in those days introduced, for example, fingerprinting and the Bertillon system of anthropometry as indispensable tools of police work. The plot divides into three parts. The first part (titled 'Perception') deals with the formation of the team and introduces Kreizler's approach; the second ('Association') demonstrates its application; and the third ('Will') follows the team's capture of the killer, whose identity is by now known. Kreizler's profession, which unites the skills of an investigator with those of a psychoanalyst, thus underlining the similarities between these two professions,[14] makes this book interesting for the present purpose by emphasizing the primacy of the symbolic order for analysis. Moreover, *The Alienist* portrays this order as the only available medium for the investigation, thanks to the fact that the investigators initially know nothing of the serial killer. They can approach him (as it turns out) only by constructing various culturally determined models and comparing them.

In this book the criminal and the detective are both at the outset distanced from the reader, for one is a serial killer, while the other is an expert alienist. The author-reader game builds directly on the method of investigation, which Kreizler teaches not only to his team but also indirectly to the reader. With its help we can try on the alienist's mask in order to attempt, in this capacity, to imagine an even more radical other, a serial killer.[15] What adds to the book's interest is that the association of the criminal psychologist with the detective explicitly highlights the question of (narrative) transference. Psychoanalysis understands it as 'a special space between the analysand and the analyst, one where the analysand's past affective life is reinvested in the dynamics of the interaction with the analyst' (Brooks 1994, 52). *The Alienist* shows the investigation as the space where the transference takes place. At first, the team's projection of the killer is solely based on their interpretation of him; after the killer's early realization of being chased, transference takes hold, for he actively intervenes in the investigation by threatening the team and by killing one of Kreizler's protégés. Kreizler teaches the team to recognize in these destructive acts the killer's only means of communicating with them; the team can use this information not only to elaborate on the killer's picture but also to test their hypotheses by provoking him into action. The transference is thus reciprocal. Further, it demonstrates that the killer's murders recall his past in the form of unconscious repetition. He acts out his past as if it were present: repetition is his way of remembering, as recollection in the intellectual sense is blocked by resistance and repression.

Yet what is more significant from the reader's perspective is, as Brooks suggests, that we may conceive of 'the text as an as-if medium, fictional ... yet speaking of the investments of desire on the part of both ... author and reader, a place of rhetorical exchange or transaction. We as readers "intervene" by the very act of reading, interpreting the text, handling it, shaping it to our ends, making it accessible to our therapies' (1984, 234). Brooks argues that the transference between author and reader is most visible when narrative deals with the problematics of its own transmission, for, by revealing the desire both to narrate and to listen, it emphasizes its role as the medium of mutual exchange (216–21). The opening of *The Alienist* questions whether the narration of the story can succeed. Its narrator, a journalist named John Moore, is resolved to tell it, but Kreizler doubts the value of the project, maintaining that 'it would only frighten and repel people' (6). The narrative frame affects the author-reader game, for, as the narrator explains, Kreizler's approach challenges one to overcome one's fear and repulsion in order to achieve a deeper understanding of the human psyche (5–6). Is the reader able to share in this experience of hunting for a 'murderous monster,' which in the end results in our coming face to face with a 'frightened child' (5)? To cut through the wealth of detail in this book, I discuss only the relationships among the victims, the murderer, and the team which directly build on the notion of mirroring.

The following excerpt describes the beginning of the investigation, and similar scenes recur. The crime is heinous, and there are no feasible suspects. Before the investigators can think about particular individuals, they have to form a sense of the type of person who is capable of committing the kind of crime with which they are dealing:

On the walkway was the body of a young person. I say 'person' because, though the physical attributes were those of an adolescent boy, the clothes ... and facial paint were those of a girl ... The face did not seem heavily beaten or bruised – the paint and powder were still intact – but where once there had been eyes there were now only bloody, cavernous sockets. A puzzling piece of flesh protruded from the mouth. A wide gash stretched across the throat, though there was little blood near the opening. Large cuts crisscrossed the abdomen, revealing the mass of the inner organs. The right hand had been chopped neatly off. At the groin there was another gaping wound, one that explained the mouth – the genitals had been cut away and stuffed between the jaws. The buttocks, too, had been shorn off, in what appeared large ... one could only call them carving strokes. (19–20)

After witnessing this sight, Moore turns away, nauseated and overcome by a profound sense of pathos. The deed seems totally senseless, and the rage it evokes renders the observers helpless. Yet to solve crimes, detectives must find means of ensuring their ability to work in the midst of monstrous events. The various skills of detection such as forensic techniques can serve as such an insulating mechanism. By teaching the team – and the reader – the basics of an alienist's approach, Kreizler shows how a criminal psychologist is able both to acquire and sustain functional detachment and to put together the criminal's profile based on the evidence at hand. Detachment both enables and protects the transference, for it is not the psychologist's ego but his or her neutrality that should mirror the patient (Gallop 1988, 272).[16]

To create the needed distance, Kreizler advises the team to subordinate their responses to the present task by asking what those responses tell them about the killer. Somewhat paradoxically, this detachment involves intimacy, for they attempt to understand the murders from the killer's perspective.[17] The key to it lies in the context(s) of his life, for Kreizler's method is based on a theory of *contextualism* that has the mechanisms of *psychological determinism* at its core. Therefore, to follow adequately the process of projecting the criminal, as readers we have to grasp the basics of this theory. By using the information the book supplies, we can summarize it as follows. Contextualism applies certain basic notions of William James, Charles Darwin, and Herbert Spencer to the human mind, conceiving of the cause-and-effect relations that mould the human psyche in a particular way. According to this theory, the origins of the psyche are in formative childhood experience. A subject's actions are idiosyncratic responses that are established through habit and learning during childhood. Those responses and actions that ensure his or her psychic and physical survival are the ones that come to dominate behaviour and orientation in life. Repetition and learning engrain them into his or her mental makeup to form stable behavioural, perceptual, and cognitive patterns. If a subject, for example, experiences only harshness and cruelty from early on, these experiences govern that person's outlook and orientation, so that it is difficult for him or her to conceive of other models than a cycle of violence, humiliation, pain, and outrage (57, 61–2, 73, 160, 296–7). As this pattern results from 'the law of habit and interest' (251), geared to sustain the psychic mechanism, it is exceedingly difficult to break and change, even if the learned patterns turn out to be counterproductive, or destructive, in adult life. The subject must follow the laws by which his or her world has always functioned, for to give up on them means abandoning one's self (251–2, 268).[18]

Kreizler introduces a thought experiment to demonstrate how one can begin to put together the cause-and-effect mechanisms of the killer's psyche. He first invites the team to think of cases in which extreme violence seems acceptable – for example, a mother protecting a child or a child protecting itself. He then argues that the difference between these examples and that of the killer lies only in context, asking the team to 'shift [its] point of view enough to grasp that every victim and situation leading up to a murder resonated within the killer to a distant experience of threat and violence and led him for reasons that we had not yet fully defined to take angry measures in his own defense' (192–3). Here we see a conscious effort to 'look awry,' that is, to place oneself imaginatively in a position outside the perspective outlined by the symbolic order, which, simultaneously, represents the team's effort to extend signification into realms that appear to lie beyond this order. The boy-prostitutes represent something pivotal to the culprit; to find out what it is, the team has to dwell on circumstances that would make his deeds appear well-founded and motivated.[19] Thus even extreme brutality can be made understandable by placing the perpetrator in a proper context. Kreizler conceives this effort as an act of imaginative identification with the child in the criminal, especially with his position in the interaction of his immediate early contacts.

Kreizler's insistence that this method's application extends signification to realms that appear meaningless emphasizes both the textual and narrative nature of the transference. It is textual because the killer's past is present only in the symbolic form of his murders and attacks on the team; it is narrative because the team uses it to construct a coherent, connected, and forceful story giving their interpretive account of that past (see Brooks 1994, 53–4). Starting with the mutilation of the bodies, they ask what the murderer sees when he looks at his victims. Although seemingly 'coherent,' the defacement seems inexplicable: the removal of the genitals suggests sexual abuse, but why should anyone remove the eyes? They take the eyes as 'the link, the key, the way in' (66) to the killer's inner world, conjecturing that the killer sees himself in his victims. Thereby the bodies become 'a mirror image of some savage set of experiences that were central to the evolution of [the] man's mind' (193).[20] What makes *The Alienist* useful for the present purpose is that it employs the mirror motif for *narrative* ends by making it the device enabling the team to put together a rough story about the killer's life and the roots of his pathology.[21] With its help they read the message he sends them through the continuation of his murders.

The mirror motif creates a whole series of mirror structures which direct the team's reasoning as well as providing it with the means of combining narrative fragments with one another. This series has at its centre the idea of the victims as doubles of the criminal. On the basis of the reversal-into-the-opposite mechanism of the mirror image, the team projects the profile of someone who is now a reversed version of the victims. Thus, by examining the tormented, they construct the image of the tormentor. The second layer in this reflexive series builds on the notion that this external relationship describes an internal condition: doubling has its origin and end solely in the killer's mind. As each victim was a mixture of compliance and saucy insubordination (267), they assume that the criminal was dominated by a similar inner split in his adolescence. The victims reflect his character, his inmost needs and experiences. Thus, the mutilation of the bodies is the killer's interpretation of what has been done to him. This image the team constructs articulates their interpretation of the killer's unconscious motivation as that of someone who has assumed the position of the castrator; the killer himself might not recognize it as his own. The third layer in the reflexive series arises from the reader's cognizance that these mirror constructions are the postulation of the investigating team, who, by looking at the victims, envisage them in front of a reflecting surface that throws back a dim image of the quarry they are after. The picture they are putting together is their narrative transcription of what the inner landscape of this serial killer looks like.

The next narrative step involves combining this image of the killer with the theory of contextualism in order to understand the factors that may contribute to his pathologically split psyche. What makes a child compliant and yet insubordinate? What mechanism causes a person to move from one binary (tortured/castrated) to its opposite (torturer/castrator)? In order to explain how the victims portray the criminal's situation as a child, the team examine dishonesty and duplicity as a child's responses to violence. By using the victims' life histories, they model a family context in which the parents have seriously maltreated the child while preserving a respectable social front (252). Brutality belongs to the shaping experiences of such a child, engraining in him a model of behaviour. He learns to abhor the characteristics and conduct that his parents punish with acts of violence. He associates the forbidden actions with the means of asserting himself, as his only way of defending himself in the family battle (114–15, 251). This pattern leads to the paradoxical situation in which the child simultaneously is deeply impregnated by self-loathing, yet pursues and cultivates prohibited actions (267). Duplicity and violence are his survival tactics. The team postulates that this cyclical pattern of betrayed trust, deceit, violence, and self-hatred binds the killer to his victims.

The team wraps up its narrative exercise by linking the killer's primary life context with the mirror motif. The pattern of duplicity and violence makes the killer desire his switch from the slave position of the tortured to the master position of the torturer.[22] Yet this reversal fails to free him from self-hatred, leading to a compulsive cycle of murders. The reason is his inability to distinguish 'I' from 'you': by killing 'he hope[s] to eradicate an intolerable element of his own personality by eradicating mirror reflections of the child he'd once been' (462).[23] At this point, the team can postulate the 'originating' mirror: the target of the killer's rage is his cruel mother; her taunting gaze has, however, turned this rage inward, resulting in the attempt to cut off unwanted psychic aspects (461–2). The gouging out of the victims' eyes thus represents the murderer's attempt to destroy the humiliating inner experience of the very first mirror that reflected him in such a hateful light.

The employment of the I-am-you method in *The Alienist* emphasizes the limits to one's embrace of the other's perspective. Two factors in particular drive this point home. The killer mimics the Sioux Indians in mutilating the bodies, but his imitation reveals ignorance of the cultural aspects of this practice, which underlines the fact that his role playing springs from his own needs. The second illustration is a conflict deriving from the team's dispute as to which parent is more likely to intimidate a child. Given the abusiveness of his own father, Kreizler finds unacceptable the suggestion that the mother wields such influence. The quarrel is resolved once he recognizes that he suffers from what William James calls the *psychologist's fallacy*, the mistaking of one's own perspective for that of the patient (295, 302). This incident works both to reinforce and illustrate the basics of the contextual theory. There is no one shared human nature enabling 'I' to project 'you' by solely probing into one's self, because the formative context is the determining shaping factor. Kreizler defines the limits of this exercise: '[y]ou can come close, perhaps, close enough to anticipate [the killer], but in the end neither you nor I nor anyone else will be able to see *just* what he sees when he looks at those children, or feel *precisely* the emotion that makes him take up the knife' (531). The only way to learn these things would be to ask the killer himself – and even he (or especially he) is unlikely to know. The separateness of persons remains. The killer's capture provides the justification for the conjectures, but as he dies before there is a chance to interview him, the team – and the reader – are forever left outside this mind, seeing it solely through various deliberately constructed narrative models. Thus, following the investigation from beginning to end enriches one of the opening epigraphs from William James: 'Whilst part of what we perceive comes through our senses from the object before us, another part (and it may be the larger part) always comes out of our own mind.'

In order to relate the depiction of this long process and its outcome to the author-reader game, we need to consider how transference addresses this bond. Brooks (1994) understands it as the dialogic relation of narrative production and interpretation, explaining it as follows: 'Something is being transmitted or transferred from the teller and is told to the listener, and to listening: it has entered into the realm of interpretation. And if the story told has been effective, if it has "taken hold," the act of transmission resembles the psychoanalytical transference, where the listener enters the story as an active participant in the creation of design and meaning, and the reader is then called upon himself to enter this transferential space' (51). In the light of the foregoing analysis, it seems worthwhile to ask how the solipsism suggested by the theory of contextualism, on the one hand, and the narrator's narrative motivation, on the other, affect the author-reader game through narrative transference.

Brooks argues that as the process of reading is fundamentally constructive – a linking up of fragments into a coherent whole – the measure of its success is 'a further opening up of the text, [the creation of] further patterns of interconnectedness and meaning' (1994, 57). *The Alienist* illustrates this argument, for the team's analysis of the transference allows them to build increasingly larger parts of the killer's life story and finally to connect them into a coherent whole. The thoroughness of this process means, I think, that the transferential relationship of the author-reader game addresses not the killer's story as such, but its broader implications. The narrator appears intent on making the reader consider the significance of imaginative identification in the context of our limited access to reality. If we are, for the most part, locked within our own minds, and if our perceptions of reality stem from the engrained patterns of our various contexts, does the attempt to place oneself in someone else's position make a difference? Can it make a difference even if its results remain uncertain? Of course, this question is set in special terms, as the someone else is a brutal serial killer, making the gap between 'I' and 'you' extraordinarily wide. Yet the team's response shows that this exercise increases understanding of the psyche, for what seemed totally senseless is endowed with some kind of meaning in the end. By using the narrator's opening and concluding remarks about his narrative motivation, the reader can determine that the author's game includes making us see the benefits of drawing the killer's profile, for even imperfect understanding, refracted through the solipsism of one's mind, functions as protection against blinding prejudice, indifference, and cruelty. In this book, solipsism, entailing the notion of one's basic solitude, works to reinforce the importance of trying to fathom other minds. Imaginative identification with the killer inspires sympathy for him, as is indicated by the narrator's musings: 'It was odd ... to think of *his* torment; odder still to realize that I had some sort of vague sympathy for the man. Yet the sentiment was in me, and it was understanding the context of his life that had put it there: of the many goals that Kreizler had outlined at the beginning of the investigation, we had at least achieved that one' (510). As the book's title signals, narrative transmission involves the reader's gradual adoption of the alienist-detective's mask, which entails the understanding that, even if for a lay person it may seem morally wrong to feel sympathy for a killer who has caused others unbearable suffering (192, 570–1), the alienist can and must retain the expert's professionally sympathetic attitude.

By associating the reader with the alienist, the author-reader game puts the reader in the place of the *subject supposed to know*. Brooks explains that in psychoanalysis the analyst's mere presence – prior to any interpretive intervention – signals to the analysand the potential and the promise of interpretation on the part of the analyst. This promise triggers the transference relation (1994, 54). In Carr's game, the positioning of the reader acknowledges and encourages our interpretive intervention, yet we need to ask what it is that we are supposed to know. *The Alienist* links up the dramatization of the transferential relationship within the fictional world with the author-reader game by characterizing the serial killer as society's dark mirror image. The whole book is framed by an overarching mirror structure, for the narrator ends by suggesting that the reader consider the killer as society's 'offspring, its sick conscience.' People, author and reader included, revel in this figure, because the killer and his like 'are the easy repositories of all that is dark in our very *social* world,' so much so that the contexts that help make serial killers are ones we tolerate in life and even enjoy reading about (592). In the final instance, then, the killer stands in a reflexive relationship with us and our (present-day) society: he is the image of the evil we would like to cut off by placing it solely in an external, alien other. By implying that he is society's own mirror image, the author reminds the reader that the relationship between 'I' and 'you' is not restricted to the individual level, but encompasses much larger structures. This game thus suggests that, in such reflexive relationships, 'I's' ability to think and feel like 'you' includes the ability to recognize oneself in general human models and in general human situations. It demonstrates that such models include the Oedipal configuration, for the killer's pathology derives from his mother's hatred of her child, the offspring of the sexual relations she abhors, as well as from his father's indifference. The theory of contextualism highlights the cultural constructedness of these basic models; yet the effect is the universalization of (Oedipal) guilt through this suggestion that we explain deviance and evil by evoking a murderous desire in each and every one of us.

The overarching mirror structure enables us to specify the nature of narrative transmission in *The Alienist*. By making the narrative message the point of reflection – that is, the reader's participation in evil through social and narrative practice – the author-reader game privileges narrative content. This means that Carr's game does not intend us, as readers, to apply the alienist's approach either to our own relationship with the author or to the reading experience. The acts of writing and reading detective stories are not included in the transferential relationship as issues to ponder. As a result, it may escape the reader's attention that Kreizler's method motivates and even justifies the author's depiction of sadistic cruelty and violence, the very topics with which the book takes issue.

I Am You: Union through Malevolent Sympathy

G.K. Chesterton explicitly discusses Father Brown's application of the I-am-you approach in the prologue and epilogue of his fourth collection of short stories, *The Secret of Father Brown* (1981c). The prologue, entitled 'The Secret of Father Brown,' depicts a meeting of the priest, Flambeau, and an American visitor, who presses the priest to divulge the 'occult' and 'esoteric' (463) secret of his approach. He agrees to do so in order to rebut what he sees as superstition and unreason. His description of mimetic identification shows it to be a highly creative process, resembling the way in which authors create characters and actors play roles. Yet the explanation accounts for less than it seems at first to do, for, unlike Carr's Kreizler, Father Brown never demonstrates exactly how the method works in practice. The eight ensuing stories are narrated by an external narrator,[24] who even focalizes them through someone other than the priest, thus placing him at a further remove from the reader. The epilogue, titled 'The Secret of Flambeau,' then returns to the discussion, which is closed by Flambeau's revelation of his identity as a reformed thief.

The structure of the collection calls attention to the relationship that the framing prologue and epilogue have to the framed stories. In Brooks's view, framed-tale structures always dramatize reading as transferential interaction by highlighting the presence of a narrator and a listener (a narratee) and the interlocutionary relations thus established. Framing makes listeners (and readers) fix on the motives of telling, which, in turn, invites them to think about their own participation in listening (and reading). What consequences does reading have? What is one supposed to do with the tale once it is read? 'As a "subject supposed to know,"' writes Brooks, 'the listener is called upon to "supplement" the story ... to articulate and even enact the meaning of the desire it expresses in ways that may be foreclosed to the speaker' (1993, 200). In Chesterton's collection, the American who desires to know Father Brown's secret illustrates curiosity as a partial motivation of the narrative transmission. That the method's application is never demonstrated step by step channels curiosity by stimulating the reader's imagination to apply the priest's explanation to the events depicted by the narrator. Lynette Hunter explains that the author 'does not come out and say "this is how it works"; he does not impose a theory on his character. We are presented with events within which Father Brown thinks and acts, and we understand from these' (1979, 141).

The narrative motive thus understood affects the author-reader game by lending it a markedly self-reflexive quality, for, unlike Carr, Chesterton explicitly intends us to apply the detective's approach to our own reading experience. After describing his method, Father Brown falls into a reverie, gazing meditatively into his cup of wine 'as if that single cup held a red sea of the blood of all men, and his soul were a diver, ever plunging in dark humility and inverted imagination, lower than its lowest monsters ... In that cup, as in a red mirror, he saw many things' (466). Under Father Brown's gaze, the cup of wine merges with the cup of the Holy Communion with its red mirror reflecting the drama of sin and redemption. Therefore, to think like him is to think *allegorically*, which directs attention away from what is read to *how* one reads. As a trope in which a second meaning is to be read beneath and concurrent with the surface story, allegory directs attention to the linking of one plane of meaning with another. Thus, in *The Secret of Father Brown*, narrative transmission aims to involve us in a self-reflexive application of the priest's method to our own reading of the stories.

In what follows I first consider Father Brown's explanation of his method and then match it with what he does in 'The Mirror of the

Magistrate.' I have chosen this opening story because Father Brown briefly comments on it in the epilogue. In closing I analyse how this approach affects the author-reader game.

The priest startles the American by claiming that 'it was I who killed all those people' (464). He attributes his secret to the adoption of an inside view, as opposed to the scientist's outside view, which, in its impartiality, dehumanizes the criminal to a mere object. He attempts to transcend the subject-object dichotomy, assimilating the other by thinking how one becomes a person who commits certain kinds of deeds. He describes this process as follows:

> Well, what you call 'the secret' is exactly the opposite. I don't try to get outside the man. I try to get inside the murderer ... Indeed it's much more than that, don't you see? I *am* inside a man. I am always inside a murderer, thinking his thoughts, wrestling with his passions; till I have bent myself into the posture of his hunched and peering hatred; till I see the world with his bloodshot and squinting eyes, looking between the blinkers of his half-witted concentration; looking up the short and sharp perspective of a straight road to a pool of blood. Till I am really a murderer. (465–6)

Chesterton grounds Father Brown's use of the I-am-you approach on the hermeneutic legacy of empathy, which comprehends the event and experience of understanding not only as involving a dialogue between 'I' and 'you' but also as aiming at an inward communion beyond the external bounds of social interaction and the separateness of persons (Morrison 1988). This exercise has observation, reflection, and experimentation as its basis. Achieving the inside view requires both time and conscious effort. Father Brown feels himself into the other by enacting a role: imitating a model taken from life, he strives to conform his thoughts, feelings, and actions with it. This process is thus both cognitive and affective. He thinks about how a crime could be done and in what style and state of mind a person could do it, adjusting and elaborating on the inner model until he believes it matches with the criminal's constitution. The approach thus postulates a basic likeness between the knower and the known as a condition for knowledge, without the knower being the object. The closure of the distance between 'I' and 'you' becomes possible by moving through various stages of increasing likeness to the point of identity. This likeness hides itself under many guises: Father Brown plays many different parts both during the solving of a case and at various times in his career. Yet the identity achieved is selective and partial, involving restricted aspects of the imitator's being. This tradition of empathy acknowledges that role playing is fundamentally limited by the fact that the imitator always remains more intimate with him- or herself than with the person (role) being emulated. Therefore, the specific goals of the role playing reflect, in the last instance, the imitator's own character (Morrison 1988, 30–1).[25]

Bearing this description in mind, how does our imitation of Father Brown shape our reading of 'The Mirror of the Magistrate'? The story is mainly focalized by a policeman and his friend who stumble on the scene of a crime. The events move from the discovery and investigation of the murder of Judge Gwynne to the trial of Osric Orm, a revolutionary poet, culminating in Father Brown's demonstration of Orm's innocence and the guilt of Gwynne's colleague. The solution builds on two clues in particular: the scene of the crime, a night-time garden illuminated with multicoloured lights, and a shattered mirror.

'But the garden itself ... showed a random glitter, like that of fading fireworks; as if a giant rocket had fallen in fire among the trees' (469), the narrator states, providing a view of this place through the policeman and his friend: 'As they advanced they were able to locate it as the light of several coloured lamps, entangled in the trees like the jewel fruits of Aladdin, and especially as the light from a small round lake or pond, which gleamed with pale colours as if a lamp were kindled under it' (469). It is characteristic of Chesterton, Martin Priestman observes, to connect the nature of the setting in a symbolic unity with the problem being investigated; Father Brown's method involves entering with gusto into the symbolic resonances of the setting, which match with the details of the crime (1990, 125, 133). His reading of the setting as the expression of the criminal's desire demonstrates, in turn, the basic principle of Chestertonian semiotics, which treats the setting as an *external reflection* of the *internal condition* of its inhabitant. This tenet draws the reader's attention to the manifold mirror structures of the story, for not only is there a mirror in its title, but also the shattered mirror in the victim's house is itself set within a larger mirror structure of the whole setting. The coincidence of the story's title with the central symbolic objects the story presents further highlights the story's self-reflexivity, for the qualities the story attributes to the mirror and the night-time garden largely apply to itself as well.

In order to enter into the setting's symbolic resonances, Father Brown identifies the dominant motif of this setting, which is light. The garden is lit. The victim lies with his head in the pond, the artificial illumination of which gives it 'the appearance of an unholy halo' (471). Orm, the prime suspect, has 'a wonderful head of hair, as yellow and radiant as the head of a huge dandelion' that is 'outstanding like a halo' (474). The recognition of the terms in which to think about the crime starts the process of imaginative identification. In order to determine who plays what role and why, Father Brown identifies himself with more than one participant. He first plays a revolutionary poet by trying to see the setting through Orm's eyes.[26] It makes him realize that, from a poet's perspective, looking at the garden 'was like looking *down* at heaven and seeing all the stars growing on trees and that luminous pond like a moon fallen flat on the fields in some happy nursery tale' (478). The inspirational setting and the poet's passion for poetry explain why Orm would never spoil his career by killing a 'conventional old fool' (584). As the murderer is none of those present on the scene when the victim was found, Father Brown can advance only by meditating on the victim. The garden as an external reflection of the victim's internal condition supplies the point of departure for role playing. Feeling himself into a man for whom 'the world [is] a blaze of electric lights, with nothing but utter darkness beyond and around it' (585), the priest identifies himself with a person whose function is to uphold and safeguard the law and conventional order to such an extent that the profession itself seems to stand for these concepts. The victim's commitment to and dependence on the standing order and his status as its representative make Father Brown conclude that '[i]t is not the revolutionary man but the respectable man who would commit any crime – to save his respectability' (585). Therefore, the murderer has to be someone fundamentally similar to the victim.

The postulated similarity opens up the significance of the shattered mirror, which, argues Father Brown, rests on 'rather a fine metaphysical point' (480). Although the pictures in mirrors usually vanish forever, this glass retained the murderer's reflection, 'hanging [it] in that twilight house like a spectre; or at least like an abstract diagram, the skeleton of an argument' (481). To conjure this embryonic narrative out of the void, Father Brown takes the victim's one distinguishing characteristic, his hatred of spying, and projects its mirror image, the very thing that is hated. A new configuration emerges between Judge Gwynne and his colleague, Sir Arthur Travers. Treason, Father Brown reasons, is the worst crime a worldly man can imagine, for it undermines the foundation of his respectability. As the prosecuting barrister, Travers accuses Orm of conspiring against the state. His vindictiveness and reputation as an ambitious, status-conscious man (476–7) bring Father Brown's exercise to an end. The similarity between victim and murderer is complemented by a likeness in appearance, as both are tall and bald men and, on the night of the murder, were dressed in white tie and tails. The priest conjectures that the murderer saw his own reflection in the mirror, but mistook it for Gwynne and, in panic, shot at the mirror. This mirror retains his picture, because he is the victim's antithetical double.[27] The story ends with the information that Travers has committed suicide, shooting 'at the same man again, but [this time] not in a mirror' (482).

Our application of Father Brown's method to our reading of the story directs attention to its mirror symbolism, especially to the fact that the physical mirror contains something metaphysical. The phrasing of Travers's having shot at the same man again but not in a mirror indicates that the duel between the two basically similar men relates to a suicidal duel within a divided self.[28] Thus the principal pairings of outer (garden) and inner (internal makeup) as well as of container (mirror) and contained (image) that structure the story all evoke the mystery of self-reflection. They highlight it as the self's encounter with its fundamental otherness in the dramatic mirror-shooting scene: the murderer mistakes his own picture for that of the victim. Through his confusion this scene effectively underlines not only that self-reflection is grounded on splitting and doubling, but also that it involves a fluidity, bordering on interchangeability, between self and other. Thus the mirror's mystery includes the realization that 'I am you and you are I' is the hallmark of the self-reflexive capacity. But in order to understand the Chestertonian interpretation of its metaphysical aspect, we need to read the scene in the manner Father Brown does.

The murderer's mistake, expressed as 'I am my enemy,' yields the allegorical key to Father Brown's thinking, and hence to the metaphysical side of self-reflection. The priest envisages each person, himself included, as governed by an internal strife between the old and new Adam, that is, the human being's sinful, fallen nature and his or her redeemed nature through God's mercy. The criminal's wickedness doubles externally that which is always already imprinted in our inmost being. In the struggle against evil, one's 'only hope is somehow or other to have captured one criminal, and kept him safe and sane under his own hat' (466). The notion of original sin, a readiness for evil grafted in everyone, provides Father Brown's ability to recognize, partake in, and assimilate, the maliciousness of the criminal through the awareness of his own inclination to evil. He can claim to *be* the criminal in a literal and not a metaphorical sense, for reasons having to do with the mind/body (spirit/flesh) division as understood by the Christian creed. He is one with the criminal, because of the sinfulness of all flesh; but, believing in Christ, he is also incorporated into the body of Christ. In this body, Christ is many (members) and the many are one in Him (Morrison 1988, 9–10). Taking this double unity literally is one of the cornerstones of the faith the priest represents, so that the one decisive factor setting him apart from the criminal, the 'actual final consent to action' (465), explaining why he repeatedly finds that 'somebody else had played the part of the murderer before [him] and done [him] out of the actual experience' (584), is, in his eyes, secondary.

Chesterton encodes the self's otherness to itself in terms of a tension-filled internal strife, which gives Father Brown's mimetic role playing its special character by infusing his empathy with a degree of malevolence. By coining the concept of *malevolent sympathy*, Morrison draws attention to the fact that strife can also be a condition and a means of union, and that human bonding can take place through emotions antithetical to love. Conflict, rivalry, and hatred are means of assimilation, for it is in the nature of hatred, as well as of love, to change us into the likeness of what we contemplate (1988, 70–1).[29] The malevolence of Father Brown's bonding with the criminal stems from the Christian injunction to love one's enemies: he loves them for what is good in them and hates them for what is evil. His assimilation of the criminal builds on this antagonism, for, loving his adversaries, he also chastises them for spiritual and moral wrongdoing. Thereby, his act of bonding is sealed by a single emotion manifested simultaneously both as love and as hatred. This description applies, of course, to his relationship to himself as well. Father Brown uses malevolent sympathy for benevolent ends, however, for his goal is the confession, repentance, and ensuing redemption of the criminal.

Envisaging self-reflection as a malevolently sympathetic activity calls attention to the means by which the inner strife is managed. Priestman notes that there runs throughout Chesterton's work 'a double insistence on the absolute distinction between good and evil and on their mirror-like resemblance ... The *doppelgänger* motif is everywhere, corresponding at the level of action to the "paradoxical" mannerisms for which Chesterton is notorious at the level of style' (1990, 123). Priestman registers the curious self-reflexivity of the author's narrative strategy, for Chesterton brings down the imaginative congruence between the crime and the atmospherics of the setting at the point of Father Brown's explanation. This strategy highlights the artifice on which the reader's pleasure has been based; however, in the context of the whole series, Priestman says, it 'produce[s] the effect of an irreconcilable split in the author himself' (127).

These observations are useful, because Priestman does not seem quite to get hold of the terms in which self-reflection works in these stories. By linking up the mirror motif with the absoluteness of distinctions, he argues that self-reflection serves as the means of division and differentiation. On the basis of Father Brown's approach it is possible to maintain, however, that the profusion of mirror imagery draws on an inverse mode of associating ideas from the one Priestman identifies. The literal sense in which the priest understands the phrase 'I am you' implies that he relies on a mode of reasoning which associates things by *contrast* (Morrison 1988, 37–40). This mode, Morrison explains, uses the contrast between two qualities or roles as a means of combining and unifying them. It underlines the implicit presence within a characteristic or a role of its defining opposite, envisaging these opposites as existing concentrically, or as nested within one another. (The yin-yang figure offers a visualization of this mode.) Father Brown's remark about the two ways of renouncing the devil illustrates this idea of contrast as a means of combination: 'One is to have a horror of him because he is so far off; and the other to have it because he is so near' (587), which is to say that at the very heart of redemption lurks the awareness of one's own readiness for evil. Or, to give another example, in 'The Man with Two Beards,' a reformed thief and murder victim is most alive when dead. When still alive physically, he was 'in a most radiant and shining sense' dead, because he was outside the judgment of the world; once physically dead, he is forever alive, thanks to being resurrected by God. In this line of thinking, the polar opposites participate in one another; although the difference between them remains, it is proportional instead of being absolute. In associating qualities by contrast one thus perceives identity as based on a both/and relationship, instead of an either/or relationship. Of course, this idea of combination also applies to the distribution of traits within one's self.[30]

That association by contrast directs Father Brown's thinking enables the reader to identify the striving for synthesis in Chesterton's metaphysics of self-reflection. The momentary and imperfect fusion of 'I' with 'you' which his approach entails points towards the belief that eventually the internal split will be bridged for good. This conviction provides the eschatological framework in which self-reflection takes place. This eschatological aspect becomes most visible in the aesthetic side of Father Brown's approach; so far the image of a worldly and heavenly body has shown us only its 'biological' side.[31] Yet as his role playing is distinctly artistic, it suggests that the inner split between the old and new Adam also involves creativity and interpretation. Hunter relates this aesthetic side of the I-am-you method to Chesterton's conception of the artist as a mystic, who, in accepting the Catholic faith, subordinates himself to an external authority. Consequently, as an artist Father Brown not only creates in alignment with this power, but, acknowledging such a power beyond him, also interprets it. This interpretive function shows the artist's human side, exposing his limitations (Hunter 1979, 134–5; 155–6). These derive from the fact that, although the priest's work as artist is in the Creator, and the Creator in it, this union remains flawed, split into two dimensions: '[t]here is always something unspoken in the creative word, something rebellious in its uttered image. There is always the Creator's hatred for flaws introduced into his work by others, always hatred by the work for standards of perfection that condemn it' (Morrison 1988, 94). Yet participating in God's creativity, the mystic artist hopes for the moment of synthesis when God, the sculptor, finally melts down his human, flawed nature, recasting it into a new form, bringing about unity among the different faculties of his mind and permanently closing the gap separating him from the Creator and his own fellow human beings.

The aesthetic side of Father Brown's approach enables us to see how the Oedipal configuration becomes manifest in Chesterton's work. The light imagery of 'The Mirror of the Magistrate' supplies the clue that provides the link between the Theseus myth, a variation of the Oedipus myth,[32] and Christian mythology. This imagery already suggests that the author stresses not the sexual differentiation of subjectification (all characters are male) but its spiritual side, which indicates a *sublimated* version of the myth. Christianity represents divine thought as light, which in the figure of Christ descends into the 'dark cave' of the physical body and reascends in His resurrection from the grave. 'In the myth of Theseus and the Minotaur,' writes Irwin, 'a human being takes on godlike qualities in his heroic overcoming of the fear of death, while in the Christian gospel a god becomes man, slays death, and gives humanity the gift of immortality. And in each case the light-in-the-cave structure evokes the human condition as the entrapment of a godlike principle of light in the physical cave of the body and human destiny as the ultimate return of this light/life to its origin, either in an undifferentiated form (as in Dionysianism) or a differentiated one (as in Christianity)' (314). Differentiation moves from the body/mind axis to the mind/spirit one, so that self-reflection necessitates the recognition of the mind's duality, which can be stated, for example, as a distinction between human and divine reason. The ability to reason divinely gives Father Brown the analytic upper hand so that he can momentarily desire from the perspective of the other. Thanks to the creativity of this process, self-reflection is distinctly aesthetic in nature.

In portraying aesthetically appealing crimes and artist-criminals, Chesterton thus evokes the fascination of negative creativity, which he then controls through the aesthetic creativity and criticism voiced by Father Brown, the artist-detective.[33] By not providing the reader with an inside view of the workings of Father Brown's mind, he challenges the reader to become the 'I' that fathoms 'you.' In this way, the I-am-you approach acquires a distinct aesthetic-spiritual function. The reader's interpretation of these stories progresses through various stages, starting with our desire to understand the process dramatized in the stories, continuing through our creative imitation of Father Brown's method, and ending in the moment of aesthetic closure, when we perceive the intricate patterning of these elements.[34] Given Chesterton's own religious framework, it is clear that, in this game, the moment of closure includes the reader's understanding that the dramas played out among victims, criminals, and detective are allegorical portrayals of the spiritual strife within us, representing our own complementary and simultaneous aspects.

Chesterton makes both the writing and the reading of detective stories meditative exercises. In playing according to the author's rules we come to understand, by following the examples of our *alter ego* in the stories, what the author and Father Brown do, not merely in a literary critical sense, but in an active manner. For by our own work and reflection, we may thus develop the actual ways of thinking for which a blueprint is set forth in Chesterton's stories, and build on them in our hearts. The employment of the I-am-you approach is fundamentally restricted by the fact that a role player always remains more intimate with him- or herself than with the other person; hence, in imitating Father Brown we are forced to turn the mirror on ourselves. And such is Chesterton's trust in the reader that he explicitly leaves room for the narrative transmission to respond to our disposition. In the prologue, the narrator refers to Father Brown's meditative vision, saying that 'all these things ... may be seen later from other angles and in other moods than his own' (467), a statement which shows that the narrator acknowledges and respects our intervention in reading. The specific goals we choose for our interpretation are, in the last instance, a reflection of our own inmost needs and capacities.[35] In meditating on these stories, then, we find that our interpretations in multiple ways reflect back on ourselves.[36]

If Chesterton's author-reader game moves us from the position of the detecting 'I' to that of the criminal 'you,' thus dramatizing our own split and doubled consciousness, then what constitutes the difference between Chesterton and Poe as well as between Chesterton's and Poe's postmodern lineage? The answer calls for a brief consideration of Poe's game. When we imitate Dupin in our reading of 'The Purloined Letter,' we inevitably realize that the application of his approach engages us in a struggle for the interpretive possession of the mystery's meaning. Poe achieves this effect by linking up interpretation with the structural positions in which role playing places us. Trying to gain the interpretive possession of 'The Purloined Letter' and thus defeat Poe, we play Dupin, only to find out that the logic of Poe's game will eventually place us in the loser's position (the Minister's place), for not only does the letter bring with it a blind spot, but also the struggle to be one up on one's opponent anticipates the opponent's retaliating move. Whatever interpretive strategy we apply as readers, the next player will adopt it in order to turn it against us and demonstrate what remains unaccounted for in our interpretation, as the analyses of this story by Jacques Lacan, Jacques Derrida, Barbara Johnson, and Irwin confirm. Thus, we can never solve the mystery Poe has designed: we can only endlessly *repeat* it. This feature makes the story metaphysical, for it has 'a mystery with a repeatable solution ... that conserves (because it endlessly refigures) the sense of the mysterious' (Irwin, 2). Irwin explains that '[i]n any detective story whose central mystery is the self-conscious description of its own workings, there will always be one more step needed, precisely because self-consciousness by its very nature can never really think its own ending, its own absence' (423). Chesterton's quarrel is not with this description of self-consciousness as such; he believes, however, that the internal antagonism on which it is grounded will eventually be resolved, although how that happens or what that state is like remains unknown – and, perhaps, even unthinkable. Because it posits an external, omniscient authority outside self-consciousness, such a belief affects interpretation by promising its eventual cessation. The familiar passage from St Paul expresses this idea in terms of the mirror image: 'For now we see through a glass, darkly, but then face to face: now I know in part; but then shall I know even as also I am known' (1 Cor. 13: 12). In contrast, the secular and aesthetic nature of the self-reflexive allegories Poe and his postmodern progeny write celebrate the unending movement of interpretation.

These three examples demonstrate that detective fiction invites us, as readers, to play different kinds of games through the representation of imaginative identification with a fictional investigator. The applications of this approach show its surprising adaptability to diverse conceptual and ideological frameworks, ranging from nineteenth-century philosophical-rational and theological concepts, to present-day psychoanalytical notions. The approach moves detectives and readers along the axis of sameness, similarity, and difference. The range is from games where we are invited to join the detective in role playing, using the results to meditate aspects of ourselves, to games in which the playing of roles is subsumed into an emotional rampage, leaving available only the role of the angry avenger, to games in which the construction of models is the means of playing. The genre does not dictate the relationship between the detecting 'I,' whether the investigator or the reader, and the criminal 'you'; rather, one discovers the relationship on a case-by-case basis. Good games highlight doubling between players, such doubling being both mentally challenging and aesthetically and emotionally pleasing. The games thus include from the start, or lead to, the acknowledgment that the twin fictional masks fit the players at the higher level, too.

The foregoing analysis shows that the representation of imaginative identification affects narrative transmission. It is worthwhile to speculate about this link in terms of the 'logic of complicity, sanction, and reassurance' that Meredith Anne Skura (1981) finds in Freud's analysis of the joke as a transference exchange. Applying what she says about it to the detective story,[37] we may characterize this genre as a displaced version of a forbidden sexual or aggressive wish, allowing its narrators to express it in an acceptable way: instead of killing someone, they tell stories about killing him or her. But the narrative cannot complete its work of displacement and yield narrators their substitute pleasure without an audience. Often the presence of a third party necessitates displacement. 'There is someone watching,' narrators say to themselves, 'so I can't kill this person. But I can get this onlooker to share the guilt with me vicariously, by acting out an attack through the characters of the story.' They cajole readers to join them in a verbal enactment of the crime that civilization prevents them from carrying out. By this means readers get the pleasure of a substitute satisfaction without exerting energy, while narrators secure their own pleasure by being reassured that their displacement has worked: their actions are acceptable and their guilt shared (180–1). In a general sense, then, imaginative identification as the ability to recognize the criminal – the embodiment of the forbidden wish – in oneself highlights the writing and reading of detective stories as a more or less self-reflexive processing of the Oedipal complex. Imaginative identification grounds the capacity for moral reflection, for, according to Freud, when children stop trying to satisfy their Oedipal wishes, which have become prohibited, they internalize the prohibition through an identification with their parents. This leads to the formation of the super-ego, constituted through the internalization of parental interdictions and demands. This differentiation of the super-ego from the ego leads to the formation of conscience and a sense of guilt (Freud 1961a and 1961b).

Finally, the game metaphor emphasizes that writing and reading detective stories always involves an antagonistic aspect. Translating Žižek's analysis of Hitchcock's films in *Looking Awry* (1991) into textual terms, we can approach the text itself as a kind of mirror; if we look awry at (or into) it, we may suddenly realize that it, as it were, gazes back at us, making us aware that what we took to be an object has turned into a subject. (Such moments are analogous to the detective's encounter with the inexplicable aspects of the crime.) Thus reading itself thematizes self-reflection, for our perception of the alienness of the text invariably leads to the perception of ourselves as differentiated from the other. And, as we have seen, the extent to which this feature is either suppressed or celebrated depends on the way in which the author has constructed the game.

2

Abduction: Interpreting Signs for Narrative Ends

The generic conventions of the detective story hold that every criminal always leaves behind traces, imprinting in one way or another the story of the crime on the fictional world; from these traces a perceptive person can read this story. To avoid exposure, criminals attempt to camouflage and manipulate or distort the signs of their crimes, anticipating the possibility that someone might investigate their transgression. Their crimes constitute the 'texts' they 'write.' They are the 'authors' of at least two stories: the authentic story of the crime and the deceptive one(s). The ideal from the culprit's perspective is a text whose existence no one would ever discover. (This is the so-called perfect crime.)[1] As criminal deeds, however, alter the state of things in the fictional world, this goal is usually impossible to attain. The next best alternatives are crime texts that are illegible, incomprehensible, and incoherent, or those that convey false and deceptive stories. The culprits aim at providing a decisive, final version of their texts, but the investigation frequently compels them to keep on manoeuvring to escape detection.

The game of detection gets under way with the beginning of the detectives' reading operation, that is, with the investigation. Their actions and their readings of a case are thus oriented by the question of 'whodunit,' and by the prerequisite of constructing the criminal's text in such a way that the construction also proves this person's authorship. By so doing, the detectives also function as 'authors' of the text about their detection. Because the exact boundaries of the crime and the code (or even the idiolect) in which it is written are obscure at the outset, gathering data marks the detectives' first entry into the solving of a crime. Knowing that the scene of the crime is at least partially a manipulated surface, they first have to observe it closely, trying to decide what items constitute clues. In some instances this task is relatively easy, as, for example, with forensic evidence. If a person has been shot, the fact of the shooting itself, together with such details as the point of penetration of the bullet and the range at which the shot has been fired, offer a starting point from which a detective can begin to build the investigation. The crime text itself foregrounds these features, explicitly suggesting them to an investigator as the basis of pertinent questions. If the victim is, in addition to being shot, naked, with chunks of his flesh cut out, as in Patricia Cornwell's police procedural *Cruel and Unusual* (1993), these factors are additional signs that the investigation team must account for.

Cruel and Unusual demonstrates – as does any detective story – that some signs are much more difficult to spot than the visible 'writing' on a victim's body. In Cornwell's book, the tiny pieces of debris on the victim's wrists and the incision marks within the wounds are not discernible to the naked eye, yet they prove to be meaningful. The protagonist, a Chief Medical Examiner, does spot them thanks to her professional knowledge, which directs her observations. But crimes usually involve still more nebulous signs, frequently pointing to human interaction. For example, the protagonist of *Cruel and Unusual* is unable to perceive that her assistant's nervous and clumsy behaviour is a symptom of something other than fatigue and the early stages of pregnancy. She fails to consider the acts and the underlying motives of certain of her colleagues as signs of the crime she is dealing with.

What adds to the intricacy of the signs of the crime is that many of them stand for such factors as the needs, desires, and goals of the persons involved. Therefore, they cannot be exhaustively fathomed and explained. The opaqueness of reality and the impossibility of attaining direct knowledge of either past events or the inner lives of the suspects make these signs only indirect points of contact with past reality. They are indicative of the deep signifying connections that explain surface phenomena. Various kinds of signs allow the detectives to make a 'leap' from directly observed states of things to a reality that can be observed only indirectly, because it lies 'deeper' or 'below the surface.' This interpretive stand entails going *beneath* or *beyond* the ostensible nature of things (Ginzburg 1983, 109). Together with this in-depth model of knowledge goes the notion that marginal and seemingly irrelevant clues are often the most important and revealing ones.

This method of reading minutiae became, from early on, one of the staples of the detective-story genre, thanks to ingenious feats of reasoning by Edgar Allan Poe's C. Auguste Dupin and Arthur Conan Doyle's

Sherlock Holmes. Holmes's reasoning is based on the notion that details are hard to manipulate, for they either escape attention entirely or seem too unimportant to bother about.[2] They receive their significance from the fact that it is relatively easy to imitate, falsify, and distort the obvious or the typical, whereas the minutiae reveal individual traits that a person repeats in a certain way by force of habit, almost unconsciously. The innermost characteristics of a person's individuality are thought to reside in these elements beyond her conscious control. Details disclose that which is typical of the individual (Ginzburg 1983, 87). To hide his identity, the murderer in Cornwell's book commits copycat murders.[3] Were it not for a tear in the expensive vest the criminal wears, leaking out pieces of eiderdown, the investigators would not have managed to identify him. With the help of this detail, taken as a sign of the culprit's narcissism and dare-devil attitude, the protagonist not only springs a trap for him but also hazards an explanation of certain key features of his psyche. Such individual features are of special importance in fictional crime detection, as the aim is not to explain the phenomenon of crime but to resolve particular cases. The definition of crime as a text also entails a focus on its individual nature, for it presupposes an idiolectal code that reveals the specificity and uniqueness of the particular case at hand. Even negative evidence, the absence of certain facts and events, may be highly significant.[4]

In what follows, I rely on *The Sign of Three* (Eco and Sebeok, eds, 1983), and in particular on Eco's essay, in explaining the basics of the conjectural method fictional detectives employ; all subsequent examples and their analyses, however, are my own.[5] In analysing this conjectural process, I am making explicit its various steps or stages; although investigators usually explain how they arrived at the solution, they seldom explicate in detail what specific rules or contextual and circumstantial selections they applied to the case. That fictional detectives unmistakably apply a conjectural method of reading and interpretation, the basics of which are assumed to be familiar to the reader, is precisely what has attracted academic readers to discuss the genre. It is certainly not an accident that Edgar Allan Poe and Arthur Conan Doyle – the two writers who are most forthcoming about the detective's reasoning process – initiated the philosophically serious examination of the genre. Such scholars as Umberto Eco, Carlo Ginzburg, or Thomas A. Sebeok maintain that reading detective fiction requires mental ability, involving such faculties as memory, attention, intelligence, inferential thought, and inventiveness. It is one of intellectual creativity, giving the reader pleasure and a sense of achievement through understanding and discovery. It is important to be precise on the focus of this game, for spotlighting the conjectural process allows for (at least) two kinds of playing between the author/detective and the reader. The more usual game is the openly competitive battle between author and reader in which the author, while following the rules of fair play, strives to preserve the mystery of the crime until the end, and the reader attempts to outwit the author. In effect, the reader plays *against* the author and the detective. In contrast, the kind of game I engage in here is based on playing *with* the author and the detective by trying to understand better, even to systematize, the method whose workings the genre demonstrates.[6] The detective functions as a model reader, but one whose various reading operations I try to elucidate in more detail than he or she (or even the author) does. The aim of this game is to contribute to a deeper appreciation of the mental ability and intellectual creativity the genre asks its reader to exercise. I also play with the previous players of this game, namely, the authors contributing essays to *The Sign of Three*, by lifting out their passing references to the narrative aspect of the abductive method and expanding on it in order to draw attention to the extent to which these games are games with narrative and narrativity, and, specifically, with the human competence to construct plots and to conceive such constructions as spatial patterns.

This narrative aspect of the detective's interpretation is evident from the early stages of the investigation onward. After gathering some data, detectives start fitting together whatever pieces of evidence they have: they look for the *narrative scaffolding* tying the separate pieces together. They search for the overarching plot pattern that governs and organizes the relations among the parts while they also search for an understanding of how the separate parts form this postulated global network. (The projected whole then helps to orient the investigation, indicating what kinds of further information or testing is still needed.) Their postulation of various plot patterns helps to elaborate the facts – the chosen narrative units – and, reciprocally, their refinement of these facts contributes to their specification of the hypothetical patterns. In other words, detectives are engaged in a process of figuration, of trying to conceive the spatial network which organizes the elements into a meaningful totality. Perceiving the narrative patterning does not yet guarantee that the crime has been solved, however, for with initial hypotheses detectives usually come up with *wrong* narrative models before they identify the one that will enable them to explain the crime adequately (i.e., so that it corresponds to the real state of things in the fictional world).

The concept of narrative theme (Ryan 1993) elucidates this complementary movement as supplying the backbone of the detection process. As the term indicates, narrative thematics is a plot-oriented approach. Narrative themes have (at least) three functions in the process of narrative construction, thanks to the flexibility they exhibit at its various levels. Moreover, they may be organized hierarchically, moving from single narrative themes to thematic sequences and, ultimately, to plot schemata. Thus, their identification creates coherence. At the most elementary level, then, narrative themes enable detective-readers to link separate motifs (such as events and incidents) to more general and abstract categories of meaning. As these themes describe primarily the interaction of agents, they indicate what kinds of actions, intentions, and results the particular motifs instantiate. Another way to express their function at this level is to characterize it as showing 'the precise narrative meaning of the elements which make up the plot' (ibid., 170). Examples are such narrative themes as 'deception,' 'vengeance,' 'broken promise,' 'violated interdiction,' and so on. The individual motifs of plot link with one another, forming sequences of various lengths, made up of specific sets of actions by characters. Thinking of plot as a series of action sequences brings out the second function of narrative themes. They help detective-readers sketch the plot's semantic skeleton by indicating its strategic points, which describe those events, actions, intentions, and results of actions that keep it moving and that are indispensable for understanding the totality it forms. Hence, narrative themes show how the separate plot units form thematic (and often stereotyped) sequences composed of various motif configurations. In Lawrence Sanders's *The First Deadly Sin* (1973), for example, each slaying by the serial murderer is initiated by his delusions of grandeur. The repetition of this key characteristic organizes the sequences depicting the acts of murder under the stereotyped plot scheme of Lucifer. This example points to the third function of narrative themes. They have a synthesizing capacity: they may be used as shorthand expressions for the abstract plot schemata subtending narratives. Such thematic conceptualizations of whole narrative patterns traditionally take the form of an adage or a character's name (the theme of Lucifer, as in Sanders's example) (Ryan 1993, 185; see also Ryan 1991, ch. 10).[7]

The complex process of identifying and classifying narrative themes as well as of organizing them hierarchically relates to the detectives' mental movement within the 'hermeneutic circle' in an attempt to bring their horizons of understanding to fit as closely as possible with that of the crime text written by the criminal. Given this notion of the interaction among the parts and the whole, it is not surprising that detective narratives usually describe the meeting of these horizons as a moment of insight, even of illumination, for then the whole and the parts are understood together.[8] This circularity, in depending on the closeness of understanding, interpretation, and application of cultural codes and rules, further explains why conjecture plays such an important role in crime solving: it enables detectives to rise above the narrowly defined meaning of facts, linking these facts to their hidden possibilities of significance. They can never amass sufficient facts to account for absolutely everything in a crime, but, by fitting together past events with the actions and motives of the people involved, they can offer an interpretation of them. And, as narrative construction plays a crucial role in this interpretation, we now turn to examine how abduction serves as a tool for this purpose.

The Abductive Method

Fictional detectives use abduction both in searching for the significance of the separate signs they encounter and in attempting to link these individual units together. Consequently, the conjectural approach might be said to be the procedure by which signs are read as the motifs of plot and are then linked to narrative themes and, ultimately, to plot patterns. As detectives are not interested in signs as such, but only as narrative components that can help them to solve a given crime, they treat objects and events as texts rather than as individual signs (Eco 1983, 204–5). Such textualization makes signs yield narratively useful units. Arthur Conan Doyle's 'The Adventure of the Blue Carbuncle' (1985a) opens with Holmes having been delivered a 'very ordinary black hat of the usual round shape, hard and much the worse for wear,' whose owner he is asked to trace. His name is known; he is a Henry Baker, but as there are 'some thousands of Bakers, and some hundreds of Henry Bakers' in London, the problem is to find the right Henry Baker. After examining the hat with a magnifying glass,[9] Holmes concludes about the 'individuality of the man' that he is

highly intellectual ... fairly well-to-do within the last three years, although he now has fallen upon evil days. He had foresight, but has less now than formerly, pointing to a moral retrogression, which, when taken with the decline of his fortunes, seems to indicate some evil influence, probably drink, at work upon him. This may account also for the obvious fact that his wife has ceased to love him. (122)

In reading out such a wealth of information from an ordinary felt hat, Holmes explains what the hat is and why it is so. In Eco's words, he 'tentatively' clarifies the reason(s) for the hat's appearance (Eco 1983, 202–4). To do this, he must decide which specific property or properties of the hat call for explanation. These properties are not available automatically, but the interpreter has to *choose* them. Holmes finds it noteworthy, for example, that the hat is covered with 'the fluffy brown dust of the house.' The whole of the explication directly depends on the feature the interpreter isolates as significant and surprising, for it triggers the explanatory process.[10] The isolated fact is then related to a general principle, rule, or law which is thought to account for it. The reasoner thus has to look for two things: the property or fact to be explained and the general rule which will interpret that property or fact. Once they are selected, the conclusion about the subject under investigation follows mechanically. C.S. Peirce calls the adoption of such an explanatory hypothesis *abduction*. We can specify how Holmes abducts the meaning of the brown fluffy dust as follows:

Rule: Wives who neglect to maintain the apparel of their husbands no longer love them.
Result: (the observed fact acting as the starting point): Henry Baker's hat is covered with the fluffy brown dust of the house.
Case: (the conclusion of applying the rule to the result): Henry Baker's wife neglects maintaining his apparel and thus no longer loves him.

Holmes defines the significance of the fluffy dust through a cultural rule concerning the manifestations of marital love. The postulated rule is regarded as the explanatory cause of the perceived effect: the lack of wifely love and thus of care account for the hat's sorry state (which lack, in turn, may have its roots in the weakened financial position and moral decline of the husband, as Holmes implies).[11] What characterizes abduction is that the fact to be explained may be indisputable, but the reasoner's choice of the rule in the light of which it is interpreted may be wrong or inappropriate. Given this hypothetical nature of abduction, Eco (1984, 40) defines it as 'the tentative and hazardous tracing of a system of signification rules which will allow the sign to acquire its meaning.' The abductive conjecture always needs to be tested, for the rule is usually selected among a number of other possible ones. In this particular case, other feasible explanations would have been the death of the wife or the bachelorhood of Mr Baker. The encounter with him confirms the general tenor of Holmes's hypotheses, as everything about the man testifies to his reduced means and decline in fortune. The exact state of the marital relationship, however, remains unverified, functioning rather as a comic flourish to a chain of clever conjecture.

In approaching the hat as a 'text,' Holmes interprets a little *story* about the fate of a man. He relates each observed feature – the dustiness, the various stains, and the battered shape – to a rule that fences off an area of meaning having to do with adversity and decay. He treats the signs he observes as the motifs of this story. Taken together these motifs strongly suggest a formulaic plot pattern about an intellectual man gone to seed. (In accordance with nineteenth-century phrenology, the hat's 'cubic capacity' stands for the intelligence of Mr Baker.) The motifs and the plot pattern, in turn, may be summarized with a thematic label that handily captures the overall trajectory of this story. This heading might be designated 'personal decline.' Once Holmes discerns the semantic range of the motifs, he is able to link them with a thematic label which condenses their significance.

Abduction represents an interpreter's bet on the meaning of a sign. It is a means of coding that which is encountered. Another way to describe abduction is to characterize it as the procedure wherewith detectives browse the *semantic encyclopaedia* at their disposal, zooming in on sections that seem promising as regards the coding of the sign to be explained. The notion of the encyclopaedia refers to what Eco (1976, 125) calls the 'Global Semantic Universe,' registering *all* possible meanings of linguistic items. Consequently, it has the form of a rhizomatic, multidimensional network. In this unordered network, every point (i.e., every structuration of content) can be connected with every other point which, according to some previous cultural conventions, can be associated with it; where the connections are not yet designed, they are, in principle, conceivable and designable (Eco 1984, 81). The encyclopaedia is, then, the semiotic postulate designed to describe the notion of unlimited semiosis. It also records sets of frames, scripts, stereotypes, and common knowledge which contain information on the use of linguistic and non-linguistic items, indicating to the interpreter which of the semantic properties of these items ought to be activated and which disregarded in a specific context. In this sense, the encyclopaedia may be said to describe the detectives' knowledge of their world.

As the encyclopaedia, however, changes with time, and, as it is virtually infinite and hence globally indescribable, it can be structured through a sum of potential local descriptions, represented by what are called *dictionaries*. A dictionary supplies a linguistic item with a concise definition, composed of a finite set of semantic markers. It circumscribes a culturally shared area of meaning within which a particular discourse should stay, given a set of specific circumstances. The dictionary functions as the interpreter's *pragmatic device* for shaping the semantic universe (Eco 1984, 85). Detectives use abductions as tools in selecting the appropriate dictionaries with the help of which the semantic range of particular signs may be determined. This selection entails deciding on the suitable contextual and circumstantial frameworks which restrict an otherwise vast semantic field. Marie-Laure Ryan (1993) even envisages a specific *thematic dictionary* which each reader draws upon in making sense of a plot. This dictionary consists of narrative themes and represents an intermediary zone of meaning within the 'pyramid of meaning,' which is flanked by extremely general cognitive categories (e.g., 'action' or 'mental reaction') on one side, and the specific contents of a text on the other. The thematic dictionary includes such narrative categories as 'challenge,' 'deal,' 'punishment,' 'retaliation,' 'prohibition,' 'betrayal' – categories which are employed in sketching the semantic skeleton of a plot, enabling the reader's comprehension of its key points. This dictionary also contains stereotypical plot formulae, making it possible for the reader to classify a narrative pattern as being of a given type (e.g., of the Faust type) (ibid., 169–70, 185). Book-length detective narratives especially demonstrate the use of thematic and other dictionaries in the search for the meaning of the pieces of evidence. The investigation proceeds through trial and error as detectives choose suitable-seeming dictionaries and explore the semantic range these dictionaries make available. The mistakes they frequently make, sometimes with embarrassing consequences, derive from the selection of a wrong dictionary or from making inappropriate contextual or coreferential selections within it.

Types of Abduction in the Service of Narrative Construction

In browsing the semantic encyclopaedia, by first choosing among dictionaries and then in employing the dictionaries deemed appropriate, fictional detectives put to use their competence in cultural signifying practices. The crime cases they encounter test this proficiency in various ways. In some instances, detectives immediately perceive what a particular case or its individual component are about and almost automatically draw on pertinent entries in a dictionary in constructing their explications. The appropriate plot outlines with their concomitant motif configurations and narrative themes lie within easy reach. But often the interpretive task proves more difficult. Complications may be caused by a detective's (temporary) inability to perceive what particular components make up the case at hand and what exactly is at stake in it. The complication may have its roots in the difficulty of fitting the pieces together, for it seems that no existing plot pattern matches the case. And at times the pieces tally equally well with more than one pattern, yielding a number of equally suitable plot schemes. The fact that abduction may thus be either a simple or a complex process underlines the way in which the conjectural effort varies in proportion to the interpretive challenge a sign or a text poses.

The diversity of the abductive labour means that the identification of motifs, narrative themes, and plot formulae demands in some cases much more work from the detectives than in others. It also raises the question of the reasons for such difficulty. Does the complexity of the abductive labour match the complexity of a given motif, narrative theme, or plot pattern recognized as its result? We can approach this question by looking more closely at the abductive process itself – the backbone of any detective's narrative construction – and, more specifically, by concentrating on its most basic stage: the detective's search for the narrative themes and plot patterns he or she deems suitable both to the crime text and to the aims of his or her interpretation. Detective fiction itself highlights this phase, for it dwells on those moments when detectives relate their observations to different narrative themes and plot patterns, evaluating the adequacy of the results.

The complexity of an abduction may be further specified by using the accessibility of the rules and laws as a demarcational criterion. Following Eco's example in 'Horns, Hooves, Insteps' (in *The Sign of Three*), I link the discussion of the different types of abduction with the detective's recognition of certain events and objects as either *imprints*, *symptoms*, or *clues*, which represent some of the most typical signs characteristically encountered in detective narratives.[12] What makes these signs useful for this discussion is the fact that each refers to a story, as each is the result of a prior event or chain of events.[13] They aptly demonstrate the nature of the task facing fictional detectives: they have to solve the crime by constructing a coherent story about past events, and, in doing so, they have to fit together pieces that are (micro)narrative in nature. Again, I am making explicit the operations fictional detectives rely on – operations which are not spelled out in detail in the texts serving as my examples. By using the facility with which a rule or law suggests itself in the explication as a distinguishing criterion, Eco (1983, 206–7; 1984, 41–3) draws a line between *overcoded, undercoded,* and *creative abductions.* There is a graded continuum of complexity from overcoded abductions to creative ones, with the former representing the most easily accessible relationship between the thing to be explained and the chosen rule and the latter the most elaborate one. These three types of abduction address the intension of the conjectural process, focusing on such factors as the coherence and unity of the explanation. The final category Eco discusses, *meta-abduction,* deals with the extension of the hypothesis, that is, the interpreter's testing of whether his or her abductions correspond to external reality. I consider the implications each has for the detective's choice of motifs, narrative themes, and plot patterns.

The following excerpt from Michael Dibdin's *Ratking* (1988) shows what is involved in reading *imprints* through overcoded abductions:

The mud surrounding the building site where Ruggiero Miletti had been murdered had proved a rich source of impressions. A preliminary investigation, completed while Zen was still present, had yielded five different footprints and two distinct sets of tyre marks. One of the two sets consistently overlaid the other, and it was distinctive, in that one of the tyres did not match the other three. Zen had imagined that this would be a rarity, but in fact four of the cars in the garage had one odd tyre. Only one configuration, however, matched that found at the murder scene. (184–5)

Aurelio Zen observes imprints of footprints and tyre marks in the soft mud. To be able to read them as the occurrence (or *token*) of a given type-expression, he has to have a precise, coded competence about imprints in general and footprints and tyre marks in particular. This competence entails the ability to recognize ready-made expressions and link them with a content made up of a pertinent class of possible imprinters. The code on which the interpreter relies is built on his or her previous experience (Eco 1983, 210). With overcoded abductions such as these, the appropriate rule suggests itself automatically or semi-automatically to the interpreter. Since the rule is readily available, the inference concerns only the decision to recognize the Result as a Case of a given Rule. Even in these instances, however, the recognition of a phenomenon as the token of a given type is not completely without a hypothetical effort and is never a matter of complete certitude (ibid., 211). Imprints can, of course, be faked and made to lie.[14] As one of the four tyres is different from the others, Zen can connect the vehicle not only with a genus (car) but also with a species of a kind (a car with one odd tyre). The imprints tell him that a car has been at the site of the murder, but they do not reveal whose car it was. In such type-to-type semiotic relationships, concrete individuals are not yet concerned (ibid.).

Zen recognizes the traces as indicative of a story, enabling the projection of a possible sequence of events. There seems to be a correspondence between the facility of choosing the pertinent rule and selecting a preliminary broad plot outline. Ruggiero Miletti has been kidnapped. His kidnappers have promised to release him alive at the remote building site. Consequently, the tracks most probably tell of the arrival and departure of the kidnappers and the murderer (whose identity may coincide). The specification of this sequence of events represents a somewhat more complex abductive process, for the tracks suggest to Zen two possibilities involving two different opponents. It is feasible for the kidnappers to have delivered Miletti to the location by car and killed him there, but it is also possible that someone else, also travelling by car, did the deed after the kidnappers left. Zen makes the imprints a motif in two separate plots. The first one centres on the murder of Miletti by his kidnappers and is characterized by the narrative theme of a broken promise. The second deals with his murder by a member of the Miletti family and centres on the theme of a double-cross. To choose between these options Zen needs more information, but the abductive leaps from clear-cut imprints to two alternative plots and their concomitant narrative themes were relatively easy to decipher, because Zen has a lot of experience of kidnapping cases. This competence involves familiarity with intertextual frames furnishing analogous stories about what kinds of things have usually happened in kidnappings. Therefore, when the construction of plot relies on overcoded abductions, the detectives' movement from signs to pertinent narrative themes and plot outlines takes place with (relative) ease, thanks to the accessibility of the rules on which the relationship stands.

It seems reasonable to assume that more complex abductions would affect a detective's selection of motifs, narrative themes, and plot formulae. We can approach this question through another example, this time involving an alleged murderess encountered in Elizabeth George's *A Great Deliverance* (1988). She has supposedly chopped off her father's head; yet the events remain clouded in mystery, for she refuses to communicate with either the police or the psychiatrist assigned to her case. We see her for the first time through Inspector Thomas Lynley's eyes:

[Roberta's] hair was filthy, foul-smelling. It was pulled back from her broad, moon-shaped face with an elastic band, but greasy tendrils had escaped imprisonment and hung forward stiffly, kissing on her neck the pockets of flesh that encased in their folds the incongruous ornament of a single, slender gold chain ... The broad face was expressionless. Suppurating pimples covered cheeks and chin. Bloated skin stretched over layers of fat that had long ago erased whatever definition her features might have had. She was dough-like, gray and unclean ... Roberta was dressed in a too-short skirt that revealed white, flabby thighs upon which the flesh, dotted by red pustules, quivered when she rocked. There were hospital slippers on her feet, but they were too small, and her sausage toes hung out, their uncut nails curling round them. (149–50)

Part of the mystery Lynley encounters is the obesity of the alleged culprit. None of the villagers can account for her acquiring gigantic proportions. He approaches her corpulence and lack of self-care and response as *symptoms* of some occurrence that has caused a serious derangement of her personality and has eventually affected the course of events at her father's farm. When signs are recognized as symptoms, the type-expression represents a class of ready-made physical or mental events that refers back to the class of their possible causes. The cause of a symptom is a feature not of the shape of its type-expression, as it is with imprints, but of its type-content. The cause is a marker of the compositional analysis of the meaning of a particular symptom-expression (Eco 1983, 211). But, given that any symptom, obesity included, can have a number of causes, Lynley must choose among alternative rules that his knowledge about the world supplies him with. Such selection among alternative explanations portrays an instance of an *undercoded abduction*. It is characteristic of undercoded abductions that the elected rule is not necessarily the correct one – or the only correct one. In these instances, the interpreter continually has to take into consideration other possible readings and can entertain her abductions only until further testing proves or disproves their validity. Thus their *under*coded nature relies on there not being a readily available explication for a given sign. The decision as to which rule is the appropriate one depends on contextual and circumstantial factors which indicate whether certain properties belonging to the meaning of a term need to be emphasized or played down. In the initial stages of the case, the psychiatrist treating Roberta suggests that food might be for her a compulsion, a stimulus, a response, a source of gratification, or even a form of sublimation, emphasizing that one cannot know more precisely until she herself indicates which interpretation is appropriate (George, 148).

Lynley and his assistant go through a slow and complicated process in solving this crime. Yet once Lynley perceives the overriding topic of the case and links it with a suitable plot pattern, he can arrange the pieces he has gathered in a rudimentary sequence and endow them with more precise meanings. He gets hold of the decisive clue by accident: while visiting the local graveyard, he stops at the grave of a baby found dead in the woods some time ago (176–7). The birth and death of this infant constitute another mystery, besides the murder, which afflicts the village community. Intrigued by the bizarre epitaph for a child on the tombstone – 'As Flame to Smoke' – Lynley traces it back to its source, one of Shakespeare's lesser known plays, *Pericles*. What further arouses his curiosity is learning that the local priest, who contacted the police about the murder, has chosen the epitaph. Lynley's decision to find the subtext is directed by an undercoded abduction concerning the significance of the inscription. By drawing on a rule according to which 'grave epitaphs express certain key aspects of a person's life or character,' Lynley hopes to throw light on the enigmatic fate of the infant. *Pericles* is a play about the theme of (father-daughter) incest and the birth of a child from this liaison. After reading the play, the detective makes another undercoded abduction on the basis of the first one, by drawing on a rule concerning intertextuality which states that 'a text may relate to another text through analogy.' He further concludes that, given the infant's age, the similarity must address the sequence of events, enabling him to read the case through the play. He infers that Roberta's father has sexually abused her, and that, as in the play, this liaison has involved the birth of a child. Therefore it seems likely that the dead infant found in the forest is this child. Although this chain of events, by suggesting a clear-cut motive, strongly implies that Roberta really did kill her father, Lynley has no proof whatsoever of the accuracy of his conjectures. The detective knows that the plot he has constructed describes only the very broad trajectory of the events. It needs to be specified and elaborated. Yet the Shakespeare analogue enables him partially to decode the symptom he initially thought was significant. He now understands that Roberta's fatness has at least one cause pointing to the sequence of events which obesity hides: pregnancy by the father.[15] (The rule he draws on may be formulated as 'Pregnant women look fat.') He cannot, however, explain why she has grown even fatter after giving birth.

Assigning narrative themes and plot patterns to motifs through undercoded abductions brings into view the process-like nature of the detectives' search for meaning. The investigative labour involved in the interpretive effort indicates that at least some kind of complexity must be involved in the motifs, their concurrent narrative themes, and the plot patterns the motifs suggest. But is there anything particularly complex in the theme of incest, given its familiarity in literature and life? There are at least two possible reasons for a detective's slowness in recognizing the overriding topic of a case and the plot pattern that lends coherence to observations and facts. The first reason has to do with what Ryan (1991, 155) calls *functional polyvalence*. This notion refers to the convergence of events and states (not necessarily adjacent) that have special strategic significance for the narrative as a whole. An example of functional polyvalence is the sexual abuse of Roberta by her father. The investigator has trouble in perceiving and naming it because this event simultaneously functions in at least three different roles: as a solution to a problem (the sexual desire the father has for small girls); as a violation of an interdiction (incest prohibition); and as an infraction justifying the punishment to come (Roberta kills him). As detective narratives deal with conflicts that frequently involve several people and their goals and interests, such nestedness of functions is very typical of them, explaining the effort a detective has in arriving at suitable narrative themes and plot patterns. In other words, the investigators do not sufficiently take into account the interactional nature of the events they are trying to explain. Hence, instead of linking a motif with just one character's domain, they should place it against the interactional network, looking for narrative themes expressing the *confluence* of actions and motives. The detective's difficulty in recognizing this confluence derives from the fact that functional polyvalence requires the detective to organize the narrative elements into what Frank calls 'an "intemporal" organization of temporality.' Kermode explains that the complexity of such an organization derives from the fact that it requires the perception of the present, memory of the past, and expectations of the future in a common pattern. Within this pattern, that which was conceived of as simply successive becomes charged with past and future (1967, 46). Lynley himself supplies the other feasible reason while reading Shakespeare's play: 'now he read and reread the lines, trying to wring a twentieth-century meaning from the seventeenth-century verse' (257). The play represents only an analogue, not a perfect replica of the crime. As can be expected, the theme of incest illustrated by the play does not in itself address the case Lynley is trying to solve, but needs to be modified and individualized to fit its features.

The validation and the modification of Lynley's tentative narrative construction happens during an emotional interview among the psychiatrist, Roberta, and Gillian, Roberta's sister. The elaboration of the past events takes place through a shared effort by these three characters, and it is significant that the investigators remain mere observers, although the narrator indicates that they can anticipate the different turns of the narrative (280–94 and 296–300).[16] At this point, the psychiatrist takes over the position and narrative function of the detective, a typical shift of roles in modern detective stories.[17] The interview represents the events from two angles by attempting to establish an understanding of what exactly happened in the past and by offering an interpretation condensing the significance of those events and actions for the participants. These perspectives may be related to motifs and narrative themes respectively. The motifs stand for the individual incidents which make up the totality of the events, whereas the narrative themes demonstrate the conceptual categories enabling the characters (and the reader) to comprehend the meaning of those events within the totality. There is a division of labour here. As direct participants, only Roberta and Gillian can supply the missing pieces of the sequence of incidents; however, these are not identical pieces, for the sisters have experienced similar, but not the same, events. Given that Roberta has been traumatized to the point of psychosis, Gillian and the psychiatrist in particular are the ones to assign the motifs to suitable narrative themes. To make the events understandable, it needs to be mentioned that Mr Teys, the murdered man, was planning to marry a widow with a young daughter, Bridie.

To illustrate the assignment of the narrative themes of the crime story, I present the schematization shown in Table 2.1. This table further demonstrates the spatiality of plot structures by showing how 'order has ceased to be a succession and has become an interconnexion of parts all mutually implied and conditioned in the whole' (Kermode 1967, 55–6). In drawing it up, I have marked down the interpretation of the events offered by the characters themselves. It is noteworthy that they continually explain the events from two sides, that of the daughters and that of the father. What emerges clearly from the interlacing of these perspectives is the general structure of plot: the existence of a problem (or a number of problems) and the attempts to solve it. The movement between these perspectives brings out the effects that the moves (acts and actions) of a character have on the domains of other characters, which then lead to countermoves. The table tries to preserve this double perspective. Therefore, the column in the middle represents plot motifs, while the left-hand column expresses the narrative themes from the viewpoint of the father and the right-hand column from that of his daughters.

TABLE 2.1   Narrative Themes in George's *A Great Deliverance*

Narrative theme (Mr Teys)	Plot motif	Narrative theme (Roberta & Gillian)
fulfilment of desire (for a child-like body and social respect)	marriage of Teys to sixteen-year-old Tessa	
problem: threat (to sense of security) and loss of satisfaction	birth of Gillian	
solution: fulfilment of desire (problem: violation of the incest prohibition)	molestation and sodomy of Gillian	problem: violation of integrity; solution: search for love and appeasement
problem: loss of satisfaction	Gillian leaves home	solution: escape, self-protection
solution: fulfilment of desire problem: violation of a pro-hibition (and justification of future punishment)	molestation, sodomy, and continued rape of Roberta	problem: violation of integrity; solution: self-blame, self-hatred
problem: fear of exposure, loss of satisfaction solution 1: cover-up	birth and murder of mutual child	problem: loss of a sense of self, inner death solution 1: gluttony
solution 2: attempt to fulfil desire	sadistic molestation without rape	solution 2: self-sacrifice (to protect Bridie)
solution 3: plans for ensuring the future fulfilment of desire	plans for new marriage by the father to Bridie's mother	solution 3: plans of protection and revenge
punishment	murder of father	solution 4: 'a great deliverance': revenge, rescue (of self and Bridie)

The first thing to ponder is what enables the characters to move from a motif to the assignment of its concomitant narrative theme. The straight-forward answer can be obtained by looking at the dictionaries Gillian and the psychiatrist employ. The sister views her own and Roberta's narratives by relating the events to her own experience. She has obtained enough distance from her past to be capable of conceptualizing it by using a sort of 'child-abuse victim's dictionary.' The psychiatrist draws on his clinical experience and professional knowledge. In contrast, the detective could not go farther in his narrative construction because of his unfamiliarity with these frames of reference. The abductive effort subtending the choice of narrative themes by these two characters is still undercoded, but there is, nevertheless, a decisive difference in comparison to the interpretive labour by the detective, for the psychiatrist and Gillian work within clearly fenced-off and overlapping areas of meaning. Although they have to choose among a number of feasible explanations, their choices stay within the same register. For example, when Lynley returns to the symptom of fatness at the end, the psychiatrist can still only suggest a number of alternatives (298), but this indecision is more a matter of adjusting and refining the undercoded abductions than of the detective's taking conjectural stabs in the dark in the hope of finding the right set of dictionaries. What greatly contributes to the psychiatrist's ease of interpretation is intertextual acquaintance: he has treated other patients with similar life stories. Therefore, he has a set of narrative patterns within easy reach which facilitate narrative construction. (At one point he comments that the behavioural strategy of the father is 'so typical, Inspector Lynley. I can't tell you how typical it is' [298].)

The division of labour between the detective and the psychiatrist in *A Great Deliverance* points to the fact that the abductive model in detective fiction represents first and foremost what might be called *practical reasoning* as opposed to theoretical reasoning, for the former weds praxis and action together. It consists of a grasp of what is necessary in, and appropriate to, a particular situation. It involves more than knowing the general rules guiding action, for it shows that understanding a rule involves understanding how to apply it. This characteristic explains the decisive importance of the choice of an appropriate dictionary or set of dictionaries in the genre. In George's book, the detective's knowledge and experience of shared cultural practices enable him to identify the general topic of the crime, whereas the psychiatrist approaches it from the angle of the expert. In both instances of reading – by uniting knowledge and experience – the abductive inference employed in fictional crime-solving resembles what Aristotle calls *phronesis*, or practical wisdom. Phronesis 'combines the generality of reflection on principles with the particularity of perception into a given situation. It is distinguished from theoretical knowing (episteme) in that it is concerned, not with something universal and eternally the same, but with something particular and changeable' (Hoy 1978, 58). Practical wisdom involves both deliberate reasoning and intuition, uniting perception, reflection, and experience.[18]

The chart shows how the fictional characters formulate narrative themes.

It is useful to compare the characters' conception to discussion of the incest theme in theoretical literature on narrative themes. George's book would seem to confirm the claim that the main function of narrative themes is to demonstrate the semantic skeleton of a plot. The themes assigned by the characters to the events bring out clearly the patterning of the crime plot. It is made up of strongly repetitious cycles, for the events are initiated and sustained by the same structure of problems: Mr Teys's fear of grown women (and of the adult world in general) which leads him to gratify his sexual needs by abusing his own children and even to plan to remarry in order to have the new wife's child at his disposal (as in Nabokov's *Lolita*). The narrative themes also demonstrate the logic whereby the events proceed. Mr Teys's solutions (sexual abuse) to his problems (inability to interact with women) create problems in the domains of his children which they, in turn, try to solve in different ways (splitting of self, escape, revenge). Moreover, the chart brings out the confluence of narrative themes. For example, Mr Teys's solution of his sexual problems provides the justification for the punishment he will receive. Finally, the narrative themes also highlight the crucial inversion of roles characterizing this plot. In the end, the murder victim emerges as the real culprit, whereas the murderer is shown to be the real victim.

What is less clear, however, is the level of abstraction in the formulation of these themes. Ryan, for example, envisages all narrative themes proper as being equally abstract; the interpreter draws them from a thematic dictionary familiar to her from her experience of narratives and plots. Therefore, Ryan claims that the assignment of narrative themes is less subject to interpretation than is the assignment of other types of themes. This assignment deals first and foremost with cognition, which also accounts for the uniformity of abstraction in the formulation of narrative themes (1993). George's book appears to justify this argument to only a limited extent. The argument seems to hold as regards the 'strategic profile' of the plot: the perception of the cycle of repetitious problems and solutions and the inversion of roles. The status of narrative themes that describe the effects of actions (division of self, inner death) is more problematic, because they are of different degrees of abstraction. They are much closer both to the concrete events and to the frame of reference employed in explaining them. They do not appear to derive from the kind of thematic dictionary Ryan has in mind. One answer is to say that they are not narrative themes. This argument does not seem satisfactory, because the characters insist on them as features that make the sequence of events comprehensible to them. The obvious conclusion is that context does, after all, affect the formulation of narrative themes.

We can throw light on this problem by returning to the theme of incest, which Inspector Lynley identified as the overriding topic of the case. This theme may be divided into a number of 'subthemes' that go together with certain culturally familiar plot patterns, as, for example, in the Oedipus and Electra formulations or the biblical narrative about Lot and his daughters. Actually, *A Great Deliverance* makes use of the religious framework, for it describes the motivation of the father from his perspective. Sexually abusing his daughters while reading the Bible, he justifies his actions by referring inaccurately to the story about Lot's daughters. He misinterprets his deed, forcing this misinterpretation on his daughters. This biblical narrative forms the subtext that Lynley and the psychiatrist have to counter, and, as we have seen, they do it through the notions supplied by modern (popular) psychology. From this angle, any resonances of a 'family romance configuration' are pathologized and firmly rejected. This frame of reference constructs stereotyped narratives about the sexual abuse of children in which certain kinds of actions (always) lead to certain kinds of results of which the 'division of self' or 'inner death' are not only typical examples but also crucial factors in driving home the narrative's point.[19] In this sense, we may say that such effects belong to the realm of narrative themes, and that they are closely connected to their frame of reference. In conclusion, George's book presents to the reader a variation of the incest theme in which its mythical versions are juxtaposed with a contemporary interpretation that treats the phenomenon in terms of pedophilia.

Narrative construction that relies on undercoded abductions involves more work for fictional detectives. When the signs they encounter are diffuse in nature, they are faced with a wealth of interpretive alternatives among which they have to choose. Besides the various options, the difficulty in identifying case-specific motif configurations and (narrative) themes depends on the 'impure' nature of these elements, for the context and the frames of reference introduce variations and modifications. I have dwelt on this type of abduction at length because it is one of the most typical of the detective-story genre.[20] Now, however, we turn to *creative abductions*, which I illustrate by discussing the solution of Agatha Christie's *Towards Zero* (1944). Generally speaking, in making creative abductions interpreters are hazarding a guess both about the rule and about the nature of their world. On the whole, the creativity and novelty of an abduction depend on the choice of and relationship between the result and the rule: the more unusual the mating of these two, or the more distant their semantic fields from one another, the more pregnant the abduction will be (Truzzi 1983, 133). In contrast, in over- and undercoded abductions the detectives choose a rule from a store of already checked, actual-world experience, feeling entitled by their knowledge of the world to think that, provided the rule is a suitable one, it already holds good in the world of their experience.

In Christie's detective story, a man saves a woman from a murder charge by reporting that on the night of the murder he was walking alone by the coast when he saw someone rise from the sea and climb up a rope to a house on an island where subsequently an old lady was murdered. At the conclusion, the accused thanks her saviour.

[Audrey] ' – did you realise *then* that you'd got some important evidence?'

'Not precisely,' said MacWhirter, 'I had to think it out ... I did not actually see a man climbing up a rope – indeed I could not have done so, for I was up on Stark Head on Sunday night, not on Monday [when the murder was committed]. I deduced what must have happened from the evidence of the suit and my suppositions were confirmed by the finding of a wet rope in the attic.'

From red Audrey had gone white ... 'Your story was all a lie?'

'Deductions would not have carried weight with the police. I had to say I saw what happened.' (189–90)

In constructing the story that frees Audrey Strange, MacWhirter has had only one *clue* to go by: the local laundromat has given him someone else's suit which reeks of rotten fish, insisting it was left there under his name. By definition, clues of this type are 'objects left by an external agent in the spot where [this agent] did something, and are somehow recognized as physically linked to that agent, so that from their actual or possible presence the actual or possible past presence of the agent can be detected' (Eco 1983, 211).[21] MacWhirter actually reads two clues from the suit. That someone left it at the laundromat in his name indicates the existence of an unknown agent who does not want his true identity to be known and who knows MacWhirter, if not personally, then at least by name.[22] The underhanded act of this agent points to his having something to conceal. The other clue is the smell of rotten fish the jacket exudes. This MacWhirter takes to indicate the presence of this same unknown agent at another spot at another time. He relates this latter clue to the following simple rule concerning the habits of people: 'You step on decayed fish but you don't put your shoulder down on it unless you have taken your clothes off to bathe at night, and no one would bathe for pleasure on a wet night in September' (186). From a smelly suit he *invents* a story involving a man who undresses in order to swim, accidentally placing his clothes on top of some rotten fish. (The events, after all, take place at a seaside resort.) However, given the chilly season of the year, the swim cannot be for pleasure. MacWhirter has only to select from his intertextual knowledge a narrative pattern involving the theme of cunning murder, acquainted as he is with the sensational events at the house on the island. Thus, he is capable of elaborating his rudimentary story about a night-time swim with the man's climbing up a rope left hanging from a window, killing an old lady, swimming back, and putting his clothes back on. All these various actions are motifs in the plot he is putting together governed by the aforementioned theme.

When narrative construction makes use of creative abductions in detective stories, it appears first and foremost to be characterized by the boldness of the act in relating a sign to a motif, narrative theme, and/or plot formula. It relies on the gap that seemingly exists between the two terms, highlighting the surprise effect that comes from their juxtaposition. Or, as in this example, it comes from the recognition of the mental dexterity involved in the demonstration that one can intelligibly derive a tale of murder from a smelly suit. The fact that there is initially no code and hence no set of rules suggests that the results may also be thematically innovative. In mainstream detective fiction, however, such novelty is kept in firm check. There is no doubt that MacWhirter's conjectural process has involved some invention, but one can nevertheless say that its creativity very quickly falls back on undercoded abductions, for the simple reason that stories about people hoisting themselves up somewhere to commit murder are very familiar within detective-story worlds. Thus, detective fiction does not so much foreground the exploration of new spheres of meaning, as emphasize the imaginative leaps detectives make in boldly uniting signs and texts with surprisingly ingenious contexts. Bonfantini and Proni (1983, 127–8) as well as Eco (1983, 217–20) point out that, on the whole, the abductions of fictional detectives seem to lack any great originality. Bonfantini and Proni explain this 'sensibility' in terms of the purpose of the investigation: it would seem too arbitrary to prove the guilt of a culprit through bold new theoretical hypotheses. Reasoning and proof of guilt must be grounded in well-tried interpretations, commonly accepted codes, and certain facts (128). Therefore, the narratives that are unwound from the mass of evidence are also mainly intertextually familiar. These restrictions endow criminal investigation with less innovation than scientific study. Yet this reservation does not mean that creative abductions are completely devoid of innovation in the detective-story genre.

Abducting World Structures

The familiarity of the rules used in reasoning about guilt and proving it is intimately connected with an additional reason for the predominance of over- and undercoded abductions over creative abductions in the mainstream detective story. The detectives' choices of suitable dictionaries to use in interpreting the signs of a crime are linked up with their understanding of the nature of the whole encyclopaedia to which these dictionaries belong. This means that the detectives' reasoning includes abductions concerning the whole *system* that welds together their separate hypotheses, endowing these hypotheses with coherence, regularity, and even aesthetic appeal. As the great scientific innovations demonstrate, the most creative abductions concern the structure and nature of the world (or even the universe), challenging us to reconsider and correct our understanding of the encyclopaedia describing our knowledge of the world. In effect, reliance on creative abductions would necessitate the author's envisaging of a fictional world that works by some other rules than those we are familiar with. Mainstream detective stories seldom, if ever, disturb readers in this way. This is an important point to note, because it sets *limits* to both the game taking place within the fictional world and the game between author and reader. Both realms would thus seem to follow a rule that could be formulated in the following fashion: Use abductions as creatively as you can in linking clues to narrative events and narrative events together, but stay within the bounds of the already known.[23]

This brings us to *meta-abductions*, the last category Eco distinguishes, concerning the verification of the results of narrative construction. In the Christie example, MacWhirter cannot know for certain that his textual hypotheses are true, for, contrary to his earlier claim, he has not been present on the location at the night of the murder. His story is thus only *textually verisimilar*: it represents a coherent and possible account of the past events. (Given the puzzle-book character of Christie's book, the story also fulfils the requirement of plausibility.) He *knows* only that the cleaners have given him the wrong suit. The sequence MacWhirter constructs represents his strongly motivated *belief* about how things must have happened. Eco (1983, 214) emphasizes that undercoded and creative abductions are *world-creating devices*, outlining a possible course of events and a set of possible agents. Meta-abduction comes into the picture with the extensional game, that is, with the reasoner's decision to relate his or her abductions to reality. Owing to their task of exposing and catching the criminal, the detectives have to engage in this activity, checking whether the hypothetical individual they have outlined as an inhabitant of the world of their *beliefs* is the same as the individual of *the actual world* they are looking for (ibid.). In the Christie example, once the culprit is confronted with this narrative construction (together with a certain amount of verbal bullying), he loses his poise and in the heat of the moment gives himself away, thus confirming the validity of MacWhirter's interpretation. From the point of view of narrative construction, meta-abductions function to test whether this construction is justified or whether it still needs to be corrected, elaborated, or even completely rejected.

Eco argues that meta-abductions most clearly bring out the difference between detective stories and scientific inquiry. In science they involve an element of risk, for they remain open for testing and falsification by subsequent study. In contrast, detective-story authors usually employ certain straightforward means of validating the detectives' conjectures (the Watson figure, the criminal's confession, the supplying of corroborative information), whereafter meta-abductions are no longer falsifiable. From a generic perspective, however, this distinction between fiction and science is not particularly significant. What is much more important is the way in which the relationship between the reasoning mind and the external world is conceived, for this connection points to the epistemological grounds that make possible any meta-abductions by a detective. This link throws further light on the use of creative abductions in the genre.

'Oscillation [of a woman] upon the pavement always means an *affaire du coeur*' ('The Case of Identity,' Doyle 1985a, 51), claims Sherlock Holmes. To be able to make such an assertion, Holmes relies on conventional assumptions about the efficacy of interpretation in moving from sensory data or narrated facts to other, intentionally or circumstantially hidden, facts, and from them to factual or moral truths. This method entails the consideration of all kinds of data as potential signs, which, when ordered and linked together, are turned into signs of the hidden order behind manifest confusion. Holmes's premise is that such an order and one true meaning of the events ultimately exist, which explains, for example, why an oscillating woman on the pavement *always* means unhappy love (Stowe 1983). Hence, Holmes makes a set of conventions pose as the 'true meaning' of the cases he solves. One can contrast these notions of the nature of reality and of the role of interpretation with the statement by Dashiell Hammett's Continental Op, explaining his views on the case he is trying to solve: 'I don't know. I don't think anybody knows. I'm telling you what I saw plus the part of what Aaronia Haldorn told me which fits in with what I saw. To fit in with what I saw, most of it must have happened very nearly as I've told you. If you want to believe that it did, all right. I don't. I'd rather believe I saw things that weren't there' (*The Dain Curse*, 1980a, 214). The principles that direct the Op centre on his conviction of the arbitrary basis of our 'truths': what we see, what we believe, and what we think is what we have created ourselves. Even the most probable solution is only one rendering of the 'reality' of a case. Solutions are for him mostly fictional projections of our need to impose order on an inexplicable and fundamentally incomprehensible universe (Gregory 1985). Peter J. Rabinowitz (1994) links the difference between these two conceptualizations of the nature of reality and the role of interpretation with what he calls the *Fort Knox notion of truth* and the *barter school of truth* respectively. The Fort Knox school, embodying notions associated with empiricism, realism, and positivism, rests on 'the twin assumptions that the truth exists and that it can be found through rational procedures' (158), whereas the barter school endorses the notion that perspective inevitably influences any account of reality, so that what 'counts as' truth is invariably a context-dependent construction. In effect, 'we *make* truth discursively and rhetorically by telling stories and negotiating among them, bartering truth claims in exchanges that are either taken up or not according to the needs of a particular social context (including its power relations)' (159–60). Hence, Hammett's work strongly anticipates the emergence of the metaphysical detective story.[24]

These epistemological postulates underlying the abductive movement from result to rule to case explain why scholars have felt that creative abductions are most likely to be found within the metaphysical detective story (see Calinescu 1993, Eco 1990, Holquist 1983, Tani 1984). The creativity has to do with the author's challenging of the reader to think about the fictional world and the playing process in some new or at least unusual terms: as readers, we can regard neither the fictional world nor our game with and against the author as functioning according to the rules and codes familiar from mainstream detective fiction and/or everyday life, but must try to decipher what system regulates the compilation of these worlds and what rules apply at the author-reader level of the game. As these rules primarily address the search for new, unsuspected possibilities of meaning and creative literary play (Calinescu 1993, 214), the use of abductions is regulated by a different kind of injunction from that in the mainstream detective story: Use abductions as creatively as you can in linking clues not only to narrative events but also to narrative conventions, and try to push and stretch the already-known into new regions of meaning. As a concluding example one can mention Eco's analysis of abduction in Borges, which he shows to be based on 'the mechanism of conjecture in a sick Spinozist Universe' (1990, 152–62). By parodying the Fort Knox notion of truth, Borges creates a world where the movement of the investigator's mind does follow the same rules as reality, but this reality is that of fiction. Hence, the logic of this world is the logic of 'the library of Babel,' so that the investigator 'discovers that what his clients experienced was a sequence of events projected by another mind. He discovers that they were already moving in the frame of a story and according to the rules of story-telling, that they were unconscious characters of a play already written by someone else' (161).

All these examples demonstrate that, among other things, the episte-mological postulates to which a fictional detective like Sherlock Holmes adheres influence the interpretational guidelines he follows, making him a very different figure from the one represented by his colleague, the Op, not to speak of Borges's detectives. These detectives do not employ the same dictionaries in searching for suitable narrative themes and plot patterns, because their conceptions about the encyclopaedia to which these dictionaries belong are different. In concluding, we can relate this difference to the significance a detective's explanatory system accords to what Kermode (1967, 17) calls the 'doctrine of consonance' that underlies the human propensity to shape the meaninglessness of pure temporal duration through plots. He explains that plots not only express our desire for consonance but also a derision about it. We invest imaginatively in coherent plot patterns which, by providing an end, make possible a satisfying consonance with the beginning and the middle. Yet we are also distrustful of such patterns, for we feel they fail to represent reality as it is. Therefore, there is a recurring need for adjustments in the interest of reality as well as control. The doctrine of consonance expresses the attempt to hold on to or restore a discredited pattern rather than abandon it. In this context, the mainstream detective story stresses this doctrine to a far greater degree than does the metaphysical one, which is markedly sceptical of the fit between plot patterns and reality.

The types of abductions through which the search for plot patterns takes place throw light only on the basic stage of retrieving narratively and thematically useful units and patterns that serve the goal of solving a crime. They tell us little, however, about the process by which fictional detectives make their narrative explanations cohere and highlight certain meanings over others, a topic to which I turn in the next chapter. Yet even this brief comparison among the varying conceptions that direct narrative construction enables us to perceive subgeneric differences between detectives. From the reader's perspective, much of the intellectual challenge and pleasure comes from playing with these figures, that is, from trying to understand how they reason, what rules they apply in their reasoning, and what system lends coherence to this process.

3

Fitting the Solution to the Mystery

The traditional view of the detective-story plot holds it to be constructed backwards. The idea of backward construction goes back to the founder of the detective-story genre, Edgar Allan Poe, according to whom the author has first to determine the solution and then to fashion the plot with that ending in view, to give it an 'indispensable air of consequence, or causation, by making the incidents, and especially the tone at all points, tend to the development of the intention' (cited in Steele 1981–2, 561).[1] This notion of plot relies on an extraordinarily tight complementarity between the parts and the whole – at least when it comes to the solution of the crime. Such reciprocity is the hallmark of the classical detective story, but the fit between the problem and the solution applies more generally to the whole genre. This mode of modelling the plot poses a specific challenge for authors, because they have to create the sense that their detectives *produce* the crime story through the reading of clues, portraying it as directly *deriving from* the interpretation of the evidence, and, in some instances, also stemming from the actions of the detective. This prerequisite of plot construction directs attention to the ways in which a writer makes a detective generate a particular solution through the reading of the crime story. The detective-story conventions also hold that not just any solution befits a crime problem, for the solution has to cover all the various aspects of the problem so that each feature is explained to the reader. A further requirement is (logical) coherence, for the solution should not exhibit any (obvious) fallacies of reasoning (Freeman 1946, Sayers 1988a and 1988b).

When we place these generic conventions shaping the relationship between the crime problem and its solution in the context of semiotic study, they link up with the question of what it takes to create a (logically) coherent plot. The authors' challenge is to have their detectives demonstrate how the narrative themes, and, eventually, the plot patterns, they choose organize the meanings that events and actions put into play. To express these meanings, detective-readers select among *topics* for the purpose of distinguishing the suitable *isotopies* for interpreting the crime text. According to Eco's definition, topics are abductive schemas that help the detective-reader to decide which semantic properties have to be actualized, whereas isotopies are the actual textual verification of these tentative hypotheses. The topic is a reading hypothesis, which the detective-reader tries to apply to the textual clues, while the isotopy is its semantic result, supported by the rule in the light of which the detective-reader has chosen to interpret it (1984, 189, 193). In Eco's view, isotopy is an umbrella term covering diverse semiotic phenomena generally definable as *coherence* at various textual levels (190). By serving the function of textual disambiguation, the choice of isotopies makes possible a uniform reading of a story (189). Eco states that isotopies represent *thematic* classifications that can be organized hierarchically (191–2).

The thematic nature of isotopies makes it appropriate to discuss the construction of a coherent solution in terms of what is called *theming* or *thematization*, which refers to the interaction of a text and its reader in terms of themes. Generally speaking, theming demonstrates how a text and its reader come together under the aegis of a theme or a cluster of themes (Wimmers 1988, 63). It relies on a number of cultural and idiosyncratic codes or subcodes which guide this process as well as supplying the principles it respects (Prince 1992, 8). The focus lies on the metathematic operations of arranging thematic elements into clusters and linking them with one another. In displaying fictional detectives' search for themes and the activity of uniting these themes to one another, detective stories put forth for our scrutiny various self-reflexive *representations of theming*, drawing attention to the protagonists' role as *themers*, or as persons who interpret themes. So this is one further way in which the genre depicts the scene of reading.

When theming addresses plot only, detective-readers link events and actions to such conceptual categories as would most profitably describe not only their significance but also their patterning. They may also relate the plot they construct to various issues in the world at large. In reading crime stories, they cannot but adhere to the general principles of theming that apply to any type of plot. Analysing representations of theming in the genre draws on these commonly shared operations, demonstrating how they are put to use by a specific detective-reader. What fictional detectives do is, of course, mirrored by what the reader of detective fiction does. Showing how these principles function does not in itself indicate, however, what is characteristic of theming in detective stories, displayed both at the level of the fictional world and at the level of the author's relationship with the reader.

The specificity of detective fiction derives from the fact that theming is always represented as involving a triadic relationship among the author, the detective, and the reader. The theming by a detective figure is both directed and controlled by the author. After all, it is the author who draws up the crime problem, determines its correct solution, and sets a given detective to establish it. The manner in which a detective-reader puts together a coherent solution is directly dependent on the author: all of the detective-reader's readerly activities are severely restricted. Therefore, there is an intimate link between the characteristics of this figure and the kinds of crime stories he or she is good at putting together. We may further hold that authors consider these crime stories worth telling in themselves. One generically specific feature would then have to do with the link between a crime story which is worth telling, the detective's theming process, and his or her characteristics. Moreover, as the fit between the problem and the solution is of such significance to the detective-story plot, we should look for generic particularity there. Two considerations seem pertinent in this context. The first has to do with the consistency of the solution. Does the requirement that the solution be logically coherent place specific constraints on a detective's theming process? The second issue also deals with the solution. Detective stories underline the difficulty of solving a crime by having the detective (or someone else) construct an apparently coherent, yet false solution. Only after trial and error is the correct solution put together. The juxtaposition of two or more solutions, only one of which is right, raises the question of what decides correctness or falseness. Can we explain this distinction in thematic terms?

There is an inevitable circularity involved in the author's relationship to the detective, as the latter cannot but generate the solution foreseen by the former. The author, of course, uses the representation of the detective's theming to challenge the reader in a battle of wits. This overt competition is, however, but one feature at this level. We may, occasionally, beat the author by conjecturing who the culprit is or how the crime was committed, but it is unlikely that we can by ourselves put together the solution with all its interlocking details. The antagonistic game of obfuscation and guessing is framed by the semiotically more challenging game concerning the drawing up and solving of the narrative enigma itself. The reader's attention is directed at the predetermined circularity of this undertaking: the author's creation of a detective whose personal characteristics and theming process together untie the knots the author has tangled up. As Calinescu observes, what makes this generation of the solution fascinating for the reader is that 'in a successful detective story information that would appear to be hermeneutically superfluous or completely neutral is made to play a *potential* (teasing, occasionally tantalizing) hermeneutic role. The game proposed by the detective story would then be one in which information, including information of cultural, semic, and symbolic nature, would be made hermeneutically significant and thus become the focus of heightened attention' (1993, 212–13). This hermeneutic singling out of clues is accompanied by procedures with the help of which these clues are ultimately strung together into a narratively and thematically coherent totality. The creation of such a totality demonstrates the *architectonics* of the detective-story plot, for usually the organizing plot pattern is comparable to a visual shape, be it a locked room, a maze, or the grid of a crossword puzzle.

I examine representations of theming in detective stories by looking in detail at two examples, pondering along the way what the specific issues are that detective-story conventions bring to bear on these representations. Fictional detectives can put the solution together either by interpreting the clues and arranging them in various patterns or by trying to make the solution emerge through their own investigative actions. I consider each manner separately. Although these means are usually intertwined, they do, roughly speaking, correspond with certain subgeneric differences. The focus on reading and interpretive operations is typical of the classical detective story, while the action-orientation of problem solving characterizes the hard-boiled tradition. (The police procedural seems to unite these two tactics through a division of labour: the police officers actively push the events forward while their forensic backup teams engage in the careful interpretation of whatever data the investigation uncovers.) The whodunit is represented by Colin Dexter, who has written a series of thirteen books depicting crime investigations by Chief Inspector Morse and his assistant, Sergeant Lewis.[2] The whole series supplies the context of the discussion, but I use one book, *The Jewel That Was Ours* (1994a), as the case-study text. Michael Dibdin's Police Inspector Aurelio Zen series, set in present-day Italy, serves as an example of the action-oriented approach to plot construction and theming. This series is a mixture of hard-boiled detective story and police procedural, with classical ingredients. Its setting and world-view are typical of the hard-boiled legacy, whereas the police context unites the book with the procedural tradition. The author's careful embedding of the clues within the text suggests the whodunit formula. I use Dibdin's fourth book, *Dead Lagoon* (1994), as the text for close reading. In both cases, the choice of a series character facilitates the analysis of the fit between the solution and the figure who produces it. Thanks to its repetitiveness, the series context not only enables the reader to identify the thematic patterns a particular writer favours, but also draws attention to the detective's stable characteristics, showing the kinds of themes against which he likes to read crimes.

In looking at these examples of plot construction and theming, I again mainly play *with* the author, interested as I am in the ways in which separate clues and the thematic categories attached to them are ultimately made to yield a consistent narrative about a crime. As previously, what justifies such an examination is the complexity of these procedures, for if we are to understand more deeply the narrative nature of the genre, then we have to be able to follow the detective's conjectural movements which ultimately produce a coherent totality in the form of an explanation. Therefore, in what follows I make explicit those thematic operations that remain mainly implicit in the detectives' process of narrative construction. As I proceed, I keep relating these observations to the reader's game with the author through the detective.

Theming as a Game of *Double Entendre*

A detective's character partly derives from the reasons making him or her the right kind of 'can opener' for an author's purposes. In Dexter's *oeuvre*, the author-narrator may be said to view Chief Inspector Morse as his beloved puppet, a fact which emerges most clearly in passages of free indirect discourse mingling the narrator's and the detective's perspectives and voices. A scene in *The Jewel That Was Ours* combines the narrator's exhortations to Morse and Morse's mental spurring of himself. A brief example suffices:

Yes, those were the facts.

So move on, Morse, to a few non-factual inferences in the problem of the Wolvercote Tongue. Move on, my son – and hypothesize! Come on, now! Who *could* have stolen it? (371)

And what about – what about the most unlikely, improbable, unthinkable ... Unthinkable? Well, *think* about it, Morse! (372)

From our point of view, the phrase 'non-factual inferences' supplies the key. Dexter's narrator has modelled Morse[3] after the (male) supersleuth tradition, making him 'an eccentric, irascible old sod' whom 'the gods had blessed ... with a brain that worked as swiftly and as cleanly as the lightning' (*The Dead of Jericho*, 1991a, 27). The inner duality typical of fictional detectives is in Morse's case coded as a combination of earthy coarseness and culture, both sides of which are engaged in the detection process. The coarse side (women, sex, alcohol, and certain forms of pornography) makes Morse familiar with the motivational side of crimes, enabling him to conjecture the kinds of passions that may seize people, leading them to commit crimes. The cultured sphere involves, above all, the appreciation of imagination. The whole Dexter series builds on a tension between ratiocination and imagination, because unembellished facts fly in the face of Morse's predilection for fancy, whence obtains his repeated difficulties in sticking to the facts.[4] The basic tenet of Morse's investigations is that any convincing construction of a crime always represents what he calls *faction*, a combination of fact and fiction (*The Riddle of the Third Mile*, 1991c, 345). The solution consists of more or less irrefutably proved facts, but it invariably includes a lot of guessing as well (e.g., *Last Seen Wearing*, 1991b, 533; *Riddle*, 344; *Service of All the Dead*, 1991e, 392). Faction weds ratiocination and the testing of hypotheses with imagination. The investigation moves back and forth between these poles: Morse first takes hold of what he takes to be facts and then shifts to various 'prodigious leaps into the dark' (*Service*, 292) belonging to the sphere of imagination. They act as the basis from which he then starts testing and elaborating.

The emphasis on imagination ties in with the kinds of cans the author gives his detective to open. As Dexter works within the whodunit tradition, he draws up the problems – and the solutions – in a particular way. The underlying model is, as expected, the puzzle. Moreover, Dexter has made Morse an expert in puzzles who approaches each case as if it were a complicated maze made up of familiar signification systems. Invariably, the novels include a scene where Morse is engaged in solving either a crossword or some other kind of puzzle, which the narrator explicitly employs as a *mise-en-abyme* of the process of crime solving. For example, the prolegomenon of *Death Is Now My Neighbour* (1996) depicts Sergeant Lewis challenging Morse to take the 'Are You Really Wise and Cultured?' test in the *Thames Valley Police Gazette*, a test which Lewis himself has already completed. Morse, as is his wont, rises to the bait and scores maximum points, making the incredulous Lewis charge him with cheating. It turns out that Morse scored so well because he was the author of the test. The whole episode mirrors the kind of thing that whodunit authors do: set and solve problems of their own making. There is thus a very close fit between the narrative model and a central characteristic of the detective.

To observe how Dexter's narrator makes Morse produce the solution of *The Jewel That Was Ours*, we turn to a detailed analysis of this detective as a themer. The book is divided into three parts. The first part deals with the theft of the Wolvercote Tongue, a rare piece of antique jewellery dating back to Alfred the Great. A Mrs Laura Stratton, participant in a Historic Cities of England tour for a group of Americans, was to donate the jewel to the Ashmolean Museum in Oxford on behalf of her deceased first husband. The theft and her death from a heart attack are detected simultaneously. The question Morse faces in the first part is whether these two incidents are linked in any way. The second part of the book complicates this problem through the murder of Dr Theodore Kemp, a historian at the museum which was to have received the jewel. Kemp had planned to achieve both scholarly merit and a great deal of publicity from the acquisition. Morse is convinced that, as the person who was to give the jewel to the Museum and the person who was to receive the jewel on the Museum's behalf have both died, there has to be a link connecting the theft and the murder. His insistence on this link becomes a leitmotif, repeated throughout the investigation (360, 391, 418, 433, 448, 451, 462, ch. 43, 486, ch. 53). He thinks that once the nature of that link is clear, he will see the pattern governing the crime and, hence, its solution (448, 451). From our perspective as readers, this leitmotif sets the broad limits of our game with the author: the solution will – must – demonstrate how these two seemingly separate crimes join together. The crime problem addresses, as it invariably does in the classical detective story, a limited group of suspects; the guilty one is to be found among the group of American tourists on the tour to England, their tutors at Oxford, of whom Kemp is one, and their tour guide. The third part of the novel gives Morse's explanation of the solution. The 'wavering-finger-of-suspicion' technique used in this novel opens up a plethora of narrative avenues, with the clues pointing to the possible existence of more than one culprit. To simplify matters, however, I concentrate solely on Morse's reconstruction of a false solution, a process which is eventually followed by his putting together the correct one.

To establish the link between the two seemingly separate crimes, Morse concentrates on the person of Kemp, his characteristics, actions, and personal history, as providing the most significant textual clues. The singling out of these clues is motivated by Kemp's being the victim of murder, for, as Morse explains, '[i]t is a commonplace in murder investigations that more may often be learned about the murderer from the *victim* than from any other source' (505). These clues do not suggest, imply, or illustrate anything by themselves, however, but have thematic relevance only after detective-readers have singled them out and linked them to a conceptual basis (i.e., to a topic). This significance is at first only potential, until detective-readers, as their reading proceeds, decide whether the crime text lends enough textual verification for this hypothesis (leading to the postulation of a narrative theme). And even if they hold on to a postulated isotopy (narrative theme), they often find that they must modify it in one way or another to arrive at a formulation that satisfies their purposes. Generally speaking, Morse does what any reader does in creating coherence among diverse textual elements: he identifies *textual clues* on the basis of what is called *thematizing attention*,[5] resorting to *operations of theming* that enable the functioning of this attention. Thematizing attention relies on 'the nature and intensity of [readers'] interests, the interpretative systems they decide to bring to bear and the value of the methodological apparatus which is used to locate, conceptualize, formulate, order and interpret these potential themes. Finally, and most importantly ... there is the rigour with which these operations are carried out' (Bremond and Pavel 1995, 190). The so-called operations of theming supply readers with very general instructions about what to do with the textual elements they select as thematically significant. Bremond (1988, 55–60) even argues that the infinitude of possible themes is opposed by the extreme limitation of these operations regulating their appearance, transformation, and possible disappearance in the interpretive activity in which readers engage during (and perhaps also after) reading.

To give an idea of what is meant by these procedures, it is worth looking briefly at the six basic thematic operations Bremond identifies.[6] He arranges them in three paired groups: *position* and *suppression*; *composition* and *decomposition*; *generalization* and *specification* (1988, 55–60). Position(ing) takes place when, on the basis of a textual element, the reader posits a new theme. This typically happens at foregrounded points in narratives such as the beginning or the end, introductions of characters, or descriptions of objects. Repetition also effectively positions textual themes. Suppression is the reverse of positioning; because the text does not offer enough support for elaborating on a theme, the themer suppresses it. Composition fuses together a number of already identified themes into a complex, composite theme, whereas decomposing describes the inverse operation whereby a theme is divided into simpler themes. Both generalization and specification move between genus and species, the former substituting a more abstract label for a number of concrete themes, and the latter narrowing a general thematic designation to address a specific one. Generalization is thus associated with composition and specification with decomposition. Position, suppression, composition, and decomposition function at the syntagmatic level of theming, enabling the formation of thematic sequences. Generalization and specification address its paradigmatic axis, that is, the selection of a theme from a class, the elements of which can occupy the same position in a given context.[7]

The one textual clue which especially baffles Morse is a phone call by Kemp from Paddington Station in London to the Oxford hotel where the American tour is staying to inform their guide that he cannot keep his luncheon-lecture date with them. Morse fails to understand why Kemp missed the train if he made the call well before departure from the station itself. He lifts up the information concerning Kemp's call into a prominent place in order to link it to a suitable topic expressing what this call is about (ch. 30).[8] In other words, he positions this 'textual' clue as significant. He realizes, however, that he cannot explain it without specifying it further. To do so, he tries to create a context for the event, again positioning two further facts about Kemp that seem significant: he was a notorious philanderer and, when discovered, his body was naked (422, 456, 463–4). By drawing on a simple rule – 'He was making love shortly before, or as, he died' – Morse concludes that the case is about adultery; yet he also thinks that 'It's Love's Old Sweet Song – that *must* come into things somewhere' (448). He thus has two related, although not identical, themes to choose between. Adultery is also kept in his view by the various amorous interests of the American tourists and their British guides. As Kemp has been killed, Morse further specifies that the crime concerns a love triangle. This situation goes together with a rudimentary plot pattern involving a set conflict: the rivalry of two persons over a third one. This particularization allows Morse to interpret the phone call as a clue to the 'wonderful opportunity' (for a lovers' meeting) Kemp saw to meet the wife of a colleague with whom Morse believes Kemp had started an affair. He takes the call to represent Kemp's clever deception of the husband, his colleague and rival, for, by not showing up, Kemp forces this man to stay with the Americans. Morse knows, however, that this colleague, Dr Downes, went home in the afternoon of the day Kemp was killed. He unites this fact with his postulation of an unexpected incident leading to a surprise exposure. Given that the chosen plot pattern also contains a clear-cut motive, jealous rage, the case seems closed (469–72).

Morse's theming demonstrates the intimate interaction among separate parts and the whole. Once he has decided that the case is about an adulterous love triangle, this thematic designation begins to exert, as it were, a magnetism drawing everything within its explanatory reach. By making each and every observation fit the pattern, the thematization acquires a strong degree of cohesion. This is what he means by his statement that 'Oh yes! I always try solving problems by starting at the end – never at the beginning' (461), for only the postulation of the overriding topic of the crime story enables the organization of the details of that story. Again, we notice how order becomes a spatial interconnection of parts that are all mutually implied and conditioned in the whole. Sergeant Lewis notes that Morse has identified a trite variation of the theme, characterizing it as follows: 'Amazing, really: you get all these statements and alibis and secret little meetings, and then really, in the end, it's just – well, it's just the same old story, isn't it? Chap goes home and finds the missus in bed with one of the neighbours' (473). On the basis of this construction, Morse has Downes arrested. For all its cohesiveness, however, this account does not tally with (fictional) reality. There is no liaison between Dr Kemp and Mrs Downes. Having chosen a wrong thematic pattern, Morse errs largely because of its cohesive force. The possibility of 'hanging' facts onto its design proves too tempting, making him forget both its hypothetical nature and its limited coverage.[9] It is characteristic of Dexter's detective to savour narrative rigour above the testing of conjectures and the careful consideration of their exact extension. (For similar examples, see *The Dead of Jericho, Last Seen Wearing*, and *The Silent World of Nicholas Quinn*.)

In the author-reader game, which includes obfuscation and guessing, it is not difficult for the reader to reject this explanation as false. For one thing, we know it is too early in the narrative to arrive at the conclusive solution. (The reconstruction of the false explanation takes place in chapter 43, while the putting together of the final, correct solution begins ten chapters later.) There are two strong additional clues that suggest its falseness. First, the explanation is rendered through free indirect discourse, combining Morse's and the narrator's registers. Typically, the explanation is depicted through direct discourse (the 'quotation' of the detective's monologue or the dialogue between this figure and, for example, the suspects); the detective is given the floor, because the solution is his or her triumph. Second, the epigraph to this chapter, 'As usual he was offering explanations for what other people had not even noticed as problems,'[10] should warn the reader about the lack of sufficient proof for this reconstruction. From the present perspective, however, what is more important is the thematic nature of this false solution. The triteness of the triangle theme cannot supply the reason for its falsity, because Dexter's other books include examples in which such a triangle does explain the crime (e.g., *Last Bus to Woodstock*, *Service of All the Dead*, and *The Secret of Annexe 3*). Nor is the false solution without narrative elegance, for the deceptive strategy it postulates and the supposed culprit's acquisition of an alibi are both rather clever: the victim deceives the murderer by using the murderer's work obligations, while the murderer uses the victim's deception as his alibi.[11] Therefore, we have to leave this question open until we have looked at the correct solution.

Failure sends Morse back to review the facts (the textual clues) and re-evaluate their contextualization and specification. As befits the whodunit conventions, a chance remark about a car accident by the Watson-like Lewis suggests to him the proper framework. Morse recognizes that his choice of the specific characteristics and events on which to concentrate has been erroneous. Instead of Kemp's sexual exploits, he should consider the man's indifference. It is well known that Kemp, driving carelessly and probably slightly drunk, was involved in a car accident some years previously, killing the driver of the other car and causing the miscarriage and crippling of his own wife. This sequence of events reveals that someone may indeed have a reason to hate Kemp intensely – at least the parents of the dead woman and Kemp's wife. The identification of a motive, profound hatred, implies that the case may be governed by the narrative theme of revenge. In whodunits, the detectives' errors typically derive from their looking at the case the wrong way up, thereby selecting a wrong perspective. In the new context, Kemp's phone call still holds a key position and retains its meaning, but it has significance to the dead woman's parents, who together murdered Kemp. As Kemp really did miss the train, the narrative theme of the sought-for opportunity pertains to the actions of this criminal pair, not the supposed deceptive strategies of Kemp.[12]

The assignment of the governing topic – revenge – clinches the case. It allows Morse to perceive that this narrative theme underwrites the motives of several characters: the parents of the dead woman, Kemp's wife, and the Strattons. His thematizing attention thus seizes on the repetition of certain textual elements, each of which would seem to reproduce this narrative theme without substantial change. By multiplying the realizations of a theme, repetition creates a visible configuration in which the repeated element finds itself highlighted (Shcheglov and Zholkovski 1987, 54). Most importantly, repetition enables Morse to posit three parallel, but not identical, *sequences*, each initiated by the separate agents' desire to harm Kemp and culminating in the realization of this wish. Which is to say that the assignment of the governing topic and its triplication make it possible for Morse to isolate those actions that contribute to the thematic modification of the crime plot. Morse also resorts to specification to evaluate how exactly the narrative theme of revenge is instantiated, demonstrating that it pertains in three different specifications to the motivation underlying the case. The Strattons are (somewhat irrationally) angry that Kemp has traced the Jewel to them, obliging them to donate it to the museum he represents. (Mrs Stratton thinks of it as 'the jewel that is ours' [519].) They devise a plan to steal it and collect the insurance money. This scheme represents the mildest form of revenge, which may be specified as 'mischief.' The motivation and the actions of the Aldriches, the dead woman's parents, illustrate the 'purest' or strongest example of the theme, for they are completely orientated towards retaliation for their loss. Mrs Kemp, by choosing not to interfere with the Aldriches' realization of their plan,[13] exemplifies the thematic specification of 'vicarious revenge.' Specification shows that the theme takes on variational manifestations that nevertheless share the same basis. This operation, however, is not enough to explain the trajectory of the events or account for the link between the theft of the Jewel and the murder of Kemp.

As with the wrong solution, the chosen narrative theme points to a suitable plot pattern. Revenge entails a configuration which is initiated when a character, either intentionally or unintentionally, harms another character, causing the latter to respond in turn with purposefully harmful action. The repetition of the motivational base enables Morse to perceive the intersecting interests of the agents and to abduct the stratagem employed to achieve their mutual goal of harming Kemp. There are two initially separate plans, one to steal the Jewel and commit insurance fraud, the other to kill Kemp in revenge. Drawing on a simple rule – 'Quid pro quo' – Morse is able to postulate the narrative theme of a deal, involving a method of cooperation which finally identifies the link he has been looking for. A deal based on cooperation relies on a *transfer of control* (Ryan 1991, 140–1), one agent turning over (some part of) the execution of a plan to another agent.[14] The successful accomplishment of the theft and the murder become possible through an exchange of criminal activity, as the Strattons and the Aldriches each graft the plan of the other party to their own. The Aldriches agree to steal the Jewel, because it forwards their own cause; and the Strattons consent to help the Aldriches,[15] for an outsider-thief makes them look innocent. Repetition of motive also explains why Mrs Kemp does not protest when the confrontation takes place in the Kemp residence, for, by not interfering, she also achieves her goal.

The identification of the motive and the recognition of the nature of the link (cooperation) uniting the two crimes does not yet clarify, however, what makes this exchange of criminal activity possible in the first place. Since the realization of the agents' plans depends on this barter, there has to be some event which accounts for it. A careful review of all the evidence shows, however, that there is absolutely nothing in the plans of the two couples that could be employed for this end. As the evidence does not supply the needed motivation, only one thing remains for Morse and the author to do – that is, postulate an *unexpected turn*. Morse hypothesizes such an incident, basing it on the physical traits of the characters, namely, Laura Stratton's loud voice and Janet Aldrich's acute hearing. He envisages a situation in which the Strattons have talked about their plan to steal the Jewel in the tourist bus, a plan which Mrs Aldrich, sitting behind them, has been able to overhear. But this is not all. To explain how the Aldriches can start realizing their plan, he needs to posit yet another coincidence. As they know neither Kemp nor his habits and living environs, their plan of execution must rely on a great deal of improvisation. Morse concludes that Janet Aldrich also overheard Kemp's phone call about his delay, which she took as the opportunity to start implementing their sketchy plan. The solution thus hinges on two pure coincidences.

The postulation of coincidence must depend on the investigator's (and author's) understanding of the structures of plot itself. Part of our shared competence in plotted narratives involves the notion that what partly sustains the action is the unexpected. We also know that it may take different forms. There are the sudden turns that deal with the goals, plans, and strategies of implementation of the agents. Only to a degree can an agent compute the probable course of events and the feasible reactions of other agents to her plans and goals. The implementation of a plan may provoke another agent to respond in surprising ways. The point is that in these instances the unexpectedness may be explained by referring to the intersubjective realm. Then there are situations to which none of these constituents apply. In detective fiction they are represented by circumstances in which detectives can neither use the evidence they have to account for a specific event nor find such evidence. The event comes, as it were, completely from outside the facts at hand. In these cases we are, of course, faced with events classified as '(pure) coincidence,' '(pure) chance,' or even a 'twist of Fate.'

The converging goals of the agents, as well as the one maxim – 'revenge is sweet' – directing their actions, endow both plots with a high degree of unity, so much so that they become one. The plot Morse (re)constructs has the following complicated trajectory:

Thanks to her reduced means of living, Laura Stratton is annoyed at having to donate (instead of, for example, selling) the Wolvercote Tongue to the Ashmolean Museum on behalf of her late first husband. During the Historic Cities of England tour the Strattons plan the theft of the Wolvercote Tongue in order to collect the insurance money. A fellow tourist, Janet Aldrich accidentally overhears Mrs Stratton talking about the plan. The Aldriches are on the tour in order to confront Dr Kemp, who is responsible for the death of their only child in a car accident near Oxford. They are embittered by his extremely lenient court sentence. The Aldriches propose to steal the Jewel for the Strattons if the Strattons render them a service in return. This plan is realized; Laura Stratton, however, dies unexpectedly of a heart attack. By chance, Janet Aldrich overhears Dr Kemp's phone call informing their tour guide that he cannot keep his luncheon-lecture date with the Americans, but will arrive at Oxford at three o'clock. Seeing the opportunity to challenge Kemp, the Aldriches hire a car, pick Kemp up from the station on the pretext that Mrs Kemp has been taken ill, and drive him to his own house. A violent quarrel ensues during which one of the Aldriches strikes Kemp. It is unclear whether Kemp dies from this blow or from the fall. Mrs Kemp, crippled by the same car accident, simply watches without interfering, because she strongly dislikes her husband. Later the same day, Janet Aldrich hands Eddie Stratton the Jewel, asking him to dispose of the body. Mrs Kemp again cooperates, but later commits suicide as a self-inflicted punishment.

At the conclusion, Morse sums up the general significance of the events. At this stage, theming glides over to what Brinker (1993, 29) calls referential reading, for Morse shifts his attention from the thematic narrative pattern to issues in the world at large. This shift is anticipated by the narrator's description of Janet Aldrich's look at her husband after the exposure of their mutual guilt: 'the woman turned towards him with eyes that were pale and desolate, yet eyes which still lit up with the glow of deep and happy love as she looked unashamedly, unrepentantly, into her husband's face; the eyes of a mother who had grieved so long and so desperately for her only daughter, a mother whose grief could never be comforted, and who had journeyed to England to avenge what she saw as an insufferable wrong – the loss of the jewel that was hers' (523). As the investigation has traced a line beginning with the loss of the Wolvercote Tongue and ending in the discovery of the loss of a daughter, the narrator and Morse contrast the object and the human being. The gem may eventually be found (although the reader knows it is unlikely), but the Aldriches will never recover '[t]he jewel that was theirs ... They won't ever get *her* back, will they?' (528). It is the daughter who is the genuine Jewel, '"priceless" in the sense of ... being unique, irreplaceable' (364). Morse initially believed that the crime illustrates the theme of 'love's old sweet song' (448), and the solution proves him right, yet his specification of this theme was incorrect, for the love is not sexual, but parental.

Now that we have before us both the reading of the clues and the solution it produces, we can take up the questions of what accounts for the distinction between the false and the correct solutions, on the one hand, and what makes Morse the right kind of 'can-opener' for Dexter's purposes, on the other. As to the reasons for Morse's initial failure, he himself refers to the subgeneric puzzle mould in accounting for it:

'I once did a crossword in which all of the clues were susceptible of two quite different solutions. A sort of *double entendre* crossword, it was. Get on the wrong wavelength with one across, and everything fits except one single interlocking letter. Brilliant puzzle – set by Ximenes in the *Observer*. That's what I did – got off on the wrong foot. And I did it again in this case, with Downes. You know what one across was? That bloody phone call! I assumed it was important, Lewis, and I was *right*. But right for the wrong reasons.' (494)

This quotation spells out how Dexter has constructed the problem. Each key clue permits at least a double interpretation, allowing the presentation of two solutions, one designated as wrong and the other as right. The reader, of course, cannot usually say which is which. The existence of two alternative conclusions brings into view the demarcational criteria Dexter employs to distinguish between them. It seems reasonable to suggest that the author's choice has to do with the narrative interest of the two stories, which means that he or she selects the more appealing story as the correct solution. Admittedly, there is a circularity to this argument, for correctness is usually bound to be more appealing than incorrectness. We may still query what factors contribute to such narrative interest and appeal. Can these characteristics be determined in thematic terms? And what about the criteria of logical coherence the who-dunit sets for the solution? These questions indicate that we have now moved from the scrutiny of the investigation game in the fictional world to the author's game with the reader. The issue about the correctness of the solution ties up nicely with what Calinescu says about correct play at this level, because it tests the skills of both author and reader: 'Correct play is ... correct as a function of the specific game being played, its rules, its traditions, its pace, its structures of expectations, the backgrounds and strengths of the players, and the quality of enjoyment that is desired from playing it' (1993, 155).

The detective-story author's challenge is to create the sense that the solution emerges from the detective's reading of the clues. In putting together the explanation, the detective relates individual motifs (made up of clues) to various narrative themes, which establish a particular narrative pattern by spelling out the significance of the actions, events, and characters' motives to which the clues point. The assignment of individual narrative themes involves the first stage of establishing the semantic network among the different motifs of plot. Hence, narrative themes come, as it were, with 'semantic hooks' that offer a tentative glimpse of the terrain the plot has yet to reveal. This characterization already suggests that if the solution is to emerge from the reading of clues, it can be established only through the detective's assignment of specific narrative themes.

To be coherent, the whodunit solution has to provide a satisfactory answer to each aspect of the problem posed. If logic in the narrative context refers to a necessary sequence of cause and effect, then the solution has to illustrate the dominant topic the detective names: the trajectory of events and actions has to enact the governing narrative theme by putting into play its concept(s). Morse maintains that the crime portrays the narrative theme of revenge. This solution is thematically coherent, for it is based on a sequence of events which demonstrates how a damaging move by an agent (car accident) leads to its recipients' ensuing hostile response (confrontation and murder).

Yet the assignment of the narrative theme of revenge does not in any way prescribe what specific actions are to be chosen to portray it. What this means is that there is not – and can never be – a logically *necessary* relationship between the events depicted and the narrative themes to which they are ascribed.[16] The very possibility of linking the same motif (phone call) to two different narrative themes attests to this fact. Actually, the whodunit requires that it should be possible to assign the events and actions to different concepts, for a good problem (riddle) feeds on ambiguity. Both the narrative theme of revenge and the link between the crimes could have been established, for example, through a sequence of events in which the Aldriches either overhear the Strattons' plan to steal the Jewel or witness the theft, after which they blackmail the other couple into assisting them. Or it could have been grounded on a sequence initiated by professional squabbles between Kemp and Downes, leading to a cycle of revenge with Downes first stealing the Jewel to thwart the success of Kemp, and Kemp replying to this check by seducing Downes's wife, which then prompts Downes to kill him. The fact that there is no logically necessary tie between events, actions, and the narrative themes to which they are assigned suggests that the right solutions in whodunits, supposedly the outcome of the detective's logical ratiocination, are in fact only the final result of long chains of undercoded abductions. And undercoded abductions are chosen from a (possibly great) number of alternative options, being thus highly open to varied interpretations. The logical coherence of the solution is therefore always based on what might be called *quasi-logic* which respects first and foremost the specific conventions of the whodunit. Moreover, the solution Morse puts together certainly invites the charge of absurdity, as it asks the reader to accept, for example, a number of quite outlandish coincidences as well as the willingness of the Strattons to participate in a much graver crime than insurance fraud. This observation, of course, reminds us that what counts as possible and probable within the confines of the whodunit differs from our everyday conceptions of verisimilitude.[17]

The reason for the incorrectness of the wrong solution derives simply from the fact that the explanation either does not cover all of the aspects of the given problem or leaves a certain key clue dangling outside its scope. Such coverage does not fundamentally address the specific *content* of the events, but has first and foremost to do with their *patterning* or *design*. There is nothing wrong with the love triangle theme as such; it simply does not fit this particular problem. That the correctness of the solution has to do with its design suggests that we are dealing with narrative *elegance*. It is thus possible to maintain that the right solution in *The Jewel That Was Ours* is actually superior to the wrong solution, as well as to the two alternative suggestions I myself outlined. The whodunit focus on narrative patterning represents, I think, the greatest challenge in the game between author and reader, because it tests the *formal imagination* of both participants. And, if, as Calinescu argues, winning, in the sense of a positive outcome, is, for the reader, 'a forceful, incisive, superior understanding of the issues raised by the text' (or the genre) (1993, 148), then in playing with a whodunit author we should try to acquire an understanding of the principles underlying an author's formal imagination as attested to by the architectural designs of his or her narratives.

We can better approach the significance of narrative design by paying closer attention to the crossword-puzzle simile evoked by Morse. Besides the ambiguity of the clues, a *double entendre* crossword is aesthetically satisfying, because all of its separate entries *interlock* eventually. Applied to the narrative context, this trait points to the design of the events. The leitmotif of the literal link between the two crimes supplies the reader with a clue to this design, the broad contours of which are indicated in Morse's explanation of the crime:

'Now one of the jobs of the police force ... is to try to establish a *pattern* in crime, if this is possible, and in this instance both Sergeant Lewis and myself found it difficult not to believe there was some *link* between the two events ... already there was a link, was there not? Dr Kemp himself! – the man who had one day been deprived of a jewel which he himself had traced to an American collector ... a jewel which once united with its mate would doubtless be the subject of some considerable historical interest, and bring some short-term celebrity ... to Kemp. Indeed a photograph of the reunited Buckle and Tongue was going to be used on the cover of his forthcoming book.' (505)

This description is a *mise-en-abyme*, suggesting that the elegance of the solution derives from the fact that it forms a totality whose design resembles that of the Wolvercote Tongue, a two-piece jewelled belt buckle: the plan of the Strattons fits like the tongue to the buckle to the plan of the Aldriches. This subtle structure points to the author's formal imagination, and we can elaborate on this design by considering it in the light of the notion of *tellability*. This line of argument maintains that the reason for such appealing complexity has less to do with the *substance* of events than with the *structuring of the semantic substance* based on tellability. This concept refers to the domain of *fabula*, or *story*, indicating what makes a narrative worth telling in the first place (Ryan 1991, 149; Prince 1987, 81).[18] In order to be tellable, Ryan points out, a narrative has to have a point or, rather, points. In this view, such points of interest are varied and distributed throughout the text. '"Narrative point,"' writes Ryan, 'becomes in this case synonymous with "narrative highlight." A theory of tellability implicitly regards plot as a sequence of peaks and valleys, and seeks out the formulae for building up the peaks' (151). This theory thus proposes that there are certain general guidelines for the *plot-internal formation* of states, events, and happenings and their interrelationships that may be said to account for narrative complexity, appeal, and elegance.

Ryan (154–9) maintains that (at least) four properties influence the tellability of the events making up a plot: *semantic opposition, functional polyvalence, semantic parallelism,* and narrative *diversification.* In *The Jewel That Was Ours* certain key events are structured as sudden turns: when Janet Aldrich overhears Laura Stratton talking about the plan to make the Jewel disappear; when she overhears Kemp's phone call; and when Mrs Kemp perceives that the Aldriches' plan allows her to have her revenge vicariously. These incidents follow the principle of *semantic opposition,* which promotes any such inversions between narrative states as sudden turns, twists of Fate, reversals in the fortune of characters, and narrative irony, contrasting the goals of the characters with the results of their actions. In Dexter's book these turns are particularly pregnant, because they represent events that enter into several distinct functional units of plot, relying on the principle of *functional polyvalence.* They stand for those points that have a special strategic significance for the plot as a whole. Overhearing the fraud plan offers the solution to the problem both couples face (how to commit the crimes they plan in the best possible way), introducing the narrative theme of a deal, in this instance based on cooperation. (Note that this theme is further motivated by the fact that, by exchanging criminal activity, the culprits come closer to committing a perfect crime, because in this way they diminish the traces implicating them in their own crime.) The confrontation at Kemp's home likewise conflates a number of functions. It solves the problem the Aldriches and Mrs Kemp share of getting even with Kemp, letting them achieve their revenge; but it also serves as the violation (of the moral prohibition against killing another person), which then justifies both Mrs Kemp's self-inflicted punishment and the exposure of the Aldriches. The existence of three separate agents, each entertaining the goal of harming another person and then realizing this plan in different ways depends on the principle of *semantic parallelism and symmetry,* which posits the multi-plication of narrative sequences presenting structural similarities but involving different participants. Finally, the principle of *diversification* juxtaposes the private realms of characters (their thoughts, wishes, plans, beliefs, dreams, and so on) with the state of things within the reality of the fictional world. The incompatibilities between this reality and the private realms create conflicts which initiate and sustain action. They also open up a variety of alternative virtual narrative paths that diverge from the real course that events take. In *The Jewel That Was Ours*, narrative diversification comes into play with the wrong solution, indicating what could have happened, but did not.

These properties of tellability, wedded to the discursive structure of the puzzle, help us to specify the basic principles of Dexterian narrative design. Ryan concedes that there is a fuzzy border, an overlap, between the domain of tellability (story) and the domain of performance (discourse), because it is through the quality of the narrative performance that the reader discerns tellability in the first place (149). She insists, however, that these two domains are basically separate. What makes this distinction pertinent in the context of the detective story is that this genre is recognized by its organization, at the discursive level, of what she calls *strategic points*, that is, all the narrative devices and stratagems with the help of which the sense of mystery is created and sustained (153). If we exploit the crossword-puzzle analogy further, Dexter attempts to make the 'virgin grid' (412) of the puzzle (i.e., the discursive structure of strategic points) yield a solution that maximizes the principles of tellability. He favours solutions that assign the key events simultaneously to two or more of these principles, because such overlap is what creates the sense of intricacy, compactness, and narrative virtuosity, the aesthetic criteria this subgenre most prizes. The result is a narrative structure in which the complexity of the devices and stratagems responsible for the creation and sustenance of the enigma are matched by the complexity of the semantic, formal properties of the events concerning the crime.

In concluding, we can reflect on the links between the principles of tellability and an author's favourite narrative strategies, indicating what makes Morse the right kind of solver of problems for Dexter's purposes. The author needs a detective whose primary tool is imagination, for the facts do not suggest the surprising coincidences leading to convoluted plotting which the detective has to posit if he is to arrive at the solution. Morse has to make daring undercoded abductions to erect the scaffolding of the explanation that is then fortified with whatever facts there are at hand.[19] Dexter provides a particularly good example of the principles of theming, because the leaps and bounds of Morse's imagination make them so explicit. In what other way can one unite such details as a loud voice, a car accident, and an antique jewel than by forcefully highlighting some meanings while suppressing a host of others? It is this taking of various disconnected narrative ingredients and demonstrating that they can be linked up with one another into a coherent totality which continually directs the reader's attention to the detective's thematic activity.

The representation of this activity is intimately connected with the principles of tellability. Throughout his *oeuvre* Dexter hangs the key events of his crime stories on *semantic opposition* and *functional polyvalence*. More specifically, the principle of semantic opposition repeatedly takes the form of coincidences and twists of fate. Murders and killings take place because the agents happen to be somewhere, witness something, hear unexpected information, or are prompted to do something out of the ordinary. The initiating impetus for committing a crime often derives from some unforeseen factor, such as pure chance or the uncomputed effects of one's actions on others. This feature brings into play functional polyvalence, for Dexter typically stages situations in which one character, happening by chance to learn something of another character, uses this knowledge to further his or her own secret ends. Coincidences and twists of fate make crime-solving difficult, for the facts at hand do not point to the existence of such an event. In addition, facts also hide a confluence of plans and motives, the disentangling of which is arduous. It is instructive to place the architectonics of Dexterian plot construction against the background of the narrator's description of *Success*, a parody of the detective story, in Nabokov's *The Real Life of Sebastian Knight*:

The meeting is or seems accidental: both happen to use the same car belonging to an amiable stranger on a day the buses went on strike. This is the formula: quite uninteresting if viewed as an actual happening, but becoming a source of remarkable mental enjoyment and excitement, when examined from a special angle. The author's task is to find out how this formula has been arrived at; and all the magic and force of his art are summoned in order to discover the exact way in which the two lines of life were made come into contact, – the whole book indeed being but a glorious gamble on causalities or, if you prefer, the probing of the aetiological secret of aleatory occurrences. (1992, 94)

Dexter's *Last Bus to Woodstock* (1994b), which uses a similar motif of an accidental meeting in a car, allows a further elaboration of what governs his probing of 'aleatory occurrences.' Dexter also uses the magic and force of his art to uncover how this chance meeting led to one murder and two suicides. And although the reconstruction of the events highlights the many 'ifs' and 'if onlys,' enabling the reader to spot the role chance plays, the premium remains firmly on *fitting* the various elements together (see ch. 31). It is the accomplishment of this feat of mental agility which Dexter celebrates in book after book, although, unlike Nabokov, he never questions and burlesques this exercise itself.[20] Therefore, Dexter's books demonstrate – and always almost, but not quite, parody – the outrageous ingenuity and bizarre logic that underlie the setting and unravelling of narrative puzzles.

Theming as a Game of Antagonistic Pursuit

The hard-boiled detective story supplies a very different context from the whodunit for the detective's theming process, for its plot is built around structures of the quest and (heroic) adventure rather than the untying of an elaborate enigma. Although the plot still moves from the introduction of the detective and the presentation of the crime, through the investigation, to a solution (but not necessarily to the apprehension of the criminal), there are important shifts of emphasis in structuration. Three changes are particularly significant. The initial crime functions as a provocation for a series of fresh problems created within the plot. Thus the significance of the past diminishes, as the investigator's actions compel the criminal to continue 'writing' the crime story. The drama of the solution is subordinated to the detective's quest for the discovery and accomplishment of some other goal, such as justice, retribution, or some social cause. The review of a series of potential suspects is replaced by a pattern of intimidation and temptation of the protagonist, which demands personal engagement. The spotlight comes to rest on the investigating character, his or her goals and evaluation of diverse situations, and the actions undertaken to pursue these goals (Cawelti 1976, 142–3). This shift brings in, at least potentially, questions having to do with the psychological motivation of the investigator's (and other characters') actions. The author's challenge, therefore, is to show how the denouement is produced through *investigative action*. Thereby, our task as readers also changes, for we are engaged not so much in deciphering what has happened in the past as in trying to make sense of what is happening now as the investigation unfolds.

The detection process takes place within a stereotyped framework governing this tradition. It builds on a clichéd vision of corruption and exploitation that have eaten their way into the very structures of society. The investigation is then portrayed against this backdrop of all-pervasive instability and insecurity that feeds on the self-interest directing people's actions. In the hard-boiled detective story, one always faces the danger of being exploited, deceived, and double-crossed. The denouement often reverberates with the detective's own sense of betrayal and personal loss, enhanced in those books in which a friend or a lover is among the culprits (as in Dashiell Hammett's *The Maltese Falcon* [1980c] or Sara Paretsky's *Burn Marks* [1990]).

The differences in the patterning of plot also affect the protagonists' theming process. Typically, the difficulty they encounter is in forming a clear picture of what exactly is at stake in a particular case. They often spend the major part of the investigation simply trying to understand what is going on. (This happens, for example, in Raymond Chandler's *Farewell, My Lovely* [1976b] and Mickey Spillane's *Kiss Me, Deadly* [1953].) Hard-boiled detectives acquire data through direct action; consequently, the investigation closely resembles a dangerous game consisting of moves and countermoves between the investigators and their opponents. The theming process is made up of this fluctuating movement, with the move-countermove structure directing the detectives' thematizing attention primarily to the behaviour and actions of the people involved. To determine their significance, they first assign the actions and reactions of their opponents to suitable conceptual categories. This task often involves assessing a particular agent's goal and his or her plan for attaining it. They then reply by engaging in such action as they think serves their own goals, which, preferably, leaves them one jump ahead of the quarry. The opponents' response provides them with additional data in the light of which their hypotheses about the case may be tested and corrected. This back-and-forth movement continues until either party decides to terminate the game. At least to some extent, this thrust-and-parry game carries over to the relationship between author and reader, as the reader attempts to conjecture what the case is about. A number of conventions are of great help: we quickly learn to be wary of the powerful, the rich, and the beautiful. Ideally, however, the author challenges us to make sense of how the domains of various characters interlace and to see how the narrative patterns result from such interaction. In what follows I am again primarily interested in the architectonics of narrative design produced through the detective's thematization as well as in the function(s) it has for the author-reader game.

To illustrate what theming is like when it takes place in the fast-paced series of checks and counterchecks, I now turn to a close reading of Michael Dibdin's *Dead Lagoon* (1994). This novel aptly suits my present purpose, for its plot consists of a complex network of intersecting and colliding interests and plans, the changing nature of which makes thematization difficult for the protagonist, Police Inspector Aurelio Zen.

He thus has continually to revise the concepts and plot patterns in the light of which he views the case. What doubles the stakes of this game is that Zen uses the investigation as a smokescreen for the pursuit of his own secret agenda. He has to evaluate the interests and plans of the other agents to be able to use them for the furtherance of his own goals. Finally, the appropriateness of *Dead Lagoon* for an examination of theming is enhanced by the protagonist's failure. He comes up with a solution that is right, but also grievously wrong, enabling us to examine a situation in which an insufficient reading is, paradoxically, narratively right. Moreover, Dibdin, like Dexter, relies very much on semantic opposition in fashioning events, using this principle, however, for different ends by making it subordinate to the principle of narrative diversification. Both principles of tellability directly influence the detective's thematization, underlining its difficulty. Dibdin further complicates the plot's design by using the principle of semantic parallelism in order to create two other narrative sequences presenting structural similarities with the crime case Zen investigates. I first examine Zen's process of theming, and, to bring out better the move-countermove structure and to demonstrate how the principles of tellability shape the plot, I write out Zen's plans and his assessment of each situation, indicating the specific topic which he assigns to a given situation. I then consider the question of his failure and close the analysis with a discussion of what makes failure nevertheless suitable for Dibdin's purposes.

Dead Lagoon depicts Aurelio Zen's return home to Venice, which holds painful memories for him, especially of his father's disappearance in the war (16, 36). He investigates the kidnapping of an American millionaire, Ivan Durridge, on behalf of the man's relatives. Such a secondary paid assignment is a criminal offence; Zen intends to use the fee to provide housing for his mother and his lover, Tania (55–6). As a pretext for his self-authorized transfer to the Venetian police, he chooses the Zulian case: Ada Zulian, a family friend, has, ever since her daughter Rosetta disappeared during the Second World War, been suffering from delusions, and is now convinced that someone is trying to kill her. Zen thus plans to kill two birds with one stone. Finally, the plot also tells of the disappearance of a large package of drugs.

The opening builds on the principles of narrative diversification and functional polyvalence. The reader, privy to Zen's intentions and goals, follows how he deceives others about his motivations (e.g., 23, 40, 45–6). The narrative theme of deception creates a situation in which the reader sees two distinct threads being woven into the plot's fabric: the state of things Zen intends to bring about and the state of things he wants others to accept as tallying with reality. The narrator further underlines the principle of diversification by using, besides Zen, Ada Zulian as focalizer, showing the fictional world through the delusions plaguing her mind. Finally, stretches of direct dialogue depict how other characters besides Zen view reality, revealing their beliefs, plans, and goals. This narrative strategy emplots the events as a line passing from the domain of one character to that of another, yielding mutually competing, even starkly contradictory, interpretations of the state of things in the fictional world. This latter aspect refers to the principle of functional polyvalence: the same events have different significance for different players.

The beginning evokes also the principle of semantic parallelism through the presentation of three similar mysteries, each dealing with the missing-person motif:[21] the disappearance of Ivan Durridge in the immediate past, and of Zen's father and Rosetta Zulian during the war. It is clear from the start that these mysteries are parallel, but also that they are unlikely to intersect, although the Durridge and the Zulian cases may both involve a crime.[22] Each mystery builds on the principle of diversification, for each involves guesses about the fate of the missing persons. This narrative strategy covers the reality of the fictional world from the detective's and the reader's view: by multiplying narrative possibilities, Dibdin makes it difficult for both to distinguish what is true (i.e., what tallies with reality) from false beliefs and fantasies. The narrator continually plays up this confusion by depicting the discrepancy between actuality and Zen's memories, imagination, and desires: 'His mind was a jumble of contradictory thoughts and feelings, an inner landscape equivalent to the one all around him: blocks of every size and shape thrown together as though at random, like bricks tipped in a heap ... Everything was turning out differently from what he had imagined' (43).[23] The stress on the principle of narrative diversification shows that the clash between appearance and reality organizes the author's game with the reader, challenging us to determine what is 'real' in this narrative. Simultaneously, this clash directs the reader's attention to the author's conception of plot's relationship to reality: how does plot model reality?

The plot can be divided into three phases. The first stage follows the Zulian and Durridge investigations, closing with the apprehension of Zulian's persecutors. The second phase depicts Zen's investigation of the murder of a local police officer, which he uses as a new screen for his covert activities. This phase ends with his identification of Durridge's kidnappers. The third phase consists of his attempts to have the guilty exposed and brought to justice, which backfires, leaving him with the disastrous consequences of having misevaluated the other players.

During the first stage of the two investigations, Zen mainly gathers information. The Zulian case turns out to be quite straightforward. Zen re-establishes himself with Ada, gaining enough of her trust so that when there is a new attack on her, she begs him for help (29–34; 82–8). The rest is simply 'positioning' and putting together scraps of information and his own observations, such as Ada's ownership of valuable property, the recently oiled waterfront door, and the visits of her nephews. Zen solves the case by relating it to the narrative theme of deception, concluding that the nephews' concern conceals a sinister purpose. He reasons that the night-time ghosts Ada encounters are these nephews, whose plan is to have her pronounced insane so that they can acquire authority over her assets. He also estimates that his own presence escalates the attacks and, to put a stop to them, he draws up this simple plan (186–92):[24]

Plan 1:
Prerequisite: Leaving Ada ostensibly unprotected.
Planned event: Attracting a new attack on Ada.
Postcondition (goal): Exposing the attackers.

This plan is a trap for the attackers, based on Zen's assessment of what his opponents are likely to do if surveillance on Ada is lifted. He correctly evaluates their tactics and catches them red-handed. His success is grounded on simply choosing from among a number of feasible plot outlines one which seems to suit this particular context. He thus makes use of specification in picking a plot dealing with exploitation in the family circle for financial gain. Satisfied with the results, Zen also expects Ada to be gratified (193). She, however, uses Zen's actions for her own benefit. By refusing to prosecute her nephews, she gains a firm hold over them, but is spared a public scandal (194–9; 202–6). It is Zen who is left looking very foolish: 'he had never expected to be outwitted by an old woman everyone agreed was crazy ... The only loser was Zen, who had been totally outsmarted' (207–8). This unexpected turn of events ex-presses two narrative themes simultaneously, related to the domains of Zen and Ada respectively. The narrative theme of action with accidental effect summarizes the turn from Zen's perspective, for the results of his actions conflict with the result as registered in his plan. From Ada's

perspective, the event presents itself as a fortuitous resolution of a problem, enabling her to achieve the goal of stopping the scary night-time
incidents through an event not even specified in her own plan-register.
This turn shows that Zen's evaluation of the player he is faced with has
been incomplete. To alleviate his anger and sense of humiliation, Zen
later on pesters Ada about the fate of her daughter, Rosetta, trying to
bargain with her: 'Give [the nephews] to me, and I'll tell you what really
happened to Rosetta' (257), which, as the reader knows, is a false promise, for Zen, at this stage, does not know this story.

Conducting the covert investigation poses more difficulties, for newspaper accounts and, later, a copy of a police report are Zen's sole sources
of information. Casual inquiries reveal only that the official police version must be wrong, for Durridge was supposedly abducted by water,
but the extremely low tide would not have allowed the use of a boat. Zen
realizes that his only chance of progress is to concentrate on the discrepancy between the official version and the local estimates of its practical
impossibility by tracing the boat allegedly used in the kidnapping
(103–8). Again, there are two sketchy, conflicting versions about what
happened. Zen finds out that the boat has recently been sold by one
Giulio Bon. He plans to proceed in the following fashion:

Plan 2:
Prerequisite: Tracing the boat.
Planned event: Interrogating the seller of the boat.
Postcondition: Acquiring new information enabling progress.

The inconsistency is the only sign of the governing topic of the kidnapping case, but as Zen can relate it to neither a narrative theme nor a plot
outline, the second plan remains very rough. It represents a typical
example of an investigator's prompting a given situation to acquire more
information. This strategy always contains an element of risk, for one
cannot foresee all the reactions one will call forth; one can only hope to be
clever enough to master the situation by turning them to one's own
advantage. Here, too, events take an unexpected turn, for a lawyer, by
pointing to procedural irregularities, terminates the interrogation before
it really starts, thus aborting the execution of Zen's plan. Zen realizes that
this incident was arranged by a fellow police officer, Enzio Gavagnin,
whom he had seen with the boat's seller at a political rally of the local
separatist party, Nuova Repubblica Veneta, the day before (140–1; 151–2).

He does attain his goal, however, although in a roundabout way, for Gavagnin's intervention suggests that he should consider terms that bring politics into the case. The disloyalty of a fellow officer, however, so enrages Zen that he improvises a plan of revenge: he follows the man Gavagnin has been interrogating and hopes, by intimidating this man, to find out something enabling him to make his colleague look ridiculous (152, 156–7). An unexpected new turn occurs, however. Angered by Zen's coercion, the man accuses him of being party to the same drug ring to which Gavagnin also belongs. This ring has murdered the man's brother for losing a package of drugs (154–5). By using this new piece of information, Zen improvises a fresh line of revenge. He sneaks into Gavagnin's office, calls a number in the colleague's personal phone book and, pretending to be Gavagnin, announces he knows where the missing drugs are (169–73). This sequence thus begins with Zen's aborted plan of execution, leading to his adoption of a counterplan aiming at retaliation.

At this stage, Zen has his first glimpse of the larger state of things: there is a drug ring with a clever system of transporting and distributing the drugs, and there are members of the Nuova Repubblica, who are somehow connected with the Durridge case. The link is the corrupt policeman Gavagnin, who is involved in both operations. Zen lacks the data to put together a more coherent picture than this. This situation terminates the first phase of the plot. Approximately halfway through the narrative, the reader can begin to form a sense of the 'system' regulating its flow of events, a system which profoundly affects the protagonist's attempts at theming. On the one hand, there is Zen with his intentions, plans, and goals and, on the other, there are the characters affected by his actions. What begins to emerge is a thrust-and-parry structure in which Zen intervenes with the current status quo, only to be answered back in ways he had not anticipated. The facts about the crime cases become slowly visible, thus establishing a point of access to the reality of the fictional world. This thrust-and-parry structure, united as it is in this narrative to the principles of semantic opposition (the many unexpected turns), and narrative diversification (the incompatibilities between fictional reality and the private domains of characters), begins to prefigure disastrous consequences for Zen. The culmination of the first part of the plot is revealing in this sense, for, before taking action in the Zulian case and before his practical joke on Gavagnin, Zen, having spent a night making love to Cristiana Morosini Dal Maschio, the daughter of a family friend, feels 'strong and vigorous, invincible and serene. The doubts and difficulties which had beset him earlier now seemed trivial. A woman had offered herself to him and he had satisfied both her and himself. What could touch him?' (169). In the light of the outcome of his actions, Zen's feeling of omnipotence acquires a strongly ironic hue, suggesting that the legend about the Zen family's 'habit of winning all the battles and then losing the war' (159) may apply this time, too. And if it does, there is a covert thematic parallelism between Zen's investigation and the historical story about the fate of his ancestors, foreshadowing his downfall.

The second stage of the plot begins with the discovery of Gavagnin's body in a cess pit. Realizing that his practical joke directly caused Gavagnin's death, Zen quickly hatches a new plan. He wants to settle the score by bringing Gavagnin's killers to justice, but he must also find a new cover for ending the Durridge case, for the semi-successful conclusion of the Zulian case threatens to end his authorization with the Venetian police (208, 212, 215–18, 226–8). His initial goal has, however, changed. He now wants only to cover his tracks so that he can remain in Venice and marry Cristiana Morosini Dal Maschio, for he has become totally besotted with her (208–9, 265, 282).[25] The new plan may be written as follows:

Plan 3:
Prerequisite: Convincing the public prosecutor that Zen knows the
    identity of Gavagnin's killers.
Planned event: Acquiring a free hand to conduct the investigation.
Postcondition #1: Settling the score with Gavagnin's killers.
Postcondition #2: Covering up any trace of Zen's involvement in
Gavagnin's death and in the Durridge case, and solving the Durridge
    case.
Postcondition #3: Creating favourable conditions enabling Zen's
    permanent transfer to the Venetian police.

To establish the prerequisite for the initiation of the plan, Zen has to lie to the public prosecutor, saying that he knows who Gavagnin's killer is (214–18). He can do so because he is able to assign this case to a straightforward topic: the murder is about the punishment of a member whom the drug ring falsely believes to be treacherous. Again, the unexpected turn builds on narrative diversification. Only Zen knows that the ring has misread Gavagnin's actions, for it took Zen's joke for real. Having received authorization, he breaks up his plan into two components. These parts may be written as follows:

Plan 4:

Component 1	Component 2
Prerequisite: Finding the missing heroin.	Prerequisite: Making the public prosecutor believe that all interrogations deal with the drug case.
Planned event: Setting a trap for the drug ring with the heroin.	Planned event: Questioning the men who landed on Durridge's island on the day he was kidnapped.
Postcondition: Bringing the ring to justice, which settles Gavagnin's death.	Postcondition: Possessing enough information to conclude what the kidnapping is about and to begin legal proceedings.

The complexity of this plan derives from the fact that its first component functions as an enabling device for the actualization of the second component. Moreover, it also entails additional subplans to create other necessary enabling relations ensuring success. As a means of resolving the problems facing Zen, it has elegance, allowing him, again, to try to 'kill two birds with one stone.' As regards Gavagnin's murder, Zen handles only the search for the missing drugs on an ossuary island, after which he delegates the case to others (248–9). The search is important, for, besides locating the drugs, the police unexpectedly find Durridge's body (239–42). The method of the search – from the air by helicopter – gives Zen an idea of how Durridge was abducted and how he died. In accord with the second component, he brings in the men who landed on Durridge's island the day he was kidnapped. By intimidating and lying to one of them, Zen finds out that three members of the Nuova Repubblica, Gavagnin included, took four foreigners to meet the millionaire just before he disappeared (278–81; 288–9). Now Zen knows that these men are responsible for Durridge's death. He also concludes that the man was abducted by air and that the person flying the helicopter was Nando Dal Maschio, an avid pilot and the charismatic leader of Nuova Repubblica. But he still has no idea what the case is about. To redress this situation, he turns to Tommaso Saoner, his childhood best friend and Dal Maschio's right-hand man, and persuades him to disclose Durridge's significance for the party (286–91).

The third phase records a series of Zen's failures and disappointments stemming from his manifold miscalculations. Zen has freely confided in Cristiana, the estranged wife of Dal Maschio, believing that his affair with her is about passionate love leading to commitment and marriage (208, 282, 304–5). Now he finds he has totally misevaluated the situation, for Cristiana has all along related everything to her husband, who has thus secretly been able to follow the investigation. Realizing that Zen has a sketchy sense of these events, Dal Maschio decides to terminate Zen's investigation and his affair with Cristiana for good. Dal Maschio first mockingly demonstrates both Cristiana's loyalty to him and the circumstantial nature of all the evidence, then freely tells Zen that the Durridge case was about establishing political allies. The party members helped the Croatian secret police to kidnap the millionaire to ensure the Croats' support of Dal Maschio's plans for making Venice an independent regional nation.[26] The Croats kidnapped Durridge (né Durić), a Serb, in order to make him stand trial both for his atrocities during the Second World War and for running guns for the Bosnian Serbs during the Bosnian war. After receiving a foretaste of his fate at Gavagnin's hands, Durridge jumped from the helicopter Dal Maschio was flying. This encounter makes Zen aware of another grave misevaluation: Tommaso Saoner has used his disclosures to warn Dal Maschio of potential danger (305–12).

Humiliated and infuriated, Zen is determined to get back at Dal Maschio. His resolve is only heightened after learning what really happened to Rosetta, Ada Zulian's daughter,[27] for he sees a connection between these wartime events and the ultra-nationalistic politics of Nuova Repubblica.[28] The final plan for bringing Dal Maschio to justice is an improvised one involving a 'psychological trap' (331) for Tommaso Saoner. The trap is based on Zen's assessment of his friend's character, for he believes that Saoner is too honest to be entangled in even semi-illegal dealings. The plan is as follows (328):

Plan 5:
Prerequisite: Barring Saoner from entering his home and challenging
    him to a mental duel.
Planned event: Pursuing Saoner through the night-time streets of
    Venice and pestering him with the details of the Durridge case.
Postcondition: Getting Saoner to testify against Dal Maschio.

To add pressure, Zen deliberately lies to Saoner about Dal Maschio's view of Saoner's abilities (338–9). The pursuit ends when Zen loses track of his friend. The novel concludes with three unexpected turns: during the final meeting with Cristiana, confirming that she has used their affair to get back at her unfaithful husband, Zen hears that Saoner has committed suicide. He then calls home, learning that his lover, Tania, has left him. Finally, on his way out of the city, he bumps into an old family friend and learns from him the truth about his own father: contrary to everyone's belief that he was heroically killed in the war, Angelo Zen deserted the army, hiding at a farm in Poland and assuming the identity of a dead Pole, and, after the borders closed, realized that his life was there with the new family he had started. Having failed to attain any of the goals he set for himself, at the novel's close Zen is left with a profound sense of alienation: 'Zen understood only that [the tourist] was asking directions to somewhere in English. He closed his eyes and tried to summon up a few words in that language. "I'm sorry," he replied with an apologetic smile, "I'm a stranger here myself"' (354).

Why do Zen's ardent, even frantic, attempts at thematization – at forming a coherent picture of what is at stake in each case he deals with in Venice – bring such disastrous results? By using Zen as the main focalizer, the narrator helps the reader to form a sense of the psychological motivation accounting for his defeat. There are at least two obvious reasons. First, Zen's initial motive for coming to Venice is morally dubious, presenting the violation of a professional rule which causes the subsequent backfiring of his plans. Having to play underhandedly places him at a disadvantage: he cannot openly gather information, and he lacks the necessary institutional support for taking effective measures. These restraints, however, are not, as such, impediments to success, as the other novels in the Zen series make clear, for in previous cases he has had to play multiple roles, involving lying and cheating to attain his goals. The decisive factor would seem to be his acting purely in his own interest, which has not happened before. This interpretation gains support from the fact that the final showdown, built on the traditional gumshoe motif of one man pursuing another through the labyrinthine streets of a city, takes place after the official termination of Zen's licence in Venice:

As the noise subsided, a church bell struck midnight. Zen smiled grimly at this signal that his official tenure in the city was at an end. If his opponents had counted on him meekly packing his bags and going when told to go, they had seriously miscalculated. He felt a weight lift from his shoulders as the twelve ponderous chimes cut through the red tape and procedural minutiae in which he had been enmeshed. As a free agent, he was much more dangerous and effective than he could have been in his official capacity. (331)

The excerpt also demonstrates the second reason for Zen's failure, deriving from his emotional entanglements. His desire to have things a certain way forms, as it were, a distorting, even a blinding, pair of spectacles through which he views other people and reality. This obsession leads to Zen's being 'dangerous and effective,' but with consequences he himself cannot foresee.

Thanks to the protagonist's limited vision, leading to his incomplete thematization of the crime story, the challenge of forming a larger view of the plot's thematic configuration moves to the reader. Indeed, such a move seems to be implied by this failure. Thus, the reader can use Zen's numerous miscalculations as the key to the overall architectonic design of the plot, which is grounded on ironic inversion: the ending demonstrates that the protagonist's actions have produced results directly opposite to what he planned and aimed at. The trajectory of the plot consists of sequences of such ironic inversions, producing the global reversal. These sequences build on the move-countermove structure of the investigation, resulting from the active plotting by the central characters. The narrative appeal of this plot resides in the tortuous, surprise-filled course of the events, as they shift back and forth between the tracks of the competing plans and goals of Zen and his various opponents. This shifting back and forth diversifies narrative paths. Of special significance in this diversification is the frequent lying and deceit in which most characters are engaged. They continually try to make others accept their misrepresentation of things as tallying with reality in order to achieve their own aims. These strategies make us privy to a plethora of embedded narratives, as, sooner or later, we can juxtapose the private plans and aspirations of one character with those of another.[29] This scurrying back and forth brings the reality of the fictional world under scrutiny, because that reality is seen from various perspectives. Dibdin's narrator uses diversification in order to demonstrate that, although Zen finds out the facts of the cases he investigates, the significance of these facts is tied to each agent's interpretation of the events. There is no one stable value system in the fictional world that would both confer meaning on events and serve as the point of arbitration in cases of dispute. The function of this narrative principle in *Dead Lagoon* is to emphasize the opaqueness of reality; because the characters have access to it only through their own perspectives, they can never master it: 'The few facts he had gleaned stood out like objects scattered at random in a dark room, illuminated by a beam of light whose brilliance only serves to emphasize the impenetrable obscurity all around' (127). What adds to the trickiness and unexpectedness of reality are other people, whose motives and goals are difficult, if not impossible, to decipher. This accounts for the protagonist's repeated sensation that appearances are all there is: 'Zen began to lose all sense of reality, as though his night's dreams, denied, were seeping out to taint his waking consciousness. He dimly remembered what he was doing and why, but only as one remembers some fact about a country one has never visited' (336–7).

The thematic density of the plot of *Dead Lagoon* is enhanced by the parallel stories about the missing persons (Ivan Durridge, Rosetta Zulian/Rosa Coin, Angelo Zen), which further develop the juxtaposition between appearance and reality through repetition. Each story centres on a duplicate identity: in Durridge's case, the veneer of a millionaire hides a war criminal; Rosetta Zulian's corpse was dressed up as that of Rosa Coin; and Angelo Zen adopted the identity of a dead Pole. These stories reverberate with what happens to Zen, as the ending demonstrates his estrangement from his former ideas of who he is. Moreover, the parallel story about Zen's ancestors, who won all the individual battles but lost the war, provides a historical precedent for the events in which Zen himself is entangled. In this sense, his conviction that 'nothing new could happen to him here, nothing real' (35) is correct, although Zen realizes too late its terrible irony.

Dibdin uses the figure of Zen and Zen's incomplete thematization to play with detective-story conventions. There is irony in the investigator's defeat; more importantly, this failure spotlights the profound epistemological uncertainties the plot brings to the fore. There is no truth about the mysteries surrounding Zen, for things are 'not merely unknown but in some essential way unknowable ... everything was a trick of light, an endlessly shifting play of appearances without form or substance. What you saw was what you got, and all you would ever get' (304). In playing the game set up by this author, we encounter the mysteries about crime leading to mysteries about the nature of reality that prove to be unsolvable. In criticizing the notion of knowability and the power of plot to describe reality accurately, Dibdin's novel moves close to the metaphysical detective story. This situation challenges our formal imagination in its own way by directing our attention to narrative design as providing the only stable structure about which things can be known, as reality remains elusive. In *Dead Lagoon* we see the elegantly interwoven narrative line twisting back and forth between the domains of the characters; these twists draw a figure in which the ending contrasts ironically with the beginning.

From the perspective of the series, there is a catch to the author's game with the reader, however. From the beginning of the series (in *Ratking*) onward, the one framing enigma evoked in each book is the mystery of the disappearance of Zen's father, which is ostensibly solved in *Dead Lagoon*. The analogy between the story about Zen's historical ancestors and the plot of *Dead Lagoon*, enticing the reader to account for Zen's failure in terms of this analogy, is undercut by the next book in the series, *Così Fan Tutti* (1996), the events of which are a rewrite of Mozart's opera. A new layer of meaning is added to the reading of *Dead Lagoon*, for in *Così Fan Tutti*, Zen again maintains that 'everything happens twice,' adding, however, 'the first time as tragedy, the second as farce' (*Così Fan Tutti*, 246). Now the plot of *Dead Lagoon* is annexed to a much larger plot configuration. Moreover, *Così Fan Tutti* reveals that, thanks to Signora Zen's marital infidelity, Angelo Zen is *not* Zen's real father.[30] This disclosure results in another reinterpretation, for, strictly speaking, Aurelio Zen is not of the Zen lineage; the similarity of fate between the unfortunate Zens and the protagonist is contingent. Hence, we realize that the picture we have formed of the plot's structuration in *Dead Lagoon* and of the connections of its various parts is open to revision, thereby demonstrating that its formal and thematic design exhibit features of the same 'pervasive instability' that the events in the fictional world do. And that challenge is definitely part of the fun of playing with this particular author.

INVESTIGATING GUILT

4

The Reading of Guilt

In John le Carré's *A Murder of Quality* (1980), Inspector Rigby, enlisting George Smiley's help, describes a murder to him: ' Stella Rode must have been struck fifteen to twenty times with a cosh or bit of piping or something. It was a terrible murder ... There are marks all over her body ... I've seen some nasty things in my time, but this is the worst' (28, 31). The cruelty of this deed makes him wonder what kind of person would engage in such brutality. The Chief thinks 'a maniac, a man who kills for pleasure or the price of a meal' (36) is responsible, but Rigby is unwilling to pursue someone he 'can't believe in' (37). The *type of crime* affects conjectures about the *type of person* to look for as a likely candidate for the *role of murderer*. A bystander's description of the victim as one who was 'trouble,' being 'the hysterical kind, self-dramatizing, weeping all over the house for days on end' (98), suggests that also the *type of victim* directs the search for the perpetrator. Smiley lists the people he has encountered as suspects, evaluating what is morally questionable in them as persons and in their relations with the victim. Thus he tries to establish a sense of what the *suspects are like in moral terms*, fitting each into the role of criminal and appraising the result. Undecided about the options, Smiley places the suspects against the setting of the murder, an exclusive public school, which to him appears an unreal and insane place (93). He has to grasp the *type of community* the Carne school represents in order to come to a conclusion not only about who the murderer is and why, but also about the kind and degree of guilt each person alone, and the community together, carries in the events.

The explicit evaluation of these basic detective-story roles in a particular setting shows Smiley to be engaged in what might be characterized as the *reading of guilt*. Detective stories represent moral evaluation as a process based on those aspects of the investigation dealing with the observation, explanation, and assessment of diffuse things as potential clues about the legal and/or moral responsibility of certain persons for a crime. This process includes the interpersonal sphere, for a criminal deed cannot be fairly judged nor can justice be served in isolation from the context in which a crime occurs. Although the genre depicts this evaluation as the outcome of a complicated process, it is, in actual fact, always controlled by various relatively simple generic conventions.[1]

In what follows I examine how this process of reading guilt functions in detective-story investigations. Like any other detective, George Smiley has to picture the human interaction in a particular setting, which suggests that there might be something akin to a 'logic' of reasoning which he draws on in evaluating guilt and responsibility. That he dwells on the character typologies of the suspects and on the moral quality of their actions implies that this 'logic' is tied up with the construction of *ethos*. To speak of ethos includes evaluating characters and their actions from a moral perspective. The notion refers to a (fictional) character's virtues and vices, that is, the strengths, capacities, and habits of behaviour, good and bad, that he or she may use for either benevolent or malevolent purposes. According to Wayne C. Booth, ethos expresses itself best in habits of choice and behaviour; therefore, its moral evaluation covers not only what a character is but also what he or she *does* (1988, 8–11).[2]

The focus on ethos is built into the criminal investigation, for detectives read various signs as indications of what the suspects are like and how they are therefore likely to act.[3] The genre spotlights the interpretive leaps detectives make from the observation of such outward clues as reactions, appearances, living environs, and possessions to the assignment of personal qualities that make up an ethos. These leaps largely depend on a detective's experience of people and crime. The association of observation with a sense of ethos that Smiley makes in watching the victim's husband in *A Murder of Quality* clearly illustrates such a leap: 'Smiley found himself continually irritated by Rode's social assumptions, and his constant struggle to conceal his origin. You could tell all the time, from every word and gesture, what he was; from the angle of his elbow as he drank his coffee, from the swift, expert pluck at the knee of his trouser leg as he sat down' (75). That Rode is a grammar-school boy from the lower middle class is easy for Smiley to conclude, thanks to his familiarity with the upper-middle-class mores from which Rode's habits differ. Often, however, the matching of observations to qualities of character requires a choice among competing possibilities. The first part of this chapter looks at how fictional detectives use their observations to construct a suspect's ethos.

Smiley's investigation shows that the victim has behaved in an odd manner. He uses her actions as the basis for picturing her ethos, conjecturing about her mode of conduct, her goals, and her manner of attaining those goals. This procedure he adopts with suspects as well. Fictional detectives try to explain behaviour and action, using these explanations to project what a person's ethos is, again using their experience of human nature and crime.[4] In the second part of this chapter I examine the principles of reasoning that use actions to build a sense of ethos.

In assessing questions of guilt and responsibility, it is not enough, however, to form a sense of ethos. In thinking about one suspect, for example, Smiley is struck by the fact that she fits the role both of murderer and of victim well, thanks to the strong sadistic streak in her ethos (93–4). Yet she is neither, which shows that conventional conceptions about a murderer's or a victim's ethos is like simply provide broad guidelines for conjecture. The construction of ethos is one means of solving crimes, but it cannot in itself supply the basis for conclusive moral evaluation, which can take place only after the identity of the perpetrator is known. The moral perspective on crime changes profoundly when detectives move from investigation proper to explanation. The knowledge of the perpetrator's identity enables the allocation of guilt and responsibility, which includes the appraisal of the ethoi not only of the suspects and the criminal but also of the victim(s), the causal relationships underlying the crime, and the moral significance the detective accords to these elements. The question is, then, what kinds of factors affect detectives' decisions about moral answerability, and how do they fit those factors together? The detectives' decisions, in turn, reveal the nature of their own moral conceptions, because they cannot allocate responsibility without judging the people involved. In *A Murder of Quality*, for instance, Smiley's assessment is mainly based on two elements: the victim's cruelty and the murderer's intolerable position, as someone completely under her power. He gives no weight whatsoever to the reasons for the victim's (moral) pathology, nor does he dwell at length on the murderer's ethos. An additional consideration is the affection he feels for the murderer's dead brother, a good friend of his. Although his conclusion is that the victim is more to blame than the murderer, he nevertheless thinks that murder calls for atonement (ch. 20). When Smiley tries to help the murderer escape, to allow him to commit suicide, he acts as an independent moral agent in evaluating the situation according to his understanding of the morally approvable line of conduct. This attempt fails, however.

There is good reason for dwelling on how fictional detectives assign guilt and responsibility, because what they do serves as the model for what readers also do while reading detective stories. In spite of this overlap, the detective's and the reader's tasks are not identical, for one of the major decisions we have to make as readers is the extent to which we accept the detective as the spokesperson for the morals endorsed by the implied author. The point of closure makes this final divergence of the detective's and reader's paths particularly evident. The detective, as a player in the events, has a field of vision that is necessarily more limited than the reader's, which expands to include the appraisal of the detective's ethos, together with the whole fictional community and its moral values. We can further elaborate on this difference by using the distinction Peter Rabinowitz makes between *narrative* and *authorial audiences*. In letting the detective guide us, we participate in the game of make-believe, thereby becoming part of the narrative audience, for whom the narrative situation is real. In joining the authorial audience, however, we draw on our awareness of the constructedness of the detective and of the fictional community, paying attention to the signals the implied author gives us for the construction of the text and the reading experience (1987, 93–104).

The reader's participation in the authorial audience introduces an additional sense in which the notion of ethos is relevant for the process of reading guilt in the detective-story context. Booth (1988) argues that the ethical criticism of literature invites us as readers to reflect on, assess, and explicate the entire range of *effects* a narrative has on *our own ethoi*, making us ponder the kind of company books provide us with during reading: what becomes of us *as* we read? How do the books we read shape our desires, direct our emotions, or challenge our patterns of perception and thinking? In Booth's view the challenge arises from the duality of interaction in which readers are engaged. The first level of this interchange consists of our effort to be fair to the narrative we are reading. Doing justice to the narrative means listening as carefully as one possibly can to the views put forth in the narrative, and trying to understand the values it promotes in the terms the implied author suggests are pertinent and valid. This first level thus largely deals with the reconstruction of the implied reader's sphere (138–49). But Booth argues that ethical criticism goes beyond piecing together this textual role. It appears that the kind of general ethical inquiry he advocates insists that readers also take a *personal* stand on what they read. This level of interaction between authors and readers thus draws in our response as actual, flesh-and-blood readers, as we are invited to reflect on our reading experience.

The reading of guilt makes us aware of yet another manner in which the detective story invites us to decipher its plot through patterning. The *minima-moralia* configuration – that is, the interplay between the basic character roles and the setting – supplies both detectives and readers with a ready-made mould with whose help they can structure the interaction within the fictional world. In order to demonstrate how such patterning is achieved, I analyse the 'logic' involved in the reading of guilt, expressed by sets of questions detectives and readers have to answer. The reader has, of course, the additional task of examining the experience and effects of being made first to construct ethoi and then to evaluate them in the light of notions about guilt and responsibility.

The reader's generic role is marked by distance, for we are required to view each and every character with suspicion, that is, as a potential murderer. What Philip Kerr's private detective says of himself applies to the reader as well: 'A suspicious nature goes with the job' (*March Violets* 1993a, 81). This task requires us to exercise our 'moral muscles,' making us aware of the elements that go into moral evaluations. This process is framed, however, by the more general question of how guilt relates to the inevitable voyeurism of being made to probe into the personal affairs of characters. Is moral evaluation reconcilable with such curiosity? In concluding this chapter I consider these issues in more detail.

Constructing Ethos on the Basis of Observations

How do detectives – and readers – begin to construct a suspect's ethos? In thinking about this question, I use Laurie King's *A Grave Talent* (1993) as an example. This novel fits my purpose well, for it represents that small-ish, though growing, subgenre of detective fiction emphasizing in-depth characterization, and, thereby, overtly raising issues typical, in more covert form, of the whole genre. The creation of complex, plausible characters underlines ethos, through which some moral issue is explored. (Other such quest-through-character novels include, for example, P.D. James's *A Taste for Death* [1989a], Dorothy L. Sayers's *Gaudy Night* [1986], Minette Walters's *The Dark Room* [1996], and Barbara Wilson's *Sisters of the Road* [1986].)[5] *A Grave Talent* uses this quest-through-character approach by preparing a role for the reader in which we are not so much expected to do what the detectives do as to follow interestedly the progress of their investigation. This strategy leaves room for thinking about ethos. The book has an external narrator, and most events are focalized through Kate Martinelli, one of the two police officers assigned to the case. As most information comes through the detectives, the reader observes how they construct the suspects' ethoi. It is up to us, however, to form a sense of the detectives' ethoi, including the reliability of their judgments.

A Grave Talent deals with the search for the murderer of three small girls. The first phases of the investigation best show a number of stable components of reading guilt in the genre. In this book it seems likely that the culprit is to be found among the inhabitants of the Road, a bohemian community near San Francisco. The investigation quickly centres on Vaun Adams, alias painter Eva Vaughn, who has previously been sentenced for strangling a child. Here are Martinelli's earliest impressions of this suspect:

Christ, she's gorgeous, was Kate's first thought, followed immediately by, She looks like one of those living dead looking blankly into the camera outside Dachau or Buchenwald. Her glossy black curls were slightly too long and tumbled onto her shoulders and around a pair of startling, icy blue eyes that revealed nothing whatsoever of the thoughts behind them. Her cheekbones were high and thin, her skin pale, her mouth a fraction too wide for the rest of the face ... Her eyes were as calm and as vulnerable as those of a dead woman, but there was a slight smile at the corners of her mouth. (58)

Kate's observations during a search of Adams's home, of her art books and a painting she has just finished, also provide information to be processed:

Books on Titian, Poussin, Bellini, and Michelangelo, and three volumes of Christian symbolism, bristling with strips of paper marking depictions of women and children, some classical, most of them Madonnas with child or Pietàs. Under the circumstances, Kate thought, a strange topic to research. (64)

A woman with brown hair and a blue dress was holding a naked child to her breast. The child was dead. The woman, the mother, had just realized that her daughter's blue, limp sprawl was final, forever. The finish was exquisite, the background detailed, the texture of the hair and fabric palpable, and the overall effect on the viewer was of a knife in the heart. (67)

The investigators – and the reader – consider what the observations about such factors as the appearance and responses, the setting, and the belongings of suspects can be made to tell them about these characters: the construction of ethos starts with the assignment of various *traits* to describe personal qualities. Chatman defines trait as an 'adjective out of the vernacular labeling a personal quality of a character, as it persists over part or whole of the story' (1978, 125), adding that '[it] is a relatively stable or abiding personal quality, which may either unfold, that is, emerge earlier or later in the course of the story, or that may disappear and be replaced by another' (126).[6] Barthes draws attention to the reader's classification of traits as a process that is affected by hesitation among several labels to find the most suitable one. As implication and inference belong to our construction of character, much has to be conjectured simply on the basis of various textual details (1974, 94–5, 190–1).[7] The reader becomes aware of this hesitation as King's detectives begin to speculate about what it indicates of a person if she is good-looking, seems anorexic, and has an impenetrable, 'dead' gaze. The suspect's intense interest in the motif of a child's death raises the question whether she takes an interest in this tragic yet conventional topic as an artist, or whether it describes her first-hand past and present 'real' experiences. The police also consider her hard-to-interpret behaviour during the preliminary interrogation (ch. 7). Their various observations allow them experimentally to view the suspect as 'a bluffer,' 'callous,' 'suicidal,' 'crazy,' and 'begging to be exposed and caught,' attributes which, taken together, might suggest that her ethos fits conventional notions of what a murderer is like. But they also remark that the very same features could mean that she is 'hesitant about a suitable line of behaviour,' 'a badly-beaten ex-con,' and 'courageous' (88), attributes which suggest an altogether different ethos, one that is a combination of uncertainty and resignation, but also of determined perseverance despite all odds.

There is no logical connection between observation and the named attribute when we classify traits; rather, we choose among a number of more or less familiar attributes that we typically relate to certain signs such as, for example, a given type of eyes. The example also demonstrates that, in selecting suitable attributes, the investigators look for a general model or stereotype to which the character may be related. The chosen model supplies a unifying framework under which other traits may acquire significance. It may even suggest what further specifying traits to look for in the character. Hence, to brand someone a crazy bluffer who unconsciously desires to be caught supplies the rudimentary profile of a psychopath. In this instance, such features as Adams's excessive tidiness or her arsenal of medicaments would help the investigators to specify the kind of psychopath she is. The model and the attributes already include an evaluative or normative dimension, entailing a prefatory assessment of ethos.

The reader's means of constructing ethos – through the construction of character – are fundamentally the same as the investigators'. James Phelan uses the variety of traits to argue that forming a sense of character results from an interplay among what he calls the *mimetic*, *synthetic*, and *thematic dimensions* of the assigned traits (or, in his term, attributes). The mimetic dimension refers to all those attributes which enable readers to picture a possible person. In assigning mimetic attributes, readers are playing the game of make-believe, whereas for fictional detectives, the suspects are, of course, flesh-and-blood people; yet in forming a sense of ethos, they also draw on notions of plausibility and verisimilitude within their world. The synthetic dimension, according to Phelan, comprises those attributes that bring to the fore the artificiality and constructedness of a fictional character: the highlighting of such traits punctures the reader's mimetic illusion. This dimension has relevance at the level of the fictional world as well, however, for detectives try out on suspects different stereotypical models of ethos. Lastly, Phelan's thematic dimension emerges from the attributes that make characters into representative figures, linking them up with some general proposition or assertion (1989, 2–9). Again, there seems to be a convergence between what readers and detectives do. Phelan points out that our understanding of people in life includes a thematic component, as we see the traits of others as defining either a type of person or a set of ideas familiar from elsewhere. 'We say,' writes Phelan, '"He's a sixties flower-child," or "She's a radical feminist," and imply that the identities of these people can be summed up by a set of ideas or values associated with those descriptions' (13). In *A Grave Talent*, for instance, the case looks different depending on whether the suspect is construed as a psychopath or a falsely suspected (and, as it turns out, wrongly convicted) ex-felon. The thematic dimension is of particular importance for the reader, for the moral statements – if any – which the narrative puts forth, depend on this dimension.

That the ethoi of a psychopath and a redeemed ex-convict can be suggested by the same observations shifts our focus to the mode of reasoning or 'logic' detectives and readers alike use in evaluating different characters in the role of the criminal. Generally speaking, investigators appear to use the following very simple guidelines – expressed here as a set of related questions – in matching their observations with conjectures about the suspects' ethoi:

- What kind (type) of person is this character?
- How does his or her 'kind' relate to the crime in question?[8]
- Is it likely that this kind of person would commit this type of crime?
- What circumstances would have to prevail to make him or her the perpetrator of this crime?

Let us see how the investigators in King's book apply this line of reasoning. As there is no telling which of the two portraits best describes their prime suspect, they conjecture that her most conspicuous trait – artistic talent – forms the cornerstone of her ethos (92–5). The following excerpt shows Martinelli weighing the possibilities that this hypothesis brings into their earlier considerations of Adams as either a psychopath or a redeemed ex-convict:

Eva Vaughn would have been a fine painter any time, any place, but nearly a decade in a tough women's prison, convicted of a crime intolerable even to the other inmates, had flayed her of her caution, had cut her loose from any of the expected possibilities. A normal woman would have gone mad, or retreated into the anonymity of ordinariness, or died. Instead, Vaun Adams, Eva Vaughn, had become empty of herself, had become a pair of all-seeing eyes and a pair of hands that held a brush, and she had channeled the pain and the beauty of life into her canvases. She was a murderer who had strangled a small girl, a child who would now be a woman of twenty-four had she lived. Nothing Vaun could be or do would make up for that, and deep down Kate could never finally forgive her. Painful as it was, she knew that her own work, her own humanity, demanded that she pit herself against the woman who had painted those magnificent visions of the human spirit. (95)

Considering Adams primarily as an artist enables the detectives to draw up her ethos, supplying them and the reader with criteria for reviewing possible guilt and moral responsibility. Or, to put it differently, once we have linked a character's ethos with a given thematic domain, we are then invited to think what guilt and responsibility might mean in its context. In this instance, Martinelli considers how an artist's ethos relates to murder. We can, in turn, pick our cue from the detective's pondering, relating notions of such an ethos to detective-story conventions. The conjunction of art and murder suggests the two familiar detective-story portraits of the artist-as-murderer[9] and the murderer-as-artist.[10] Although overlapping, these motifs differ in that the former is an artist by profession who may commit murder either for non-artistic reasons or, possibly, as an artistic experiment. The latter, though not an artist by profession, is a person for whom murder is the primary medium of an art which he or she regards as more 'genuine' or aesthetically 'inventive' than the work of officially recognized artists. Martinelli's musings (92–5) further define this model in the context of crime by allowing the reader to relate the artist to two opposing notions familiar from Romanticism. The murderer-as-artist is sinister and destructive, while his or her opposite is the benevolent guardian of life. Both figures actually function as harbingers of higher truths, but whereas the destructive artist illuminates life from outside morality, the life-affirming artist works within it. These two Romantic artist stereotypes hence imply that art may be seen either as antagonistic to ethics (a realm with its own laws, where beauty eclipses goodness as a pertinent criterion) or as harmonious with it (a realm whose laws correspond with the laws of ethics, so that beauty is goodness). The citation above spells out these options by focusing on the baffling incongruity between the perceptive paintings and the (past) violence of this artist. The reader can envisage at least two satisfactory explanations. One holds that Adams was once violent, but has attained the profundity of her renditions through remorse and suffering; the other pictures this depth as springing from her familiarity with causing pain and death. Serial killers, portrayed as gifted murderer-artists, are examples of the destructive type, but artistic talent may actually be indicative of Adams's innocence – even of the crime for which she was previously incarcerated. It is also possible that this character represents some combination of these two models.

Connecting the suspect's ethos to the broad cultural model of the artist begins to particularize her 'kind' and its possible association with crime, but it does not offer clear guidelines for deciding whether she would be likely to commit the type of crime under investigation, or for determining what circumstances would push her into it. Further reflection on her guilt can proceed by clarifying the type of artistry she expresses. Such reasoning is based on notions about a basic harmony between personal qualities and action according to which everything a person does expresses in some way his or her ethos. Thus, painting is as intimate as handwriting: the painter invariably exposes his or her ethos on canvas. The topics of Adams's paintings are 'classically simple: a man, a woman, some children, a kitchen' (100). They are representational, going against the mainstream in their traditional techniques. Many contain disquieting overtones of menace and ambiguity, but the overall impression is that all are of 'devastating honesty' (101), without the distorting perspective of hatred or any other such 'negative' passion. Instead, even when agony and passion are depicted, the painter remains detached. The high ethical quality of her work speaks for her. Art seems to offer her an all-encompassing outlet for emotions, making it difficult to conceive of any situation or circumstances that would move her to crime. Moreover, in propelling herself into personal and artistic freedom in the face of overwhelming odds, this character has shown considerable inner strength. Therefore, it does not seem likely that an artist of this kind is capable of the type of crime under investigation. In fact, this conclusion casts doubt upon her guilt even of the murder for which she was previously convicted. These considerations, however, remain at this stage open.

Acquiring a sense of ethos in detective stories unites the three components of character construction that Phelan analyses. By showing Adams at work and by describing both her paintings and other people's reactions to them, the narrator creates a plausible, lifelike artist character. The investigation further foregrounds this mimetic dimension, for the criminal's various traits have to be combined in such a way that they fit the crime at hand; moreover, his or her ethos has to be plausible and verisimilar in the generic context. The narration emphasizes the synthetic qualities of constructing ethos by having the investigators relate the suspect's attributes to cultural conceptions about artists.[11] The matching of observations with types of character shows the conformity ethos has with culturally constructed models. From early on, the significance of the artist motif indicates what the relevant thematic issues are.

Neither readers nor detectives can, however, go farther than this on the basis of observation, which provides only the starting point for drawing up the ethos of a character. The action-orientation of detective fiction requires the scrutiny not only of what suspects have done in the past, but also of what they are doing right now and will probably do in the future. Decisions about guilt and responsibility cannot be grounded solely in what people are like; they must also be based on what they have actually done or left undone. This focus on action draws attention to those traits characters either choose or, for some reason, are compelled to foster in themselves. Phelan argues that action and, more generally speaking, plot, affect the reader's understanding of the functions characters and characterization serve in a given narrative, for the synthetic, mimetic, and thematic dimensions of character are seldom equally important. He shows that, in creating an arresting portrait of the duke, Browning's poem 'My Last Duchess' underlines the mimetic dimension, whereas Golding's *Lord of the Flies* spotlights the thematic dimension in order to drive home the notion of inherent evil in human nature. The primacy of one dimension over the other cannot, however, be decided without a careful examination of the plot, for plot shows which of the dimensions are actually put into play during the course of the narrative. Hence, in order to identify traits with narrative impact, Phelan differentiates between dimensions and *functions*. Dimensions are the mimetic, synthetic, or thematic attributes characters may be said to have when considered in isolation from the work in which they appear, while functions are the particular *applications* of those attributes made through the progression of plot. Dimensions are thus converted into functions by plot (8–9). Although the reader of detective fiction can always construct moral – thematic – propositions on the basis of the detective's search for the guilty person and the allocation of guilt, the moral (thematic) functions of character may, nevertheless, remain secondary. As with Phelan's Browning example, authors may take the moral propositions of their narratives for granted, presuming their truth independently of the reading experience and subordinating them, for example, to the creation of a lifelike character portrait.[12] We must keep in mind this distinction between dimensions and functions in our further analysis of King's book.

Projecting the Agent's Ethos from Action

The majority of detective-story crimes involve someone acting against somebody else by injuring the other's interests, property, or person, generating thereby the roles of criminal and victim. As crime takes place in the interpersonal sphere, investigators have to 'read' it as a network of interactional relations among the suspects, taking into account their goals and the actions they undertake to achieve them. *A Grave Talent* demonstrates how the construction of ethos is enriched through the consideration of actions. After having acquired incriminating evidence against Adams (108–9), the police are about to arrest her. The discovery of this evidence is surprising, for it had begun to seem that the painter was innocent. There is, however, a further twist to the plot when the police unexpectedly find her on the verge of death. Now they have to decide whether to treat the event as 'an attempted suicide' or as 'an attempted murder.' Each implies a different scenario. If the event is branded as a suicide attempt, then Adams is both the perpetrator and the victim of her own deed. The act implies her mental collapse in the face of police suspicion, and it may also be an indirect admission of her guilt. If she is the victim of a murder attempt, however, someone else is to blame for this and perhaps other events (ch. 13).

I have already alluded to Barthes's (1974) suggestion that the same process of classification, familiar from the search for suitable character attributes, affects the analysis of action. The example shows that when dealing with acts and actions, our classification of them entails the rudiments of a moral assessment. To commit suicide is not (or is no longer) legally wrong; and its moral wrongness or wickedness depends on the specific view of life from which it is judged. To commit murder in the circumstances described in King's book is certainly both legally and morally wrong and reprehensible. The fact that the classification of actions influences what an event looks like only underlines the importance of having the means to analyse actions and, through this scrutiny, to examine the interaction among suspects. How do fictional detectives do this?

One of the guidelines in much detective fiction seems to consist of a two-way deliberation. The investigators attempt to match their sense of a character's ethos to the specific act under scrutiny, asking if it is likely that a person of this type would do such a thing. But they also consider the situation by looking at the act itself, asking what it tells about the person who would do it. In this particular instance, the detectives equate the act of suicide with the ethos of 'a guilt-ridden psychopath' and the murder attempt with the ethos of 'the victim of an attempted murder.'[13] (The latter alternative remains neutral as to the artist's responsibility for strangling the children.) The decision is in this case straightforward, for the investigators may refer to external circumstances: a pot of stew has been left on a burning stove. Knowing the importance of her art for the suspect, the investigators conclude that she would never endanger her life's work by fire (171). Hence, they choose to interpret the act as attempted murder, not suicide, which throws them back to square one in their investigation, for now they no longer have a prime suspect.

The second part of the book deploys a new angle on the construction of ethos, based on the mode of reasoning used in explaining action. It shows how an act can serve as the basis for projecting an agent's ethos. As this act is usually morally wrong, detectives try to identify a fitting combination of reprehensible traits in someone's ethos. Moreover, action brings such factors as motives and goals into consideration. Again, we can begin to schematize this strategy with the help of a number of simple questions such as the following:

- What did the agent want to achieve by committing this action?
- Why did the agent think it necessary or profitable to undertake just this action?
- What exactly constitutes a satisfactory end of action for the agent?

By adopting the acting agent's perspective, investigators try to imagine themselves in his or her position. The questions imply that the answers are to be found both in the past, as the motive for crime often lies in former squabbles, and in the future, because the perpetrator envisages crime as opening up better prospects (such as personal gain) than exist at present.

Although these questions are not always overtly spelled out, they invariably direct the search for the perpetrator. Similarly, the steps in this mode of reasoning are seldom made explicit, yet they can be made visible, as in the present discussion of King's novel. Hence, my description of the reasoning of King's investigators recreates the process they follow in order to reach the solution. In starting over, the police consider whether the stranglings of the children and the murder attempt against Adams are connected. They look at the case from the artist's position, asking who would want her dead. A re-evaluation of the facts ensues. In accounting for the situation, they attempt to fill in each of the terms in the following simple formula:

An agent has the goal (G), which is the object of her desire.
The agent believes that G will not be attained, unless she takes action (A).

The agent does / undertakes to do A.

(Knuuttila 1989, 210; my translation)

This formula represents a mode of reasoning the aim of which is to explain the action of an agent. It postulates the agent as having a particular goal (G), which will fulfil a particular desire. It also assumes that this agent holds that neither her goal nor her desire will lead to action unless she has some idea about how to achieve this goal. She has a goal (G) and a belief (B) that a certain action (A) will bring about this desired goal. The computational logic is that of *practical reasoning*, and the explanatory model has the form of the so-called Aristotelian *practical syllogism*. The practical syllogism, Martha C. Nussbaum explains, may be defined as a schema for the teleological explanation of human activity, designed to show us what factors must be considered – what states ascribed to an agent – to give an adequate explanation of an action. Sometimes these states are conscious, and the account corresponds to an agent's actual deliberation; even when this is not so, however, the states are supposed to have psychological reality, and to be sufficient conditions for the occurrence of the action (Nussbaum 1978, 174). The practical syllogism may be applied either to help an agent plan what she herself ought to do to realize her goals or to speculate about the actions of other agents (ibid., 176).

In King's book, the detectives have to conjecture simultaneously about a number of factors: the unknown agent's desire and goal and the means through which this person believes he (as it turns out) can attain this goal. To sketch these components, they start with the facts at hand. Adams has been imprisoned for strangling a child. Three girls have recently been strangled and each has been found close to the artist's house. If she is innocent, it seems likely that someone else has committed these copycat murders, trying to make her look like the perpetrator. Staging the murder attempt as suicide, meant to look like her admission of guilt, further speaks of this strong desire to hurt her. The consideration of these facts already contains the rudiments for filling in the syllogism:

> A still-unknown agent has the goal of causing Vaun Adams to suffer; to see her suffer is his desire.
> The agent believes that this goal will be achieved if he commits crimes which make it seem that Vaun Adams is the culprit.
> _____
> The agent starts strangling little girls and implicating Vaun Adams as the culprit.

The murdered children function as means to a 'higher' goal for this agent, although doubtless he also likes strangling little girls. Both investigators characterize the contents of this syllogism as 'farfetched' and a 'crazy idea,' describing a line of action that only a 'madman' would undertake (129–30) because it implies an unusually intense hatred that brooks no obstacle. Yet this hypothesis seems to make sense of the events.[14] The investigators' next hypothesis then concerns the agent's means for achieving this state. Usually, there is more than just one route to achieving a goal, but the agent's own understanding of its constituents helps him or her to compare means and choose those that best fit the criteria the agent regards as primary, be they effectiveness, speed, elegance, or some other such property. Hence, the practical syllogism functions as a model of reasoning back from a desired goal to the first action necessary (or available) for its achievement that is in the agent's power (Nussbaum 1978, 190).[15] The example illustrates this feature. From the information they gather, the police conclude that the criminal decides to revive the past by committing crimes similar to the one for which Adams was incarcerated, most likely because this strategy will implicate the artist and give her tormentor the sadistic satisfaction of watching the net tighten around her. But this route does not bring in the desired result fast enough, as the police are slow to connect the events with Adams. The agent then changes tactics to ensure success and his own safety by staging Adams's suicide.

The practical syllogism enables investigators to interpret an action or a sequence of actions by ascribing to an agent a desire, a goal, and a belief about how to achieve the desired state in the best possible manner. It also gives them a specific idea of the kind of person to start looking for. In the example, the analysis of the stranglings and the murder attempt sketches the picture of a sinister person who is moved by profound hatred and is capable of careful, intelligent planning and of biding his time in order to get what he wants (147, 171–3, 184, 186). The practical syllogism is designed to explain rational and deliberate action: agents are responsible for the actions they undertake.[16] It does not, however, account for why an agent desires certain things. This desire may, for example, spring from a response to a prior action by someone else. To understand this explanatory feature, detectives have to analyse the interpersonal sphere.

The projection of the agent's ethos from actions validates the conjecture about a psychopath's involvement, and the real criminal is relatively quickly identified in *A Grave Talent*.[17] As the murderer's ethos conforms to a conventional view of psychopaths as vicious, beastly, and amoral, the matching of his various attributes to this stereotype is not particularly interesting. Yet to facilitate the ensuing discussion, an outline of the roots of the crime is in order. At the bottom of things is a love affair between Adams and Andy Lewis, a high school classmate. When she breaks off the relationship, the jilted lover plots his revenge, which involves strangling a child and framing Adams as the culprit. Thus, Lewis is the perpetrator of the crime for which the artist has been punished. The recent murders stem from his fury at Adams's survival and artistic success, which make him try to destroy her for the second time. Again, it is possible for us to explicate the detectives' mode of conjecture, which follows approximately the following lines: 'I want to make Vaun Adams suffer. If I am really to damage her, I must kill her. In her case, symbolic death is more damaging than physical death. By depriving her of the possibility of freely doing her art work, I will kill her mentally, which will ultimately lead to her physical death' (see pages 130, 185–6, and 266). The elaboration of the goal and the underlying desire throw light on the chosen strategy – killing children; implicating Adams and getting her incarcerated appear to this agent the best means to ensure that mental shrivelling leading to physical death will take place.

Projecting a suspect's ethos from actions shows us what dimensions of this ethos we are to read as functions contributing to the ethical assertions that a given narrative puts forth. As the reading and evaluation of guilt are thematic in nature, we are, of course, interested in how King's narrator uses the construction of ethos for making ethical statements. Phelan maintains that there are two basic strategies for developing thematic functions from thematic dimensions. 'In works that strive to give characters a strong overt mimetic function,' he writes, 'thematic functions develop from thematic dimensions as a character's traits and actions also demonstrate, usually implicitly, some proposition or propositions about the class of people or dramatized ideas' (1989, 13). In contrast, '[i]n works where the artificiality or the synthetic nature of characters is more overt, thematic dimensions get developed into functions somewhat differently; the representative quality of the attributes or ideas will usually be explicitly revealed in the action or narrative discourse' (13). Although King's narrator strives to create a strong mimetic effect,[18] the ethical statements become available primarily through the synthetic functions of the characters. The mode of reasoning in which the genre engages investigators and readers explains why the synthetic component of characterization acquires such a central status: a focus on typologies of ethos and likelihoods of action is inevitably accompanied by an allegorical pull, which limits the depth of detective-story characterization.

A Grave Talent demonstrates this feature well, for the construction of the criminal's ethos from his actions shows that the story of the crime deals with what a psychopath has already done and is still trying to do to an artist-victim. The stranglings and Adams's suffering derive from her identity as an artist, for it is her prizing of her art above everything else that has infuriated the criminal. The juxtaposition of the artist-victim and the criminal-psychopath demonstrates which dimensions in their ethoi become the kind of functions Phelan talks about. Given that the psycho-path's murders serve 'as a means of building an elaborate and creative revenge' (266), his being a murderer-as-artist figure is made explicit. The narrator uses these two stereotypes in order to draw the reader's atten-tion to art and its ethical significance.

The narrator further interweaves the question of art into the criminal investigation by making it a central facet in the evaluation of guilt and responsibility. The artist is certainly not legally responsible for any of the events ensuing after her liaison with and rejection of her psychopathic lover. But the narrator raises the question of whether she can somehow be held morally responsible for them, because a caricature she painted of the murderer kindled his hate and fury. The following description of this painting shows how this question is introduced into the crime case:

It was a caricature ... At first view it was the portrait of a young man with whom the artist was both in love and in lust. Gradually, however, the slight exaggera-tions asserted themselves, and soon Hawkin knew that she was not painting how she felt looking at Andy Lewis but rather how Andy Lewis imagined women in general felt looking at him ... Suddenly Lee Cooper's words came back to him: Vaun was 'more likely to commit a devastating murder of someone's self-image on canvas ...' This painting was her weapon, the victim as yet quite unaware that the murderous blow had been struck. Hawkin could see that anyone knowing Lewis, and truly seeing this portrait, would never take the man seriously again. It spoke volumes about Lewis's methods that he had not killed Vaun outright when he first realized what she had done. To Lewis, mere death was not sufficient revenge: hell must come first. (268–9)

If we want to do justice to the narrator's and the characters' views, the question of responsibility cannot be settled outside the context of values depicted in the book. Analysing the final allotment of guilt and responsi-bility underlines the importance of closure – in the sense of having all the relevant facts at hand – in making this assessment. Simultaneously, this scrutiny enables us to consider the manner in which the narrator devel-ops ethical assertions through the analysis of ethos.

Ethos as the Basis for Assigning Guilt and Responsibility

In order to determine blame and answerability, we need to consider the interplay among characters and their fictional community. We recall that this perspective brings together the constitutive components of the detective story: setting, crime, and the interaction among basic roles as sustained by plot. The interplay of these components can be charted by examining a number of interactional patterns among the individual elements. With the help of King's book, I briefly outline some things we should observe to structure this interplay. Again, the analysis of these patterns reveals something of the process in which investigators and readers engage when they try to assess guilt on the basis of ethos. We may distinguish two general sets of patterns: the first concerns the victim and the criminal in their communal context, while the second pertains to the detective's relationship to these characters and the community.

I have already stated that *A Grave Talent* deals with what a psychopathic murderer-artist does to an artist-victim. We can begin to enrich our analysis of the ethical significance of these ethoi and their interaction by considering the following general questions describing the relationships among the victim, the criminal, and their communal context:

- What role and status does the community accord to the victim and the criminal? How do the victim and the criminal themselves perceive their role and status in the community?
- What is the criminal's (and possibly the victim's) understanding of the criminal deed as compared to communal values? What attitude does the community take to this deed?

It is striking that the stereotypes to which the artist-victim[19] and the psychopath-murderer conform in *A Grave Talent* are basically similar, for each is portrayed as an outsider in the community, thanks to a 'deviance' in ethos. The lives of both expose shortcomings in the functioning of the community. The murderer, Andy Lewis, is an outsider because of his refusal to have anyone set any kinds of limits on his behaviour. He always punishes a person who responds negatively to him either by inflicting physical harm or by damaging property. Such traits, which imply an insufficient internalization of the basic norms regulating social life and suggest the incapacity to be a full member of any community are, of course, typical ingredients in the ethos of a fictional psychopath. It is integral to such an ethos that these characters follow an idiosyncratic system of values deriving solely from their own desires. Lewis further demonstrates the familiar traits associated with fictional psychopaths in his attitude to divergence from social norms. It is not clear whether he even understands that many of his actions are deviant, as he always blames others for any trouble he encounters. In his reasoning, the killings really are the artist's fault, or, as he puts it: 'All of this happened because of you, you goddamned bitch ... you're going to live knowing that because of your precious fucking painting people died ... when I'm finished with you all you'll ever be able to paint is blood and death, and you did it, you did it, Vaunie, it was you' (324–5).

A psychopath like Lewis tests the effectiveness of the police and legal machineries in detective stories. Typically, such a character has killed numerous people without getting caught. There have been strong suspicions of Lewis in the past, but lack of evidence has hindered official interference. Or, if there has been evidence, the victim has refused to testify against him out of either infatuation or fear. A frustrated county sheriff once even badly beat Lewis, but to no avail (182–6). An additional explanation for the lack of evidence against Lewis derives from the ethos associated with this stereotype. Lewis is the kind of psychopath who is not only extremely clever at keeping up a 'normal' front (209), but also a great charmer of women (184, 201). The powerlessness of the police machinery to spot such criminals is exacerbated by the indifference and sloppiness of the legal system, as the trial against Adams is intended to show. As the case seems straightforward, there is no real investigation of the events. There are two incriminating pieces of evidence against her: her previous experimentation with drugs and a painting of the murdered child, portrayed in exactly the same position in which the child was later found dead (140–1). The book thus suggests that the systems designed to protect the community function inefficiently.

The two stereotypical outsiders illuminate the fictional community from two directions in *A Grave Talent*: the psychopath demonstrates what it is to refuse to accept communal norms, indeed actively to rebel against them, whereas the artist shows that it is possible to be outside the community in a manner that ultimately benefits it, thanks to the insights and aesthetic experiences her paintings make available. The opposition between the 'bad' outsider and the 'good' one thus structures the reader's understanding of these characters. The fact that the community takes a long time to evaluate these two figures correctly suggests that it carries at least some responsibility for past events itself. This community comes across as insensitive and indifferent, for the seeming normality of the psychopath protects him, while the artist's conspicuous talent singles her out as an oddity whom few people try to understand, and fewer still try to help. Adams's own parents, for example, wanted to rid her of her talent, taking her to various psychiatrists in search of a 'cure.'

As the murders are connected with the victim's art, King's book scrutinizes the artist's ethos together with art. The title depicts artistic talent as *grave*, and the characters describe it as something which has eaten the artist up, so that she 'can never be normal, never be free and happy, not while this "gift" has her' (162). The artist herself refers to the 'burden of this gift' that has (almost) ruined her whole life (312). The significance of art is further underlined by the artist's refusal to continue working after hearing that the murders stem from Lewis's hatred of her and her art (262–3). Hence, the construction of the artist's ethos is central for identifying the main ethical values of the novel, motivating, for example, the descriptions of, and quotes from, critical assessments of her work (93–5; 97–102; 152–4; 230–1; 268–9). This focus calls on the reader to build on the ethos of the Romantic artist figure with whom Adams is associated in order to connect art with its suggested 'grave' overtones.

As a 'natural artist' and an 'artist by birth' – to borrow terms familiar from Romantic theory of art (Abrams 1953, 24) – Adams prizes her art above everything else. The descriptions of her paintings demonstrate that she has an innate sensibility and an ability to perceive how 'things really are.' Her artist's mind can modify, even transform, the images everyone sees to fit her own experience of them, so that ultimately her paintings reveal to observant viewers what these images are truly like (see Abrams, 55). Her visionary talent includes distance, the capability of looking at people and things with a sort of 'X-ray vision,' the purpose of which is to reveal 'the inner things that make a person work as well as the outer way he looks, and how the two come together' (155). The artist's responsibility is first and foremost to this experience, which is grounded on the search for, and the examination of, the truth, and which remains elusive to the lay-person's eye without the artist's guidance. These qualities of the artist's ethos explain why Lewis is enraged by the portrait Adams has painted of him, for it exposes his ethos on canvas for anyone to see, expressing the painter's explicit moral evaluation of the model. The artist's dedication to truth, however, is usually not disparaging or demeaning in nature, for even in disclosing (moral) shortcomings, she remains respectful, even affectionate, towards the things she depicts (155).

The association of Adams with the Romantic artist is particularly significant because it shows the reader how the narrator conceives of the underpinnings of any ethos. Adams's compulsion to paint from early on (303–7) attests to the fact that her talent evolves spontaneously from an internal source of energy: it effectuates its own growth. The plant imagery, emphasizing the organic nature of the artist's gift, is typical of

Romantic theories of art (Abrams, 171–3). Schelling's description of the artist's inner pressure describes concisely this ethos in King's book:

An artist, with respect to that which is genuinely objective in his production, seems to be under the influence of a power that sunders him from all other men and forces him to express or represent things that he himself does not entirely fathom, and whose significance is infinite. (Quoted in Abrams 1953, 209–10)

The concept this quotation refers to accounts for the punning title of the book. As an organic, heavily personified force over which artists have little control, artistic talent 'possesses' them, directing their lives in almost any way it wants. Lack of control, the involuntary or automatic nature of artistic composition, the (partial) mystery of the result, and social isolation are all features which potentially lead to the artist's suffering and to various sacrifices he or she has to make for the sake of art. The extraordinariness of art and of the artist's creativity tends to endow his or her life with extremes of feeling and experience. This artist's suffering is, of course, augmented with each stage of the murderer's scheme of revenge. Social exclusion and Adams's brief experimentation with drugs make her suffer from feelings of guilt, so that she thinks she deserves the prison sentence. Hence, she has had to pay an unusually high price for what she is, while fighting for the right to express herself. Again, the insensitivity of her community is emphasized. Moreover, the motto for the epilogue reinforces this notion of the artist's suffering and personal sacrifice: 'Works of art are always products of having been in danger, of having gone to the very end.' (The motto is from a letter by Rilke.)

By using the portrayal of the artist's ethos, *A Grave Talent* appears to promote the notion that the motives and behaviour of people can be explained in the light of what they are like by 'nature,'[20] which is never fully explicable. This concept gains support from, among other things, the motto for the third part of the book: 'At birth our death is sealed, / and our end is consequent / upon our beginning' (Marcus Manil[i]us, *Astronomics*). This view applies to all characters. The culprit is characterized as being thoroughly bad, 'a monster inside a man's body' (282), and the ultimate inexplicability and innateness of his evil are accepted (209, 259). (The roots of his pathology are briefly linked to the untimely death of his father and the weakness of his mother [151].) The extraordinariness of the artist's talent is equally inscrutable and inherent. Strong support for this notion of the innate moral quality of ethos comes from the evaluation of responsibility. We remember that the caricature of the murderer raises the question of whether the artist somehow shares the moral responsibility for the tragic events. The answer supplied by the events and the evaluation of the characters is negative. The explanation offered by the artist's psychiatrist seems to come closest to the narrator's view of the allotment of guilt:

Vaun doesn't need to do anything deliberately to change people's lives. Perhaps a better image is that of a black hole ... so massive they influence the motions of everything around them in space, so immensely powerful that even light particles can't escape, so that they cannot even be seen except by inference, by reading the erratic movements of nearby planets and stars. Vaun passes by, utterly tied up with her own inner workings, and people begin to wobble. Tommy Chesler makes adult friends for the first time in his life. John Tyler gets serious. Angie Dodson looks at her hobbies and sees a mature form of art. Andy Lewis is nudged from criminality to pathology ... And none of it deliberate. Vaun is as passive and as powerful as a force of nature. Her only deliberate actions are on canvas, and even then she would insist that there's no choice, only the recognition of what's needed next. (209–10)

The artist unwittingly draws out that which is already in people, waiting to get out. Her relationship with others resembles the sculptor's vision of the finished sculpture in yet unformed matter. In painting Lewis's caricature she portrays him as he is – a trickster in love with himself. The artist is not to blame, and neither is art. Thanks to their unusual gift, artists of this kind are particularly valuable to their communities, as their work enables others to see what people and life are like, fostering ethos, for example, by increasing the viewer's self-understanding. But the artist's own nature, as distinct from her work, may also influence others. The basic quality of a person's ethos affects that of others: a good person encourages the good in others, while a bad person threatens to harm or even destroy the other. Yet the events also demonstrate that a good person may unwittingly bring out the evil of the bad person, as happens with Lewis.

King's book further illustrates these views on ethos by making the reader focus on the investigators, Kate Martinelli and Al Hawkin. As they are the main focalizers, many of the insights concerning ethos emerge from their reflections. We can again formulate a number of questions in order to assess the detective's role and status in light of the narrator's moral values:

- What relationship does the detective perceive between a crime and communal values? What role and status does the detective give to the victim and the criminal?
- What is the detective's understanding of his or her role: for example, what means are acceptable in pursuing the criminal?
- How do the detective's values compare with communal values, on the one hand, and with the evidence we have of the implied author's values, on the other?

In *A Grave Talent*, the investigators evaluate the victim and the culprit in a straightforward manner, adhering to the familiar binary of good and bad. They understand the value of Adams's art, appreciating her perseverance. They are troubled by the laxity and oversights of the police and the judicial system in the handling of the Adams case (141, 229). The reader quickly perceives that there is no serious friction between the ethoi and values of these characters and the narrator. Yet there is an additional focus on ethos that is brought up through the initial strains in the working partnership of these officers, and, more importantly, through the personal choices they have to make as the investigation proceeds. These choices develop the organic notion of ethos, probing into the question of whether a person has both the willingness and the courage to become what he or she basically is. This personal question is made part of the professional problematic the police face, for they have to decide on the method of capture.[21] They know the murderer will try to kill Adams again, but have no idea of his whereabouts or even exactly what he looks like.

The narrator examines the detective's ethos mainly through the female officer. Being extremely guarded about herself and her life, she is similar to the artist, for, as a lesbian, she is also an outsider.[22] As is typical of much feminist detective fiction, the moral focal point is in some respects a socially marginalized figure. The evaluation of the suspects makes the female officer think about who she herself is and whether her reticence is ethically right. The test comes with the decision to use the artist as a bait for flushing the murderer out of hiding. This unorthodox method requires Kate Martinelli to allow the artist to stay in the home Kate shares with her domestic partner, thus disclosing her sexual orientation. The consequences are devastating, for the safety system breaks down, and the murderer cripples Martinelli's partner. Yet, as each of the characters involved in setting the trap judged it necessary, the plot shows that the principle of taking risks for the sake of what one is, and what one believes in, has an application beyond the world of art. It figures among the moral values supported by the novel. The book thus promotes the notion that to do anything well and to occupy fully a certain role (such as an artist's or a police investigator's), one has to be willing to lay oneself on the line. Being and action have to support each other.

This remark illuminates the role the community plays in King's novel. The alternative communes depicted in the book implicitly criticize what might be called 'mainstream' society. The San Franciscan gay community and the bohemian Tyler's Road where the artist lives are shown to be far more tolerant and supportive of difference than society at large. These subcultures promote and foster traditional ethical values such as friendship, caring, and sharing, allowing their members to be or become the persons they are. The perceptiveness of the outsider position is further apparent in that the female officer and her partner recognize more readily than others the force and the beauty of the artist's paintings, appreciating their value for the individual viewer and the whole community. Yet there is the possibility of a change for the better even within rigid, conservative structures, as the working partnership between the two officers, moving from hostility to friendship, demonstrates. This change, however, emphasizes that positive moral values can subsist and flourish only in the care of individuals.

The major ethical statement of *A Grave Talent*, promoting the courageous cultivation of the good inclinations with which one has been endowed in order to become fully what one is, emerges primarily through the interplay of the ethoi of the artist-victim, the psychopathic murderer-as-artist, and the lesbian detective. These typologizing labels make explicit the cultural material out of which the characters are constructed. The novel is thus an artist parable set in a detective-story context: the focus on the artist's ethos builds her up as a visionary whose art shows how beauty and truth come together. The focus on the lesbian detective and her personal choice enlarges the notion of art, emphasizing that the cultivation of one's inherent qualities is the cultivation of the ability to see and understand life more deeply. Generally speaking, personal choices of attitude and action in the face of adversity reveal what characters are made of. This analysis identifies the narrator's main ethical values, as demonstrated by the reading of guilt and the evaluation of responsibility; the next phase appraises the reading experience that makes them available.[23]

Engaging the Reader's Ethos

What happens to us while we are reading a book such as King's *A Grave Talent*? Booth's emphasis on the reader's ethos comes from the key metaphor of *friendship* that he uses to describe the reading encounter, an encounter which, according to him, is to be evaluated in much the same way as we evaluate our real-life friendships. It seems profitable to draw on Booth's general framework, especially since he proposes some measures to help the reader give form to and assess the reading experience.[24] He emphasizes that the ethical distinctions applied to this experience do not depend on choices among traditional moral virtues. If it were so, we could not explain why many of the books we love are beneficial to us, even though they are clearly immoral in many respects (1988, 179). Another reason, which makes the consideration of the reading experience relevant to our inquiry, is the inbuilt bias in Booth's evaluative apparatus against popular, formulaic narratives. He maintains, for example, that '[o]nly a special kind of reader, importing interests not insisted upon by the work itself, will ever be tempted to go on unpacking the secrets of a particular mystery after the first reading. And only an especially well-made mystery can support for an hour such continued demands for more reward' (183–4).[25] With its emphasis on a balanced appraisal of the reading experience, Booth implies that the 'ethical games' authors and readers play are based on the rereading approach, which he regards as alien to formulaic literature. This bias derives from Aristotle, who holds that there are three different grounds for friendship: pleasure, usefulness, and good character. In Booth's view, detective fiction falls into the first category, which, by definition, can provide a few hours of pleasant company, but no more.[26]

Booth's criteria for assessing what he calls the *friendship offerings* of different books are the following. It is evident that not all of them are equally pertinent to all books:

1. the *quantity* of invitations they offer readers;
2. the degree of *responsibility* they grant us (the level of reciprocity between author and reader);
3. the degree of *intimacy* in the friendship;
4. the *intensity* of the engagement expected or required of readers;
5. the *coherence*, or consistency, of the proffered world;
6. the *distance* between the fictional world and our world;
7. the *range of kinds* of activities suggested, invited, or demanded of readers. (179–80)

Given our specific focus, one criterion would seem to rise above others: the degree of responsibility a narrative grants the reader. This category deals with the reciprocity (or hierarchy) distinguishing authors who make readers their equals from those who posit readers as either their inferiors or their superiors (184). The scale of reciprocity overlaps with the scale of quantity, drawing attention to the amount and kind of work the reader is required to do,[27] and suggesting that 'the fullest friendships on this scale are with [authors] who seem wholly engaged in the same kind of significant activity that they expect of us' (187). Booth's specification of such activity is meaningful for us, for he argues that traditionally it has 'included that most important of all "reading" challenges, the interpretation of moral character,' elucidated through a character's efforts to make moral choices. 'In tracing those efforts,' he continues, 'we readers stretch our own capacities for thinking about how life should be lived, as we join those more elevated judges, the implied authors ... [whose practice] impl[ies] that we might become their equals in discernment if we only practiced long enough' (187). Does not this description come close to the generic task the detective story invites its readers to take on?

We can now apply Booth's criteria to King's *A Grave Talent*, beginning with the degree of responsibility and the range of activities demanded of the reader (criteria two and seven), as they most immediately concern the generic task of reading and evaluating guilt. Obviously, as the foregoing analysis of the novel suggests, this task is a rather complex one, drawing on ways of reasoning familiar to us from everyday life. Although the hypothesizing typical of the whodunit is absent in this novel, as readers we must exercise our knowledge of how to form a sense of ethos. We must also know and be able to apply the various stages involved in the reading of guilt as well as the principles of evaluating guilt in order to follow the plot adequately. Our task, however, is made easy by the narrator's helpfulness in using the investigators to guide our reading. Moreover, certain key structures, such as the outsider status uniting the victim, criminal, and detective, or the similarity of the moral choices that the artist and the female detective make, are relatively easy to spot. To adapt these two Boothian criteria to reflect the moral complexity of the detective-story context, we need to ask two interrelated questions: what attitude does King's narrator take to the intrusiveness of the criminal investigation, and how does the reading process relate to the inherent voyeurism of that investigation?

Reading detective fiction is fraught with moral ambiguity, for the genre always exhibits vice as more exciting than virtue and depends on the transgression of laws and norms for its existence. Our choice of detective narratives as reading material thus signals our desire to spend time immersed in crime and its investigation. We *want* there to be a crime and an intellectually interesting or suspenseful, adventurous process of solving it. And we also desire to be told in the end how and where the chips of guilt fall. All critics who consider this desire (Auden 1988, Pederson-Krag 1983, Porter 1981 and 1988, Rycroft 1968, Žižek 1991) point to its ambivalence. Ostensibly, the genre would seem to reinstate certain very widely accepted values such as the sanctity of human life, the need for justice, the need to accept responsibility for one's actions, and the importance of truth. Yet whatever 'positive' or widely endorsed value is put forth, such promotion always has a transgressive act as its starting point. And the interest in crime is wedded to an investigation which is intrusive. Under the cover of detection the reader is invited, along with the detective, to pry and to peep into the private and intimate affairs of the characters, all in the name of the urgent need to uncover the perpetrator. (The generic cliché is that crime, and murder in particular, abolishes every right to privacy.) The genre thus fosters a clear-cut voyeurism, and Porter (1988), for example, quips that anyone with the sensibilities above those of a Peeping Tom will let detective stories lie. Being poised between a fascination with criminality and the exorcism of this interest through the criminal's exposure, detective narratives may actually appeal to us as readers – even seduce us – in ways that are in themselves morally dubious.

The narrator of *A Grave Talent* solves this generic moral dilemma with two rather clever strategies. First, the construction and exploration of ethos primarily takes place through probing into morally commendable characters, especially the artist-victim and the female detective. The desire to know and uncover is directed at qualities that are portrayed as morally admirable and durable: perseverance, courage, and honesty. Moreover, as regards the intended victim, the narrator limits curiosity by focusing solely on her identity as an artist. The titillation of voyeurism concerns more directly the ethos of the female detective, as her being a lesbian is a sexual secret revealed during the events; yet voyeurism is kept in check by the conventional love-story setup between the partners. Second, by making the primary focalizer a character who is reliable, fair, and capable of self-reflection, the narrator builds an important analogue between this character's attitude and that of the artist towards the things she depicts: it is '[l]ike you were being taken apart, a little impersonally but with respect, and affection' (155). The 'artist parable' aspect of the book is, I think, meant to suggest to the reader the appropriate manner in which to view the characters – apart from the criminal, that is.[28] Such a distanced and respectful attitude keeps curiosity within bounds, safeguarding the integrity of the characters.

We can briefly outline what the reading experience looks like in light of the other Boothian criteria. The anticipated intimacy and intensity of the reading engagement are clearly significant, deriving from the character-orientation of the novel. We are evidently expected to take an interest in, and care for, the characters we encounter, becoming concerned about their fate. As they are shown from different perspectives, we gain insight into what they are like. Much of the intensity issues from the twists and turns of the plot, which keep us turning the pages to learn who is guilty of what. The last three criteria in Booth's list address, in a roundabout way, the construction of characters in terms of guilt. They all refer to the reader's constructive effort to follow the narrative and put together its fictional world. Some narratives demand of the reader a more extensive set of skills and a greater array of knowledge than others. In these respects, *A Grave Talent* provides quite effortless reading. The world it depicts is close to our everyday world and, although not all readers have first-hand experience of bohemian and gay communities, fictional representations of such lifestyles abound in various media. Similarly, the central ethoi correspond to widely familiar cultural stereotypes. Although the plot contains many twists and turns, making sense of it poses no difficulty whatsoever. The author uses everyday language and a straightward prose style. These features greatly facilitate the reader's construction of ethos and our conjectures about the nature and final distribution of guilt in the book.

How high does a book such as *A Grave Talent* score when viewed according to Boothian criteria? Booth appreciates the 'toil' involved in reading (although, at the same time, he refrains from extolling avant-garde, experimental, or notoriously difficult works of literature); hence the familiar ('the already-read') and the easy-to-read aspects of King's book would not seem to suggest a high ranking. There is, however, a way to sidestep such an automatically disparaging conclusion by taking seriously – which Booth himself, unfortunately, does not do – the idea of literature as 'a botanical garden full of many beautiful species, each species implicitly bearing standards of excellence within its kind' (56). Against this background, we could claim that the 'already-read' and the 'easy-to-read' are significant narrative strategies in formulaic literature, because reading for relaxation and entertainment usually proceeds at a faster pace than reading for study, for example. One might argue, as does

Roberts (1990, ch. 1), that formulaic literature works with the stereotypical, in order to make readily available for reflection the various components of its given topic. Such strategies do not, as such, preclude the
contemplation of moral issues. The question pertains, rather, to differences in means and strategies. In thinking about the role of the stereotypical in King's book, I take as my aid Booth's rather elusive notion of
the *mean*, understood to refer to a balance in the given quality (or group
of qualities) which his criteria describe. The claim is that 'we can always
discern, on any scale, kinds of excess that for most readers will destroy a
proffered gift' (181).[29] In order to relate my evaluation of the ethical
merits or shortcomings of King's book to the strategies typical of formulaic literature, I try to attune the Boothian criteria and his idea of the mean
to what is valued as ethical (and aesthetic) within the detective-story
genre. I briefly analyse the construction of ethos in *A Grave Talent* by
relating it to the role that stereotype plays in this kind of literature.

Cawelti talks of 'stereotype vitalization' as a significant aesthetic criterion, designed to describe the variations on a thematic structure typical of
narrative formulae. Roberts (1990, 134–45) argues that this strategy usually incorporates an ethical aspect as well. Briefly put, stereotype enrichment refers to the means with which an author creates characters,
especially to the fit between general models and the individualizing
features employed in their actualization (Cawelti 1976, 10–12).[30] Amossy
(1984) maintains that ideally the realization breaks the mould, forcing
readers to examine both the stereotype and its modification. As this
method is often used for critical ends, it frequently demands an ethical
assessment of our previous experiences of the particular stereotype as
well as a scrutiny of its 'revitalization.' (It is noteworthy that the stereotype under examination need not be ethically superior to other speci-
mens of the tradition.) Roberts argues that, with the help of this layered
and inherently comparative approach, authors can not only draw readers' attention to the constituents of the genre in which they are writing,
but can also invite readers to criticize (or praise) these constituents (1990,
140–1).

Stereotype vitalization seems a particularly pertinent strategy for the
major requirement of King's book, which is the construction of ethos. My
reconstruction of the victim as an artist and the culprit as a psychopath
has shown the conformity to the general model. Now is the moment to
reverse the focus, asking whether any elements in the compilation of
traits escape the clutches of the stereotype. In what follows, I concentrate
only on the artist figure.

The conjunction of art and murder is an old one (see Black 1991). King's decision to eschew the more usual choice of concentrating on the murderer as an artist or the detective as an artist (or both) in order to focus on the artist as a victim is interesting in the generic context, thanks to the relative rarity of this association.[31] This choice directs attention to the combination of the two facets: how does the fact that the artist is the victim affect her as an artist, and vice versa? There are two frequently (but not necessarily) intertwining reasons for the artist's being a victim: the murderer's envy of the artistic gift, together with the ensuing rivalry over who is the better artist, and sexual jealousy. The relationship between Adams and Lewis combines both facets, for Lewis, enraged by Adams's rejection of him and adamant that no one else will ever have her, creates his own destructive art by murdering several children. Yet Adams continually remains one move up on him, thanks to her status as the 'true' artist. Although she is, as we have seen, the victim of her uncontrollable talent, it also gives her an inner strength which a mock-artist such as Lewis lacks. This strength shows best in her ability to will her own destruction, as she does while serving her term in prison and during the showdown with Lewis, when she challenges him to kill her. Ultimately, this will may be directed against the idea of art itself, which Adams embodies, allowing her to pass beyond the culturally conditioned limits of artistic expression, and to achieve the experience of a pre-aesthetic 'reality' (324–5). Thus, even in the face of death, the gift ensures her victory over her tormentor. The artist is encapsulated in a private world with her art, which may enslave her, but also protects her from evil – that is, from being inwardly marred or harmed by wickedness.

How successful is King's stereotype vitalization? And in what sense can we talk of the reader's ethical response to this construct? *A Grave Talent* treats the idea of the artist as victim from many angles, developing notions that remain implicit in other detective stories using this figure. In this sense it vitalizes the stereotype familiar from the generic context. We can use this context to ponder the ethical aspects of constructing ethos. Portraying either detectives or murderers as artists, to start with the more familiar use of the artist figure, allows the author to examine the detective's creative mental processes (ratiocination, intuition) or the murderer's attempts to transcend the limits of signification. As well, the similarity between the skills, methods, and ways of reasoning of these two antithetical figures allows the author to analyse the tensions between the aesthetic and the ethical. When King's handling of Adams is inserted into this context, a number of ethically disturbing features begin to appear, such as the *glorification* of certain characters and the *sentimentalization* of the relationship between ethics and aesthetics.

Glorification is part and parcel of the discursive strategies typical of popular fictions, as Cawelti (1976, 18) and Roberts (1990, 133–9) maintain, especially the strategies used in character construction. We like reading about characters who are in one way or another better (or worse) than we are, so the argument goes, allowing us to indulge in various satisfying, vicarious fantasies. The super-sleuths as well as the atrocious serial killers are examples of this strategy. What sets such detective-artists as C. Auguste Dupin, Father Brown, or Sherlock Holmes apart from Vaun Adams is the distance from which they are viewed. As their abilities are being praised, these figures are simultaneously also undercut in some way (for example, through irony or parody). Hannah Charney argues that this distanced angle of vision is the hallmark of the (classical) detective narrative, ensuring the balance between aesthetics and ethics (or even the pleasure and reality principles), a strategy which prompts the reader to treat the given character critically (1981, 33). In contrast, Adams is not only the 'greatest artist of the Post-Picasso age,' perhaps even of the whole century (102), but is also beautiful, intelligent, courageous, and so on. Interestingly enough, the narrator cannot sustain the kind of distanced attitude to the artist which is otherwise suggested as the ethically appropriate attitude to life. Therefore, the characterization of Adams smacks of hero-worship, for there is too perfect a fit between the cultural model and the fictional figure. The glorification of the artist also accounts for the sentimentalized exploration of the links between art and murder. Art is unproblematically presented as the realm of goodness, truth, and beauty, or the realm where ethics and aesthetics meet and coexist in harmony. The sentimentalization shows best in Adams's position as a courageous victim, defending the fortress of art and, therefore, of ethics as well.

Portraying the detective and the murderer as artists frequently implies the author's projection of his or her own qualities as artist onto the detective or criminal. In reading King's book, one cannot escape the idea that the portrayal of the artist as victim is meant to draw the reader's attention to King's own writing, with King somehow juxtaposing her book and the notion of art promoted in it. It might be that she supposes that her narrative does for detective stories what Vaun Adams's art is said to do for art; that is, raise it to new artistic heights. This strategy is typical of detective-fiction authors who, in order to gain more respect for their craft, employ artist figures to this end (P.D. James's Adam Dalgliesh is a good example).[32]

My assessment of the ethics of King's *A Grave Talent* situates itself in the generic context. The (implied) author of this book clearly has ethical designs on the reader, inviting us to construct and evaluate the ethoi of the characters and to assess them in terms of guilt and moral responsibility. The artist figure is used to focus this moral scrutiny on art both in its narrow sense of the world of art and in its general sense of the art of living a morally commendable life.

This examination started out from the conviction that the rereading strategy on which Booth's ethical theory builds is not, as he thinks, alien to this genre, but part of the familiar game between author and reader. In playing the 'ethical game' with this (implied) author, I have made use of the Boothian notion of the mean, but, by relating it to the narrative strategy of stereotype vitalization, I have made this notion work within one literary kind. This modified notion of the mean allows us as readers to attune our ethical assessment to the rules of the particular game we are playing, achieving a balance that neither presupposes the generally poor quality of detective fiction nor asserts the superiority of this form to 'serious' fiction.[33] This analysis shows that, in light of the generic background, the author does not make the best of her chosen ingredients, for she holds up a simplified and sentimentalized version of some of the issues the conjunction of art and murder raises. And if the author's version is evaluated in terms of the question of guilt, then we see that it adheres to a black-and-white portrayal of how blame and praise are to be distributed. I thus criticize King for being too emotionally attached to her central character and of being too impervious to the sinister aspects of the artist figure, of which there is an acute awareness within the detective-story genre.

5

Putting Together an
Ethical View of Life

'Ah, my friend, one may live in a big house and yet have no comfort,'
observes Hercule Poirot of the scene of the crime in Agatha Christie's *The
Mysterious Affair at Styles* (1954), neatly summing up the sense of life
embedded in the whodunit legacy. The affluent mansion is the emblem
of the social standing characters hanker after in this tradition, and it is
their mutual competition for such a standing which triggers crimes,
introducing a disquieting instability into the social fabric. The spacious
but uncomfortable house also functions as the conventional image of the
self, constructed at the interface of the various roles characters play in
this world. As one role frequently masks another, selfhood is presented
as an uneasy layering of roles, with the subject trying to play each of them
as convincingly as possible. In this context, the function of criminal
investigations is to establish who is the rightful occupant of the contested
mansion, to determine which of the roles being played by the characters
fit their proper social standing, and, finally, to unmask and perhaps
punish the ones who have used role playing for criminal purposes.

By seeing good social and economic standing as signs of moral rectitude, a view which derives from a system of living that promises people
the continued enjoyment of the lifestyle they have personally earned by
competition with others (Knight 1980), whodunits express a sense of
value, a sense of what matters ethically and what does not. As literature
always represents life *as* something, Nussbaum argues, this 'as' must be
seen not only in the paraphrasable content, but also in the form and style
which in themselves express choices and selections, setting up, in the
reader, certain activities and transactions rather than others. In advocat-
ing the ethical relevance of literature, Nussbaum strongly underlines its
reciprocal interlacing of form and content which channels and shapes

reading. Literature has a special status in ethical deliberation by self-reflexively keeping in the reader's view this triad of form, content, and reading experience, with each component contributing separately and in conjunction with the other two components to the (ethical) *view of life* a literary work puts forth for the reader's consideration (1990, ch.1).

Nussbaum's brief characterization of Greek tragedy in *Love's Knowledge* (1990, 17) usefully elucidates how such an 'ethical view of life' emerges from the reading (viewing) experience. Of all the elements that make up the view typical of this genre, she emphasizes that of plot construction as the one that engages the reader's attention most strongly. Plot is significant, for it structures a complex set of 'beliefs' about life and human fate in a manner that underlines the decisive influence of chance events on human lives, the conflicts of value to which these events push characters, and the emotional turmoil to which their choices lead. 'The tragic genre,' Nussbaum writes, 'depends on such beliefs for its very structure and literary shape: for its habit is to tell stories of reversals happening to good but not invulnerable people, and to tell these stories as if they matter for all human beings' (17). This inextricable interlacing of form (plot) and content (set of beliefs) generates appropriate emotional reactions (fear and pity), with the tragic view of life resulting from all three components.

Nussbaum suggests a barrage of specific questions for studying these three components and their interaction (1990, 30–5), the aim of which is to establish, through careful close reading, the 'expressive and statement-making functions' (8) of these elements. According to Nussbaum, the 'responsibility of the literary artist ... is to discover the forms and terms that fittingly and honorably express, adequately state, the *ideas* that it is his or her design to put forward' (5–6; my italics). Thus conceived, the analysis of a text's (ethical) view of life aims at formulating the conceptions to which the various components give rise: the view emerging from them would seem to equal the text's *thematic network*.[1] As the institutions of both morality and ethical theory supply the conceptual background against which Nussbaum examines the work and its reading experience, her analysis cannot but be thematic in character.

By engaging in the kind of scrutiny Nussbaum advocates, let us try to characterize the 'ethical view of life' of the whodunit, based on its content, form, and reading experience. Its formal strategy is to represent the interpersonal conflicts leading to crimes as challenging puzzles, laid out for the reader's bafflement and amusement, while its stylistic register renders a 'polished version of polite middle-class English speech,' correlating with commitments characteristic of this class (Porter 1981, 136). Reading the whodunit is tied up with similar allegiances, for the rules regulating the relation between writer and reader conform to the principle of fair play, familiar from a middle-class conception of sportsmanship (Lovitt 1990, 68). To engage in the whodunit game as the genre usually demands, the reader has to accept a number of elements such as, for example, the following notions about crime: crime, even murder, evokes practically no other emotion than curiosity about the perpetrator's identity (and possibly method and motive); murder is not really shocking as an act, but as a sign that someone is upwardly mobile in an inappropriate way (or that someone has a guilty secret to hide); the punishment of the culprit is secondary to the revelation of his or her identity; and crime is the site for the criminal's and the detective's ingenuity rather than for moral indignation as regards its planning, committing, covering up, and solving. All in all, authors and readers agree that there has to be a moral transgression – the worse the better[2] – for this game to take off, but without the distressing features such a transgression contains in real life. Yet equally significant is the mutual understanding that, despite the ludic handling, crime *matters*: it *must* be solved. This basic tenet, emphasizing the importance of knowing the truth (what happened and why) rather than considerations of justice and punishment, forms the backbone of the whodunit.[3] Hence this game is, in the first instance, epistemological and only secondarily ethical.

The whodunit's ethical view of life seems to rely on a mixture of immorality and its containment through the exposure of the criminal. But we cannot determine this subgenre's ethical relevance by simply examining its formal and structural qualities or the features of its reading experience. The game-like nature of the whodunit suggests that to understand the function of any textual component, or even the characteristics of the reading experience, we should first tune ourselves into the rules governing the relationship between the author and the reader. Otherwise it is difficult to say what meaning the elements of this view of life have. These rules are grounded in generic practices, although they are not identical with them. Rather, they arise from a conjunction of *generic conventions* and *interpretive strategies*, telling the reader what things to look for and especially how to make these things signify. These rules thereby enable the whodunit reader's own moves in the game against the author.[4]

Conceiving of the detective-story reader as the player of a game against the author constitutes the reading experience as a fluctuation between general fixed interpretive guidelines, functioning as rules of thumb, and the reader's situational judgment. As cumulative summaries of particular decisions, the guidelines indicate what generic features to pick out as worthy of attention and how to ascribe significance to them. In adopting such rules, the reader acknowledges that choices of this sort have, with other detective narratives, appropriately reflected the relevant complexities of the generic particulars, yet we can (even should) disregard them if these rules fail to function, following, instead, our intuition about what is fitting to the narrative at hand. The rules themselves are plural and often incommensurable: they may conflict with one another.[5] The specifics of a detective narrative may call these rules into question, necessitating the reader's revision, even abandonment, of them. Envisaged as an interaction among generic components, conventional rules, and the perception of the particular, the reader-player's stance is one of practical deliberation: on the basis of our prior experience of the generic tradition, our choice of which rules to apply – or to modify – resides in a perception that responds flexibly to the concrete particulars. This emphasis on generic mutability, indeterminacy, and particularity brings to the fore the fact that the game against the author always involves the reader's *interpretation* of what is salient and important in it, throwing light on our own responsiveness and flexibility as players of a literary game.[6]

One ground rule cutting across all subgeneric variations concerns the special authority the detective enjoys. Engaged in an often dangerous contest with the criminal, this figure is a gamester, who also functions as an emblem of the reader's own activities of trying to make sense of the events narrated. But more importantly, as the one choosing and implementing crime-solving means and strategies, and as the one declaring judgment and explaining the solution to the crime, the detective always both enacts and explicates an ethical view of life. Many critics mistakenly interpret this rule as indicating that this figure embodies, even 'incarnates,' the moral code of a work or of a whole series endorsed by the narrator (e.g., Cawelti 1976, chs 4 and 6; Grella 1988a and 1988b; Porter 1981, ch. 8). In fact, this figure is but one, although a central, component in the game between the author and the reader. There is no guarantee that the investigator represents the author's moral views; instead, this figure may, for example, serve to mislead the reader into reaching conclusions which are refuted and even mocked in the end.[7] In the author's game with the reader, the detective functions as a central textual component with whose help the narrator instructs, manipulates, or cajoles the reader into forming this or that ethical view of life. We may interpret this ground rule broadly as involving the reader's task of evaluating morally a detective's investigative performance.

I examine the ethical views of life put forward in the detective-story genre by considering the detective and his or her investigative perform-ance as the author's most stable means of illustrating and voicing such views. I place this performance and its results in the context I have established of the game between the author and the reader. The genre includes two partly overlapping games, of which the first is the game of make-believe between the detective and the criminal within the fictional world. The second is the author-reader game, comprising the author's handling of generic narrative strategies and conventions – including the detective – and the reader's capability of identifying what these strate-gies are and how the author uses them.[8]

To do justice to the complexity of subgeneric variation, I examine and compare with one another the two most important forms of the genre: the whodunit and the hard-boiled narrative. Thanks to their widespread familiarity, their different rules are well known. In the whodunit, the game between the detective-pursuers and the criminal-pursued resem-bles a clever cat's pursuit of a resourceful mouse, a pursuit without the moral complexities or qualms typical of hard-boiled investigations. The ideological – and moral – void Fredric Jameson (1983, 124) identifies as being characteristic of the detective-story genre best fits the whodunit tradition, for the game is as fixed and 'natural' as is the cat's hunger for the mouse. A similar teasing attitude distinguishes the author's game with the reader, as the author implants correct, ambiguous, and false clues into the narrative fabric, setting the crime problem in such a way that the denouement springs some sort of surprise on the reader. In contrast, the hard-boiled game, emerging from a context of all-pervasive corruption, does provoke considerations about various moral issues. The author, instead of teasing the reader, challenges us to think not only about these issues but also about the narrative framework in which they are set. The comparison of these subgenres will show that detective fiction has no uniform ethical view of life; subgenerically differing sets of rules produce divergent results. I examine two typical cases from each tradition: these 'business as usual' examples provide a good opportunity for observing how detectives function at the two levels of the detective-story game.

The Play's the Thing: Indifference and Ethics in the Whodunit

Ruth Rendell's *Wolf to the Slaughter* (1967), a typical whodunit puzzle, allows us to consider detective figures and their investigative performance in terms of the particular game configuration of this subgenre. The obvious place to look for promptings to ethical consideration is the author's manipulation of cultural stereotypes and generally accepted preconceptions and prejudices to keep the reader from guessing the solution. These manipulative strategies interlace with the whodunit's self-conscious creation of a 'reality' which is primarily discursive. A number of scholars argue that in order for this game between the author and the reader to function, we have to tune ourselves into what might be called 'middle-class morality' (Barnard 1980, 5; Grossvogel 1983; Knight 1980, 107; Priestman 1990, 153).[9] Let us now explore this idea with the help of Rendell's detective narrative.

As is typical of Rendell, *Wolf to the Slaughter* has two plots: the main narrative line deals with the investigation, while the subplot depicts the love affair of an aspiring young policeman involved in it. These two plots come together at the end, when it is revealed that the policeman's lover is the culprit, an outcome deeply disappointing to Wexford, Rendell's series investigator, for the policeman was his protégé. The investigation ends in the capture of the culprit and the policeman's resignation from his job. Because inference plays a key role as an investigative method both in the fictional world and in the game between the author and the reader, I analyse the conjectures the detectives make and the ones Rendell's narrator[10] entices the reader to entertain.

The narrator safeguards the solution through a careful handling of what Bennett calls *confidence* and *confidentiality*. Confidence is the degree to which the reader can rely on the truthfulness of the presentation of events; it controls the quality of the information the reader receives. Confidentiality regulates the quantity of information shared by the detective and reader (1979, 250–7). The Rendell reader can trust the narrator's manipulation of facts to follow the rules of fair play, whereas confidentiality is a trickier question. The narrator typically establishes a relation of confidentiality with the reader by supplying important narrative information solely to us, while still enticing us to reason along the same lines as the investigators. This strategy leads us to think we know or understand more about the case than the investigators, while actually we are lured into a wrong conjectural avenue. In *Wolf to the Slaughter* the narrator establishes confidentiality by obliquely describing the crime to the reader and by letting only the reader follow the policeman's love affair. The opening illustrates this strategy well: it depicts a man and a girl on their way somewhere to meet someone unspecified; the man plays with a flick knife, boasting it might come in handy if things fail to go their way. After a significant gap, we are told the following:

When things went wrong, hideously wrong, he had a terrible sense of fate, of inevitability. It would have happened sometime, sooner or later, this way or the other. They got into their coats somehow and he tried to staunch the blood with his scarf.

'A doctor,' she kept moaning, 'a doctor or a hospital.' He didn't want that, not if it could be avoided. The knife was back in his pocket and all he wanted was air and to feel the rain on his face and to get to the car. (10–11)

The narrator evokes a scenario in which the reader imagines a bleeding girl and a callous man who refuses her plea for help. The epigraphs framing the narrative and the few lines of Romantic poetry quoted by a character imbue this opening scene with a morbidly elegiac tinge, emphasizing the quirks of fate and the passion of erotic love. The investigation then starts as a missing-person case, centring on the disappearance of a wealthy 'playgirl,' Ann Margolis. Thanks to the narrator's confidentiality, we think we know what has happened: we now follow to see how the police will arrive at the same conclusion and how the investigation fills in the few crucial gaps, most notably, the culprit's identity. The main means the police have for solving the crime are conjectures about the alleged victim's ethos and the suspects' line of action, for the better they understand the victim, the easier it will be to locate her body and her murderer. They put together a picture of a carefree, yet caring, sexually liberated young woman who, under her happy-go-lucky veneer, shows a middle-class shrewdness about money matters. In looking for her they find a sordid room with bloodstains on the carpet; thinking that they are dealing with a sexual crime, they hypothesize that some villain has first engaged in a bit of easy sex with the missing woman and has then robbed and murdered her (43), an interpretation with which the reader concurs.

This scenario elicits the first explicitly moralizing response from Wexford and Burden, for neither condones promiscuity;[11] it spills guilt over to the victim, as her behaviour, it is thought, has contributed to this outcome. Yet both the investigators and the reader remain doubtful about this version: the police because the alleged victim ill fits the type who lets herself be murdered (66), and the reader also because it is still too early in the narrative to know things for certain. After a number of turns, involving false suspects and wrong conjectures, the investigators realize they have all along been mistaken about who exactly is involved in the case. This misconception is the reader's as well, for the narrator's confidentiality in the opening scene was limited. At this point the police and the reader learn the identity of the knife-carrying man, and are getting to know of his habit of carving up his lovers to enhance his sexual pleasure. These facts and the depiction of the crime would seem to confirm the reader's conjecture about a sex-related killing with the missing woman in the role of the self-evident victim and the sadistic man as an equally obvious culprit, but the convention of the surprise ending is reason to doubt this scenario. Our doubt is increased by the fact that Burden, Rendell's Watson-figure, endorses this interpretation. Thus, close to the end, we realize that, for all our cleverness, we have been reduced to a 'Watson' and now must wait for the supersleuth to spell out the correct answer. The surprise ending builds on a reversal of roles, based on an importation of a convention of the hard-boiled detective narrative: finally identifying the crime, along with its victim and perpetrator, Wexford proves that the policeman's beautiful girlfriend has killed the violent man. The missing woman, whose character the police and the reader have been busily constructing, has nothing whatsoever to do with the crime, while the 'Botticelli girl,' whom the narrator has been keeping under the reader's gaze all the while, is the one to blame.

Focalization partly accounts for the narrator's strategy of keeping the reader from guessing the solution, for the culprit is shown only through the eyes of male characters (the besotted lover's, but also Wexford's), which emphasizes the girl's innocent beauty. The narrator also underlines her sordid living conditions, further strengthening the view of her as an exquisite thing in the midst of tawdriness. Confidentiality again plays a role, for by making us privy to the change of the calculating and cynical young policeman into a committed lover, the author directs our attention to the sweetness of love, instead of its darker depths. Had we noticed a number of straightforward, yet insignificant-seeming clues, we could have worked out the solution. More significantly, we should have observed more carefully the narrator's use of narrative and cultural conventions and stereotypes. For one thing, it is typical for the main and subplot lines to intersect at the end, and a handy way to do this is to plant the culprit in the subplot. Also, the culprit's looks[12] betray her, for the allure of her beauty functions as the sign of her corruption and evil. The reader should have remembered that cultural stereotype, extremely typical of the hard-boiled detective story, which constructs madonna-like female characters as attractively masked sources of depravity. Looks alone do not explain this fixing of guilt, however. The morally dubious nature of beauty goes together with the notion of love, which emphasizes love's irrational, passionate, and enslaving nature. Such love lies outside the bounds of morality, forming a source of temptation for anyone caught in its throes. The poetry quotations, used as epigraphs, were there to remind the reader of the dangers erotic passion may entail. Finally, the title of the book gives an explicit clue to the reversal of roles on which the solution builds.

What is the reader to make of this manipulation of narrative and cultural material, and what moral relevance can it have? And how does the author-reader game make the whodunit's ethical view of life emerge? The convention of providing as unexpected and surprising an ending as possible occupies a central place, for it proves that the author has succeeded in outwitting the reader. In Caillois's view, the whodunit rules decree that 'the murderer's identity must challenge not only moral norms but what ordinarily pass for rational and material possibilities' (1983, 8). This striving is at the root of what Priestman calls the *innate schizophrenic formula* of much detective fiction. It is grounded in the gap between the fact of crime and the detached manner of handling it. Its schizophrenic nature derives from a careful separation of the fascination with 'real' crime from the fantasy of more or less infallible detection, which in itself is the reverse of realistic. The juxtaposition of these two elements leads to their uneasy coexistence; in the whodunit, according to Priestman, the overall effect of their pairing is to make us indifferent to the social, moral, or political issues the crimes depicted (possibly) raise (1990, 6). The primary concern of the whodunit is to develop and resolve the narrative problem as ingeniously as possible. The schizophrenic formula thus creates a tension between ethics and aesthetics that cannot but influence what the ethical view of life is like in the whodunit.

Rendell illustrates this strategic indifference well, for in her books she uses many different kinds of textual materials, including hard-boiled conventions, to wring out their most surprising or shocking angle. There is nothing in her books which is not a visible citation of something else. The Kingsmarkham community is an updated version of the Golden Age country village; the detectives use easily identifiable cultural grids as means of crime solving; and the crime cases are often structured on some specific aspect of the cited textual material. In this last category one can mention, for example, *A Guilty Thing Surprised* (1970), which portrays a crime involving a biographer of Wordsworth and builds the solution on an analogue between his and the poet's incestuous love for a sister; *From Doon with Death* (1964) quotes Victorian poetry extensively to make the verses provide a revelation about lesbian love; *The Veiled One* (1988) and

An Unkindness of Ravens (1985) make Jungian and Freudian psychology fit the whodunit conventions. The author employs the cited texts for the operative reason of making her whodunits as ingenious as possible; the ideological implications of this material remain a secondary consideration.

I elaborate on the significance the schizophrenic formula has for the ethical view of life of the whodunit by considering the two interconnected levels of the game configuration. The first level is the game of make-believe played by detective and criminal, and the second is the game of obfuscation and guessing played by author and reader. Finally, I discuss very briefly the means we use as readers to distance ourselves from the presented view of life, submitting it to 'ideological critique.' It is useful to look at these issues separately.

As regards the game that takes place in the fictional world, the function of the detective is to emphasize that solving the crime and exposing the criminal are important for the moral well-being of the fictional community. The solution also allocates guilt to the parties concerned and evaluates its degree. In *Wolf to the Slaughter*, Wexford's condemnation of the female culprit is comprehensive, with its roots lying at least partly in her father's petty infringements against the law. The dictum 'Like father, like daughter' governs his stance, as if the inclination to crime were a genetic property. Also, the victim's guiltiness is considerable, for he is a psychopath who the police think only got what was coming to him. Next in the scales of guilt comes Wexford's protégé for having compromised his duty as a policeman, failing to perceive the obvious links his girlfriend has to the case.[13] Finally, there is the bemused but tired scorn Wexford and Burden feel for the general foolishness of people. These evaluations show the protagonists' perception of their own role: they are the guardians of law and order, ensuring the upkeep of basic moral decency. This is a mechanical attitude to morality, for it prioritizes the technical sense of guilt without placing it in a wider context; therefore, the traditional binaries of good and bad, right and wrong, usually remain intact. Yet this attitude already speaks for there being at least a conventional acquiescence in moral issues, even if they are understood in a very crude and sketchy sense.

The game between author and reader includes the author's supply and placement of straightforward, ambiguous, and wrong clues.[14] Each clue type may make use of stereotypes, clichés, and general preconceptions and prejudices, but what is of crucial importance is the *manner* in which these elements are employed. In discussing the obfuscation strategies of Agatha Christie, David I. Grossvogel gives an insightful description of her handling of narrative information; as his observations have more general significance, it is worthwhile to quote him at length:

The canniest person in *The Mysterious Affair at Styles* is neither the criminal ... [nor] Hercule Poirot either: it is Agatha Christie herself. She moves in a world she knows so well she can pretend not to be part of it, counting on the reader's prejudice that associates [the reader] with her characters, while she herself avoids contamination. Her mode allows her to show the guilty and innocent in what appears to be the same light by dissociating herself ostensibly from the convention on which she relies, while in reality she knows she is casting suspicion on those who should not be suspected. Farmer Raikes' wife is a gypsy, but pretty enough to turn the appreciative (if empty) head of Hastings: the narrator [i.e., Hastings] seems quite ready to become a part of the immorality that appears to radiate from her, but the author has done nothing more than provide us with factual evidence about her origins and encounters. That Hastings (and the reader) should fall sway, with the rest, to a belief suggested by the word 'gypsy' is a consequence that Agatha Christie will not reject but that she has done nothing to encourage. (1979, 47–8)

The relevance of 'middle-class morality' for the whodunit begins to emerge. If we understand this vague concept to refer to another (equally vague) notion of 'hegemonic ideology,' we perceive that generally accepted and endorsed – or at least widely circulated – conceptions form, as it were, the board on which the game takes place. As the whodunits are predominantly located in (upper)-middle-class settings, we gear ourselves to think along lines appropriate to these surroundings, borrowing the logic of our reasoning from them. As Cawelti (1976, 111–16) shows, we readily process whodunit cases in the light of what we think of as satisfying the 'deeper emotional structure of the classical formula' (114), opting for any views that seem to promote reason, order, and responsibility. Hence, it is easy, for example, to construe loose sexual behaviour as a taboo in Rendell's middle-class world and see the missing playgirl in *Wolf to the Slaughter* as the proper victim. Our mistakes as readers mostly derive from a belief in our own competence within this logic; while the author is busy bending the familiar tenets to work against us, we are made to dig our own (hermeneutic) grave. And even if we should take precautions, trying to engage in the game as a purely semiotic undertaking, we tend to forget that our opponent is, to borrow Eco's (1979, 162) characterization, first and foremost a *cynical tale-engineer*.

The game between author and reader relies to a large extent on the functioning of conventional moral norms. On the basis of various clues, we attempt to appraise what could be good and bad, laudable and blameworthy in the middle-class world whose crimes we are investigating. The manipulation of these norms does not mean, however, that the author would thereby lead us outside conventional morality; instead, the solutions are bent back into its grooves. In *Wolf to the Slaughter*, for example, the playgirl, once found (alive), is shown to be a basically sound character: her sexual mores were a red herring, and, in spite of her consumerist attitude towards money and men, she is kind and caring. In reflecting upon the strategies of obfuscation from the perspective of the ending, we become aware of the particular stereotypes and prejudices we have been made to entertain, but there is seldom (if ever) any in-depth criticism of these elements. Rather, the manipulative narrative strategy creates a distance that is, as Hannah Charney (1981, ch. 1) argues, ironic, or even sarcastic. As a result, the detectives, all other characters, and the whole fictional world become pieces in a game: the whodunit is not a literature of (emotional) 'identification,' but an exercise in narrative and cultural 'mythology.'[15]

This 'mythological' character of the whodunit is central to the ethical view of life this subgenre puts forward, deriving from the double perspective on which it is structured. On the one hand, as in all make-believe, the reader has to step into this game by naturalizing the textual signs of the whodunit's status as a game between author and reader. We have to regard the fictional world as an imaginary alternative to our system of reality; for the duration of reading, while we are playing with the author, we must behave as if the fictional world were the actual world. As this world is to a large extent modelled after our system of reality, stepping into the game of make-believe is easy, and is further facilitated by the fact that fictional crime solving directly depends on familiar conjectural schemas, which use well-known cultural conventions and stereotypes as material. Hence, while reading, we encounter the very same notions, beliefs, and prejudices as in our own system of reality. On the other hand, a crucial component of the author-reader game is our awareness of it as a game of obfuscation and reasoning, whereby we are required to regard the fictional world, with its characters, situations, actions, and locales, as the many different game tokens to be arranged into an aesthetically and narratively satisfying pattern. Given these two perspectives, reading the whodunit may be described as a constant *fluctuation* between the game of make-believe and the framing game between author and reader. To read the whodunit as intended, the reader has to keep moving from one realm to the other. Take, for example, the figure of the culprit in *Wolf to the Slaughter*. In the fictional world, the characters model her after the pictures of the great Renaissance painters; in the framing game the reader has to recode this model as the more modern figure of the beautiful but wicked blonde. Compare this figure, then, with that of the dark playgirl, first coded as an immoral man-eater in the fictional world, but then recoded as a liberal tenderheart at the higher game level.

If this fluctuation is characteristic of the whodunit's signification process, how does it effect the ethical view of life arising from it? The first thing to note is that this movement gives the fictional world an ambiguous standing, for it simultaneously expresses a 'full' meaning (in accordance with the realistic illusion that governs its compilation), while also supplying an 'empty' form for the author-reader game. And, if we are to believe Barthes, this constantly 'moving turnstile' fluctuation, presenting alternately the meaning of the signifier and its form, is the mode of signification typical of modern, commodified 'myths' (1973, 133).[16] The fictional world is always there to supply the formal grounds for the game between author and reader; this game is itself always there to outdistance and ironize the fictional world. The effect of this signification mode for the ethical view of life derives from the fact that both these 'levels' are intimately tied up with *values*. Barthes explains that the first-order signification system, here conceived of as comprising the fictional world, is itself associated with a whole complex of values, which the second-order system, that is, the game between author and reader, treats as form, calling for signification to fill it with new values (1973, 131–4). In the whodunit this first system, itself grounded in middle-class values, is stocked with the very same values as in the second system; in the author-reader game, however, our attention is redirected so that we see the first system from another perspective. The resulting ethical view of life may be described as one of *middle-class vertigo*. This value basis actually enables the play of obfuscation and guessing, for author and reader need a common ground for playing the game. And as the components of the fictional world are the tokens, they, too, have to conform to these same values. The reader's vertigo arises from being made to see one thing from shifting perspectives, as if through a kaleidoscope.

This feature explains the schizophrenic formula: the whodunit game can afford indifference, because its underlying bedrock of values is reinforced through repetition at all levels. The game also imbues the whodunit's ethical view of life with at least some complexity, for individual detective puzzles present this value basis from shifting angles of vision. Thanks to its basic mode of signification, this view of life – whatever its specific modifications in particular narratives – is inevitably bound up with middle-class 'hegemony.'[17] This value basis has a specific role in the game between author and reader, for, in order to compete successfully with the author, the reader has to know that they are both steeped in narrative and cultural 'mythology,' the clever handling of which *is* the game they are engaged in.[18]

The whodunit author would, however, seem to have two different ways of manipulating these values. I briefly compare Christie's *The Mysterious Affair at Styles* (Grossvogel's example) and Rendell's *Wolf to the Slaughter* in order to demonstrate this difference. What unites these books is the familiar detective-story motif of criminal cooperation between two persons. In Christie's book, murder results from the scheming of a pair of lovers hankering after money; while in Rendell's book, the culprit tries to use the young policeman's infatuation to avoid getting caught. Christie concentrates on features that can be explained about the couple's motives for cooperation: infatuation, greed, wickedness. Poirot sums up the case by saying that the criminals 'had already arranged their infamous plot – that he should marry this rich, but rather foolish old lady, induce her to make a will leaving her money to him, and then gain their ends by a very cleverly conceived crime' (185). Rendell emphasizes the engulfing emotion making the young policeman lose himself in the girl: 'He had reached a stage when his paramount wish was to be alone with her in silence, holding her to him, and in silence enclosing her mouth with his' (145). The symbiotic stasis he dreams of is literally a silent state, for its bliss lies beyond signification. His infatuation brings forth the deepest motivation for the majority of Rendellian crimes, springing from the real of desire. The characterization of criminal cooperation as *folie à deux*, a state of mutual, self-feeding madness, is typical of Rendell.[19]

The effect of the ending demonstrates the difference between the two strategies of manipulating the middle-class value base. Christie presents a world where the detective explains criminal deviance with the help of a shared, middle-class symbolic system. Interestingly enough, however, its very stability points to its being culturally constructed, and, in this sense, a 'fiction.' Her criminals are deeply committed to the system which they break; they transgress according to its laws, wanting just those things its ethics forbids them to pursue. This same commitment transports itself to the narrator's stance, so that in designing both the fictional world and the strategies of obfuscation, the narrator, who manipulates the whole exercise in cunning deception, is nevertheless touched by the deviant striving of her criminals, precisely because she and the reader share this striving. Following Slavoj Žižek (1996), we can say that this approach is that of the *ironist* who, by treating outward signs as symptoms of a hidden agenda, interprets them as proofs of the agent's inevitable immersion in the symbolizing systems of his or her culture. The ironist suspects that all displays of indifference, disdain, and calculation are so many masks hiding an agent's genuine attachment or commitment to the things he or she ostensibly holds in contempt. If we exaggerate a little, the ironist believes in the basic 'benevolence' of the acting agent, because even the worst of the agent's deeds and attitudes find their explanation in the context of shared cultural systems. The ironist, Žižek says, 'entertains a suspicion that perhaps reality itself is not real but always-already structured as a fiction, dominated, regulated by an unconscious fantasy' (207–8).

Rendell's strategy, in contrast, is to construct a world in which middle-class values cannot guide criminal behaviour, because, being under the sway of desire, that behaviour follows a(n il)logic of its own. Her criminals may hanker after the trappings of the affluent lifestyle, but most of all they want the giddy, intoxicating immersion in the pleasure of infatuation or of power. The middle-class symbolic system represented by her series investigators provides the fragile footholds from whose vantage point we can perceive the abyss of desire opening in front of us. Unlike Christie, then, Rendell can use different frameworks ranging from Romanticism to modern psychology – she can even build the solution so that it demonstrates the basic correctness of Freud's theory of female sexuality (*An Unkindness of Ravens*) – because all of these frameworks remain only the incomplete efforts of various signifying systems to explain what is basically unexplainable.[20] Taking our cue again from Žižek, we can designate this approach as that of the *cynic*, who denounces and mocks all expressions of authority, commitment, and emotion as so many poses masking the agent's purely self-serving ends. The cynic is convinced of the agent's basic 'malevolence,' stemming from such pleasure-seeking self-interest as surpasses the signifying capacity of our symbolizing systems. The cynic believes only in the 'real of *jouissance*' (201), 'reduc[ing] all ideological chimeras to raw reality, searching for the real ground of elevated ideological fictions' (207–8).[21] It is the profound distrust of symbolization that allows the cynic to reveal the mechanism of the functioning of ideology without in the least affecting its efficiency: the cynic openly declares that she knows what she is doing but keeps doing it nevertheless (200–3).

The difference between Christie and Rendell brings into view the change that has taken place over the years in the whodunit author's manipulation of the middle-class values on which the subgenre's ethical view of life is based. Perhaps we can relate this change to Žižek's sketchy musings on the broader links irony and cynicism have with the cultural productions of modernism and postmodernism respectively (1996, 200–2). Modernism, Žižek claims, cherishes the belief that 'reflection somehow affects its object' so that 'once a symptom is properly interpreted, it should dissolve.' Christie's work fits this loose definition, as her detective stories express a belief in the effectiveness of identifying the causes behind crime. The detective's explanation serves to banish, or at least curb, similar impulses in the reader and in characters other than the culprit, because the narrator assumes that all share the same symbolic system. And if postmodernism, as seen by Žižek, starts out from the conviction that reflection shows the object for what it is, so that the interpretation of a symptom mainly explains why it functions the way it does without causing real change, then Rendell may be characterized as a postmodernist, for whatever account her detectives offer for crimes, it can never alter the real of desire.

This distinction between irony and cynicism as narrative strategies affects the way the reader gains access to an ideological critique. This critique analyses the (ethical) world-view of a narrative (genre), made up of beliefs and values, in order to demonstrate how this world-view relates to beliefs and values in the world at large. Given that irony and cynicism provide two perspectives on the world depicted, the reader's perception of the limits of the system of values underlying this world follows two different routes. As the ironic narrative strategy assumes the efficacy of a symbolizing system based on shared values and beliefs, the reader can see its limits simply by placing it against some other system. The cynical strategy, in contrast, invites a different approach. In denying the efficacy of the meaning-endowing systems it nevertheless employs, this strategy posits areas of desire that stand for the 'real' reality. Žižek says that the cynic's (ideological) error lies in her naïve belief that, because signifying systems are constructed, they do not work. Hence, the reader may turn a cynic's strategy against itself by pondering how the areas of desire, supposedly outside signification, actually hold the narrator's system of values together, thus ensuring its functioning.

The 'expressive and statement-making functions' of form and the 'sets of beliefs' (Nussbaum 1990, 8, 17) which the whodunit puts into play during the reading experience are based on a specific set of values.

Although critics maintain that the hard-boiled narrative is based on similar values, its game configuration differs so widely from that of the whodunit that it views these values from an entirely different perspective. This difference will become clear as we look at the characteristics of the hard-boiled literary game and the ethical view(s) of life emerging from it.

Tough Games: Moral Murkiness and the Hard-Boiled Narrative

The whodunit legacy emphasizes the curbing function of moral rules and prescriptions. By presenting crimes as rising from an individual's inability ('genetic deficiency') or unwillingness (personal hubris) to conform to these guidelines, it makes policing a matter of safeguarding the community from a deviant individual (Charney 1980, 61–3; Knight 1980, 115, 124, 128; Porter 1981, 161). The game in which the hard-boiled narrative engages the reader has an altogether different point of departure. The reader knows from the outset that the investigation will reveal the ubiquity of moral corruption in the fictional world. We also know that at first either corrupt social institutions or professional criminals (or both) seem to be responsible for the particular crime a detective is working on; but we can be almost sure that the ending will finally show private persons to be the ones to blame. Our safe bets as to the culprit's identity include the detective's client, friend, colleague, or lover. The hard-boiled game taking place in the fictional world thus moves between two concentric realms of guilt: institutional moral decay and professional crime encircle the private transgressions that are singled out for scrutiny (Jameson 1983, 142–5). This double focus changes the nature of the reader's game, for the explicit inclusion of social structures as (causal) factors in crime suggests that this subgenre gives weight to various moral questions.[22]

As the function of crime as a puzzle to be solved diminishes (without vanishing altogether), the reader's interest centres on the adventurous, even deadly dangerous, progress of the investigation. The focal point in the reader's game with the author is, therefore, the hard-boiled detective: we observe how an investigator's moral code is established and elaborated through that individual person's functioning as an investigator. The narrative conventions stress the significance of such a moral code, for the solution frequently demands that the investigator take on the role of a judge or even that of an avenger (Cawelti 1976, 142; Grella 1988b). Ross Macdonald's series investigator Lew Archer aptly describes the role the detective and the reader share by remarking that 'most of my work is watching people and judging them' (1986, 85). Unlike in the whodunit, however, the watching and judging are action-oriented: the investigator's evaluations are revealed in what he or she does. In turn, the reader's first task is to watch investigators work their way through their tangled cases, evaluating their choices, actions, and conclusions.[23]

The structure of hard-boiled narration – which, whether first-person or third-person, is noted for its 'reportorial lyricism'[24] – customarily aims at creating a blatant discrepancy between the sordidness and violence of the events and the highly aestheticized and stylized, even 'poetic,' manner of narration, thus creating two different perspectives on the hard-boiled world. This structure differs from that of the whodunit, which constructs the relationship between author and reader on the basis of obfuscation. Hence, the second major task set for the reader in the game with the author arises from this discrepancy between narration and the narrated: the reader's task is to evaluate the qualities of the narration and to reflect on how these two perspectives interact in a given narrative.

To elucidate how the ethical view of life typical of the hard-boiled novel emerges, I first discuss the reader's entry into the game of make-believe through an evaluation of a detective's investigative conduct and the moral code he or she relies on. I then consider the reader's assessment of how narration affects this game level. I use Ross Macdonald's *The Moving Target* (1986), a typical hard-boiled narrative, as my example. In drawing up the basics of the game formations, I refer to the tradition familiar from the three 'Founding Fathers': Dashiell Hammett, Raymond Chandler, and Ross Macdonald. Later permutations – the 'perverted' revenge fantasies of the 1950s (Mickey Spillane), the sentimentalized and nostalgic quests of the 1970s (Robert B. Parker), and the many present-day feminist detective stories (Sara Paretsky, Sue Grafton) – build on this legacy. Choosing a book by Macdonald means discussing the author-reader game in terms of first-person (intra- and homodiegetic) narration.[25] Although this mode does not cover the whole subgenre, it represents the best-known variation of it. A simplified outline of the fast-moving plot of this novel follows.

Lew Archer is commissioned to find a missing millionaire, Ralph Sampson. He notes the tenseness of his household: the millionaire's daughter, Miranda, is infatuated with his private pilot, whereas the millionaire's lawyer, Archer's former colleague, is besotted with Miranda. Following a tenuous lead, the investigator tracks down a criminal gang who might have kidnapped Sampson. A ransom letter arrives. The family decides to hand the money over to ensure Sampson's safety. Archer's task is to observe the courier, whom he identifies as one of the gang. Minutes later, the courier is killed by another member of this gang. Archer seeks out their leader; the confrontation reveals that the leader knows nothing of the kidnapping, but decides to cut in on the game. He orders Archer to be killed; instead, Archer kills the henchman. The final stage begins with Archer accusing Sampson's pilot of the kidnapping; the pilot admits the charge and threatens to kill Archer. Having over-heard the confrontation, the lawyer intervenes by shooting the pilot. Archer goes looking for the pilot's accomplice and lover, Betty; hearing of her lover's death, Betty reveals Sampson's location. Archer calls for help from the lawyer and the police. He is attacked at Sampson's hideaway, and, after coming to, he finds Sampson dead. Various facts make him conclude that the lawyer, married to Miranda on the very same day, murdered Sampson in order to acquire the fortune she inherits on her father's death.

Throughout the narrative the reader notices the friction between Arch-er's knowledge of what would be a correct line of procedure and what he needs to do to solve the case, as, for example, when Archer plies an alcoholic with alcohol to acquire information.[26] Given the corruption of the hard-boiled world, the reader understands that moral juggling belongs to the investigator's work, for his opponents never respect traditional morality. We may therefore expect the investigator also to break these rules: the manner in which and the reasons for which he breaks them thus become the issue. From this friction derives the code of *professionalism* central to the subgenre, which entails personal non-involvement and infringing morality only to the extent necessary to do the job.[27] The code blends toughness with sentimentality. Toughness involves control over personal feelings and sexual desires in professional situations, and a stoic acceptance of (one's own) death. Toughness also includes the notion that the detective's self-worth and the quality of his character are tested in violent action. The sentimental side of this code stresses such factors as loyalty, the determination to help, pity, or per-sonal ideals as the motivation for persevering with a case. Adherence to this code frequently results in the detective's loneliness and isolation from the rest of the community (Cawelti 1976; Grella 1988b; Margolies 1982; Parker 1984; Porter 1981; Slotkin 1988).

The Moving Target shows this code in action; it provides for the reader's consideration the most extreme, albeit typical, example of conflict, one in which the investigator is compelled to break the fundamental moral rule against killing. We follow the birth of Archer's decision to slay the criminal gang's henchman, the mental spurring on he needs to undertake the act, and the actual killing (125–9). In doing so, we understand that we are meant to consider the mitigating circumstances, for the deed is in self-defence: it seems inevitable that, unless Archer kills the criminal gang's henchman, this man will kill him. We also perceive that Archer consciously musters up sufficient aggression to assault the hitman.[28] This fact speaks for the 'appropriateness' and professionalism of his emotional attitude in the situation, for the deed is done without personal hatred. The detective does what he must to survive, even, after breaking free from captivity, himself trying to save his opponent (128). Yet to decide on the quality of Archer's ethos, the reader needs to relate the killing to his system of values and his goals as an investigator, because the code of professionalism alone seldom covers all the values that govern a detective's work.[29] The supplementing of the professional code with other values accounts for many differences between hard-boiled investigators. An earlier scene describing Archer's dream gives the reader an important clue to the investigator's personal code. This dream is thematically tied to the scene of the killing through the image of wading in filth, which is allegorical in the dream, but concrete in Archer's struggle for life under water with Puddler. Part of the dream goes as follows:

The room was a whitewashed corridor slanting down into the bowels of the earth. I followed it down to the underground river of filth that ran under the city. There was no turning back. I had to wade the excremental river. Fortunately, I had my stilts with me. They carried me untainted, wrapped in cellophane, to the landing on the other side. I tossed my stilts away – they were also crutches – and mounted a chrome-plated escalator that gleamed like the jaws of death. Smoothly and surely it lifted me through all the zones of evil to a rose-embowered gate, which a maid in gingham opened for me, singing *Home, Sweet Home*. (111)

The exaggerated, too-perfect details of the dream betray that it is the (ironic) fantasy of what Archer himself would like to be, whereas during the underwater killing he is up to his neck in dirt.[30] He has no stilts-cum-crutches to keep him untainted, for working in the morally grey area of law enforcement and functioning as an insulating buffer zone between criminals and ordinary people invariably infects hard-boiled detectives, forcing them to do things people normally never need to do. Two things about the hard-boiled game formation are particularly noteworthy in this context. First, the reader's task of putting together the investigator's ethos demands alertness to patternings and parallels such as the one just

cited. Second, the subgeneric conventions ascribe a standard interpretation to the inevitable gap between ideals and the reality of (private)
policing: the investigator's willing submission to the moral complexities
of his profession identifies him as the kind of 'hero' the hard-boiled
world – and, perhaps, by analogy, the reader's system of reality – needs.
The typical practice of emphasizing this gap is intended to keep the
reader's attention on the protagonist's system of values. As the ending
requires that the investigator either take a personal stand or enact a
punishment of some sort, the reader may best evaluate this system in the
light of the conclusion.

In *The Moving Target* Archer grades guilt according to the standing and
goals of the people involved. Customarily, his evaluation of outright
crooks is the briefest, as they belong to the criminal structures infesting
society. In keeping with the pattern Jameson identifies, the crimes committed by ordinary persons are of interest because they enable one to trace
the agents' shift from one moral position to another. Therefore, Archer
concentrates on explaining the kidnapping and the two murders. Similarly
motivated, these crimes elucidate the nature of the hard-boiled world.

One of the two kidnappers maintains that love is the motivating source
of the crime, for she wants a new life outside California with her accomplice, the pilot. By kidnapping the millionaire they aim to secure a nest
egg for life, justifying their deed by their victim's own immorality. Archer,
however, believes simple greed is the motive (166). The underlying postulation that love needs the accoutrements of money to be fulfilling
presents a typical motive for crime in the hard-boiled world. It is the
conjunction of money, the power money brings, and love (or, rather,
sexual attraction) that, for Archer, explains the kidnapping. It is noteworthy, however, that the kidnapper objects to this interpretation.

The allure of the triad of money, power, and sex also directs the
lawyer's fate, which follows the pattern of the fall of the upright man. A
self-made man, his professional success has failed to bring him wealth,
and his work for rich, unscrupulous people such as the millionaire has, in
Archer's opinion, corrupted him by instilling in him social envy and
ambition (183). Archer maintains that the kidnapping offers the lawyer
an unexpected opportunity to attain his goals: he shoots the pilot, ostensibly to protect Archer's life, but really to remove his rival for the love of
the millionaire's daughter; he stages the millionaire's murder to look as
though the kidnappers committed it, to ensure that the daughter, whom
he has hastily married, inherits half of her father's fortune. But although
the lawyer acted on the spur of the moment, in Archer's view his deeds

have been shrewdly calculated. Archer's final, harsh, and punitive judgment of the lawyer is prompted not only by the man's deeds, but also by his bad faith and hypocrisy – his refusal to admit his motives and take responsibility for his actions, and his betrayal of public and professional trust (175–9, 184–5).

Archer is particularly incensed with the lawyer for breaking the rule against killing. For Archer, the sanctity of human life is the basic tenet sustaining moral integrity: letting go of this principle means violating the primary boundary setting humans off from animals. Archer portrays human relations as a battle played out in a 'steel-and-concrete jungle' (127). This nature/culture dichotomy characterizes the moral agent as internally divided, torn between 'natural appetites' and the limits culture sets on the agent's behaviour. By extension, moral integrity is inherently *fragile* because, for the duration of his or her life, the agent is caught between internal pressures and external events over which he or she has little control. Thus, moral rectitude requires constant nurturing and self-conscious protection. This view follows Archer's understanding of human nature as impregnated with an innate propensity for evil, which any mishap – '[e]nvironment, opportunity, economic pressure, a piece of bad luck, a wrong friend' (85) – may activate. For this reason Archer is cynical about people's motives (166–8, 176–9, 185).

Because moral integrity is inherently fragile, the private domain is seen as the locus of guilt in hard-boiled narratives. When all are morally tarnished, and many are out-and-out criminals, a story about the fall of a good, or even an ordinary, person is a jarring event. Moreover, in this and in other books by Macdonald, the culprit resembles the investigator, from which we infer that anyone can fall. A person's goodness and moral integrity do not protect him or her from temptation, opportunity, or chance events. Furthermore, a person's moral fibre can be tested only in situations of conflict and personal crisis – as when one unexpectedly meets 'something utterly new. Something naked and bright, a moving target in the road' (86). This image, giving the novel its name, reveals the existential slant of its moral value system.[31]

To sum up, in *The Moving Target* the typical hard-boiled professional code is supported by a system of values that recognizes the instability of human ethos. By contrast with the whodunit, the hard-boiled narrative identifies the deciding factor in moral evaluation as not so much what a person is as what she does. The stress on doing as the decisive criterion in moral arbitration allows the reader to evaluate Archer on his own terms, making us see that he is, through his own actions, party to the endemic moral corruption. Situated at the very point where the moral codes of law enforcement and the criminal order intersect, he cannot choose but do things that are not strictly legal. His persistent striving to do what is right in the face of overwhelming odds attests to his sorrowful lot, characterized by a tragic double-bind. The fact that, in book after book, he perseveres in attempting to do good lends him, in the end, a heroic status.

In carrying out the reader's task of reflecting on the detective's ethics, are we to conclude that this figure serves as some kind of moral 'model'? The standard American argument is that he is to be assessed in Chandlerian terms as the 'best man in his world and a good enough man for any world' (1946, 20), or as 'a traditional man of virtue in an amoral and corrupt world' (Cawelti 1976, 152) (see also Grella 1988b; Porter 1981; Parker 1984; Slotkin 1988). However, although Macdonald's investigator has moral integrity,[32] it is difficult to fit Hammett's and Spillane's protagonists, for example, into this scheme. The subgenre neither uniformly invests the detective with moral rectitude nor suggests a stable notion of virtue. Instead, its ethical view of life centres on the detective's *duality*, manifested as a combination of antithetical traits: good and bad, rational and irrational, unfeeling and emotional, animal and human, and so on. Duality, of course, is the constituting principle of all fictional detectives, but the hard-boiled subgenre brings it into sharp focus by revealing the investigator as the point of intersection of two antagonistic codes. The subgeneric ethical view of life includes two set features: first, to investigate crimes requires the investigator to break moral rules and place himself or herself in the interstices of conflicting codes and values; second, the various situations of moral conflict provoked by the investigation throw light on the detective's system of values through his or her choices and actions. Thus, the reader's task involves evaluating an investigator's ethos and determining towards which pole (virtue versus vice) it tends.

Stressing this duality helps us see how the revenge formula, whose best-known representative is Mickey Spillane, emerges from this same setup. There seem to be two broad variants. The first is illustrated by Hammett's *Red Harvest* (1929), in which the protagonist, incensed by the criminals' violence against him, forgets his professionalism, becomes emotionally entangled, and orchestrates a veritable bloodbath. The point of such narratives is that walking the tightrope between two codes and being personally threatened in one's work make it hard for the detective to suppress his or her criminal side. The other variant is the Spillane type of narrative, which is based on an inversion of the signs conventionally taken to represent moral rectitude in an investigator. This narrative feeds on violence, emotional frenzy, and hatred as tokens of moral strength, justifying the worst deeds in the name of 'good.' Mike Hammer summarizes this type when he remarks on his own role that 'I was the evil that opposed other evil, leaving the good and the meek in the middle to live and inherit the world!'[33] The broad contours of the hard-boiled ethos are thus staked out between limited and necessary moral infringements, represented by a detective who, although forced to compromise, tries to hold on to conventional moral values, and the wholesale endorsement of the criminal code as the only means of effectively cleaning up evil and corruption, represented by a detective who is morally indistinguishable from the criminals he or she chases.

What does this duality look like when it is inserted into the context of the reader's second task in the hard-boiled game, the evaluation of narration? We may first note that the typical discrepancy between the sordidness of the fictional world and the aestheticized manner of narration suggests the binary of 'reality' or 'life' versus art as one structuring principle of this game. But its function remains to be determined. I approach this issue in the framework of the first-person narration of *The Moving Target*. In the conventional patterning of the hard-boiled plot, only at the end does the detective discover the real nature of the case he or she has been investigating. The conclusion, therefore, makes an appropriate starting point. The plot's rhythm of exposure (the term is Cawelti's 1976, 147) – which reaches its climax in the ending – is dramatized by a set style of narration, exemplified in the closing lines of *The Moving Target*:

As we rolled down the hill, I could see all the lights of the city. They didn't seem quite real. The stars and the house lights were firefly gleams, sparks of cold fire suspended in the black void. The real thing in my world was the girl beside me, warm and shuddering and lost.

I could have put my arms around her and taken her over. She was that lost, that vulnerable. But if I had, she'd have hated me in a week. In six months I might have hated Miranda. I kept my hands to myself and let her lick her wounds. She used my shoulder to cry on as she would have used anyone's.

Her crying was settling down to a steady rhythm, rocking itself to sleep. The sheriff's radio car passed us at the foot of the hill and turned up toward the house where Graves [the lawyer] was waiting. (185–6)

The whole lengthy closing chapter is narrated in a fashion which expresses disappointment, defeat, a sense of betrayal, and sorrow. The feeling of loss and the accompanying tone of lament derive from a number of things: the solving of the case has revealed the badly tangled, even perverted, nature of human relationships and the immorality of social structures and institutions; the protagonist has faltered in the execution of his task;[34] the damage done cannot be repaired. The careful stylization of the endings proposes one explanation for the narrative thrust subtending the hard-boiled subgenre. The strategy of underlining the sordidness of reality while still describing it 'artfully' suggests that narration functions as the narrator's means of *self-realization*.[35] This interweaving of the aesthetic with the sordid does not, of course, emerge only in the ending, but infects the whole narrative as seen in similes, metaphors, and descriptions. This strategy requires the reader to move back and forth between the violence and immorality of the fictional world and the perspicuity, sensitivity, and imagination of the narrator through whose eyes we view this world. From this fluctuation arises our task of relating the tone and aim of the narration to the events narrated.

Describing narrative motivation in terms of self-realization implies that narration functions as a means for hard-boiled narrators to draw the past out of themselves by transforming prior experience into symbolic form; at times it serves the purpose of recovering the coherence of their inner world.[36] The first-person narrative structure, Kenneth Bruffee notes, implies an important contrast between the meaning-endowing act the narrator accomplishes in telling the tale, and that which he achieved during the fictional past (1983, 52). The contrast is built into the subgeneric setup, for the plot records the detectives' gradual process of understanding what is at stake in the crimes they are solving. It is actually their lack of knowledge that frequently bars them from acting 'heroically'; they engage in actions the meaning and (tragic) consequences of which they can apprehend only in retrospect. But this contrast is not always rendered directly; instead, it often arises from the reader's observation of the narrator's 'formative impulse' as the key to his or her ethos. This means that the reader is to pay attention to how the narrator's symbol-making impulse and storyteller's art shape how the narrator renders his or her experience and perceives the objective world (Bruffee 1983, 52, 59).

The Moving Target, for example, begins and ends with the narrator's perception of the unreality of things (see, e.g., 1, 16, 30, 55, 185); his narrative is an attempt to probe this unreality. As if in contrast to this stated sense of unreality, the narration is mostly strictly factual, with long stretches of dialogue interrupted by brief descriptions of locales, people, or the thoughts of the investigator. The 'formative impulse' manifests itself as a need to describe the unreality of things as precisely as possible. The sparseness of the narrator's commentary suggests that such things as the patterning of the events (for instance, the linking of the lawyer's fate to the motif of the fall of the upright man) and the rhythm of narration (bouts of action interrupted by thoughtful reflection) function as keys to this impulse, for they create a sense of a narrator who shows carefully arranged glimpses of life to the reader while he himself ostensibly stands in the wings. This strategy leaves us room to draw our own conclusions; moreover, as narration relies more on 'showing' than 'telling,' it has the effect of making us experience that sensation of strangeness which affected Archer while the investigation was going on and which still does, even as his narration closes. Narration gives his experience form without doing away with the mystery of human desire which initiated it. It is this vision he wishes to share with the reader. More generally, the 'formative impulse' of *The Moving Target* suggests that if there is any kind of putting things right, the reader finds it at this narrative level of experience. Thus, the art-versus-life opposition in writers such as Macdonald and Chandler brings forth an ethical view of life which stresses the power of art to make a meaningless world – a world of apparently senseless trouble, sordidness, and sorrow – meaningful through the act of narration.

It is this belief in the power of art and narrative that considerably modifies the cynicism characterizing the hard-boiled investigator's attitude to life.[37] The scepticism about lofty motives goes together with qualities that undermine it, betraying the investigator's commitment to the quest. Although narrative has lost its social function, it has acquired another meaning: it is the hard-boiled investigator's only means of ordering chaotic and fragmented experiences and of achieving a sense of self and self-control, however fragile. As the level of narration reveals a basic belief in the power of symbolizing activity to give coherence and meaning to the individual's experience, it represents the hard-boiled version of the ironic strategy that was discussed in the context of the whodunit.

Given the hard-boiled emphasis on the duality of the detective figure, we must examine what the interspersing of reality and art looks like at the other end of the moral scale, the revenge narrative. The rhythm of exposure structuring the pace of the hard-boiled plot shows in the emotional crescendo of hateful frenzy as the protagonist undertakes increasingly violent actions, an escalation which is accompanied by a certain apocalyptic quality in the narrative voice. The ending is a fusion of violent action (the investigator kills the main opponent) and the narrator's perversely elegiac emphasis on death and destruction. The narrative motivation may still be described in terms of self-realization or self-recovery, even self-justification, because of the taxing emotional burden of the bloody rampage which the investigator-narrator has barely survived. The form-giving function of art figures strongly in the revenge mode as well, for the investigation constantly threatens to take the investigator to a realm beyond signification. The oscillation between experience and the narrator's 'formative impulse' is an attempt to structure those regions of the investigator's psyche which defy structuration: lust, hatred, and rage.[38] The binary of art versus reality is thus reversed in revenge stories, for art can only approximate the reality of consuming emotional turmoil.

This characterization already implies the logical conclusion of the cynical narrative strategy in the hard-boiled narrative: the disappearance of the detective's moral code and the increasing loss of narrative's power to make sense of self and the world. We see this tactic at work in, for example, A.J. Holt's *Watch Me* (1995), which culminates in the metamorphosis of a female FBI computer expert into a serial killer, shorn of her career, identity, and beliefs:

Somewhere between Albuquerque and here, Jay Fletcher had disappeared ... You couldn't be Jay Fletcher anymore; you just couldn't. Mom was a tattoo on Jeffrey Dahmer's arm and Apple Pie was something you used as a sex aid. Nothing worked now; the world was running on empty ...
The center cannot hold.
And here she was, right at that center, a stranger.
The center cannot hold.
She turned away from the mirror; afraid that she would have to give herself a name. Give what she was doing a name. It felt as though she was spinning off into space, everything that she had been, was, or ever could be falling away like the scraps of her own hair on the cold tiles of the bathroom floor. (478)

One of the prime functions of the investigator's moral code is to draw a boundary between what is (still) permitted and what is absolutely forbidden. This line is important for, as the example illustrates, breaking the ultimate limit set by the code breaks the investigator's sense of self. This shattering effect stems from the subject's confrontation with what she thought she could never have believed, desired, or done, leading to the realization that she no longer can be what she hoped to be, or what she thought she was. In extreme cases, such as Jay Fletcher's in this example, there is no vocabulary in which she could still tell a coherent story about herself (see Žižek 1992, 162). But the investigator's experience of the loss of self, leading to decentred emptiness, is not, of course, enough to characterize the cynical tactic, which addresses primarily the narrator's attitude. Not unlike the Rendellian narrator, Holt's narrator evokes various frameworks against which the violence of the protagonist and her serial-killer opponents may be related; these include a childhood in a sadistic Catholic orphanage, sexual abuse, rape, the Vietnam war, and the all-embracing corruption of American society. Yet the striking feature of the narrator's handling of this material is that, while ostensibly explaining the characters' motives (Jay Fletcher wants revenge because she was raped as a teenager and nobody cared), it does not, and is not even meant to, explain anything. Instead, these details function as a conventional background to the depiction of various murders, committed because '[s]ome, a few were simply addicted to killing ... They did it because it felt good, gave them pleasure' (486).

The ethical view of life expressed in the hard-boiled narrative has its basis in moral murkiness, which is reflected in different ways in the game of make-believe and the author-reader game. The violent game of investigation tarnishes the investigator; the reader ponders the quality of this figure's ethos by observing his (or her) choices and actions. The framework of (first-person) narration adds a further layer to the ethos under the reader's scrutiny. That the range of moral murkiness extends from limited moral infringements to a wholesale endorsement of wickedness indicates that we cannot attach the ethical view of life to any particular moral position; instead, we know the broad contours where we as readers can expect it to settle in an individual narrative. A similar openness characterizes the function of narration, which engages the reader in the narrator's personal reasons for telling his or her own story. Again, we are familiar with this motive of self-realization, but what specific 'formative impulse' it illustrates remains for the reader to decide on a case-by-case basis. The game's 'logic' derives, nevertheless, from the reader's fitting together of the investigator's and the narrator's levels of experience.[39]

Although the ethical view of life of the hard-boiled detective story does not settle in any particular moral position, we may nevertheless note that both the game of make-believe and the author-reader game, by laying such great stress on the *individual*, rely on at least one stable value. In this sense, the ethical view may be said to be linked with a traditional American ideological heritage. The plot is patterned as a search for self-fulfilment by the characters, as all seek their own private good; their clashing interests result in crimes. In an atmosphere of mutual distrust, the investigator needs to be self-reliant and self-sufficient. In a context of institutional corruption crime is treated as an individual affair. Narration is a means of self-realization, self-recovery, or self-justification, conveying the vision of a single person. The reader is preoccupied with the evaluation of individuals as acting agents and as narrators. The result is a narrative form which, either nostalgically or critically, treats the facets of individualism without being able even to envisage, let alone move on to, other options.

6

The Anatomy of Good and Evil in Agatha Christie

'I want you to think of this place as a stage set' (175) Miss Marple advises the other characters in *They Do It with Mirrors* (1971), suggesting they give thought to 'what exactly is *behind* the scene' (176). She thereby points to the central organizing image of the *theatre* in Christie's work, for everyone plays roles in this author's world.[1] Her characters resemble a theatrical company, comprising a dramatis personae of such stock social and comic types as the tyrannical landholder, the English rose, the siren-with-a-past, the army colonel, the secretary-companion, the endearing rascal, and so on. The Shakespearean notion that 'all the world's a stage' has a literal meaning in her books, for her various settings serve as the staging for plays of impersonation, which make deception, intrigue, and crime possible. What enhances this sense of theatre is the closed nature of her typical settings: the manor house, the country village, the fashionable city dwelling, the holiday resort, the exclusive girls' school, or the train. All the physical objects are props in this theatre; the stage has a stable design with the scene of the crime occupying the centre, while the other locations are arranged around it like structures marking the borders of a discrete world. The whodunit depicts a world of exclusion where only the upper and middle echelons of society are allowed, which works to impose a certain order on reality, and which then becomes indistinguishable from this supposed order. Critics refer to the plays staged in these restricted milieus as either comedies of manners in the country-house tradition (Grella 1988a; Priestman 1990, ch. 9), (comic) fairy tales (Bargainnier 1980, 5; Maida and Spornick 1982, 34–5), or Everyman morality tales (Wagoner 1986, 37).

Miss Marple points out that in this world *impersonation* or *the playing of roles* – the pretence of being someone other than one is – avails itself of 'conjuring tricks,' as when 'they do it with mirrors' so that it 'looks like one person and is really two' (175, 176). While the image of the theatre as an organizing principle indicates that Christie's characters love role playing, the comparison to magical tricks suggests that there is something underhanded and unethical about such imitation. Indeed, the frequent occurrence of murder, its cunning execution, and the mystery of the criminal's identity testify that at least some characters use role playing for criminal ends. At the beginning of the investigation it seems either that no one can be guilty (and a wandering maniac did it) or that everyone is guilty, which casts a strong doubt on whether anyone is what he claims to be. At times, even the victim turns out to be someone other than who he or she was assumed to be.[2] Murder rocks the status quo because it destroys the community's ability to draw clear distinctions among its members – that is, to determine, who has what role and position in the social setup. A primary function of the investigation is to re-establish the communal ability to differentiate, and it achieves this goal through a general unmasking of all those who pose as what they are not. Ironically, in order to bring about the disclosure of such imitators, Christie's detectives often feel compelled to follow the criminal's lead in assuming a false role. Thus, the same method that caused the communal illness is used to cure it.

Whatever their specific aim, impersonators always play on notions of *sameness and difference* in trying to convince others that they are the *same* as the role they emulate and, therefore, *distinctly different from* what they in actual fact are. The term 'role playing' suggests that the impersonators have a *model* in mind which serves for them as the guiding example of how to be a certain kind of person. This model may be a culturally familiar stereotype or even a particular person in the impersonators' vicinity. Miss Marple draws her listeners' attention to the similarity between role playing and magic tricks done with mirrors, for both involve *manipulated doubling*. She thereby refers to another key image Christie uses to describe her theatre. In fostering the illusion that they *are* the models they emulate, impersonators rely on the reversal-into-the-opposite mechanism characterizing the mirror image. As their goals are either shady or downright evil, they must calculate what type of role would let them pursue these goals without raising the suspicions of others. Often the safest strategy seems to involve playing the direct opposite of the role one would like to have: in effect, imitating one's own (antithetical) mirror image. The mirror imagery thus functions as a *mise-en-abyme* within Christie's theatre.

The general proliferation of role playing implies that there must be something in Christie's world encouraging duplicity, for, as Hercule Poirot remarks, 'you can only develop a thing of which the seed is already present' (*Curtain* [1977], 173). This seed derives from the double nature of human consciousness, which the author, not surprisingly, codes as the inherent tension between good and bad. But the active 'developing' of this seed is tied up with contexts calling forth rivalry among the members of the community. Situations continually arise in which their desires and goals clash, enticing a large number of characters to resort to impersonation in order to ensure that they, at least, will get what they want. Such an epidemic of impersonation threatens to abolish the community's sense of the roles its members rightfully play and the positions they properly occupy. This epidemic erupts into murder, at which point the detective's task of re-creating the needed conditions for differentiation begins. Role playing thus frequently presents a moral dilemma in the whodunit world: '[t]he question is, are these people themselves, or are they somebody else?' (*After the Funeral* [1956a], 184). Because the order of the world depicted depends on careful differentiation, that order is constantly threatened by a pull towards sameness. It cannot, for example, tolerate many people who have the same social role and the status associated with it. The tension between the (assumed) necessity of differentiation and the simultaneous fascination with sameness implies, in turn, that the moral complications involved in playing arise from a confusion about the distribution of *moral binaries* among characters. By changing their own appearance and often that of others as well, impersonators try to impose a false and deceptive pattern on reality, one that shows them as innocent and someone else as the guilty party.[3] Given the shady goals underlying impersonation, this practice may be characterized as a play with such conventional pairings as good versus bad, innocence versus guilt, right versus wrong, order versus chaos, rationality versus irrationality, and so on.

In patterning the various binary oppositions among set character figures, the detective narrative typically uses numerical/geometrical structures made up of *doubles*, *triangles*, and *quadrangles* in order to portray the *interactional relations* obtaining among them. Each structure, as Irwin (1994, 2–8) shows, involves mutually reflective mirror relationships. Doubling is involved in the antagonistic opposition between the detective and the criminal, turning each into the antithetical double of the other. Doubling also serves as the common method of apprehending the criminal through the detective's re-creation of the criminal's thought processes so as to anticipate the criminal's next move and end up one jump ahead of him or her. It is possible, however, that the positional difference of these set figures is the sole distinguishing criterion between agents who may in every other respect be similar. The canonical example of doubling based on fundamental similarity is, of course, the relationship between C. Auguste Dupin and Minister D— in Poe's 'The Purloined Letter.' That fictional detectives may outwit their opponents because their minds are so much alike suggests immediately that their supposed black-and-white dichotomy might not be so simple after all.

The triangle with its three positional slots describes the interactive, communal field within which detective-story crimes take place.[4] This pattern is also based on doubling, for each of the three positions functions as one pole of a mutually constitutive opposition with one of the other positions: thus, each position is subject to being reversed into its opposite (Irwin 1994, 6). The introduction of a third term, however, serves to complicate the distribution of moral characteristics: we can have a structure in which the set characters represent three different terms, such as good, neutral (or a combination of good and bad), and bad. The most obvious character triangle consists of the victim, the criminal, and the detective, but other triangles are typical as well, such as that made up of the criminal, the police, and the private detective. Moreover, a triangle may consist of a structure in which one *term* of a binary pair is doubled, as when one character standing for the good is opposed by two characters representing the bad. It is worth noting that in this situation there is some significant distinction between the doubled characters, so that the binary term (e.g., bad) which they represent is made internally more specific in one way or another. Obviously, this feature introduces an enrichment of the moral configuration. The most typical example is the triangular relationship among the victim, the criminal, and the scapegoat (with the last two as the doubled pair).

The quadrangular structure has significance in describing interactive patterns, for it stands for those configurations in which one of the *roles* is doubled, such as, for example, a crime involving two accomplices, a victim, and a scapegoat.[5] If the quadrangle is thought of as being constituted by two opposing triangles, each the mirror-image of the other, we see that each position functions as a mutually constitutive opposition with one of the three other positions, and is thus subject to being reversed into its two opposites. The quadrangle's special character is based on the fact that characters, most often the culprits, try to represent a quadrangular pattern as a triangular one, because success may depend on hiding the doubling of one of the roles.

The examination of these geometrical generic patterns has so far been mainly confined to the metaphysical detective narrative (Derrida 1988; Irwin 1994; Johnson 1988; Lacan 1988), where they have been treated as figurations of self-consciousness and the act of (self-)analysis. This subgenre's preoccupation with the self shows clearly in the blurring and collapsing of the central roles of detective, criminal, and victim into two or even just one, an act which explicitly shows the splitting/doubling linking these roles (Merivale 1968 and 1997b). Given the fact that splitting/doubling involves a play with moral binaries, the strategy of making either one character (or two characters who are essentially one) enact all these roles may be said to include an ethical dimension, for it effectively demonstrates the play of these moral binaries *within* the self. Although we can find these geometrical patterns in the whodunit as well, they supposedly serve a different thematic function there. The whodunit is generally thought to distribute moral binaries in such a way that the detective represents the good and its derivatives (the master terms), while the criminal embodies the pole of evil (the slave terms) (see, e.g., Eco 1979; Grella 1988a; Porter 1981, 94–6). By keeping the set roles apart, this particular subgenre presumably *externalizes* evil and guilt by locating it solely in the criminal, whose unmasking and expulsion exonerate the fictional community. Thereby, maintains Žižek, the conclusion victimizes the criminal by turning this figure into a scapegoat carrying the weight of collective guilt – including the reader's own morally ambiguous desire to indulge in narratives dealing with murder and its investigation (Žižek 1991; see also Heissenbüttel 1983).

In what follows, I examine the interactional relations, initiated and sustained by plot, among the set characters of detective fiction by observing the kinds of geometrical, mutually reflective constellations they form. In order to highlight the organizing force of the geometrical structures, I frequently draw the patterns they form. In so doing, I am particularly interested in the moral positions the set characters are made to symbolize through their interaction. In using John T. Irwin's analysis of the metaphysical detective story in his magisterial *The Mystery to a Solution: Poe, Borges, and the Analytical Detective Story* (1994) as my aid, I am deflecting his examination back on to classical detective fiction. What does the ethical view of life of this earlier subgenre look like when it is reflected against the background of its newer highbrow relative? The work of

Agatha Christie will function as a synecdochal example of the who-dunit.[6] Is there something like a system to Christie's patterning of moral binaries that draws the boundaries of her world? In examining her work, I first concentrate on the analysis of the geometrical patterns from the criminal's perspective in order to show how good and bad interact through the committing of a crime. If the criminal functions as the reversed mirror-image of victims, scapegoats, and detectives, then this angle promises to elucidate a process that starts with the acknowledgment of similarity, but ends up rejecting it, opting, instead, for careful differentiation among positions and players. After looking at the functions of the criminal and the community, I discuss the detective's communal role.

My analysis concludes with a consideration of the author's and read-er's roles, for, as Irwin suggests, the generic character roles serve as masks which in turn are counters in the battle of wits between these two contestants (1994, 386). While the reader can only indirectly play a role, in the theatrical sense, through the characters, Miss Marple's description of the *theatre-goer's* position provides a clue as to what we should take into account while reading: 'You're here in the audience looking at the people on the stage. Mrs Serrocold and myself and Mrs Strete, and Gina and Stephen – and just like on the stage there are entrances and exits and the characters go out to different places. Only you don't think when you're in the audience where they are really going to. They go out "to the front door" or "to the kitchen" and when the door opens you see a little bit of painted backcloth' (175–6). By singling out the double structure of stage and backstage, Miss Marple alludes to the reader's task of envisaging the world of Christie's whodunits. Knight (1980, 110–13) and Priestman (1990, 152–4) argue that the creation of this sense is the author's primary purpose. The reader's forgetfulness of the existence of the backstage is what makes detecting the criminal difficult; but it is the comparison of this world to the theatre which makes the reading experience highly ambiguous from the moral perspective. Priestman puts his finger on the source of this ambiguity by remarking that Christie's attraction stems from 'her instinctive ability to express two aspects of this facade-structure simultaneously: the notion of a community, even a home, to be run with dedication and efficiency; and the simultaneous knowledge that the dedication is to a morally empty world' (153). This self-reflexive awareness that the theatre with its make-believe and dramatic masks is all there is raises doubts about the (assumed) ethical stability of the reader's position. How effectively does the narrator insulate us from the criminal's infectious influence?

Geometrical Patterns in *Evil under the Sun*

As teenager Linda Marshall examines herself in a mirror, her thoughts wander to her new stepmother, calling forth '[a] big dark burning wave of hatred against Arlena' (20), and making her think she could kill Arlena. During Linda's musings, the mirror shows her a new, totally alien side of herself: she is faced with her evil double.[7] This new experience stems from her interaction with Arlena, whose contemptuously amused glance also serves as a mirror, making Linda see herself as a clumsy, ugly, immature, and insignificant teenager. Linda's deep resentment is shared by Christine Redfern, whose husband is madly in love with Arlena Marshall. The two adult women form an antithetical pair: Arlena is vivacious and extraordinarily beautiful with a deep tan and flaming red hair, while Christine is mousy and anaemically pretty with extremely white skin and ash-blond hair. Their respective spouses constitute another pair of doubles, with Kenneth Marshall representing the cuckold and Patrick Redfern the unfaithful husband. Add yet another woman to the mix, the dark-haired Rosamund Darnley, a pleasant-looking woman with a strong attraction to Kenneth Marshall, and we have the tension-filled opening situation of *Evil under the Sun* (1941), 'the classic Christie marital triangle plot set in a West Country seaside resort, with a particular play on the alikeness of sunbathing bodies, and dead ones' (Barnard 1980, 139).

As the biblical allusion of the book's title indicates, evil 'walks the earth' (10), challenging the small company of seaside guests, Hercule Poirot, and the reader to assess the manifold mirror relationships in order to perceive how, exactly, moral binaries are distributed among characters. Or, 'one sorts the colours' (137), by noting the seemingly clear differences between the good woman (whose first name contains an allusion not only to Christ but also to Christie herself) and the bad woman; the cuckolded husband and the betraying husband; and the dominating stepmother (Arlena) and the downtrodden stepchild (Linda). The reader may note, however, that the oppositions are not coded in the usual terms of black versus white, but as the conflict between red ('the Scarlet Woman' or 'the whore of Babylon') and white, with emphasis on red as the colour of the devil (146). But what complicates the reader's endeavour to sort out colours is that there are features suggesting underlying similarities between the supposed opposites as well. All female characters, for example, are united by the colour red: Arlena and Linda have red hair, while the names *Red*fern and *Rosa*mund also allude to it.

Christine and Rosamund are linked with one another through the colour white, as Christine's natural colour and Rosamund's professional alias, Rose *Mond* ('moon' in German), refer to the white associated with the moon. Moreover, Arlena's white bathing suit figures centrally in the crime. Because each woman combines red and white, this suggests that the reader must sort out the colours by tracing what qualities are associated with them and by establishing their morally proper blending. In other words, we need to introduce difference into sameness by finding suitable distinguishing criteria for doing so.

It is useful to sketch the marital triangle expressing the opening situation in order to see how the author codes the moral qualities associated with each of its nodes. This coding is important, because it shows the kinds of moral terms Christie uses to describe crime in the communal life she depicts. To spot the appropriate terms, we simply take our cue from the characters and the narrator. The opening of the novel displays a scene on the beach, with characters offering observations of one another. The first appearance of Arlena Marshall supplies two significant clues, for she is described as someone who 'looks rather a beast' and as 'a personification of evil' (11), a characterization that is a little later on repeated by alluding to her as 'a man-eating tiger' (19) who is 'bad' (20). Poirot even denies her human nature altogether, thinking of her face as that of a 'sleek happy cat – it was animal, not human' (37). This portrayal suggests that the combination of animal and evil forms one pole of pertinent moral binaries, which is further reinforced by the description of the suffering wife as 'the kind that thinks that mind has a pull over matter' (19), and by implication, as someone who thinks and who is therefore human and good. By introducing the opposition of human versus animal as well as that between mind and body, interlaced with the opposition of good versus bad, Christie employs the typical generic strategy of associating evil with animality. We remember that in Poe's first detective story, 'Murders in the Rue Morgue,' the murder was committed by an animal. Irwin maintains that this relationship has significance for Poe's project of analysing reflexive self-consciousness as part of the larger task of differentiating 'man from animal by defining the essentially "human" (i.e., mental, self-conscious) element in man as opposed to the animal (bodily) element' (65–6). Christie parts ways with the metaphysical (or analytic) detective story by employing these terms first and foremost to depict a *social* or *communal* configuration. But the detective's (and the reader's) task remains the same as with Poe: to restore (or to evaluate) the proper relationship between mind and body. Figure 6.1 shows the initial situation of the novel with its marital triangle.

Femme Fatale (body)

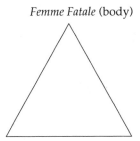

Unfaithful Husband (body/mind)   Suffering Wife (mind)

FIGURE 6.1   Initial Marital Triangle

Representing the animal, the alluring *femme fatale* (Arlena Marshall) epitomizes stupidity (characters remark that she has no brains [69]), as well as cruelty. With instinct overruling reason, the body directing the mind, she is without moral sense, an embodiment of animality, and is thus by nature incapable of marital fidelity. Consequently, this figure would seem to symbolize the destructive reversal of the proper relationship between mind and body in the human being. The suffering and betrayed wife (Christine Redfern) appears to represent the *femme fatale's* reversed mirror opposite, who not only has brains but is also courageous, resolute, loyal, and devoted. Christie uses this contrast to suggest the dominance of the white of reason over the red of instinct. (Red is, after all, the colour of blood.) The betraying husband (Patrick Redfern) is a combination of these qualities, for in him the animal side has momentarily taken hold of the human side. Through comparing this figure to a dog, the narrator, nevertheless, emphasizes that he is capable of a moral quality Christie prizes in humans: loyalty (47, 49, 77, 97). On the basis of other characters' remarks, it seems that the fluctuation between animal and human is especially typical of men, for they are easily allured by spectacular beauty, but eventually return faithfully to their (less beautiful) spouses.

What complicates this configuration is that the evil, man-eating tiger actually turns out to be the victim. Her body is found on a ledge in front of Pixy's Cove, a cave which is the heart of a labyrinthlike rock formation. She has been strangled, which provides a further link with Poe's legacy, for this method of assault is a variation of the severing of Mme L'Espanaye's head from her body in 'Murders in the Rue Morgue' (1944a), alluding, of course, to the separation of a higher portion (head) from the lower (body). Moreover, Christie's victim is forced to hide *in* the heart of the rock-labyrinth shortly before her death: probably a reference to the Minotaur (another man-eater with an animal head and human torso), a significant symbol of the destructive reversal of mind and body in the analytic detective story.[8] The same master/slave reversal characterizes the manlike killer in Poe's first detective story (Irwin, 197–8). As Christie's victim is like Poe's criminal, Christie seems to invert Poe's strategy by starting from the very point where Poe ended: the revelation of the destructive reversal where instinct takes over from reason. In both instances, the cause of crime is described through mirror imagery. In Poe, the owner's discovery of his ape attempting to shave itself in front of a mirror sends the ape on its disastrous flight, whereas Christie's victim is said to exist only 'in the light of a man's admiration' (72). The crucial difference between the two writers shows that Christie is not as self-reflexively cunning as she first seems, for Poe uses antithetical doubling to examine questions of self-reflection, while Christie employs it to structure a communal configuration. The author teases the reader by making the victim seem at first a criminal of sorts, thereby indicating to her that the real 'Minotaur' must also be masquerading as someone else. But she is also implying something else: namely, the need to make distinctions within the notion of animality itself. Finally, she makes the victim's inhumanity serve her communal perspective by emphasizing how the community must defend the humanity of each and every victim, even if morally bad.

The whodunit tradition actually encourages making the victim unpleasant, for, as Grella (1988a, 96–7) points out, it rejects emotional identification with this figure by imbuing him or her with some *moral* flaw. Often the victim is either a blocking figure (the tyrannical spouse or parent) or someone who openly enjoys his or her socially superior position. Thus, from the moral perspective the victim and the murderer share fundamental moral similarities (both are bad), while they are also different, thanks to the decisive positional difference between them (killer versus victim), which is usually further underlined through the revelation of some distinguishing (moral) criterion. Because the criminal frames reality in a deceptive manner through role playing, this crucial distinction is difficult to perceive. Žižek (1991, 54–6) draws attention to how the criminal imposes a 'loony' framework on reality, the purpose of which is to lure others to read falsely the intersubjective dimension of signification. 'The truth,' writes Žižek, 'lies not "beyond" the domain of deception, it lies in the "intention," in the intersubjective function of the very deception' (57).[9] In *Evil under the Sun*, the criminal first makes others think that an outsider killed the victim, but then makes the clues point to a particular person, the *scapegoat*.

If the victim and the murderer are similar in whodunits, so also are the murderer and the scapegoat, for the latter must appear to have a plausible motive (i.e., 'the seed already present') for committing the crime in order to function convincingly in this role.[10] Here is yet another relation of similarity into which the detective and the reader need to introduce difference in order to keep the roles apart. The scapegoat, Linda Marshall, 'sees red' in looking at her stepmother, vehemently resenting her; to make the stepmother die, she prepares a wax doll of her for voodoo practice, pricking the doll with needles. The false framework the criminal imposes on reality yields a scene in which 'a trapped animal' (143) kills another animal out of red-hot hatred, tinged with Oedipal jealousy. ('And Father at home – with Arlena there. All – all sort of bottled up and not – and not *there*' [20].) The scapegoat plays into the criminal's hands by trying to kill herself, leaving behind a letter of confession (100). Through the scapegoat, the criminal attempts to convey the sense that it is the purely animal and instinctual strain in the human being which accounts for the crime, constructing a situation in which the moral binaries stay intact and firmly separate. The white of reason seems to triumph over the red of animal ferocity, as it looks as though the crime were grounded on the absence of the human dimension.

As is only to be expected, the solution builds on a chain of reversals turning the initial situation into its opposite. The first concerns the comprehension of the initial situation, the marital triangle, which involves manipulation of inclusion and exclusion: the crime is based on deceiving others about who are 'inside,' by being paired with one another, and who is left outside. This kind of deception typically includes the *doubling* of the criminal's role, which is Christie's favourite trick.[11] It relies on the cooperation of a pair of accomplices – most often a man and a woman, as in *Evil under the Sun*, although pairs consisting of the same sex are also possible (father and son in *They Do It with Mirrors*; mother and daughter in *Murder on the Links* and in 'The Stymphalean Birds' [*The Labours of Hercules*]). *Evil under the Sun* demonstrates how this typical situation develops.[12] A pair of lovers choose a wealthy woman as their mutual victim. The man makes love to, or marries, this other woman, while the female accomplice plays the jilted and wronged lover. The intention is to make the actual insider look like an outsider, which directs sympathy towards this person.[13]

How does the revelation of the truth change our conception of the original marital triangle? The recoding of the nodes of this triangle shows how Christie differentiates between kinds of evil. The victim (Arlena) driven by purely animal instincts is opposed by a female double (Christine) characterized by qualities associated with the mind; on closer scrutiny, she also turns out to have an animal side to her, but one which she has carefully concealed. She advertises her learning to others by letting them know that she is a teacher; however, the ending reveals that she teaches *sports* and is 'agile like a cat' (171). The colour white associated with her is further specified by such qualities as 'not one who sees red' (75), 'not passionate' (67), and 'cold blooded and cruel' (175). The surprise inversion occurs, however, when her former alias, Christine[14] Deverill, is disclosed, for it shows that her whiteness actually conceals the Scarlet Woman. The devilishness of this figure has to do with her forcing her reason to serve the ends of bestiality. The good is made to bow to, and further the cause of, the bad, through the use of reason. This characterization applies more generally not only to Christie but also to the whole whodunit tradition, which repeatedly emphasizes the cleverness of the criminal. The root of evil resides neither in murderous desire nor even in violent acts, but in the criminal's subjection of the faculty of reason to the service of (pure) bestiality, the aims of which will always remain antithetical to human morality. The criminals are reprehensible because of their misuse and waste of their unique human inheritance. Notice that the male accomplice continues to represent a 'diluted' version of his female counterpart, being incapable of controlling his bestiality by his reason to the same degree as his female accomplice. As might be expected, he is the weak link who eventually 'loses his head completely' (179), becoming 'transformed, suffused with blood, blind with rage' and revealing 'the face of a killer – of a tiger' (168).

The female criminal's former alias, *Christine Deverill*, suggests, however, that good and bad may coexist in this figure. Indeed, she embodies many features Christie holds as morally admirable, such as intelligence, courage, and loyalty and devotion in love. The author's criminals are very seldom embodiments of evil, which is to say that the distinction between good and bad in her world is not a matter of separate and intact binaries, but a matter of the appropriate combination and hierarchy of both qualities within a single figure. The disruptiveness of crime derives from the fact that it seriously threatens the community's ability to distinguish what hierarchical combination is appropriate. The central mistake of the criminals, leading to the uncovering of their guilt, stems from their imperfect understanding of the mirror mechanism they exploit in committing their crimes. The error arises from forgetting that the mirror image involves not only doubling, but also *splitting*. In another Christie book, Poirot gives an insightful description of this flaw which finally betrays, in one way or another, the impersonating criminal. Addressing the criminal, he says:

But mannerisms are remembered, and Cora [the victim] had certain very definite mannerisms, all of which you had practised carefully before the glass. And it was there, strangely enough, that you made your first mistake. *You forgot that a mirror image is reversed.* When you saw in the glass the perfect reproduction of Cora's bird-like sidewise tilt of the head, you didn't realize that it was actually *the wrong way round*. You saw, let us say, Cora inclining her head to the *right* – but you forgot that actually your own head was inclined to the *left* to produce that effect *in the glass*. (*After the Funeral* [1956a], 187)

Being dominated by the slave terms of a dichotomy, Christie's criminals think that those governed by their master terms are their 'simple' antithetical doubles, constituted solely by these master terms. Thus, the criminals choose a role directly opposite to what they are: the enemy plays the best friend, the poisoner plays the trusted family doctor. But criminals fail to remember that the role or the person they emulate is actually constituted by two sides, with the inner organization of this role being the reversed version of that organization obtaining within themselves. It is as if the culprits believed that good is the simple absence of evil, whereas with Christie the good as demonstrated in and by a human being always involves the proper hierarchy of these qualities. This view derives from her belief in a theological explanation of original sin as the primary cause of evil, in accordance with which she clearly thinks that a human being can never overcome her animal side, but should learn to control and live with it.

In considering the final fixing of the moral configuration in *Evil under the Sun*, we can specify Christie's conception of the appropriate combination of antithetical traits in the human being by looking at the quadrangle consisting of the four female figures[15] of the victim (Arlena Marshall), the beast-murderess (Christine Redfern), the scapegoat (Linda Marshall), and the new queen (Rosamund Darnley), who serves as the sign of restored order (see Figure 6.2).[16]

This pattern describing the moral relationships among the figures is formed by two opposing triads functioning as mirror images of one another (cf Irwin, 42). The triad of animal queen, beast, and scapegoat has

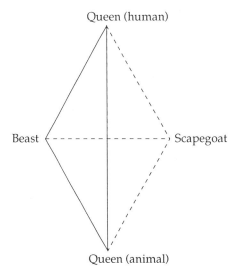

Queen (human)

Beast

Scapegoat

Queen (animal)

FIGURE 6.2   The Moral Configuration of the Conclusion

the following significance: as the queen of the beasts, the tiger is the master in relation to other female felines, but a slave in relation to the human master, the scapegoat. The scapegoat is set apart from pure bestiality through having a *conscience*, which enables a *sense of guilt*. Both these features stand as signs of the human being's, but also the community's, basic capacity for reflection about good and evil that involves the notion of taking responsibility for one's acts. But the community treats the human scapegoat like an animal, as the 'slave' who serves the community's shared need of purification from guilt. In *Evil under the Sun*, the scapegoat, described as 'a colt' (19), 'a gazelle' (145), and 'a trapped animal' (143), confesses to a murder she did not commit, because she suffers from guilt at having actively harboured hatred against the victim. She thus accepts responsibility for feelings shared by her community, but from which the community shields itself. An additional reason is her wish to protect her father from suspicion, showing her willingness for self-sacrifice. Through this figure Christie shows a young person in the transitional stage, caught, for the first time, between her animal instincts and her moral awareness of the need to curb them and keep them in check. Finally, the role of the human queen represents the elevation of the human over both the animal in the human being (the scapegoat) and the animal world (the beast). The human queen embodies the proper hierarchy of the two sides, with reason and mind directing the body. This pattern has a diamond shape, for the addition of the fourth figure, the animal double of the human queen, turns the triangle on its head to produce an inverted mirror image. Since the false queen, represented by Christine Redfern, tries to take over the position of the true queen by exercising the ultimate form of animal mastery (murder) over another human being, her accession to the queen's role involves, in effect, her reversal into the role of the beast.

In interpreting this pattern, we need to note the difference between this diagram and the similar one typical of the metaphysical detective story. Irwin draws a similar pattern for Borges's short story 'Ibn Hakkan al-Bokhari, Dead in His Labyrinth' (1978). In this story, King Ibn Hakkan is killed by his cousin Zaid, who, by assuming the dead man's identity, literally doubles his victim. Again, the emphasis is on the self's relation to itself. Christie's communal emphasis comes through her use of the generic royalist terms (as introduced by Poe in 'The Purloined Letter') to exemplify social order. The victim poses as the rightful queen (the representative of social order) without truly being one, whereas the female criminal tries to instal herself in this position, although her ethos, too, is unsuitable. Only the ending establishes who the character with the right moral qualities is. In this instance, she is a combination of the colours black, white, and red. We can link this colour combination to the black, white, and red transformation process familiar from alchemy as the sign of the union of opposites.[17] This process starts with blackening, symbolizing the animal in the human being, goes on to whitening, representing purification, and ends up in reddening, the mystical conjunction of opposites (Irwin, 52–5). In the figure of the new queen, Christie emphasizes the mastery of mind over body without, however, rejecting the body altogether: black, white, and red coexist harmoniously, although hierarchically. In her thinking, the acceptance of the animal within the human is necessary for human well-being.

Being the locus of social mastery, the position at the apex of the diamond shape is subject to interpersonal rivalry. The rightful occupant of the position at the top is established through the love story Christie – like other whodunit writers – typically interweaves into the crime plot, the purpose of which is to illustrate the suitable proportion and relative positioning of the two sides of the human being. As in traditional comedies, the love interest is tied up with the reinstatement of order, which becomes possible through the solving of the crime. But in keeping with the comic legacy, the lovers, variations of the King and Queen figures, must first prove their worth as the representatives of the proper (ethical) standing of things. The names of these particular lovers – Kenneth *Marshall* and *Rosa*mund *Darn*ley (alias *Rosa Mond*) – support their status as representatives of the restored order. According to *The Concise Oxford Dictionary of Current English*, to 'marshal' is to arrange in systematic order, guide ceremonially, or arrange in order of priority, meanings which all point to the notion of social order as the careful arrangement of sets of hierarchies. The marshal usually arranges in order the members of, for example, a parade. In addition, the marshal is, of course, a law-enforcement officer in certain countries. In Christie's novel, all of these connotations suggest that Kenneth Marshall serves as a kind of king figure. The female counterpart's name refers not only to the traditional representative of the (white) moon, married to the sun-King, but also to the repairing function – of 'darning' – that the marriage of the king and queen has in the social fabric.[18] The love story is important for Christie, because she uses the union of the lovers as the conventional symbol of the reconciliation of mind and body, a restoration of wholeness by means of a union of male and female, which also functions as the reproduction, on the individual level, of the proper standing of the whole social order as well.

The reconciliation between the two sides of the human being with which Christie usually ends her narratives shows that it is part of what she holds to be ethically commendable. This state, however, is constantly threatened by disruption. Somewhat paradoxically, by ending on the notion of order, she shows why its upkeep is an almost impossible task. By looking further at the patterns of interaction within her social fabric, we see how the pull towards crime is built into those very patterns. Like Poe, Christie is engaged in setting the human (good) apart not only from animality (inhumanity) but also from godliness (superhumanity); we next examine what distinctions among these realms she makes in order for the moral system of her world to function.

Desiring That Which Others Desire

Christie's criminals are usually one step down the social ladder from their primary victims. Being down only one notch is important, as they must be able to frequent the same social spheres as their victims. This subordinate position suggests that the relationship between the criminal and the victim is structured as the slave's attempt to topple the master. Their striving for ascendancy demonstrates that Christie's criminals transgress in order to be and have *more* than their own station of life permits.

The author repeatedly employs three different sets of images for describing the *more* her criminals attempt to achieve through crime. These images express a conception of the self's position within the social fabric that relates to the differentiation between the human and the godly. In the first example, the criminal explains what initially moved him to crime, revealing a typical fantasy criminals have of the self's social position by using the royalist imagery with which we are already familiar:

I wish I could make you understand about my meeting with Rebecca [the heiress] and my marriage. Gerda [the first wife] understood. The only way I can put it is that it was like Royalty. I had the chance of marrying a Queen and playing the part of Prince Consort or even King. I looked on my marriage to Gerda as morganatic. (*One, Two, Buckle My Shoe* [1940], 244)

In the two following excerpts, the criminal's fantasy of the self is described in terms of religious imagery, especially the antagonism between God and Satan.

'He wanted,' said the Bishop, 'to be God.' (*They Do It with Mirrors* [1971], 182)

He'd gone mad on creation ... He said to me, laughing – 'Get thee beyond me, Satan. Go and join your police friends.' And I knew then, quite certainly. *It was the other way round.* I said to myself: 'I am leaving *you behind* me, Satan.' A Satan young and beautiful as Lucifer can appear to mortals ... (*Hallowe'en Party* [1970], 187)

The third set of terms we typically find in Christie's work depicts the criminal's ideal self-concept in narcissistic terms:

Josephine and only Josephine fitted in with all the necessary qualifications. Her vanity, her persistent self-importance, her delight in talking, her reiteration of how clever *she* was, and how stupid the police were ... She had been Leonides' grandchild, she had resembled him in brain and cunning – but where his love had gone outwards to family and friends, hers had turned inward to herself. (*Crooked House* [1959a], 186, 188)

As for love – he loved only himself. He was Narcissus. (*Hallowe'en Party* [1970], 185)

These three sets of images suggest the kinds of slave terms indicating moral binaries that Christie uses to describe the criminal: the moral derivatives associated with the usurpation of royal power, with Satan-Lucifer's usurpation of divine power, and with the self-centred solipsism of Narcissus. Whether conceived of in terms of celestial or secular authority or the total mastery and self-sufficiency of the self, her criminals are always engaged in efforts to extend their reach. In *Evil under the Sun*, this striving is aptly described as 'having a head for heights'; the criminals boldly and without giddiness imagine themselves as being at least a head higher than they are. The criminals are thus conventional overreacher figures like Marlowe's Dr Faustus, whose hubris likewise tends to be followed by nemesis. We can elucidate the *more* Christie's characters hanker after as ultimately involving the search for the *transcendence of self* or, in cases of revenge, a vindication of their own self-concept.[19] Underneath lies the fantasy of an autonomous and omnipotent self always having everything its own way. Simultaneously, this fantasy involves the notion of metaphysical autonomy, with the human being replacing God. Such a self *needs* the hierarchical social fabric with its distinctions and differences, because these discriminations make its magnificence and dazzling supremacy visible to others.

These images give us valuable clues as to how Christie interlaces the mind/body distinction with associations of animality (inhumanity) and 'godliness,' perhaps more fittingly characterized as 'superhumanity.'[20] Given that the act of murder can be characterized as the ultimate form of animal mastery over another person (Irwin, 41), then the criminals' wicked but extremely clever use of reason in planning this act reveals that they see themselves as 'supermen' who have the right to stoop to the level of bestiality in order to reach higher planes. It is as if for them the human plane of existence were absent and the only direction available were upward; paradoxically, however, they move upward by first taking a plummeting detour downward. Moreover, as the prominent banker-criminal's explanation in the first excerpt suggests, many of Christie's criminals hold that the upward movement of their aspirations justifies their bestial act, for the very notion of being 'higher up' seems to go together with ethically approved qualities. Both these extreme poles are, of course, outside the morality recognized by the human community and are thus, in this sense, strongly similar. The figure of the criminal combines the worst qualities of both mind and body.

Viewed from Christie's communal perspective, the encouragement of these strands is clearly morally reprehensible. Human beings are not God and they are not meant to live in solipsistic self-enclosure. The human plane lies in the middle, being flanked by bestiality on one side and by godliness on the other. By emphasizing the communal nature of this plane, Christie characterizes it as one of interaction between fellow beings. But by insisting on the essentially *hierarchical* nature of this interaction, Christie embeds her world with the seeds of its own destruction. Its theatricality is directly tied up with interpersonal ranking, for nearly all the characters have to play various roles in order to fare well in this game. But in what way does impersonation betray the instability of Christie's moral system?

Criminals use role playing to ensure the realization of their transgressive goals. We can distinguish two basic variations for creating a dramatic mask that relate to the mirror image: the *manipulated character ethos* strategy and the *assimilative* or *metamorphic* strategy. What distinguishes the tactics from one another is that the manipulated character ethos aims at deceiving others about the impersonator's moral qualities, whereas the metamorphic strategy aims at deceiving others as to the criminal's identity, and only secondarily as to his or her moral qualities. The question of whether the characters are 'themselves or somebody else' can have two different, though related, answers, corresponding to the two problem types of the genre: the problem of character ethos, that is, whether a person is the *type* of person he or she claims to be; and the problem of identity, that is, whether a person is *who* he or she claims to be.[21]

Based on the reversal-into-the-opposite mechanism of the mirror image, both strategies include the idea of imitating a *model*, whether this model is conceived of as a stereotypical role (character ethos) or as a particular person (identity). As this model is opposite to the criminals' actual constitution (and/or goals), they try for a time to imitate their own mirror image. The choice of the role model and its imitation are directed by assumptions about the correspondence of the model's qualities with his or her social status: criminals try to convince others that the qualities of the model they emulate match the social status of this model.

The importance of such correspondence derives from the hierarchical nature of Christie's world, the structure of which is like a pyramid with only a privileged few at the top. Its pyramid structure suggests the notion of traditional royalism, with God as the ultimate source of power, the king and the queen as the earthly representatives of the celestial authority, and the different classes aligned under this earthly authority. In this scheme of things, the top social status is ideally coupled with the very best of (moral) qualities, because this position, embodied by those occupying it, serves as an inclusive *social model* for the general public of the proper way to lead one's life within a particular sociocultural context. [22] Reference to modelling builds on the Girardian idea that those occupying this top position exemplify one's proper relationship to oneself and the kinds of things that are worth pursuing within their culture. In other words, they model ways both of *being* and of *having*. Integral to this notion of modelling is a specific kind of mirror relationship, where one always uses another person as one's mirror, taking one's cue for being and having from this other. One looks at the other, observing how the other is and what kinds of things the other wants, and then emulates this model. Ideally, social order is based on carefully controlled reflecting relationships, where those at the top look up to God as their model, those immediately beneath the top look up to those looking up to God, and so on, down to the lowest social level. The ensuing harmony in such a rigidly hierarchical society may be described as being based on what René Girard calls *external mediation*, the channelling of desire along strictly regulated lines so that all individuals and the social classes they represent remain in their appointed places. He describes such mediation in the following fashion:

The stairs of Degree [cultural order] are not for climbing; each one is the equivalent of a little world inside the big one; all steps are connected from the top down, but they do not freely communicate on the way up. The people on the lower steps look up to the people above them and are likely to choose them as models, but in a purely ideal sense. They must select their concrete object of desire inside their own worlds, and rivalry is impossible. The imitators would prefer to select the objects of their models, but Degree prevents them from doing so. As long as it is vigorous, the transgression of its rules seems impossible, even unthinkable. (1991, 165)

This description no longer applies to the world Christie portrays, except as a longed-for but forever lost ideal, one which the detective's solution attempts in vain to restore. The stability of its order has been disrupted by the community's inability to prevent destructive rivalry among its members. The author depicts situations of widespread competition as the spur to actions that aim either at diminishing the distance between the model and the imitator or at maintaining the relation of inequality while reversing the roles to the imitator's own advantage. In looking up the social ladder, Christie's criminals see either obstacles or rivals standing between them and what they desire. They reason that, if it were not for the persons they cast as victims, they would already be and have what they aspire to. This attitude betrays the shift from external mediation to what Girard calls *internal mediation*, where the distance between models and imitators has greatly diminished. In Christie's world, criminal-imitators believe in the hierarchical superiority of the *position* occupied by the victim, but they refuse to acknowledge the victim's *personal* supremacy. It is this position together with its conventional trimmings that they desire. Furthermore, they no longer think that social advantage is permanent, but that it should be overcome if possible. With this belief in the impermanency of social and ethical positions, rivalry and violence enter the picture. Cultural order begins to crumble when members of a community attempt to seize office, position, or power independently of cultural rules and cultural tradition, a process which invariably starts from the top echelon of society, then spreads downward (Girard 1991, 164–5).

The refusal to accept the model's personal superiority is based on a changed conception of difference and sameness. In a world where order was based on external mediation, the imitator, in looking at the model located one notch above him or her in the social hierarchy, saw a person whose status and qualities he or she believed to be fundamentally differ-ent from his or her own. This assumed difference protected him or her from the temptation of rivalry, whereupon he or she adapted the model's qualities to fit his or her own sphere. In these reflexive relationships, the master/slave opposition remained intact, because the imitator-slave was granted the possibility of becoming a master(ful imitator) and hence a model of successful imitation within his or her own orbit. By contrast, in Christie's world changes in the sociocultural context have disrupted the kinds of (imaginary and arbitrary) social differences and barriers that formerly constituted the apparent stability of social order. The acquisitive individualism and upward mobility of Christie's world work to empha-size a contradictory message, based on the notion of the fundamental equality (sameness) of all people, while simultaneously a number of decisive but purely arbitrary distinctions are posited as setting them apart. In a world where individuals are no longer defined (solely) by the place they occupy by virtue of their birth or some other stable though arbitrary factor, the spirit of competition becomes increasingly inflamed; everything rests on comparisons that are necessarily unstable and inse-cure, since there are only a few fixed points of reference. Therefore, the idea of positional difference as the sign of these arbitrary distinctions and of personal supremacy remains, but few are willing to admit that some-one else's characteristics are actually a better fit for this position than their own. The author thus juggles between the ideology of rigid hierarchy, on the one hand, and the contradictory ideology of equality and competitive individualism, on the other. Consequently, there is a telling confusion in the social norms and systems of belief of her world, for these norms and systems promote hierarchical differentiation while simultaneously encouraging and promoting upward mobility – and then punishing it.

With the help of the following three excerpts we can probe further into the mirror relationship obtaining between the murderer and the victim. In the first, the criminal herself describes how she saw her victim:

'I knew it was a Vermeer. I *knew* it! *She* didn't know! Talking about Rembrandts and Italian Primitives and unable to recognize a Vermeer when it was under her nose! Always prating about Art – and really knowing nothing about it! She was a thoroughly stupid woman. Always maundering on about this place – about Enderby, and what they did there as children, and about Richard and Timothy and Laura and all the rest of them. Rolling in money always! Always the best of everything those children had!' (*After the Funeral* [1956a], 188–9)

The second excerpt demonstrates how other characters evaluate a friendship that has turned into deadly antagonism:

'Do you remember telling me, Charles, that Evans mentioned that Captain Trevelyan [the victim] used to send in solutions of competitions in [Burnaby's, i.e., the murderer's] name? [Trevelyan] thought Sittaford House too grand an address. Well – that's what he did in that Football Competition that you gave Major Burnaby five thousand pounds for. It was Captain Trevelyan's solution really, and he sent it in in Burnaby's name. No.1, The Cottages, Sittaford, sounded much better, he thought.' (*The Sittaford Mystery* [1956c], 196)

In the third excerpt Poirot explains to others the mental makeup of the murder victim:

'Let us, if we can, think ourselves into the mental condition of Mrs Boynton. A human creature born with immense ambition, with a yearning to dominate and to impress her personality on other people. She neither sublimated that intense craving for power – nor did she seek to master it – no, mesdames and messieurs, *she fed it* … And remember this, *Mrs. Boynton was not an ordinary blackmailer*. She did not want money. She wanted the pleasure of torturing her victim for a while and then she would have enjoyed revealing the truth in the most spectacular fashion!' (*Appointment with Death* [1946a], 184, 188)

The murderer's perspective as depicted by Christie resembles what Girard calls the *disciple's situation*, based as it is on a profound envy, the vexation and ill-will roused by considering another's success, or qualities, or some other feature, as well as the hostile longing to possess what is another's. Girard usefully elucidates the nature of envy by explaining that it 'subordinates a desired *something* to the *someone* who enjoys a privileged relationship with it. Envy covets the superior *being* that neither the someone nor something alone, but the conjunction of the two seems to possess. Envy involuntarily testifies to a lack of *being* that puts the envious to shame, especially since the enthronement of metaphysical pride during the Renaissance' (1991, 4). The significance of this characterization lies in Girard's suggestion that envy is actually based on a triangular configuration instead of a dyadic one, for he posits that it consists of a subject (the criminal), the object of the subject's desire (a prestigious social position with its typical trimmings), and an agent who serves as the 'model' of the subject's desire (the victim) (1966, 1–10). Envy would thus have as its initiating thrust the subject's belief that the model is already the kind of person he or she would like to be, because the model either is q, has r, knows s, or does t, where the specific attributes q, r, s, and t are typical characteristics of a superior social kind (Livingston 1992, 43). It is a belief of this kind that first singles out a particular person as the model of desire for the subject. Envy has its root in the subject's conviction of a hierarchical (i.e., positional) difference between self and other. In Christie's world, this belief includes an ambiguous mixture of fascination with, and hatred of, the model: fascination deriving from the model's assumed positional characteristics, and hatred, resulting in murder, thanks to the subject's belief that if it were not for the model, he or she would be or have what the model currently is or has.[23]

The striking thing about these illustrations is that each singles out *reciprocal mirroring* as the underlying cause for the events leading to crime: both the criminal and the victim use one another as mirrors. This is the fixed riveting of the slave to the master and vice versa. The slave sees in the master what he or she wants to be and have, whereas the master craves for the slave's recognition of his or her position in order to feel like a master. The victims need their rivals, because they thrive on the envious glance of those in inferior positions, finding proof of their superiority in such a reflecting surface, whereas the criminals only wait for the right moment to reverse the situation.[24] The three victims described in these excerpts have gleefully let the murderer (and others) feel his or her inferiority, which is invariably based on some objectively insignificant difference. This situation is based on an intersubjective dynamic Girard calls *double mediation* in which two agents serve reciprocally as each other's models (or mirrors). This dynamic takes place in a context where both agents desire a similar object, and where it is impossible for both of these desires to be successfully realized (1966, 101–4). In Christie's world, rivalry stems first and foremost from complex social comparisons. The ultimate object of desire is a person's *rank* or *status* in relation to others, and not material advantage as such, for money, country mansions, and the leisurely lifestyle simply function as the conventional signs of such a status. Obviously, the very top houses only a privileged few, which incites competition for this position. That social comparisons are in actual fact grounded in objectively insignificant differences implies a moral emptiness at the base of Christie's world.

The idea of double mediation builds on the reciprocity of mirroring between agents. Viewed from the criminal's perspective, this notion seems easily verifiable. In looking upward from an inferior social position, criminals hanker after a higher ranking through eliminating the rivals standing in their way. The value system turns victims into mirrors whose function is to model what is desirable, regardless of their personal characteristics. What is less easy to perceive is how criminals may serve as models for victims. The explanation derives from the communal awareness of competition as demonstrated by the envious glances in which the top brass bask. These envious mirrors show the victims that what they already are and have is truly worth being and having. To keep sustaining this sense of superiority, they simply model themselves after the picture they see in the longing and coveting glance of another.[25] What characterizes double mediation, Girard maintains, is the curious, blinding misconception about its nature that plagues each participant. The parties usually recognize that they desire similar things, but they believe their desires arise spontaneously from within themselves. It is the mediated nature of desire they fail to perceive: in order to know what to desire in the first place, they look to others for a model to imitate. Should they see that their desire is refracted through another, they would understand why the other seems like an obstacle-rival (1966, 101–4).

Because it is based on the drawing of hierarchical and arbitrary differences between people, which causes rivalry among them, the very order of Christie's world supplies the breeding ground for crime. What is more, there is a close proximity, even a fundamental sameness, between the rivals. In *After the Funeral*, for example, the victim takes pride in her knowledge of art, whereas the culprit has been trained in art by her artist-father. In *Crooked House*, *A Pocket Full of Rye*, and *The ABC Murders*, the murderers and their victims come from the same family line. In *Peril at End House*, the criminal and the victim even share the same first and last names (and are cousins to boot). This feature suggests that the moral distinctions between the agents shrink down to a very limited number of qualities.[26] The paucity of moral differentiations may thus partly account for the moral emptiness of Christie's world.

In concluding our examination of Christie's social fabric, we need to consider the most significant point where her work differs from the tradition of the metaphysical detective story.[27] This difference allows her to admit freely the pull towards crime evoked by hierarchy, while simultaneously it enables her to safeguard the notion of hierarchy itself. To perceive how she juggles admission and denial, we must once again consider the human-versus-animal opposition, especially as demonstrated by acts of violence. As the novel *Evil under the Sun* is by now familiar to us, we return to it for further clues.

In this book, the rightful king and queen figures are doubled by their sinister criminal counterparts. Before their reconciliation, each of the true lovers must overcome the suspicion that the other is the murderer. Not surprisingly, the mirror again figures in events, for the man gives the woman an alibi by claiming to have seen her reflection in a mirror, establishing her presence in his room. The mirror image points to the knowledge each has of the other's concealed side, expressed in acts of violence. The king figure observes of the queen figure that she 'used to get into the most frightful rages. You half choked me once when you flew at me in a temper' (26); and again, 'don't you remember when you nearly killed that boy about that dog once? How you hung on to my throat and wouldn't let go?' (181). Similarly, she knows of the stories about his going 'mad with rage' (181). And such violent acts by the true representatives of social order seem rather the rule than the exception in the author's work. An extreme example occurs in *Taken at the Flood*, where the king figure not only frames the murderer as the scapegoat for a manslaughter he himself committed, but also nearly chokes the queen figure to death in a fit of jealous rage. This appears a most peculiar characteristic indeed, making one wonder whether there really is anything substantial distinguishing the true and false symbols of order from one another.

For a further clue to this question we go to another Christie novel, *Appointment with Death* [1946a], set in the midst of claustrophobic family tensions, where the answer is explicitly spelled out. In this book, Poirot describes the strategy chosen by a wife who wants to save her husband from the clutches of his tyrannical mother.

'There was one last desperate throw. *You could go away with another man.* Jealousy and the instinct of possession are two of the most deeply rooted fundamental instincts in man. You showed your wisdom in trying to reach that deep, underground, savage instinct. If Lennox would let you go to another man without an effort – then he must indeed be beyond human aid, and you might as well try to make a new life elsewhere.' (172)

Poirot praises the wife for her understanding of the basic fact about humankind: humans will jealously desire that which another desires. By implying that she can be lost to another man, she incites jealousy over herself as a love object worth having, simply because someone else wants her too. We can relate this inflaming of jealousy (or envy) to the difference between the true and false symbols of order. By referring to 'deeply rooted savage instincts,' Christie alludes to the *natural* condition of the human being, whereby the true king and queen become the representatives of a *natural order*. In this scheme of things, violence is understandable and even somehow acceptable, given that it is of the right kind: it is as natural to become enraged in the throes of jealousy as it is natural to be passionately angry when someone threatens one's rightful possessions. These things are in accordance with what might be called *natural morality*. Christie emphatically stresses that even the *desire to kill* is part and parcel of the human being's natural state: 'Everyone is a potential murderer. In everyone there arises from time to time the *wish* to kill.' The continuation of the analysis of murderous desire is equally significant, for it suggests that the wish to kill is decisively different from the will to kill; moreover, adult human beings have what Christie calls 'the normal decent resistance' to protect themselves against this wish (*Curtain*, 169–70). This is a shrewd move on the author's part, for now she has made the distinction between a murderer and a non-murderer a simple matter of an individual's choice: some people act on this desire while others do not, as becomes apparent from Poirot's soothing of the intended scapegoat in *Evil under the Sun*:

'The wish to kill and the action of killing are two different things. If in your bedroom instead of a little wax figure you had had your stepmother bound and helpless and a dagger in your hand instead of a pin, you would not have pushed it into her heart! *Something within you would have said "no."* ... To make the wax figures and stick in the pins it is silly, yes – but it does something useful too. You took the hate out of yourself and put it into that little figure. And with the pin and the fire you destroyed – not your stepmother – but the hate you bore her.' (*Evil under the Sun*, 180; my italics)

Christie equates healthy cultural order with natural order. Linda Marshall is its 'healthy' representative in that she is not only capable of blazing anger but also of using her symbolizing ability in a creative way in order *not* to take the step leading from wish to concrete action. (In anticipation, let us note that Poirot's words may function as an allusion to Christie's conception of what the reader is doing while reading detective stories.) In this context, it is the mind and its use of reason that begin to appear suspiciously sinister, easily associated with deviance. Indeed, the female criminal's characterization in *Evil under the Sun* as 'not one who sees red,' 'not passionate,' and 'cold blooded' refers to such a notion, because these traits reveal her unnaturalness. The criminals' use of reason is aberrant, because it enables them to renounce their human nature. It is not that their goals are any different from those of others, for others, too, are motivated by greed and jealousy. The reprehensible thing is the elaborate manipulation of one's own nature: to attain what they naturally want, they use their reason in a way that bends their natural instincts to fit strategies that are unnatural. The deviant use of reason explains, for example, how a woman can calculatingly use her justifiable jealousy to push her man into the arms of another woman in the name of financial gain. Thus, such distinctions as spontaneity versus calculation and passion versus coolness further elaborate the division between mind and body.

By evoking human nature as the basic underlying explanatory cause, Christie can camouflage the role her hierarchical ideal of society plays in engendering crime. She needs the conception of a natural order, based on natural instincts, to support her view that crimes have nothing to do with, for example, the economic order with its distribution of wealth and opportunity. She frequently explains the criminal's deviance as stemming from heredity, as nature always produces a certain number of malformed creatures, but she usually denies that such moral malformation is caused by insanity.[28] The author uses the natural/unnatural distinction to draw the communal boundary between inside and outside: because the natural order of society depends on the normal and healthy balance between the use of reason and animal instincts, both the criminal and the detective are outsiders to this community, thanks to their unnatural overdevelopment of the faculty of reason. We now turn to examine the champion of the natural order, who himself remains, however, to some degree, an alien to it.

Hercules and the Mark of Cain

The description of the criminal's idealized self-concept should sound a warning bell in the reader's mind, thanks to its surprising similarity to the notion of selfhood Christie's detectives either implicitly project, or openly boast of. Hercule Poirot's extreme vanity and pompous self-importance are clichés,[29] but such a seemingly modest figure as Miss Marple also exhibits those features. *A Caribbean Mystery*, for example, ends with a character's awed veneration of her with the quotation 'Ave Caesar, nos morituri te salutamus'[30] (1966a, 224), while at the end of *A Pocket Full of Rye*, Miss Marple's pity for the victim and anger at the culprit are superseded by 'the triumph of a specialist who has success-fully reconstructed an extinct animal from a fragment of jawbone and a couple of teeth' (1958, 191). How are we to understand the detective's egotism and narcissism, if these characteristics lead others to crime? Such an intimacy of the supersleuth with the (super)criminal casts doubt on Priestman's argument, according to which the reader is barred from contact with the otherness represented by the criminal because the detective's triumphant self always eclipses whatever meanings are associated with the criminal (1990, ch. 8). Christie's detectives demonstrate that, as readers of the soft-boiled tradition, we need not necessarily ponder the criminal's 'otherness' for the simple reason that it may lie under our nose, embodied in the detective. Thus Christie teases us with the strategy about the 'secret' of criminal desire also used by Poe's Minister D—: she hides it in full view.

In further examining this strategy we can look at the most difficult struggle depicted in the whodunit: the committing of the grandest crime imaginable, the so-called *perfect crime*, and the master sleuth's solution (at which point, of course, it ceases to be perfect). Although many of Christie's culprits aim at such perfection (Dr Sheppard in *The Murder of Roger Ackroyd*, Nigel Strange in *Towards Zero*, and Franklin Clarke in *The ABC Murders*, to mention a few), none attains quite the same level of cunning as the mysterious and self-reflexively named X in *Curtain: Poirot's Last Case* (1977). A number of facts testify to the author's clarity about the underpinnings of her own work. The title underlines the theatrical na-ture of her world, besides proclaiming the end to the series about Poirot. By choosing a perfect crime case, staged at the very place where the series began, Styles Manor at Styles St Mary, Christie concludes by focusing on the reciprocity of the primary players. Written in the 1940s and designed for posthumous publication (but actually first published in 1975, just before Christie's death in 1976), we can expect this particular case to elucidate how the perfect criminal functions as the mirror image of the master sleuth.

Poirot introduces the problem in *Curtain* by using newspaper accounts of a string of suspicious deaths or clear-cut murders in which there is no doubt about the culprits' identity and responsibility. Yet he enigmatically proclaims that these persons were not really accountable for their deeds, but that there was a devilishly inventive serial killer involved in each event, a person X, who deserves the real blame. Poirot fears that X plans to strike next at Styles Manor. The cleverness of X shows in technique, for X plans only 'complete' crimes: 'there is a motive for the crime, there is an opportunity, there is means, and there is, last and more important, the guilty person all ready for the dock' (62). By thoroughly erasing his (as it turns out) participation in the crime, X (whose name is Stephen Norton) achieves a degree of perfection unknown in any other Christie criminal. After stating the problem, the narrative then depicts the efforts of Poirot and Hastings to prevent murders from happening at Styles. The surprise solution, revealed after Poirot's death, discloses Poirot as the master criminal's final victim: the detective has not been able to think of any way of stopping the criminal other than killing him. Making the detective a murderer is the finest victory in the master criminal's career, even though it means his own demise.[31] What is more, Poirot's written confession shows that, although unwittingly, Hastings, too, has caused the death of a would-be murderer, one of Norton's intended victims.

Norton, as the master criminal, functions by simply installing himself somewhere, knowing that prospective victims will soon emerge. The indiscriminate nature of his malice shows how perceptive he is about the drift of envious desire in his community. His strategy is to inflame his victim's envy either by insinuating that the victim cannot be what he or she truly is on account of someone else's thwarting influence or by feeding the victim's indignation at not having that which he or she wants (170). By playing on the victim's weakness long enough, he tries to effect the transformation from the wish to kill to concrete action. Norton's success thus depends on the separation of *legal* and *moral* responsibility: he is eminently responsible in a moral sense, but never legally accountable, for his victims have committed the murders.[32]

The fact that the perfect criminal's responsibility is solely moral in nature effectively underlines the role of envious desire as the root of all evil in Christie's world, which, in turn, accounts for its moral emptiness.[33] Inherent in all and sundry, envy – a form of the human desire for supremacy – seems to be the equivalent, for Christie, of original sin. The portrait of the perfect criminal is instructive in further elucidating this fantasy. His almost perfect success derives from what Girard calls the *askesis* or *hiding* of desire (1966, 153), so that others are lulled into thinking he is the very embodiment of the insignificant man he plays. Even X's name, Stephen Norton, is common and not distinctive, especially when contrasted with the more exotic names of many another Christie murderer (e.g., Bellefort, Blacklock, Fortescue, Gilchrist, Serrocold, Strange). The culprit poses as 'someone whom everyone likes and despises,' with this scorn issuing from his 'seem[ing] to have had at no time any gift for asserting himself or for impressing his personality on other people' (171).[34] He parades his antithetical mirror-opposite, the picture of a 'gentle-hearted, loving man' in front of others, while he in actual fact is a 'secret sadist,' 'an addict of pain, of mental torture' (172). In a context in which most people are trying to impress their personalities on others, a nobody like the culprit seems dull and unthreatening. Because he seems untouched by the general desire for personal and social ascendancy, no one (except Poirot) ever suspects him. The fiendishness of the *askesis* of his desire derives from his *not needing others* to acknowledge his manipulative skills. He never boasts of his exploits, not even when the detective finally confronts him (and then he simply smirks). In this sense, he is closer than any other character to the ideal of narcissistic self-sufficiency.

This distinction between the master detective and the master criminal suggests that the visibility of envious desire serves an important function in upholding order and stability in Christie's world. As long as one's aspiration to ascendancy is worn on one's sleeve, it can be controlled and kept in check by others who have the same desire. The frustrated children who openly resent the remarriage of their parent (which hinders them from getting their hands on money) are better insulated against the murderous pull of desire than the seemingly besotted but secretly resentful new spouse. In this context, the vain and self-satisfied detective articulates and displays the desire common to the community. Intimately familiar with the shared ideal self-concept, this figure is particularly well-equipped not only to diagnose envious desire in others but also to remove the cancerous growth from the community. More importantly, the detective serves as a model of desire whose exemplary status derives from a proper channelling of his own desire. All Christie's detectives acknowledge God as a higher authority. Thereby, they indicate that vertical transcendence, the mimesis of a model out of the imitator's reach, is the guarantee of stability and order, because it keeps envy in check. This is a 'democratic' way of solving the competition among the members of a community, because they always remain equally inferior in comparison to celestial authority.[35]

Poirot's own motive for murder combines a sense of weakness and envy, both of which arise from the criminal's clever strategy for putting himself out of the law's reach. For the detective, the criminal's gravest transgression is his assuming the position that should be reserved for the ultimate model, God, which turns the criminal into God's reversed image, Satan, playing with what is basest in the human being. By admitting that Norton's crimes were truly perfect, while his own was not (184), Poirot emphasizes that he does *not* aspire to usurp this position. A further defence for his deed is the need to protect the community. His strategy of self-justification, however, strongly suggests that the murder is not as altruistic as Poirot would like Hastings to believe. For one thing, like all Christie's criminals, he hides his true intention under role playing. His carefully groomed hair and moustache (both of which are false) foster the illusion of the intactness of the outer shell, whereas his pretence of being an invalid (which he is not) implies the fatally diminished strength of the inner man. As with many other criminals, the success of the detective's plan requires his assuming his victim's identity for a while. There is the murder itself, committed by Poirot's shooting the victim symmetrically in the exact centre of his forehead, which reminds Hastings of the *brand of Cain* (188). Finally, there is Poirot's justification: 'I do not believe that a man should take the law into his own hands ... But on the other hand, I *am* the law!' (187). The symmetrical wound, intended by Poirot as a clue to his own guilt, refers to another judge-turned-executor, Justice Wargrave of *And Then There Were None* (1963), who, to make others believe he is dead, paints a fake shot wound on his own forehead. Both these figures are motivated by their identification with the law and, hence, with God, an identification that is further reinforced by their assuming the right to wear the brand of Cain. All these features together suggest that Poirot, too, is motivated by a profound envy, incited by the thought that someone else might occupy a position directly opposite to his own and get away with it unpunished. Poirot's place is right under God, whereas Norton's is aligned with that of God's rival, Satan.

To punish himself for his deed, Poirot commits suicide by putting his medicine out of reach. There is, however, a further twist to the ending.

Girard observes that in the novelistic tradition he examines, '[t]he ultimate meaning of desire is death but death is not the novel's ultimate meaning' (1966, 290). While the wages of transgressive ascendancy leading to murder is the death of that which is most preciously human in the culprit, Christie ends in another key with Poirot. The final section of his confession shows what this key is:

'I do not know, Hastings, if what I have done is justified or not justified. No – I do not know ... By taking Norton's life, I have saved other lives – innocent lives. But still I do not know ... It is perhaps right that I should not know. I have always been so sure – too sure. But now I am very humble and I say like a little child "I do not know ..."

'Goodbye, *cher ami*. I have moved the amylnitrate ampoules away from beside my bed. I prefer to leave myself in the hands of the *bon Dieu*. May his punishment, or his mercy, be swift!' (187)

This is the situation Girard calls the hero's *conversion in death* (1966, 292), which explains why death is not the ultimate meaning of the novels he discusses. It includes the hero's contradiction or denial of his or her former ideas, and, in particular, of the specific fantasy of selfhood inspired by his or her pride. Pride is replaced by humility (Girard, 292–3). By admitting his former arrogance and his ignorance of how his act is to be assessed, Poirot, for the first time in the series, humbles himself. Significantly, he who has always insisted on being *radically different from* all other characters, thanks to his superior, almost godlike, mental abilities, now implicitly acknowledges his fundamental *sameness* with them, as the very same desire driving others to commit crimes also drove him to murder. The repudiation of pride further underlines such sameness, for it means letting go of the idealized self-concept of omnipotence and self-sufficiency: before God we are all equal. It also involves the acceptance of the childlike position of the human being as regards God (which differs from Poirot's former conception of himself as the 'adult' representative of a celestial authority that verges on eclipsing its model). The notion of (God's) mercy cuts through hierarchies and personal qualities, for mercy is bestowed upon a person *in spite of* what he or she is. It cannot be earned or bought. Girard maintains that the final vision expressed in the hero's conversion in death invariably reveals the author's own vision (296–7). This conclusion to *Curtain* and to the whole Poirot series thus enables Christie to show her reader that she can recognize the (master)criminal in and through the detective figure and vice versa. By ending on the notion of the 'brand of Cain' (the very last words of the novel), she envisages the human being marked as a murderer in the fashion of Cain, but, like Cain, as one who has God's protection, for the brand's biblical purpose was to prevent the onset of a cycle of revenge. The brand of Cain suggests that the criminal is a person like the detective: the Self (Poirot) and Other (criminal) are, if not united until the end, still fundamentally similar throughout the series.

Playing the Author's Game

Žižek (1991) argues that the ending of a whodunit presents the reader with a specific ethical fantasy. This fantasy is based on the communal dimension of murder that binds a group of individuals together as suspects whose shared sense of guilt could have made any one of them the murderer, for each had motive and opportunity. The detective's role, according to Žižek, is to dissolve the impasse of such universalized, free-floating guilt by fixing it on one particular character, thus exculpating all others, the reader included. Žižek's interest lies in defining the space where the external, material reality of the detective story overlaps with the inner psychic reality examined by psychoanalysis. His question is, 'how does the transposition of the analytic procedure onto "external" reality bear on the domain of the "inner" libidinal economy?' (59). His answer goes as follows:

[T]he detective's act consists in annihilating the libidinal possibility, the 'inner' truth that each one in the group might have been the murderer (i.e., that we *are* murderers in the unconscious of our desire, insofar as the actual murderer realizes the desire of the group constituted by the corpse) on the level of 'reality' (where the culprit singled out is the murderer and thus the guarantee of *our* innocence). Herein lies the fundamental untruth, the existential falsity of the detective's 'solution': the detective plays upon the difference between the factual truth (the accuracy of facts) and the 'inner' truth concerning our desire. On behalf of the accuracy of facts, he compromises the 'inner,' libidinal truth and discharges us of all guilt for the realization of our desire, insofar as this realization is imputed to the culprit alone. (1991, 59)

Žižek's argument makes use of the distinction between generality and particularity, whereby showing a particular person to have committed the act of murder obliterates general guilt. Christie would answer Žižek by insisting on the crucial difference between the universal desire or wish to kill and the act itself. She concedes that everyone is a murderer in his or her desire, but maintains that there has to be something in addition to this desire transforming it into concrete action, which is the focus of the genre. Žižek, in turn, might retort that Christie still dodges the real issue by refusing to acknowledge that readers use fictive murder cases as their own *imaginative acting-out* of this fantasy of committing murder. The particularization of guilt at the end camouflages the fact that the whole murder case initially derived from this generally shared impetus, rather than from the moral deviance of an individual character. In concluding our 'anatomy' of the moral constitution of Christie's whodunit world, we relate the external realm of the fictional world to the inner, psychic landscape of the reader. Is the *reader* discharged of any and all guilt, thanks to its externalization through the criminal?

The striking thing about Žižek's analysis is its triangular nature, for in constructing the problem of guilt he involves the suspects, the detective, and the reader. Each node of this triangle is characterized by a degree of blindness to guilt: the suspects see that each of them is potentially the killer, but they lack the means to differentiate this threatening sameness; readers see that the suspects distrust one another and, by using their knowledge of detective-story conventions, try to differentiate among them; finally, the detective occupies the position enabling him or her to bring guilt home to a character whom neither the innocent suspects nor the reader mistrusted (or, at least, whom neither mistrusted any more than they mistrusted anyone else). Žižek's point is that the position which in psychoanalytic configurations is the one of maximum lucidity is, willy-nilly, that of maximum blindness in the detective story, for it guards difference (innocence) by vehemently denying sameness (guilt). As Žižek closely follows the example of Lacan's examination of Poe's 'The Purloined Letter,' it is only to be expected that Derrida's (1988) critique of Lacan also applies to Žižek. The notable thing about the triangular configuration is that it envisages a position *outside* the triangle from whose vantage point the interactional pattern of the triangle emerges. According to Derrida, this fourth position is constituted by *the scene of writing* (or narration), making the triangle into a quadrangle. Indeed, Žižek ignores this fourth perspective, thus overlooking the fact that the reader's ultimate contestant is not the detective but the author. Therefore, the question of the reader's guilt should be considered in light of the reader's relationship to the author.

I pointed out in chapter 1 that author and reader can never directly meet one another, but can only imaginatively identify with each other through the fictive encounter between detective and criminal. Irwin (387) draws the quadrangular pattern shown in Figure 6.3 to demonstrate how doubling between detective and criminal is repeated at the higher level by doubling between author and reader. (The broken line indicates the indirectness of their encounter. Notice that the viewpoint is the author's, so that the detective represents his/her right [morally good] side and the criminal the left [morally bad] side.):

Authors confront readers indirectly through their two opposing masks

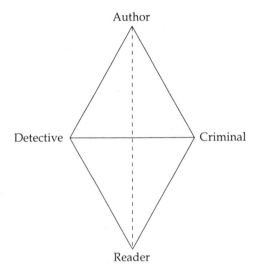

FIGURE 6.3   The Author-Reader Relationship. Adapted from John T. Irwin, *The Mystery to a Solution: Poe, Borges, and the Analytic Detective Story*, p. 387. Johns Hopkins University Press, 1994. Reproduced by permission.

of detective and criminal in a triangular structure constituted by author, detective, and criminal. Similarly, readers engage authors through these same masks in a triangular structure of reader, detective, and criminal. Consequently, authors and readers square off as specular doubles, each intending to outwit a self-projected image of the other. The figure demonstrates the authors' doubling: on the one hand, they are aligned with the criminal through the concocting of the crime problem, while on the other, they are like detectives in unravelling the mysteries of their own making. Christie's best-known example of hiding behind the criminal's mask is her use of the Watson-like narrator who turns out to be the criminal in *The Murder of Roger Ackroyd*. Poe, in turn, suggests that neither role is primary, for while authors are devising the crime problem, they have simultaneously to think through its solution. They take up both roles in imagination: they think like both detectives and criminals, drawing on both their good and bad side. The writing of detective stories entails the authors' exploitation of their own duplicity. But this description pertains to readers as well, for in order to engage in the battle of wits with authors, they, too, have to be able to think like detectives and criminals. What this means is that only if readers can get in touch with the good and the bad in and through themselves, can they approach the same qualities in someone else. Readers must thus use their self-knowledge and the figures of the two main fictional characters as the means of projecting upon themselves the narrative profile and strategies of their opponents, the authors.

If this interpretation of the specular encounter between authors and readers via the primary fictional antagonists is correct, then we can conclude that the whodunit always starts out with the shared awareness of evil and guilt within ourselves. The solution exonerates neither the author nor the reader, for the criminal is the representation of their shared evil side. Instead, the various solutions show that at this particular time the shared evil side has certain specific characteristics. Particularization is thus not a clever means of dodging universal guilt, but a means of showing under what kind of mask evil is hiding this time. There is, however, a specific twist to the whodunit's coding of this battle between good and evil. The central idea of this coding is expressed in Chesterton's short story 'The Blue Cross,' where Valentin, the French supersleuth, remarks that '[t]he criminal is the creative artist; the detective only the critic' (1981a, 12). The whodunit presents evil as active, creative, inventive, and ingenious, leaving to good the considerably duller role of criticism and confinement. The subgenre exhibits a fascination with evil, especially with its capacity to scheme cleverly and to clothe its schemes in poetic garb and structures. If the whodunit can be thought of as a cultural means to work through – as well as to play with – the battle between good and bad being waged inside the human being, then perhaps this play can be thought of in terms of 'self-patrolling,' where both the author and the reader let their evil side go, then send their good side to pursue it until the good overcomes and curbs the bad. For the duration of the story they can enjoy the attractive caprices of evil, while knowing that it will eventually be subordinated to good.

In this battle of wits the reader is always at a disadvantage, for the mystery is of the author's making: the reader must play the author's game. Authors attempt to maintain their upper hand from start to finish, guarding their positionally higher status *vis-à-vis* the reader, which suggests that the battle itself strongly resembles the general striving to ascendancy familiar from Christie's world. Christie thus pushes the reader into the position occupied by her criminal-slaves, while she herself – potentially, at least – fills that of the victim-masters. If Christie wins the battle, she then basks in the admiring – and perhaps also envious – applause of her reader. The reader, in turn, can beat the author at her own game by guessing the solution (i.e., the identity of the perpetrator), but also by spotting logical flaws, narrative oversights, and ethically and/or aesthetically better solutions.[36] Thus, in the last instance, as Irwin suggests, the battle of wits involves the whodunit authors' challenge to the reader to examine how they have constructed the games they play with us (388–90).[37] From the ethical perspective, an integral part of the reader's contribution is to do what I have just done: sketch the contours of Christie's world through an examination of her interactive patterns and her use of moral binaries. Whether the flesh-and-blood reader concurs with the author's suggestion of the proper combination of good and evil within the human being's inner landscape is something that lies outside the author's jurisdiction.

7

Symbolic Exchanges with Death: Raymond Chandler

Agatha Christie's use of the theatre metaphor brings out the ritualistic nature of her society, where impersonation is based on the knowledge of conventions and the clever employment of reason. In Raymond Chandler's world, the traditional theatrical terms lose their descriptive power, thanks largely to the fact that society no longer cares to monitor who is playing what role and by what means. The metaphors of the 'big production' take their place, emphasizing the importance of money, power, business relations, and competition. Because competition is now open, accepted, and universal, people need not hide their desire for social ascendancy. It effects a wheel-of-fortune-like rotation in the social fabric: some are ascending, others are already on top, while still others are on their way down. With so many people vying for the same or similar goals, it is difficult, if not impossible, for them to foresee the moves their rivals will make. Any role playing that still takes place arises from one person's attempt to mislead others about either his or her true goal or the means he or she intends to use to reach it. Money and the power it brings, while securing top-notch positions for affluent persons, also mark them as crooks of sorts, for the hard-boiled dictum holds that there is no clean way to make a fortune; it always involves the use of force and violence. Hence, the criminal underworld and the highest echelons of society not only resemble one another but intertwine at many points.

Open rivalry reverses the way in which the mind/body and human/animal distinctions interrelate. In the whodunit, when criminals succumb to their animal, bodily side, it also means that they must draw on their human rationality. The hard-boiled novel, in contrast, no longer places a premium on the ingenious use of reason as the supreme sign of humanity. Competition feeds the bodily and animal sides of the human being that are manifested in, for example, greed, the exploitation of others, and the use of violence. The things that mark the human realm off from the animal are primarily moral qualities such as integrity, loyalty, honour, and kindness. Given the 'animality' of his adversaries and the deadly danger in which the solving of crimes places the detective, he has to resort to his animal side in his profession. The test of his ethos is whether he can harness his animality to the continued service of his morality.

Chandler interprets his protagonist's encounter with the immoral and chaotic hard-boiled world in terms of the chivalric-quest romance, where the hero is a knightlike figure engaged in the search for a hidden truth (1946).[1] The search for and the eventual revelation of this truth structure the adventure-oriented plot, illuminate the detective's ethos, and motivate the act of narration. Invariably, the Marlowe stories trace Philip Marlowe's descent from moderately optimistic knighthood to a despairing recognition of his own impotence and the obsoleteness of knightly virtue. The contact with the longed-for truth makes the detective confront corruption, hollowness, and horror (Rabinowitz 1980, 233, 235). Chandler uses romance motifs in order to depict the aftermath of the American dream, conveying 'the fallen state of the world after the dream has not only merely become tawdry and tarnished but exists only as a debased passion' (Lid 1969, 155). R.W. Lid specifies this debased passion as arising from the author's portrayal of the schizoid aspects of American culture and 'the ways in which the base and ideal and their manifestations are so closely intertwined as to be inseparable' (156). This idea of the almost inseparable fusion of opposites informs the author's novels, for his major characters are engaged in private quests after ideals that blind them not so much to the baseness of reality, as to the emptiness of the chosen ideals themselves. Chandler's novels may thus be described as *inverted quest romances*.

Marlowe's repeated experience of the discrepancy between his knightly ideals and reality is reflected in his function as the narrator conveying a retrospective rendition of the complex, even deadly, events in which he himself was personally engaged. The act of narration serves as his means of coming to terms with disappointing and painful past experiences. The crime problem of Chandler's novels, the missing-person case,[2] is intimately connected with the manner in which the narrator repeatedly shapes the narrative line so that its twists and turns form the general pattern of the labyrinth. Its shape emerges from the way in which the narrator makes the narrative line proceed: the beginning of the search for the missing person marks the entry into the maze; the various narrative events, especially the sudden turns, take the detective into its different corridors, bringing him, step by step, closer to the heart of the maze; this centre is marked by Marlowe's finding out who caused the death (or the betrayal leading to death) of the missing person, enabling him finally to work his way out. In this narrative construction, the narrator habitually draws the same fundamentally circular figure, as the pursuit of the missing person constitutes both the entry into the maze and its exit point. This manner of figuration underlines the archetypal model of narration and the significance of the labyrinth's centre (the main enigmatic event revealing the fate of the missing person) as the answer to the problem orienting the detective's quest.[3]

'[T]he process of shadowing – detective story terminology, reified and taken literally –' writes Patricia Merivale, 'takes the form of repeating the movements and actions of the man pursued, thus turning the detective into a shadow, or mirror image, of him' (1999, 109). Philip Marlowe's search for the missing person spotlights this person's identity, for his or her fate derives from who and what he or she is. The investigation, by making the detective take up the missing person's position and repeat his or her actions, gradually turns the search for the other into a search for self. The questions initially directing the search – Who is the missing person? What happened to him (or her)? – give way to queries concerning the detective's own identity and fate (Who am I? What will become of me?). In Chandler's detective stories, this question of identity always takes on an ethical hue, because Marlowe's sense of self is intimately tied up with his work. His job as a private investigator makes him define himself against society's values as well as his own. Given the pervasive corruption, sustaining a sense of self tests his faith in his own values and principles, calling on him to evaluate his actions in the light of his own moral code.

The ubiquitous corruption of the hard-boiled world has the effect of moving characters from one role to another. The client or the friend may be the criminal, or it may be difficult to distinguish the police from criminals. Most important, the detective, in looking for the missing person, is made to enact three roles: as a professional finder-out, he is often forced to act like a criminal; in addition, the investigation constantly threatens to turn him into a victim. The motif of the missing person prompts the play with identities, suggesting the *potential* sameness of the roles of detective, criminal, and victim.[4] In what follows, I examine the moral view of life subtending Chandler's inverted quest romances with the help of the generic geometrical patterns analysed by Irwin. I have directed Irwin's findings to the mainstream detective story in my scrutiny of Christie's work, but the hard-boiled context is different enough from the whodunit to require a separate discussion. The crime problem and the first-person narrative are perhaps the two most important differences. The missing-person case with the inevitable *doubling* obtaining between the detective and his quarry draws the reader's attention to dyadic relationships based on the mirror mechanism. The generic roles of detective, criminal, and victim highlight the *triangular* patterns revealing what doubling looks like when it is inserted into the interactional (social) context. Finally, the instability of roles implies that the roles themselves may be doubled, so that what looks like a triangular situation is actually a *quadrangular* one, complicating the interpretation of the moral qualities used in describing the generic positions. What moral significance do these various reciprocal mirroring relationships acquire in Chandler's work? How does the moral coding of the generic roles influence the exploration of the detective's identity in the context of his values? What ethical significance does the narrator's manner of narration – the encirclement of the enigmatic event, eventually revealing the fate of the missing person – have for his moral view of life?

'A man was looking up at the [neon] sign too,' the narrator tells the reader at the beginning of *Farewell, My Lovely* (1976b); '[h]e was looking up at the dusty windows with a sort of ecstatic fixity of expression, like a hunky immigrant catching his first sight of the Statue of Liberty' (1). Another narrator, Nick Carraway of F. Scott Fitzgerald's *The Great Gatsby* (1950), witnesses his enigmatic neighbour 'stretch[ing] out his arms toward the dark water in a curious way, and, as far as I was from him, I could have sworn he was trembling. Involuntarily I glanced seaward – and distinguished nothing except a single green light, minute and far away, that might have been the end of a dock' (27–8). The notable links between Fitzgerald's romance and Chandler's work[5] concern not only the quests in which characters are engaged but also the distinctly *elegiac* tone of narration. Like Nick Carraway, Philip Marlowe detects the 'heightened sensitivity to the promises of life' in some of the characters he encounters, a sensitivity eventually leading them to death. In order to make sense of the events, the narrator attempts to probe into 'what preyed on [this person], what foul dust floated in the wake of his dreams that temporarily closed out my interest in the abortive sorrows and short-winded elations of men' (*The Great Gatsby*, 8). As the Chandlerian narrator's encirclement of the central enigma takes on this elegiac tone, we have to consider how elegy, as both narrative process and cause, relates to the narrator's moral view of life.

In discussing Poe's 'The Man of the Crowd,' Merivale shows how the reader is incorporated in the detective-story play with identities: 'From the reader's point of view, I am following (as I read), and mirroring as I follow, the movement of a man who is detective, criminal and victim in one' (1999, 107). As the man in Poe's story is also the narrator, the effect is the blurring of the boundary between the narrator and the reader, which transmits some of the protagonist-narrator's guilty inquisitiveness to the reader. In the metaphysical variant, Umberto Eco claims, this transmission serves a moral purpose: 'Any true detection should prove that we are the guilty party' (1985, 81). Readers of the metaphysical detective story cannot delude themselves that they are insulated from guilt and moral responsibility. Does this characterization pertain to Chandler's readers as well, as they follow the detective-narrator's shift from one position to another in his search for the hidden truth?

I use Chandler's most explicitly elegiac work, *The Long Goodbye*, as a point of departure for the analysis of his moral view of life. I then examine the significance the elegiac framework has for this view of life and conclude by considering how the narrator's narrative figuration of his experience relates to the role he prepares for the reader.

Geometrical Patterns in *The Long Goodbye*

The Long Goodbye has a typical Chandlerian plot structure, with two seemingly separate mysteries that converge at the end. The first mystery has its roots in Marlowe's 'accidental friendship' (132) with Terry Lennox, a semi-drunkard who has remarried his former wife, Sylvia Lennox, a rich and promiscuous woman. The marriage is a relationship of convenience for the couple: he gains the easy lifestyle of the rich, while she has a respectable front behind which she can live as she pleases. The first crime is the brutal murder of Sylvia Lennox, for which Terry Lennox is the obvious suspect. Convinced of his friend's innocence, Marlowe helps him to escape to Mexico. The police suspect Marlowe of having acted as an accessory and detain him in jail, where he proves both his loyalty to Lennox and his professional trustworthiness by enduring brutality at the hands of the police. Then, suddenly, with Lennox's unexpected confession and suicide, the case dissolves. To persuade Marlowe of his guilt, Lennox mails him an informal version of the confession together with his lucky charm, a five-thousand-dollar note. After the official termination of the Lennox case, Marlowe is approached by a publisher worried about Roger Wade, a best-selling writer of historical romances who has gone missing. Wade has not been able to finish his latest manuscript, for it seems that he is obsessed with a guilty secret which makes him drink excessively and behave erratically. Marlowe refuses the case, but the writer's ravishing wife, Eileen Wade, manages to persuade the detective to look for him. The second mystery concerns the strange tensions of the Wade household, in which Marlowe becomes embroiled. They culminate in the alleged suicide of Roger Wade, which seems to stem from his guilt for having killed Sylvia Lennox, with whom he has had an affair. The suicide appears to prove that Marlowe's trust in his friend has been justified. The ending, however, provides a surprising twist to this interpretation.

Marlowe's strong but inexplicit attachment to Lennox is part of the mystery feeding the plot, for he professes not to understand it fully: 'I'm supposed to be tough but there was something about the guy that got me. I didn't know what it was unless it was the white hair and the scarred face and the clear voice and the politeness' (5). The description of this friendship, with Marlowe first benevolently helping Lennox and then spending time with him in various bars, evokes a sense of male bonding, which from the start, however, involves the invisible presence of a third party, because Lennox continually brings his marriage into the conversation. The absent Sylvia Lennox, with whom the detective has had only the briefest contact (1–2, 10–11), always overshadows the male interaction. Lennox's brief remarks about his marriage help the reader to structure the interactional field, supplying us with suggestions about the pertinent moral terms we can use to code the positions the characters occupy *vis-à-vis* each other. Hence we can draw the diagram shown in Figure 7.1 revolving around the notions of exploitation versus beneficence.

Lennox characterizes his wife as 'an absolute bitch' and 'a tramp' (18), knowing that she needs him as a respectable front. Her attitude to him is indifference, for, from her perspective, their relationship is based on use-value: if he fails to deliver what she wants, she simply dumps him (as happens during the opening scene of the narrative). This exploitation of others for selfish reasons and according to whim represents the moral degeneration in human relations typical of the hard-boiled detective story. Lennox, whose role Marlowe sums up as that of the 'kept poodle' (16), is poised between exploitation and beneficence: he is weak, admitting that he likes being wealthy and privileged even at a high personal

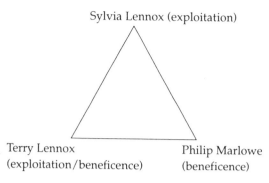

FIGURE 7.1   The Initial Situation

cost, yet decent enough to feel sympathy with and compassion for his unhappy wife.[6] Given Lennox's morally compromising status as a kept man, Marlowe would like to 'save' him from his wife.[7]

Instead of explaining the opening situation in terms of Marlowe's homosexuality, as, for example, Mason (1977) does, its undeniable homoeroticism might at first be linked with the kind of doubling familiar from traditional accounts of friendship envisaging the *male philos as another oneself*. Marlowe's kindness and loyalty to Lennox indicate that his ideal is based on disinterested benefit, sharing, and mutuality, expressing what he thinks relations between men are at their best.[8] The significance of the male dyadic bond in the interactional triad emerges sharply against the unsatisfactoriness of the marital tie, for the things that are lacking in the relationships between the sexes are compensated for in the interaction between persons of the same sex.[9] Marlowe is drawn to Lennox because he exhibits aspects of Marlowe's own character – or what he would like to think of as his character: British reticence, the stiff upper lip, the code of the gentleman, and pride, all of which the detective takes as hopeful signs of the possibility of the continuation of chivalry in the New World (Beekman 1973, 167; Lid 1969, 171–3; Speir 1981, 67, 115). But Lennox is Marlowe's double in morally indeterminate aspects as well, for he is a bout-drinker; this liking for alcohol is something Marlowe shares with him. Lennox's drinking derives from self-loathing, as he knows he has betrayed his full potential. He observes of himself that he is 'a weak character, without guts or ambition,' but he has had his moment of heroic glory in the war when he saved the lives of his comrades (18). Such self-hatred is typical of Marlowe, as well. This trait enjoys the status of an ambiguous virtue, because it stands as the proof of self-awareness, of the capacity to 'take a long hard look at [oneself] and see what is there' (152).[10] The position Marlowe occupies in the triad represents the morally commendable characteristics of male friendship: unselfish beneficence, loyalty, and reliability. The mutually reflective relationships among these three positions thus show that the promiscuous wife is the detective's direct antithesis, standing for all that he is not, whereas the husband portrays a *weaker* version of the detective.

From the opening of the narrative, then, Chandler constructs the interactional field in a manner that associates the moral qualities marking off the human realm with doubling between male characters. While the misogyny of the hard-boiled tradition is a well-established and fairly obvious fact (see, e.g., Cawelti 1976, 153–61; Christianson 1990; Porter 1981, 183–8), it suffices, at this stage, for us simply to notice this typical mistrust of women as figuring among the starting points of *The Long Goodbye*. For now, we can relate this mistrust to Chandler's inversion of the quest-romance conventions, involving his repeated portrayal of romantic love as problematic in human relations. Simultaneously, it is worth keeping in mind the ambiguous, fear-filled treatment of women in Poe's Dupin stories: the only role reserved for women is the role of victim of male assault.

Marlowe's quest in *The Long Goodbye* stems from his dedication to Lennox. He feels guilty for not having done everything in his power to help Lennox, even claiming to be responsible for his friend's death (124, 143). Loyalty, grief, and guilt together engage him in the long process of saying goodbye from which the book takes its name. The detective's quest acquires the nature of a rite of homage, for, to prove his loyalty, he undertakes to clear the name of the friend whom he believes innocent.[11] 'Lennox was your pal,' Marlowe says to Lennox's gangster friend: 'He got dead. He got buried like a dog without even a name over the dirt where they put his body' (285). The power Sylvia Lennox's father wields and the letter Lennox sends to Marlowe before his death make Marlowe believe that Lennox bravely accepted the role of scapegoat, sacrificing himself on behalf of Sylvia's family. In other words, he thinks that Lennox has repeated that 'one big moment in his life, one perfect swing on the high trapeze' (18) when he saved the lives of his comrades in the war. There is more to this rite, however, because the sense of personal guilt is heightened by professional failure, thanks to pressure from the police and Lennox's father-in-law.

In order to succeed in his rite of homage, however, Marlowe has to resort to professional means, because proving Lennox's innocence is impossible by using the means the codes of friendship and chivalry put at his disposal. This impasse makes him resort to the hard-boiled professional code, which includes the notion of the detective's honouring of his debt to a client, if he feels he has failed to serve the client's best interest (Žižek 1991, 61–2). Ideally, the revelation of the truth about the crime means the paying off of this professional debt. Central to the novel is thus the *splitting* of Marlowe into two sides: a *friend* and a *professional*. Not surprisingly, it is matched by Lennox's inner division into a *friend* and a *client*. Johanna Smith (1989) draws attention to the fact that, from the beginning, Marlowe's relationship with Lennox joins personal with professional responses. For example, in describing their first meeting Marlowe says that 'Terry Lennox made me plenty of trouble. But after all that's my line of work' (3). Each side makes a different kind of relationship available to him: the professional bond, based on what Smith calls the *economy of exchange*, places him with others on a plane of just and mutual exchange established by bargaining; whereas friendship, following the *economy of expenditure*, enables the unconditional give and take characterizing personal, intimate relations. But friendship also involves exchanges; although ideally just and equal, they nevertheless threaten to introduce an imbalance of power into the relationship (Smith, 592–5).

This tension-filled split begins to show when, after his wife's murder, Lennox comes to Marlowe for professional help (ch. 5). Marlowe, however, wanting to protect his professional standing and licence, emphasizes that he helps Lennox as a friend: 'We are friends and I did what you asked me without much thought. Why wouldn't I? You are not paying me anything' (25). As this act endangers Marlowe's professional standing, he feels that it is he who pays. As Smith (603–4) points out, the police inquiry brings out this feeling, for Marlowe refuses to reveal Lennox's whereabouts because he has 'got a reasonable amount of sentiment invested in him' (33), later specifying this amount as an investment of 'time and money in him, and three days in the icehouse, not to mention a slug on the jaw and a punch in the neck that I felt everytime I swallowed' (58). In effect, Marlowe believes that he now 'owned a piece of [Lennox]' (58). The situation is complicated, however, by the parting at the airport, because Lennox tells him that 'if things get tough, you have a blank check. You don't owe me a thing ... I left five C notes [$500] in your coffee can,' to which Marlowe replies, 'I'd rather you hadn't' (27). From the private detective's angle, money represents a sensitive medium, for his main marketable commodity is his loyalty and commitment to the client, which obligates him to guard the client's best interests. Everything about money – how clients offer it, how much they are willing to pay, and on what terms – are potential signs of their ulterior goals. The money bothers Marlowe, because it threatens to turn friendship into a professional relationship. Lennox's farewell letter, including one bill of five thousand dollars ('a portrait of Madison'), makes things worse, because Marlowe feels he has been paid twice: 'I had too much of his money. He had made a fool of me but he had paid well for the privilege' (130). The large sum of money, ostensibly 'a token of esteem for a pretty decent guy' that 'is not intended to buy anything' (67), betrays Lennox's guilt, for he pays Marlowe in the manner of a client. As Smith remarks, Lennox's investment reverses the former power positions, so that Marlowe can redress the imbalance only by mourning, but finds it impossible 'to reach the emotional equivalent of five thousand dollars,' so that the money 'becomes a gift whose goal is humiliating, defying, and *obligating* a rival'; the recipient can discharge this obligation only with a more valuable gift – that is, by returning this one with interest (Smith, 604).[12]

Marlowe's split into a friend and a professional in the pursuit of his quest helps us to see in what sense we can talk of mimetic modelling in this novel. The split itself suggests that there are two incompatible models vying for his allegiance. The first model is linked with masculine friendship. There is Lennox's act of self-sacrifice, which Marlowe values. His rite of homage resembles the squire's attempt to clear the knight's name, showing to the world the true nature of the knight's noble act. But this is not all. A journalist's astonishment – 'I don't figure what made it worth your time. Lennox wasn't that much man' – drawing Marlowe's curt response – 'What's that got to do with it?' (280) – indicates what else is at stake. Marlowe fixes on Lennox as a model, because the model allows him to construct a specific type of relationship with this person that, in turn, corresponds to a more *abstract* and *idealized model relationship* in his mind. This model relationship is an intrinsic part of the knightly ideals Marlowe prizes and imitates. In this case, the ultimate model in the imitator's mind is his conception of the culturally designated role of the friend which *he himself* tries to match through his relationship with Lennox. Thus Lennox, as the actual 'physical' friend, need not be the only or the best example of the type; it is enough that he is a sufficiently good example (Girard 1966, 4–6; Livingston 1992, 43). Indeed, given the corruption of Marlowe's world, he is lucky to find someone to fix on who even remotely represents chivalric characteristics. This kind of fixation gives the imitator the opportunity to *transcend himself* by trying to live up to the venerated ideal of the general model he has in mind. In a sense, then, Lennox is simply instrumental to Marlowe's underlying motivation, allowing him the chance to prove to himself that he is also a chivalrous man with sound ethical principles. Marlowe's rite of homage thus engages him in secret rivalry with Lennox by challenging him to prove that he can match Lennox's assumed gallantry.[13] Hence, the mirror mechanism on which Marlowe's imitation is based has something of a Platonic quality, for the physical embodiment of the model is only a shadowy and tainted version of the abstract ideal.

The second abstract model is, of course, that of the hard-boiled professional, who sells his skills and services for money, offering also intangible moral qualities such as 'principles' and the willingness to protect the client's interest at his own personal discomfiture and cost (Smith, 594). The adoption of this second model places Marlowe in open rivalry with the police, who also adhere to this model. Yet it is Marlowe's repeated insistence throughout the series that his acknowledgment of the knightly model – his being 'a romantic' (229), a 'shopsoiled Galahad' – gives him a moral advantage over the police. The pragmatism of the police's adaptation of the hard-boiled model makes them yield to the pressures of power and money. In contrast, Marlowe maintains that his hard-boiled chivalry serves truth and justice, a claim which this quest is again meant to prove.

The beginning of the quest emphasizes Marlowe as Lennox's mirror image. If the friendship did not hide Lennox's weak side (his readiness to exploit others for his own benefit), while underlining Marlowe's strong side (his beneficence and loyalty), then the quest brings to view Marlowe's weak side, showing how his beneficence covers a readiness to use others for the furtherance of his own goals. This characteristic is close to the pragmatism he despises. The doubling initiating the plot of *The Long Goodbye* thus includes, for all Marlowe's professed idealism, morally ambiguous features; similarly, as his project of clearing Lennox's name proceeds, the inner split between friendship and professionalism deepens to such a degree that the quest itself begins to acquire an increasingly dubious moral hue.

The second part of the novel places Marlowe's quest in the context of a new mystery dealing with the problems of the Wade household: the author's hard drinking, which seems to stem from a gnawing sense of guilt; his alleged violence towards his wife; and the wife's anxious, but powerless, concern for him. There is reciprocal liking between Roger Wade and Marlowe (122, 152), but it does not amount to friendship, because the detective's acts of loyalty are 'something even a fool doesn't do twice' (178). Yet the relationship is not strictly professional, either, for

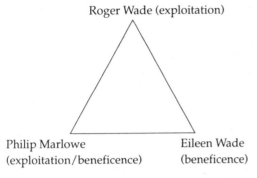

Roger Wade (exploitation)

Philip Marlowe   Eileen Wade
(exploitation/beneficence)   (beneficence)

FIGURE 7.2   A Modified Repetition of the Initial Situation

Marlowe never accepts any money for his various acts of kindness to the Wades. His readiness to help them appears to have its source in the few casual hints dropped by Wade that make him understand that the writer is somehow mixed up in the Lennox case. Therefore, the possibility of finding out more about it keeps him coming back to the Wades. This case again places Marlowe in a triangular pattern consisting of a married couple and himself. Initially, however, it seems to shift the positions of the participants (see Figure 7.2).

The husband's position is characterized by exploitation, for Roger Wade's erratic behaviour demonstrates that he is oblivious to his fate to the point of actively seeking self-destruction. He also seems to have lost all interest in his marriage and his wife. Marlowe's position is now explicitly divided. On the one hand, he sympathizes with the wife's predicament, and on the other, he acknowledges and appreciates the integrity and honesty of the husband's character. What further contributes to his divided stance is his sexual attraction to Eileen Wade. Yet in spite of the kindness Marlowe shows to Wade, there is a camouflaged exploitation beneath his beneficence, for, whenever he can, he pressures the writer to reveal what he knows of Sylvia Lennox's murder (168, 171–2). For a time, Eileen Wade appears to occupy the most morally commendable place in the interaction. She seems the antithesis of the murdered woman with her dreamlike (71), unclassifiable, and almost paralysing (73) beauty, reflecting her character as a concerned and loyal wife who tries to get help for her husband. She repeatedly declares her love for him, but it bothers Marlowe that she withdraws at those crucial points when her caring is most needed (164). Hence, for a while it is difficult for Marlowe to decide whether the wife simply hovers between beneficent loyalty and exhausted apathy towards her husband, or whether the marital relationship requires reassessment with information that for the time being remains inaccessible to him.

As is to be expected, the solution effects a reinterpretation of the interactional relations by revealing that Sylvia Lennox was murdered by Eileen Wade. It uncovers the existence of a quadrangular configuration, for it discloses that Terry Lennox and Roger Wade have, at different points in their lives, each had an affair with both Sylvia Lennox and Eileen Wade. Eileen Wade and Terry Lennox, alias Paul Marston, were married during the war, but the marriage ended with the alleged death of Marston-Lennox in 1942. Eileen then remarries and settles in Los Angeles where, to her shock, she finds Marston-Lennox alive and married to Sylvia Lennox. Later on, she discovers that Roger Wade is having a casual affair with Sylvia Lennox; thinking that this woman has robbed her of two men, Eileen Wade kills her in revenge. Guessing that Lennox knows about her guilt, she hires Marlowe in order to determine how much he, as Lennox's friend, has learned about the murder. Sensing that Roger Wade either knows or guesses the truth, she murders Wade, but frames the scene as suicide, intending it as an indirect admission of his guilt. She tries, moreover, to implicate Marlowe in the event. The ending confirms that Lennox correctly conjectured Eileen Wade's guilt but was reluctant to turn her in. He protected himself by first promising his father-in-law to play the fall-guy. He then made a secret deal with his gangster friends who helped him to fake his suicide and have plastic surgery in order to change his looks to fit his new, Mexican identity as Cisco Maioranos.

The solution reveals a quadrangular configuration, with Roger Wade facing Terry Lennox and Eileen Wade facing Sylvia Lennox. While it describes the relations behind the two murders, it does not show the detective's role in the events. As they largely stem from Marlowe's striving to prove the innocence of his friend, the diagram describing the outcome of the case ought to reflect the moral challenge he encounters in assessing who occupies the position of scapegoat. The doubling of this role derives from Marlowe's initial misevalution of his friend. Both the murderer and the friend have used him; also, he fears that the murderer stands a chance of escaping from the law. Therefore, the diagram should show how the detective's moral decisions, based on the knowledge of the truth, situate him in the interaction. I thus draw the final interactional relationships as a quadrangle including the three main male figures (Lennox, Wade, Marlowe) and the female murderer (Eileen Wade) (see Figure 7.3). The pattern is formed by two opposing triads that are mirror

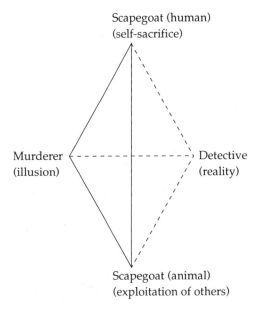

FIGURE 7.3   Marlowe's Final Evaluation of Guilt

images of one another; moreover, the positions at each end of the vertical and horizontal axes also mirror each other. In interpreting this diagram, we are especially interested in those qualities that distinguish the moral (the human) from the immoral or amoral (the animal) in the light of Marlowe's chivalric code. With this focus in mind, we first look at each position separately, comparing it then to its direct opposite.

The scapegoat in its human – moral – sense (Roger Wade) acts, in the light of Marlowe's code, in the manner of traditional chivalry: self-sacrifice. Because being the scapegoat brands one as guilty in the eyes of others, while one is actually innocent, one's acceptance of this role is based on self-denial. Wade's indifference and feelings of guilt mask the kind of integrity and loyalty the detective prizes, for Wade sells neither himself nor his wife to outsiders, even though he knows his reticence will lead to his own destruction. The most striking quality of the scapegoat-victim is his ability to face the truth about himself and his dreams and aspirations. Wade acknowledges his failure as a writer, the realm where he would most like to have excelled (141–2, 198, 205), conceding also his failure as a husband (172, 199). Jerry Speir explains Wade's acceptance of the role of scapegoat-victim as stemming from the 'competing pressures of his writer's drive to explain, to make sense of the world, and his ... impulse to hide his own guilt and protect those for whom he cares,' so that he finally verges on madness (1981, 75). The implication is that, in the end, he deliberately embraces the emptiness of his life by readily throwing himself into death (270). Wade's death is actually a kind of suicide, for he knows his wife will kill him and does nothing to ward off this fate. Looking at the events from Wade's viewpoint, however, it is not likely that he has any chivalric ideal in mind in accepting his fate, which emphasizes that this diagram shows positions which adhere to the detective's values. Wade's own comprehension of his situation would rather seem to correspond to that which Žižek attributes to the *femme fatale* in the hard-boiled genre (1991, 65–6), involving the realization that all the things around which he has spun a web of significance – his own subjectivity included – arise from his needs and the needs of others, whereas in fact these things have no inner 'essence' or meaning.

The addition of the immoral – animal – scapegoat (Terry Lennox) represents the inversion of male chivalric virtue, turning the upper triangle on its head, and making the two scapegoat figures each other's antithetical images. Lennox's moral perversion shows in his willing acceptance of the role of scapegoat without the right ethical attitude to go with it.[14] He exploits Marlowe and the Potter family, simply donning the mask of a scapegoat in order to buy time to get himself a new mask, that is, a new identity. His moral cowardice makes him indirectly responsible for Roger Wade's death (309). In retrospect, both Marlowe and the reader can say that the clue to Lennox's true character was there from the beginning, for the opening of the narrative refers to the 'plastic job' done to him: the Germans have operated on the *right* side of his face (standing for the morally good), which has given his face a crooked one-sidedness (3). The second plastic surgery, giving him a third identity (or possibly even a fourth one, as Paul Marston may not be his right name), leaves his face with scars on both sides, emphasizing the fact that he is a mere hollow mask of a man.[15] Lennox's looks reflect his relationship to reality. Like Wade, he also has accepted reality's fundamental emptiness, but he endows reality with a different meaning. His relation to it is based on what might be called opportunistic drift. He makes his own emptiness the mirror of general emptiness, matching external meaninglessness with its inner equivalent. This attitude grounds itself on delusion by its refusal to probe reality: it simply substitutes the former plenitude of being with hollowness of being, taking the latter notion as the cornerstone of the framework holding things together.

As the murderer, Eileen Wade represents the bestial in the human being. Quite fittingly, after shooting Sylvia Lennox, she mutilates the body with the statuette of a monkey. Somewhat paradoxically, her animality stems directly from her romantic goal: keeping faith in her first love (149–50, 178). She fosters this memory, even to the extent of trying to keep herself sexually chaste. This memory, however, is false through and through. Eileen Wade knows that Marston-Lennox had been captured by the Germans during the war, but she finds this fact incompatible with the story she has woven around their love – 'the wild, mysterious, improbable kind of love that never comes but once' (150). In her fabricated version of reality, Marston, the 'lover [she] gave to death' (270), dies young and heroic in the snow of Norway.[16] It is this contrived memory which she cherishes as a sacred shrine, endowing it even with a special relic, a necklace she falsely claims to have received from Marston. When she accidentally encounters Marston, 'the empty shell of the man [she] loved and married' (270) and 'a friend of gamblers, the husband of a rich whore, a spoiled and ruined man, and probably some kind of crook in his past life' (271), she holds on to the dream despite her knowledge of its utter falseness. The murder of Sylvia Lennox represents her attempt to negate truth by taking revenge on the reality that tries to shatter her faith. Ironically, the reader learns that neither the marriage nor she herself ever meant much to Marston-Lennox (308): Eileen Wade's belief in having experienced perfect love is a one-sided fantasy. Her romantic dream turns her into a murderous beast. Her suicide thus stands for the height of self-delusion, for it is the final gesture which might help her to safeguard her illusion: 'The tragedy of life ... is not that the beautiful things die young, but that they grow old and mean. It will not happen to me' (271).

The murderer's private dream, leading to her skewed perception of reality, helps to explain the detective's position as *her* antithetical mirror image. One of the surprises of the novel is this *shift* in mirror relationships, for at first Marlowe, believing in Lennox's good side, thinks that this ostensible victim is his double. (Lennox, however, has all along counted on Marlowe's bad side, on his being indifferent to truth and opportunistic.) The ending shows that the female murderer's mirror image is a truer reflection, for Eileen Wade's romantic dream and Marlowe's chivalrous quest are similar: they both believe they are loyally keeping faith. Moreover, the object of their faith is the *same* man, a fact which shows that Marlowe is again engaged in a hidden rivalry with a woman over this man. The rivalry is not sexual so much as 'metaphysical,' because it concerns the manner in which one imitates the chivalric or romantic ideals. Marlowe is, however, in one respect the murderer's antithetical image, for, unlike Eileen Wade, he wants to find out the truth, being ready to accept it, whatever it is, without embellishments – or so it at least seems. Illusion thus gives way to reality. The position Marlowe appears to hold in the diagram is, therefore, that of traditional maximum moral insight; but whether this description in truth applies to him needs further consideration.

The events demonstrate that it is Marlowe's imitation of the knightly model that ironically pushes him into committing actions that are morally dubious. The further irony is that he can act as a friend only by acting as a professional. This brings out his (moral) indifference, leading to his exploitation of others. For example, in trying to find out where guilt lies, he turns the quality he admires in Roger Wade – his ability to 'take a long hard look at himself' (152) – against Wade by forcing him several times into self-appraisal, which then results in destructive drinking (Smith, 605). He even uses Wade as a bait to confirm his suspicions of where guilt really lies: hence, it is Marlowe who sacrifices Wade in order to find out the truth (200–6). He confronts Eileen Wade privately, forcing her to 'take a good long quiet look at herself' (278), which leads to her suicide. Marlowe himself claims that he cannot think of any other way to clear the reputation of an innocent man (260–1; 266–9). He then already knows, or can make a fair guess, about the Lennox case, realizing he has been played for a sucker. Therefore, in manoeuvring the events, he acts on the basis of his sense of justice; as he knows no jury would convict the murderer, the confrontation is his own private revenge (260), considerably diminishing the difference between him and the murderer. Finally, the novel ends in Marlowe's curt rejection of Lennox: 'Pick up your money, Señor Maioranos. It has too much blood on it ... You bought a lot of me, Terry. For a smile and a nod and a wave of the hand and a few quiet drinks in a quiet bar here and there' (310, 311). Returning the money is Marlowe's gesture of freeing himself from any debt whatsoever to this 'moral defeatist' (310). Simultaneously, he forces Lennox to 'take a long hard look at himself,' which gives Marlowe the moral upper hand: 'It's just that you're not here any more. You're long gone. You've got nice clothes and perfume and you're as elegant as a fifty-dollar whore' (311).

The Long Goodbye plays with the missing-person motif by proliferating it. Paul Marston is the brave soldier gone missing in the Second World War, who then surfaces for a brief moment as Terry Lennox, only to go missing again in Mexico (and resurface with another new identity).

Riddled with guilt and anxiety, Roger Wade goes missing in order to try to escape momentarily the truth about his wife. In tracing both physically and imaginatively the movements of these men, Philip Marlowe uncovers the core event from which the crimes issue: the story of a wartime love affair, which means next to nothing to the man and everything to the woman. The search for the missing men and the rite of homage establish reflective relationships between the male figures and Marlowe, whereas the murderer's romantic dream turns her into his mirror image. The detective's emphasis on the ethical importance of the ability to 'take a long hard look at [oneself]' raises the question of how the search for the Other relates to the concomitant search for the Self. The outcome of the quest shows that no matter at whom the detective looks, the reflections he sees of himself prove profoundly unsettling: a man with many masks, the friend has no stable core;[17] the despairing victim throws his life away; the murderer is mad. The disquieting feature from the detective's perspective is that these reflections of himself do not fit his ideal of 'being a romantic,' because they proclaim the *death of the kind of moral subject* that goes together with this ideal. Marlowe's own shift from the pose of a tough professional to a sentimental friend, to the disillusioned sucker, and back to the hard-boiled professional, argues Smith, shows that the emptiness of subjectivity also applies to him (607). She claims, however, that the hard-boiled pose is the one that seems validated, because the only friendship that Marlowe has left is with the police. The plot traces the hostility between Marlowe and his cop friend, Bernie Ohls, over the handling of the Lennox case. This animosity resolves itself in mutual recognition of manliness and toughness, which restores the professional friendship between these men (Smith, 606–7). The novel ends in Marlowe's resigned acceptance of this situation: 'I never saw any of them again – except the cops. No way has yet been invented to say goodbye to them' (312). What makes this identification with the hard-boiled professional model ambiguous is that, with its help, Marlowe can dodge his own moral responsibility for the deaths of Roger and Eileen Wade.[18] Thus his ability and willingness to take a 'long hard look at himself' seem definitively thwarted.

Contrary to Smith's conclusion, however, it is not certain whether the hard-boiled pose has the final word. In explaining to Lennox that he will not say goodbye because 'I said it to you when it meant something. I said it when it was sad and lonely and final' (311), Marlowe is referring, of course, to his rite of homage. But this characterization simultaneously alludes to the whole of his *narrative*, which is his 'sad and lonely and final' goodbye to a friendship turned sour. Given the nature of his world and of his own morally compromising actions, Marlowe realizes that he cannot achieve transcendence as a chivalrous hard-boiled detective; the distinctly elegiac mode of his narration implies that he transmits this striving to his function as *narrator*. But does the role of narrator salvage him, restoring him morally in his own and the reader's eyes? Can he achieve a lasting friendship with the reader?

Encounters with Death

The Long Goodbye is a story about a quest leading to the death of a friendship. In this sense it is typical of Chandler's whole *oeuvre*, for Marlowe's quests invariably include encounters with death. The novels usually conclude with a brief, eulogizing reflection on death and its meaning that the title, and often also the opening scene of the narrative, has already foreshadowed.[19] *The Long Goodbye*, however, differs from the preceding books in the series by deliteralizing the notion of death, and, consequently, threatening to shatter Marlowe's project as narrator.

The lasting preoccupation with death derives from the protagonist's profession as a private investigator: because the investigation rocks the precarious status quo, a deadly menace looms over the detective.[20] In Chandler's novels, the knightly principles form the demanding code of ethics which sets the detective-narrator in conflict with his society, for it is these ethics which expose him to danger. All hard-boiled detective stories – as distinguished from whodunits – tell about the investigator's own brushes with and near escapes from death. The knock-out blows Marlowe receives give him valuable first-hand experience of what it might be like to die and be dead. Central to this experience is the losing of consciousness and the subsequent return to life. The narrator invariably depicts the falling into unconsciousness as a dive into nothingness, emptiness, and darkness, while portraying the coming to as a woozy and painful process of reorientation and the gradual regaining of the sense of self.[21]

As these encounters with death are intimately linked with Marlowe's search for the hidden truth, dealing with the fate of the missing person, they are pivotal for his narrative motivation. We can use the typical hard-boiled motif of *aphanisis* (eclipse, blackout) (Žižek 1992, 161) as an important clue to this motivation. Žižek explains that the loss of memory and consciousness always threatens the hard-boiled subject's self-identity, making him wonder whether he is 'the unconscious tool of an alien force which acts through him' (161). Such self-doubt derives from the fact that while the detective is unconscious, bad things happen, as the following excerpts from Chandler's *The Lady in the Lake* (1976d) demonstrate:

The scene exploded into fire and darkness. I didn't even remember being slugged. Fire and darkness and just before the darkness a sharp flash of nausea. (171)

Never sit with your back to a green curtain. It always turns out badly. Something always happens. Who had I said that to? A girl with a gun. A girl with a clear empty face and dark brown hair that had been blond.

I looked around for her. She was still there. She was lying on the pulled-down twin bed.

She was wearing a pair of tan stockings and nothing else. Her hair was tumbled. There were dark bruises on her throat. Her mouth was open and a swollen tongue filled it to over-flowing. Her eyes bulged and the whites of them were not white.

Across her naked belly four angry scratches leered crimson red against the whiteness of the flesh. Deep angry scratches, gouged out by four bitter finger-nails. (173)

The purpose of this setup is to frame Marlowe for the murder of the woman; knowing he is not responsible, his dangerous task is to prove this fact. In such extreme cases as Hammett's *Red Harvest*, the detective's *aphanisis* is more radical, for he has good reason to think that he himself may be the murderer.[22] From the present perspective, the important point to ponder is the function of these states of *aphanisis* in the subject's definition of himself. If the subject's sense of the coherence of his self is always imaginary, argues Žižek, then *aphanisis* represents the subject's encounter with some 'strange body' – that is, a belief, desire, or proposition – which he cannot incorporate into this sense. In effect, this threatening belief or desire may be said to form the subject's 'core,' because he constitutes his (imaginary) sense of self by evading it at all cost. The meeting with this feared 'strange body' leads to the subject's self-erasure. *Aphanisis* has a direct link with narration, because, as long as the subject steers clear of the desires and beliefs he cannot embrace in his sense of self, he is able to go on telling a coherent and intelligible story about himself (Žižek, 162). As a state of unconsciousness and self-erasure, *aphanisis* thus profoundly defies the subject's symbolizing ability.

That the knockout blows together with the 'bad turns' events take during the detective's state of unconsciousness defy symbolization does not mean that they could not eventually be symbolized, even if only partially and imperfectly. Marlowe continually places himself in danger and subsequently tells of its consequences. This suggests that an effort to control those frightening aspects of reality which threaten his sense of self motivates his narration. Given that his identity is intimately tied up with the moral values directing his work, making sense of past events through the telling of his own story acquires moral significance. As Marlowe's narrative line goes full circle in the labyrinth it builds, the question becomes what ethical relevance this manner of encirclement can be said to have? His function as the narrator underlines his authority in his search for the ethical meaning behind the hidden truth.[23]

What is the hidden and feared truth the protagonist finds at the centre of the maze? Rabinowitz characterizes it as 'a hollowness and a horror' (1980, 235), while Jameson describes it as 'the reality of death itself, stale death, reaching out to remind the living of its own moldering resting place' (1983, 148). Death, as the most radical annihilation of self, poses the greatest threat to the protagonist-narrator. The narrator has, however, some means at his disposal for symbolizing this horror of death. The truth about the fate of the missing person invariably includes the betrayal and/or murder of this person (and frequently also others) by a woman, portrayed as a combination of the human and the animal. With her human torso and animal head, she is an inverted variation of the Minotaur, the man-eating monster of the Theseus myth. Usually, although not exclusively, her victim is a man. The heart of the Chandlerian labyrinth houses a woman who causes multiple deaths.[24] She is further linked with death by the fact that she herself often dies before the case is over. Her criminal monstrosity acquires further significance in the light of the detective's moral principles. In the context of chivalry, the woman should be virtuous in mind and body: sexually chaste and faithful in love. As the passive love object, she should validate and reward the man's aspirations to transcend himself. In contrast to this traditional model, in Chandler's world the woman represents the perversion of this ideal, for she is promiscuous, calculating, deceitful, and revengeful. Scratch the surface of a Helen Grayle and you find the cheap night-club singer Velma Valento. Founded on reciprocity and dependence on the other, love makes the lover vulnerable. The woman's gravest moral fault is her exploitation of the man's vulnerability in love for purely self-serving purposes. The Chandlerian woman threatens not only to soil and mock the knightly principles but to nullify them altogether.

Death is not, however, exclusively caused by women in the hard-boiled detective story, as the excerpt from *The Lady in the Lake* demonstrates. In Chandler's books, many men are killers (the murders they commit often derive from the primary murder by a woman) and, when victims of murder, they are also obviously party to dying and death. Using *The Big Sleep* as his example, Rabinowitz (1980; 1988, 193–208) argues that its real villain is not Carmen Sternwood, the deranged female nymphomaniac, but Marlowe's antithetical mirror image, the gangster Eddie Mars, who, while not literally a killer, is behind most of the violence that takes place. This division of guilt and responsibility between men and women seems to be intimately linked with the double-plot structure Jameson identifies in Chandler's books. The crimes taking place at the micro level of society always stem from the perversion of sexual relationships, whereas corruption at the macro level derives primarily from the misuse of power and illegal means of making money. The significant feature of Chandler's *oeuvre* is that the characteristics leading to murder at the micro level are invariably coded as *feminine*, whereas the traits associated with murders at the macro level are distinctly *masculine*, for the wheelings and dealings of the world of money and the power struggles of the underworld rely on traditional combat tactics. As a remote-control murderer, Eddie Mars is a rational businessman, whereas Carmen Sternwood is a hysterical nymphet at the point of total breakdown.

The gendering of death into two masculine and feminine realms allows the narrator to represent murder at the level of personal relationships in such a manner that killing is equated with becoming feminized. In so doing, the narrator adheres to the tradition of the detective-story genre, which associates death with various conventional feminine-coded meanings, such as the instinctual, the unconscious, the bodily, the chaotic, and the inanimate. The hard-boiled cop Degarmo, the 'sex-killer' (179) of *The Lady in the Lake*, is feminized – that is, he loses his rationality and self-control – through his passion for his multiple-killer ex-wife. In recoding the generic roles, the hard-boiled detective story differs from the Poe lineage. In Poe, only the woman occupies the role of victim, while the man takes up the positions of detective and criminal; the hard-boiled tradition criminalizes the woman (at the micro level of society), leaving for the man the roles of detective and victim. This recoding gives the criminal woman a semi-active role, for she is active in relation to the victim, but ultimately passive in relation to the detective (Irwin 1994, 70). By associating the woman with the man-devouring Minotaur, Chandler emphasizes the threat that the feminine-coded non-rational elements of the self have, ever since Poe, been thought to pose for the various masculine-coded rational elements in the detective story (such as reason, consciousness, and order).

The double-gendering of death allows the narrator to engage in a complex shuffling of meanings. By coding the violence at the macro level as masculine, he represents it as the larger framework within which personal tragedies take place. Because of the power of the agents of this violence, Marlowe can expose its workings but cannot correct the situation: his male antagonists are disempowering, even 'castrating,' in this sense. It is against this background that Marlowe's elegiac narrative tone acquires its significance, because it fixes his attention on the *male victim* whose death is caused by a woman. Typically, elegy laments the death of a friend of the *same sex* as the narrator; as in virtually all instances both are men, it foregrounds a masculine-coded approach to death, whatever its cause. The doubling of Marlowe by the victim enables us to read the (moral) fantasy of saying goodbye to him. In the elegy, the narrator's plaint for the dead is also a plaint for the inevitability of his own death, saturated with such feelings as impotence, inadequacy, spiritual emptiness, and rage in the face of death. The aim of this act of lamenting is to restore the narrator's vitality, enabling him to go on living, for it serves as the means of solving the vexing questions that have to do with identity, self-concept, and his manner of being in the world (Bruffee 1983, 43–5). To escape permanent emasculation, the narrator uses the elegiac narrative framework and the male victims of female aggression – his doubles – as the means of getting in and out of the narrative labyrinth he constructs. In this context, what Irwin says of the mythical Minotaur's general significance in the genre highlights what is at stake in Marlowe's strivings: 'for the hero to defeat the killer animal is for him to defeat the animal in himself, that irrational part which in its instinctual terror of death threatens to overwhelm the rational and bring about the destruction it fears' (Irwin, 244). How does Chandler's protagonist-narrator succeed in this task?

The conclusion to Marlowe's quest brings to the fore the profound ambiguity in his attitude to the missing person he has been tracing: he triumphs over this person, because his resourcefulness saves his life; but, being alive, he is nevertheless denied something his dead double has.[25] It is this 'something' that constitutes the hold, even the 'advantage,' the missing person has over him. The narrator's fantasy is that, by dying, the double has not only acquired an experience of death but has also gained the concomitant retrospective knowledge it brings of life's significance. This is the knowledge that is denied to us during our lives, forming the source of the narrator's curiosity and envy. The location of Marlowe's eulogizing remarks at the end of his narratives underlines the fact that death writes *finis* to life, thereby conferring on it its meaning. The narrator seems to believe, or, rather, to hope, that he achieves some kind of contact with the dead – and the concomitant learning of life's significance – through his commemorative act of narration.[26]

The psychic restoration of Marlowe thus involves his imaginative following of the missing person, in his work as detective and in his function as narrator, into the deadly encounter with the murderous woman. His identification with this person enables him to experience the double's fate vicariously and, in this way, to come into contact with dying and death. The elegiac tradition builds on a situation in which the narrator is still *here*, among the living, whereas his friend is *there*, among the dead. The structure of his narration thus makes it possible for him to construct a position in which he can occupy *two* places at once, being both here among the living as the narrator and there among the dead through his double. His narrative act defies the impossibility of knowing about death, experiencing it, and then returning to tell about it. For this fantasy project, the gender of the double and the masculinely coded narrative model are important, because they provide the means for the narrator to encircle the central event of the murder (or betrayal leading to death) of a man by a woman in such a way that it supplies footholds for the construction of meaning. The male double and the masculinity of the elegy serve as the male version of Ariadne's thread. Given that the woman stands for death as that total otherness beyond signification – even to the point of representing the effacement of the symbolic textures of the hard-boiled culture (Žižek 1991, 63–4)[27] – the narrator's spinning of a male web around death reveals his attempt to rescue this realm from the fright and danger its feminine associations bring to it. This web enables him to narrate such events; were he forced to rely on the feminine-coded elements of death, there would be only a radical void and absence, with nothing to tell.

The Chandlerian narrator's saying goodbye to his double brings to the fore the special characteristic embedded in the context of elegy, for it seems to make possible the narrator's exchange with the dead: he gives the double (the dead) immortality through the act of commemorative narration, while the double gives him the chance to work through certain frightening aspects of life and its ultimate end. The ethical significance of the narrative act lies in its allowing the narrator some form of transcendence. Given the immoral or amoral nature of the woman, transcendence cannot take place through romantic love. From the narrator's perspective, it can happen through the fantasy of a reciprocal movement with the dead double, representing a symbolic exchange where each party approaches the other with a gift specific to the position each holds in the context of eulogy. This notion of a symbolic exchange with a dead person suggests that the Chandlerian narrator uses the male victims in order to attempt to establish a specific relationship with the dead and death.[28] Marlowe's narration tries to turn something that has, in the modern world, become a biological fact into a reciprocal relation, where death is an element in a mutual exchange between the living and the dead. The narrator's gift to the double is the whole of his elegiac narrative. The narrator's hope is that his double's countergift, achieved through identification and the act of narration, is the intimation of what dying is like and what it means to be dead. From the narrator-protagonist's viewpoint, this situation would be consoling, making the thought of his own death less frightening.

The threat of death and the violence of detective work function as the rite of initiation into the interaction with the dead and death. The decisive factor is that, even in the state of unconsciousness, Marlowe still lives. Hence, this state is comparable to sleep, which, in turn, might be what being dead is like.[29] But, as the narrator never describes his recollections of this state in any detail, being unconscious remains a mysterious experience in a similar fashion to being dead. Thus the only knowledge of death the narrator can gain and impart to the reader relies on the combined effect of his identification with the double, the story about this double's death, the protagonist's own brushes with death, and the whole of his elegiac, commemorative narrative.

The symbolic operation the narrator would like to establish through narration is the dispelling of the disjunction of life and death. There are, however, elements within his narratives that testify to the continued failure of this project, pointing to fissures in the narrative fabric.[30] The exchange characterizing the primitive's relationship with the dead is typically one that involves the notion of the fluidity of being: the partners are indistinguishable from each other. It is only with the internalization of such notions as that of the soul and individual consciousness, argues Jean Baudrillard, that the human being became alienated from her shadow, in consequence of which the double began to figure the subject's own discontinuity in death and madness. The double began to portend the subject's own death (1993, 142). Concomitant with this alienation goes the type of symbolic exchange modern society has introduced: death is now redeemed by an individual labour of mourning. Thereby, the subject's engagement with death becomes an economic process involving redemption, labour, debt, and the individual. Baudrillard remarks that this change 'entails a considerable difference in enjoyment: we trade with our dead in a kind of melancholy, while the primitives live with their dead under the auspices of the ritual and the feast' (135). Melancholy rather than ritual feasting gives Marlowe's narrative voice its tone, suggesting that his flirtations with death ultimately return to a markedly individualistic interpretation of this phenomenon. Moreover, the events depicted in *The Long Goodbye* are disturbing, for Terry Lennox is the only double who actually 'returns' from the dead, talking the language of self-interest that spoils the fantasy Marlowe has been nursing. This double's treachery suggests that the other doubles, too, are the narrator's projections. Moreover, Lennox's betrayal further implies that death threatens to hollow out life before finally taking over completely.[31] These features indicate that for all the significance the narrator gives to his various doubles, his relationship with the reader forms the ultimate framework for considering the progress of his elegiac narrative.

Remember Me When I Am Gone Away: Elegiac Patterns in Chandler's Fiction

The seriality of Chandler's fiction brings forcibly to view the moral bias of elegy. We see this feature in his use of first-person narration, a typical feature of elegy. First-person narration represents other characters more or less externally, but, as Knight argues, Chandler takes this externalization to its limit, as all other characters are completely controlled by Marlowe's personalized depiction of actions, dialogue, and setting. In each scene, characters act only upon the detective, and the reader is always presented solely with that which feeds directly into Marlowe's consciousness (1980, 145–6). The effect of this strategy is to heighten the status of the protagonist-narrator as the one stable centre of the world narrated. Priestman connects this characteristic with Chandler's troubled attitude to the relations between the detective-narrative formula and 'serious' literature, referring to the writer's attempt to use the conventional form as a 'pretext,' an indifferent initial text over which a 'richer' literary text can be draped (1990, 172). Again, the effect is, according to Priestman, the highlighting of Marlowe's own narrative voice as the unifying key to the reading experience, dramatizing Chandler's striving to make him the hero-narrator who is absolutely everything (175).

These arguments supply the broad outline for Chandler's use of doubling in the Marlowe stories. The double's death always makes the narrator aware of his own approaching death, so that narrative is his way of coming to terms with the fright and insecurity of death. There is the implication in Bruffee's (1983) analysis of the elegy that the narrator, in confronting and working through his obsession and fear, intends his narrative to suggest to the reader one tested way of dealing with these issues. In Marlowe's stories the male victim seems ultimately to serve as the initial motivation for elegiac narratives whose primary function is to sing the praise of the singer himself. The narrator uses the elegiac thrust as a recognizable background against which his function as narrator emerges in a distinctive manner. The dead doubles, together with the knowledge of life and death Marlowe hopes they could give him, highlight such traits as his sensitivity, compassion, and thoughtfulness. The extreme self-centredness of his narrative voice betrays, however, that the elegy of the double is ultimately intended as a model for an elegy for himself. The narrator uses the awareness of his own impending death, part and parcel of the elegiac mode, as a prompting for the reader to remember him when he is gone. The whole narrative series is the effigy he builds of and for himself, meant to remain standing to his memory after his death. By remembering and doing homage to his dead doubles, the narrator shows his readers how they are to linger over him fondly in their thoughts after his time has come: he desires himself to be worth a story told by his interlocutors. Chandler's work thus makes us aware of yet another role doubling plays in the detective-story genre. Instead of imaginatively identifying with the criminal, the detective-narrator feels himself into the victim, using this relationship as the motivation for his narrative transaction with the reader.

The elegiac narrator always uses the Other in order to define the self; moreover, elegies invariably are more about 'me' than about 'him' – the person in whose honour the elegy is ostensibly sung. What makes Chandler's narratives part company with an elegy such as Fitzgerald's *The Great Gatsby*, for example, is the difference in the authors' handling of the mirror mechanism associated with doubling. In *The Great Gatsby*, Nick Carraway is at first riveted by Gatsby's 'extraordinary gift for hope, a romantic readiness such as I had never found in any other person' (8); he sees in Gatsby an idealized version of what he himself would like to be. As Nick learns more, he gradually realizes that Gatsby is a distorting reflective surface, because Gatsby's self-concept is based on an imaginary identification with a romantic dream. The relation aiming at sameness eventually gives way to a relation emphasizing difference. In contrast, the Chandlerian narrator ostensibly starts out by underlining his difference from his double, for he is the 'I' that is following a distinct 'you'; he further emphasizes this seeming difference by triumphing over the double (i.e., by staying alive). Yet by insisting that 'I would be you had I not taken care,' he sees in the double *only* a picture of himself. Difference gradually gives way to sameness, for what the double is as himself is not as important as what he is as the narrator's projection.

The mirror relationships between the protagonist-narrator and the central male double play an important role in the narrator's elegiac motivation. At the beginning of his narrative, Nick Carraway tells the reader that Gatsby, who 'represented everything for which I have an unaffected scorn,' made him change his mind: 'No – Gatsby turned out all right at the end; it is what preyed on Gatsby, what foul dust floated in the wake of his dreams that temporarily closed out my interest in the abortive sorrows and short-winded elations of men' (8). It is because the narrator has reached the point where Gatsby no longer functions as his mirror image that he can evaluate and appreciate this man, without, however, embracing Gatsby's quest and values. The closing situation seems different in Chandler. As the dead double remains Marlowe's mirror image at, and beyond, the ending, his elegies seem to be designed to prove that 'No – I turned out all right; *it is what preyed on me*, what foul dust floated in the wake of my dreams that led to the morally unfortunate consequences of my quest.'[32]

The protagonist-narrator's relationship to his dead double suggests a brief comparison of Chandler's work with the metaphysical detective story as well. Such books as Vladimir Nabokov's *The Real Life of Sebastian Knight* (1992) and Paul Auster's *The Locked Room* (1988) also insist on the doubling of the 'detective' figure and the missing person he pursues.[33] What sets these books apart both from Chandler and Fitzgerald is that they depict the mirror mechanism in yet another way. The detective's identification with, and subsequent idealization of, his quarry leads eventually to the realization of the basic interchangeability of one identity for the other, thanks to the instability of the very concept of identity. Now the 'narrating I' is 'he' and 'he' is the 'narrating I,' because the narrator knows that any concept of identity is always based on imaginary identification. Thus, such a metaphysical detective narrative accomplishes the task that is only hinted at in Chandler's stories: the give and take between the living and the dead doubles.[34]

The notion of self exhibited in Chandler's *oeuvre* does not stress the self's autonomy or coherence so much as its distinctiveness. Philip Marlowe's self is not notable for its coherence or free-standing nature, but for its aesthetic memorability. Each and every characteristic of his narrative voice – the episodic and loosely connected events of the plot held together by the unifying force of his presence, the detailed descriptions of people and places, and the elaborate and witty similes for which this voice is famous – is intended to impress on the reader the sense of its uniqueness and rarity. Marlowe's basic narrative motivation may thus be described as fundamentally *narcissistic*, for he constructs the *reader's* role as one which serves as his *admiring mirror*. The narrator's use of the detective-story conventions as the pretext for aesthetic play and bravura sets the narrator and the reader firmly apart from the narrated world and its events, elevating them to a plane where they may together view these elements as rendered through the narrator's discerning and perceptive voice. This striving to create a confidential and exclusive relationship with the reader explains why all interactional relationships within the narrated world always return to a dyadic bond in Chandler's works. Because the position of readers is the narrator's projection, a place he constructs for them within his narrative web, the reciprocal bond reveals itself as the result of a narcissistic self's longing for a narrowly defined kind of response from the envisaged interlocutor who is to admire – and perhaps also envy – the narrator's aesthetic discernment and skill. That the readers' envisaged response has its specific rewards has not escaped Knight, who argues that that response verifies their intellectual and cultural superiority (1980, 138). These rewards cannot, however, camouflage the fact that the game this narrator constructs always leaves him one up on his readers.

This characterization throws further light on the difference between Chandler's work and the metaphysical detective story, which seems to arise from what might be called the exclusiveness of the aesthetic. By indicating either that all selves are locked rooms or, conversely, that one can enjoy the undulations of any soul if one exercises one's imaginative muscles, Auster and Nabokov include the reader in the narrative experience as a near equal. In Auster's book, the narrator's frustration with his double and the obscurity of his quest become in equal measure the reader's preoccupations; if the impenetrable enclosure of the double's and the narrator's selves direct our attention to the inscrutability of our own self, then at least this experience is something that is (universally) shared. In Nabokov's book, the narrator's obsession and rivalry with Knight give way to the warmer emotion of love and his realization of the possibility of understanding someone else's aesthetic experiences to the point of their becoming one's own. Similarly, by following the undulations of V.'s narrative, we may make the imaginative aesthetic leap from our own self into another's. With Chandler, in contrast, this emphasis on mutuality seems to be lacking. Instead, the central focus is that the narrative voice is distinctly Marlowe's and his alone. The reader's task is to appreciate this voice and understand its superiority in comparison to other hard-boiled voices, but it is not to share in its achievement as an equal. There is room for one and only one original Philip Marlowe. Given this lack of reciprocity, it is hard to conceive of the narrator as the reader's true friend.

As long as the reader accepts the textually embedded role, the elegiac effigy the narrator builds of, and for, himself stands intact. But what makes the narrator's position fragile is its narcissistic character, for it is so strongly dependent on the reader's response. Thus the narrator, who in the course of his stories spends so much time approving and rejecting the characters and phenomena he encounters, invests the reader with similar evaluative power with regard to himself. Should the flesh-and-blood reader refuse to function as the narrator's admiring mirror, the elegiac fantasy will fail to work in the intended way. The reader may, nevertheless, have sympathy for the desire to be remembered that runs through this author's work.

Coming to an End

This study examines the various ways in which reading detective fiction, at each narrative level, represents an elaborate process of figuration. It conceives of reading as a continual oscillation between moving forward and stopping this movement in order to reflect upon the fragments one has gathered, their interrelationships, and the whole they construct together. The purpose of this fluctuation is for the reader to comprehend the different figures of design that structure and organize the detective-story plot. As a concordant structure, this plot patterns the narrated material so that the reader grasps the relations of the plot's beginning, middle, and end during reading. The reader may then arrange the inter-relations of these plot elements with the help of various spatial configurations in order to perceive the compositional structure and the architectonics of a work. Detective fiction self-consciously emphasizes its spatial aspects, for example, in the form of various geometrical patterns that help the reader to organize and map textual structures. The genre's specificity shows in the fact that all these formal designs divulge both the narrative and the thematic design of the plot. In fact, readers use narrative form to make sense of various moral issues.

As knowledge of the whole is essential to understanding any of the parts, reading detective stories follows a retrospective logic which involves the reader's attempt to achieve a synchronic-spatial view of a work. Such a strategy is typical of rereading. As regards the genre, rereading addresses the reader's treatment of a text as an example of its kind, so that reading entails a constant comparison between this particular text and similar texts held in the reader's memory. On the basis of our generic competence, we make forecasts of a given narrative's development and outcome, a response which strengthens the notion of reading as a process of continuous hypothesizing and revising. The specificity of detective fiction lies in the fact that it stages writing and reading 'contests' at each narrative level, contests which reflect the functioning of narrative transmission in the genre. These contests make us aware of how the cat-and-mouse pursuit in the fictional world carries over and affects our own interaction with the author. The starting point is that the primary agents at each level always act in the dual role of writer and reader. To be able to function in both roles, they have to have an idea of what the opponent is like, a process which involves imagining or inventing this opponent. On the basis of this projection, each agent plans the strategy that will ensure the reaching of the goals he or she has set. Thus the author-reader relationship is always tinged with at least some degree of antagonism. As readers, our aim is to try and discover the logical pattern that our adversary's plotting adheres to, until we can form a sense of its overall organization. This projection of the opponent's moves is like a literary game in which narrative information is processed to figure out both formal and thematic designs.

The overall design of my own study builds on what Donald P. Spence (1987) calls a *recursive operator*, a device based on repetition, the purpose of which is to draw the reader's notice to regular patterns in narrative material (190). Spence explains that a recursive narrative pattern appeals to us partly because it depends heavily on repetition, but also because a recursive operator determines the shape of the data (190). The recursive operator at work in this study is the detective's and the reader's mutual attempt to turn a transgressive piece of action into a piece of narrative truth through the process of figuration. As Spence points out, recursion has a spiral-like structure, thanks to the fact that the recursive operator always operates on itself (193). What this means is that each time we interpret a recursive narrative, we cannot help applying the terms on which the operator works to our reading; yet by doing so, we add a further layer to the narrative which makes our own interpretation differ from the one represented in the text. Poe's 'The Purloined Letter' is a prime example of such a spiral, for, by inviting the reader to consider the act of analysis, it makes us realize that our own interpretation is based on the act of analysis of the act of analysis (see Johnson 1988). Johnson says that the result is 'an asymmetrical, abysmal structure,' in which 'no analysis ... can intervene without transforming and repeating other elements in the sequence, which is thus not a stable sequence, but which nevertheless produces certain regular effects' (213–14). In concluding, I would briefly like to dwell on what happens in narrative transmission when a reader – the detective or the reader – turns into a writer-narrator in the light of this recursive operator.

The writing and reading 'contests' taking place at each narrative level demonstrate the relationship between *sjuzet* and *fabula*, the basic components of plot. The repetition of this relationship ensues from the Chinese-box-like structure of narration that characterizes the genre. As we have seen, at the inmost heart of this structure is the criminal's story (*fabula*) which is reconstructed by the detective's investigation (*sjuzet*). In trying to answer the question 'Whodunit?' detectives are in a state of belatedness in relation to the criminal, for their journeys are repetitions, which gain meaning from this attachment to the criminal's prior journey. Detectives retrace their predecessor's traces and thus uncover and construct the meaning of the criminal's story. They not only repeat the adversary's story, however, but also take it as the motivating force of their own narratives. Their stories are never primary, but attach themselves to the criminal's story, seeking there narrative authority. They frame the criminal's story by enclosing, confining, and limiting it. By doing so, they complicate it by telling how they came to know it, thus adding another layer of plot and eventually transforming the relation of telling to told, so that it is finally less the criminal's story that they tell than their own stories, inhabited by the criminal's story (see Brooks 1984, 255). Here we see, of course, the recursive operator at work.

Brooks interprets this loyalty of the follower to the forerunner as the inevitable loyalty of *sjuzet* to *fabula*, of telling to told. The conclusion he draws from this situation is that it is 'only through repetition that narrative plot gains motivation and the implication of meaning, as if, in the absence of any definable meaning in either *fabula* or *sjuzet*, it were in the fact of repetition of one by the other that meaning could be made to inhere' (254). There is, however, a specific twist to this 'stitching' of *sjuzet* to *fabula* in the detective story. My examination demonstrates that the crucial feature about the detectives' retelling is that they retell a story that was *mistold* the first time. I took as my starting point the fact that the 'correct' telling of this story the second time around involves the detective's examination of the question of guilt and responsibility. The criminal's narrative is transgressive in nature, introducing disorder, even chaos, into the fictional world. Detectives have a communal task to determine the perpetrator's identity and to assign guilt to the parties involved. Society expects them to try and tell the criminal's story 'correctly'; this effort gives legitimacy to their actions. Telling another's story correctly requires only partial faithfulness to the criminal's experience.

As the implementation of imaginative identification demonstrates, detectives need to understand this experience in order to be able to evaluate how it affects the narrative explanation they put together as well as the moral evaluation they offer. But given that their task is primarily practical, they need not necessarily understand everything about their adversary's experience and story.

The social and practical nature of the detective's reading task requires that, in the retelling, the criminal's story is told in more or less conventional semantics and syntax. Even if a detective's version includes gaps and incoherencies, it nevertheless must render the crime understandable in the specific circumstances so that guilt and responsibility may be evaluated and allotted. The retelling has to be such that action can, at least in principle, ensue from it. (Whether it in fact leads to action is another matter.) The consequence of having a criminally 'wrong' and a communally 'right' version of a crime highlights, of course, not only the separation of *fabula* from *sjuzet* but also the fact that *sjuzet* is always an *interpretation* of *fabula*; moreover, in detective fiction it presents a socially commissioned, defined, and limited interpretation of *fabula*. In this genre there is thus always a disjunction between these two levels: the follower is only partially faithful to the forerunner. Again, this feature reinforces the functioning of the recursive operator, for, through imaginative identification with the opponent, the detective applies the specific terms of the opponent's strategy, but in a manner that undoes the results of that strategy.

The disjunction between the criminal's story and the detective's retelling of it has specific consequences for the Chinese-box-like structure of narration typical of the genre. At its core is the criminal's deed, which he or she presents to others as a definitive interpretation of the events, while in fact it is false. The detective reinterprets this interpretation. First-person narrators such as 'Watsons' or third-person narrators then offer their own interpretations of the detective's interpretation. And, at the most complex level of this structure, the reader communicates with the author, conscious of the disjunction among all these different versions, constructing yet another interpretive level. Each interpreter's specific challenge is to put together an account that spells out as fully as possible the narrative and moral interconnections among the components and the totality they form together. Thus, narrative transmission primarily concerns each and every participant's *conclusive interpretation* of another's story at each narrative level. The criminal's transgressive action shows dimly through each level as though in a palimpsest; what is foregrounded, however, is this *compulsion of figuration*, of taking another's story and refitting its components into a more coherent, aesthetically and ethically elegant totality. This game more than anything is about interpretive mastery and insight. Thus, reading detective fiction engenders what Brooks describes as 'an interminable process of analysis and interpretation, a dynamics of transference in which the reader is asked not only to understand the story, but to contemplate it: to make it fuller, more powerfully ordered, and therefore more hermeneutic' (1984, 260).

Sweeney (1990) explains that this recursive spiral means that detective fiction reflects not only its own narrative mechanisms, but also the interpretive processes that might disclose them. The employment of an investigative method inevitably reduces the object under study by excluding from its design all those details it cannot account for. Thematization, which contributes to the creation of coherence, further enhances such exclusion. Thanks to these features, the genre reflects the inevitable subjectivity of analysis: the choice of method, its employment, and the striving towards coherence all disclose the interpreter's ethos. Moreover, not only does the detective narrative reflect its own analysis, but this analysis in turn also reflects the narrative. Sweeney concludes that an examination of detective fiction is thus helplessly and inevitably self-reflexive, a situation which the locked-room mystery aptly describes. It is impossible to separate the criticism of a narrative text from the text itself and from all its elements and properties. Therefore, detective fiction reflects the analysis of its own narrative mysteries as well as the mysteries of our own analysis, which is itself solipsistic and self-reflexive.

Nowhere else is this subjectivity of interpretation more visible than in the endings of detective stories. They invoke the feeling of absurdity arising from the disproportion between the elaborate ordering systems employed and the triviality of their effect, which Brooks aptly describes as someone having 'designed a machine to produce work far smaller than the energy put into it' (1984, 241). This disproportion, of course, highlights the constructedness of the solution, drawing the reader's attention to the functioning of the detective-story plot. But in equal measure it underlines the subjectivity of all interpretation. At each narrative level, each interpreter spells out as clearly and unambiguously as possible what he or she thinks is the case. As the detective's example demonstrates, the genre represents this process as one which requires the interpreter to pin down meaning and take responsibility for his or her interpretation. Demanding exactitude and coherence today may, in fact, evoke its own kind of dread. Although this process engenders a feeling of satisfaction, it also entails a tinge of sadness by making interpreters aware of their own limitations. The endings of detective stories demonstrate that with the particular capabilities of an interpreter, applied in a given context, and with specific information at hand, the outcome is what the detective – and, subsequently, the reader – can construct. It thereby draws attention to the confines one mind can postulate among various components in order to construct meaningful wholes.

Can one ascribe some general purpose to this compulsion of figuration with which the detective narrative engages its readers? Obviously, it has ritual-like features, based as it is on the repetition of the familiar and the already-known. Its familiarity largely derives from its traditional narrative form, which readers learn to process from early on. Reading the genre may impart a sense of reassurance, as readers go through well-rehearsed motions, encountering ideas, notions, and beliefs familiar also from everyday life. Such shared knowledge of the 'game tokens' is, of course, what makes the game possible in the first place. It is this context of the almost overly familiar which suggests that the purpose of reading the genre can be thought of in terms of that well-known generic motif, the purloined letter. This motif, based on the idea that that which is directly under our noses is almost invisible in its visibility, applies to the general intention of the genre. Because reading it engages readers in a metalevel reflection on conjecture, plotting and plot, and the construction of views of life, it invites them to think about what it is that they know – or think they know – about these issues and how that knowledge becomes accessible. The best detective narratives use the familiar, the well-known, and that which goes without saying in order either to probe into the features giving them this quality of familiarity or to question our supposed familiarity with such things. Thus, reading detective fiction is about spotting the purloined letter, hidden in full view in the processes of conjectural thinking, narrative construction, and moral reflection: the reader's reward is seeing the already known from unexpected and pleasurable angles.

Notes

Introduction

1 For an overview of the academic criticism of the genre, see Pyrhönen 1994.
2 I thank S.E. Sweeney for drawing my attention to this context.
3 My associating the concept of spatial form with plot requires a comment on the controversy surrounding this concept. I draw on Frank Kermode's (1967) and Peter Brooks's (1984) discussions of plot as an organizing and shaping force of narrative. Both reject the notion of spatial form on the grounds that it fails to do justice to the temporal nature of narrative. I find Frank's (1991, 84–101) response to Kermode's criticism convincing, for he shows the disagreement to be terminological rather than substantial. The quarrel concerns the term 'spatial,' for Kermode comprehends it as atemporal, which, however, is a misunderstanding. Spatiality does not, in Frank's sense, exclude time as a dimension of understanding, but refers to the reader's perception of the concord among a narrative's beginning, middle, and end in a moment of time: the formal and thematic design of plot. Thus, the term does not allude to a pattern in space, but to the perception of an organized narrative pattern as comprehended *in* and *over* time.
4 Usually, however, the story of the crime overlaps with the story of the investigation, because the investigation, by closing in on the truth, compels the criminal to commit new crimes.
5 Calinescu's term for this level is *game with rules* (127), but since by definition all games have rules, I prefer to use a term that emphasizes the level where the game takes place.
6 Calinescu distinguishes between *involvement* and *absorption* in reading. Being involved, Calinescu explains, entails an emotional commitment, as a result of which the reader is transported to another world. It entails the reader's participation in the experience of fictive people through some sort

of fantasy; moreover, we may identify or empathize with them or, at the least, be there and watch them (164). In contrast, absorption is a state of high concentration, lacking the kind of personal immersion typical of involvement. It is thus markedly self-reflexive, more imaginatively detached, and more intellectual (164).

7 The notable exception is the 'double switch-back,' in which the most likely suspect does, after all, prove to be guilty. This pattern starts with the realization of the particular suspect's strong motive, which may even be underlined by the suspect him- or herself. This suspect, however, is usually capable of providing (faked) evidence which makes it seem impossible for him or her to have committed the crime. Thereby, the detective's suspicions are directed at other characters. Only towards the end can the detective see through the culprit's deceptive strategies and expose his or her guilt. A good example of this pattern is Christie's *Murder at the Vicarage* (1930).

8 The transfer of the investigative task from the community to a special corps – the police, private investigators – took place during the latter part of the nineteenth century in Western democracies. For analyses on how detective fiction reflects this social change, see Knight 1980; Miller 1988; Palmer 1978; Porter 1981; and Woods 1990.

9 It is noteworthy that situations of contradiction also involve deliberation as to which rules take precedence over others *within* a code.

10 Historical changes and the effects of the cultural context make literary genres highly transitory in nature. Genres inevitably represent heterogeneous classes, for no absolute causal, genetic bond ties together the various texts taken to belong to a given genre during its different phases. A specific period may, moreover, contain a number of diverging generic variants. The absence of identical, obligatory traits and the historical variability of definitional criteria underline the fact that the various texts integrated into a genre are linked by so-called family resemblances. They do not necessarily share the same characteristic(s), but a specific text shares certain features with some texts in the genre and a set of other traits with other texts in it. The fuzziness of generic demarcations shows also in the fact that most texts are traversed by more than one generic tradition and cannot thus be referred to one single class. This characteristic suggests that generic constituents and traits cover only certain – albeit significant – portions of the texts in question, instead of their totality. The generic model is never a global one (Schaeffer 1989).

1 Projecting the Criminal

1 I take this designation from Karl Morrison's *'I Am You': The Hermeneutics of*

Empathy in Western Literature, Theology, and Art (1988) without adopting his sense of the term. He traces the persistence of a cultural tradition interpreting empathy as a distinctive combination of cognitive and affective processes and aiming to close the gap separating 'I' from 'you.' Fictional detectives rarely aim at the kind of personal participation in the other's condition that Morrison describes.

2 The self looks at itself and the specular image *returns* this gaze whereby the self now functions as the mirror for the mirror image. The fact that the image looks back brings with it the realization of the act of reflection. As the self reflects itself, it can, through the mirror image, see itself reflecting itself. The self is one with itself while it simultaneously is also different from itself. Splitting thus both generates and sustains internal difference, a sense of interior otherness.

3 In using the master/slave terminology, I follow Irwin, who relates his discussion of the mirror image to Hegel's notion of the origin of personal identity as a master/slave conflict within a split and doubled consciousness (Irwin, ch. 5).

4 Doležel distinguishes the double from the *doppelgänger*, defining the latter as follows: 'in one and the same world there are two individuals (X and Y) with distinct personal identities, but sharing a set of properties in such a manner and to such a degree that they are indistinguishable: X = Y' (95). In the detective story the *doppelgänger* relationship most often involves the criminal and the victim: the criminal adopts the victim's identity and role, confusing others as to who is who. It is only after the detective demonstrates that one person is actually two that the epistemic confusion is cleared away.

5 Discussing Chesterton as a mainstream detective-story writer may raise questions, for Howard Haycraft first introduced the term *metaphysical detective story* (1974, 76) in order to describe the marvellous nature and the theological-philosophical intentions of the Father Brown stories. We will see, however, that Chesterton is a significant precursor, but not a full member, of the *modern* metaphysical camp. (Although Chesterton has had a great impact on Borges, Irwin alludes to him only briefly in his book.)

6 In 'The Purloined Letter,' the Queen of France hides a compromising letter from the King by leaving it in full view on her table; Minister D— steals it from her, in the King's presence, while she helplessly watches. Failing to find it, the Prefect of Police appeals to Dupin, who concludes that the Minister's strategy of hiding is the same as the Queen's: the letter hangs in full view in a card-rack, only refolded and re-addressed. Dupin replaces it with a substitute letter declaring his hatred of the Minister due to an unspecified

wrong he once has caused Dupin. Ironically, Dupin's possession of the letter blinds him to his knowledge of its effect: in giving way to his rage he replicates the Minister's actions against the Queen. He is vulnerable to self-delusion, as were the Queen and the Minister before him, for each thinks that having the letter gives them a non-reversible advantage over others.

7 The symbolic order is, in Lacan's theory, the order of signifiers.

8 Hammer envisages this hidden master in the following way: 'Someplace at the top of the heap was a person. From him the fear radiated like from the center of a spiderweb. He sat on his throne and made a motion of his hand and somebody died. He made another motion and somebody was twisted until they screamed. A nod of his head did something that sent a guy leaping from a roof because he couldn't take it anymore' (34).

9 For example, Hammer compares himself and a gangster to dogs: 'The little hairs on the back of his neck went up straight like happens to a dog when he meets another dog, only on this mutt the skin under the hair happened to be a pale, pale yellow' (85). As with animals of prey, Hammer's lips peel back over his teeth in response to aggression (e.g., 83, 108, 138), and he likens women to cats (e.g., 19, 87, 93).

10 This fantasy of 'seamless' mirroring as a reinforcement of the male self-image expresses the function Hammer accords to women in general and to their relation to him in particular. Consider his description of Dr Soberin's nurse, which begins as a generalized description of a beautiful woman, but ends up in being focused upon his effect on her: 'Some women are just pretty. Some are just beautiful. Some are just gorgeous. Some are like her ... She's got eyes to go with the hair and they sweep over you and laugh because she knows how you feel. And only for a moment do the eyes show disappointment because somehow the cigarette gets lit as if she hadn't been there at all and the smoke from *my* mouth smooths out any expression *I* might have let show through' (62; my italics). Not only does the woman as mirror image confirm Hammer's self-image as a unified totality, but her contentment is also dependent on his gaze; should he fail to look at her, she will lack the substance nurturing her.

11 Lily Carver's name is a textual clue to the inversion of her inward constitution: the snow-white Lily, smelling of rubbing alcohol, 'disturbing because of its unusual pungent purity' (129), is actually a bloody Carver, a murderer. Moreover, like such names as Hammer and Spade, it has the ring of masculine pragmatism.

12 The book's anti-Oedipal character is tied up with its protagonist's paranoia. His belief in the infiltration of the criminal woman into the symbolic order

signals the disintegration of the paternal function ensuring social order. As Žižek suggests, this vacuum is filled by the 'irrational' maternal superego, 'arbitrary, wicked, blocking "normal" sexual relationship,' that is possible only under the paternal metaphor (99). Cawelti (156–61) relates this situation to the widespread male anxiety concerning the influx of women into work life during and after the Second World War.

13 *Historiographical detection* represents a specific branch of the genre, which has flourished in recent years. Carr's book is an example of that variant, which examines a specific historical era through the detection of a crime. Another good illustration is Keith Oatley's *The Case of Emily V.* (1993), which adds a new case study to the existing stock of Freud's analyses of female hysteria. The book brings together Freud, Sherlock Holmes, and Emily V., each of whom interpret the same events within their own system of reference. The other variant reopens an unsolved historical (or pseudohistorical) mystery, demonstrating how a detective puts together a new solution in the light of various textual documents. Examples include Josephine Tey's *The Daughter of Time* (1996), Colin Dexter's *The Wench is Dead* (1994c), and Veronica Ross's *The Anastasia Connection* (1996).

14 See Ginzburg 1983 and Žižek 1991 for discussions of these similarities.

15 Dupin and Minister D— together with Holmes and Professor Moriarty are the classic examples of antagonists representing idealized versions of a human being's two sides. Pairing a criminal psychologist with a serial killer is a modernization of this fantasy. The serial killer has first-hand experience of extensive psychic damage and can use it to his or her advantage, while the psychologist's expertise includes the recognition and restraint, in himself or herself, of the drives tormenting the adversary.

16 Jane Gallop (1988) explains that in psychoanalysis the analyst is the analysand's mirror, not his or her likeness or double. This distinction of the mirror from the mirror image emphasizes that the analyst's task is to be a reflecting surface that is in itself devoid of any content. 'In the ethical imperative to be in the symbolic, the charge is to look into the mirror and see not the image but the mirror itself' (272). Neutrality fosters the transference by making explicit that the images the analysand brings into the interaction are his or her own projections. Let it be noted, however, that the transferential relationship between Kreizler's team and the killer lacks the psychoanalytical contract forbidding the parties to harm one another.

17 The narrator explains Kreizler's views of imaginative identification as follows: 'From that moment on, [Kreizler] said, we must make every possible effort to rid ourselves of preconceptions about human behavior. We must try not to see the world through our own eyes, nor to judge it by our own val-

ues, but through and by those of our killer. *His* experience, the context of *his* life, was all that mattered' (160).

18 Kreizler quotes from William James's *Principles of Psychology* to illustrate this idea: 'The character has set like plaster, never to soften again ... Habit dooms us all to fight out the battle of life upon the lines of our nurture and our early choice, and to make the best of a pursuit that disagrees, because there is no other for which we are fitted, and it is too late to begin again' (151–2). While James acknowledges the power of free will to overcome psychic disturbances, Kreizler argues that change is possible only if one is able to alter one's life context and thereby learn new modes of thought and action (57, 268).

19 The team concretizes the idea of the contextual model by using the chalkboard in creating the picture of their 'imaginary man' (73). The board is divided into three sections, bearing the headings 'childhood' (with the subentry of 'molding violence and/or molestation'), 'interval,' and 'aspects of the crime.' They list all the physical and psychological clues on this board, profiling the culprit by revising, combining, and cross-referencing the entries. Thus their interpretive actions demonstrate the spatiality of an explanatory pattern. To interpret the clues, they draw on experience, read literature on psychology and psychopathology, and consult various experts. The case histories of and interviews with other murderers supply valuable interpretive guidelines. The creation of a coherent explanation makes reading the book resemble the experience of looking through a kaleidoscope and seeing shifting and overlapping patterns.

20 This notion is elaborated in the following fashion: 'Whether we took the biological approach, and concentrated on the formation of what Professor James called "neural pathways," or the philosophical route, which would lead into a discussion of the development of the soul, we would arrive at the same conclusion: the idea of a man for whom violence was not only deeply ingrained behavior but the starting point of his meaningful experiences. What he saw when he looked at those dead children was only a representation of what he felt had been done to him – even if only psychically – at some point deep in his past' (193).

21 Brooks argues that psychoanalysis throws light on the narratological distinction between *story* and *discourse* by illustrating the fact that '[n]arrative comes into being only through the work of interpretive discourse on story, seen as the raw material ..., which becomes coherent and explanatory only as the narrating orders it in discourse' (1994, 56).

22 This transformation is highlighted by the fact that the killer adopts a new identity during the course of the book.

23 The killer's compulsion illustrates the motto for the second part of the book from James's *The Principles of Psychology*: 'The same outer object may suggest either of many realities formerly associated with it – for in the vicissitudes of our outer experience we are constantly liable to meet the same thing in the midst of differing companions.' Unable to distinguish himself from his victims, the killer sees one and the same thing wherever he looks.

24 Or, in Gerard Genette's terms, an extra- and heterodiegetic narrator, defined by narrative level (extradiegetic; i.e., a narrator in the first degree) and by its relationship to the story (heterodiegetic; i.e., a narrator absent from the story) (1980, 248).

25 For a general description of the hermeneutics of empathy, see Morrison 1988, chs 1 and 2.

26 Father Brown explains this process as follows: 'Now I set myself conscientiously down to *be* a revolutionary poet ... I tried to clear my mind of such elements of sanity and constructive common sense as I have had the luck to learn or inherit. I shut down and darkened all the skylights through which comes the good daylight of heaven; I imagined a mind lit only by a red light from below; a fire rending rocks and cleaving abysses *upwards*' (584).

27 Travers's name is already a textual clue, for it expresses being at fault or being the wrong way.

28 The title, 'The Mirror of the Magistrate,' contains an echo of an early Renaissance manual of how magistrates should behave. The mirror in the story is both literal (the broken glass in the Judge's house) and allegorical (the book indicating the conventional good behaviour of a professional). The latter aspect adds to the irony of the radically unconventional actions of an ultra-conventional man in order to safeguard his conventionality.

29 The malevolence of participation does not necessarily predetermine its results. Antagonistic identification may lead detectives to an understanding on the basis of which they decide, for example, to let the criminal go. This happens frequently in feminist detective stories when the culprit is a mistreated woman or child.

30 Association by contrast creates a fundamental instability between any contrasting pair, for the interdependence of its poles makes movement along, and fluctuation between, the poles very easy. It explains why the standard detective-story roles of detective, criminal, and victim are highly flexible, indeed overlapping in Chesterton's work. The stories present three variations of this coexistence. 'The Mirror of the Magistrate' illustrates the case where two characters are antithetical doubles. In such cases, the binary pairs of a trait or a role are embodied by two externally separate agents. In the second case, one and the same person illustrates both ends of a contrasting

pair, but at different stages. 'The Blue Cross' and 'The Secret Garden' (1981a) show how Valentin turns from the greatest of French detectives into a cunning murderer, while 'The Blue Cross,' 'The Queer Feet,' and 'The Flying Stars' (1981a) record an inverse movement by demonstrating Flambeau's conversion from the most artistic of all thieves to a consulting detective. The third instance involves persons who simultaneously embody both opposites, as does James Musgrave in 'The Worst Crime in the World' (1981c). After killing his father, Musgrave poses both as himself (the culprit) and as his father (the victim). And, as was already noted, Father Brown's inner makeup also consists of a tension between his sinful and redeemed natures.

31 Morrison (1988) draws attention to the fact that the hermeneutic tradition of empathy uses two different kinds of metaphors to describe the processes of understanding. What he calls the *biological paradigm* relies on various metaphors relating to biological reproduction, whereas the *aesthetic paradigm* uses metaphors of artistic creation (see ch. 1).

32 Oedipus and Theseus are related figures. Their similarity emerges through each man's relationship to three other figures: father, mother, and a part-human, part-animal monster whose death the hero causes. As heroes of consciousness, they are parabolic expressions of the development and stabilization of individual self-consciousness. A prominent theme in their stories is the relationship between self-recognition or self-knowledge, on the one hand, and self-mastery on the other (Irwin, 207–8).

33 Valentin's often-quoted observation in 'The Blue Cross' that 'the criminal is the creative artist; the detective only the critic' (1981a, 12) does not apply to Father Brown, who unites creativity and criticism. Hunter points out that Chesterton distinguishes between the artistry of criminals and that of madmen. Criminals are creative, because they create not only for gain but also for the sake of aesthetic pleasure. By seeking an audience – the law, religion – they implicitly acknowledge the existence of an outside authority. In contrast, madmen are utterly self-centred and egotistical, which is why their crimes lack creativity. Chesterton emphasizes that if criminals persist in crime, they will ultimately turn into madmen (Hunter 1979, 154–5). Only mystic artists are capable of sustained creativity as well as of critical acumen, developing their self-reflexive awareness of human shortcomings in their own creativity as well as in that of others.

34 In the hermeneutic tradition of empathy, aesthetic closure serves as a continual assurance of truth, i.e., of the validity of interpretation. Morrison explains this notion by analogy with *catharsis*, which requires 'first of all, a poet of special gifts, or a touch of madness, and secondly, an esthetic partici-

pation by spectators in the play as though it were reality. The play became a transparent medium through which spectators relived a poet's vision, and, in so doing, regained his original inspiration' (1988, 28).

35 Imaginative identification with the other may still change the personifier by making her conscious of characteristics she has never before perceived in herself. Consider, for example, the detective's thoughts about the serial killer in Kerr's *A Philosophical Investigation*: 'Rather it was that she felt fascinated by him. Her imagination had been roused by him. Through him she had come to learn certain things about the world. About herself' (254). At the end of the case she summarizes its meaning for her: 'Things were different now. She had stopped hating. It was time to be compassionate. To care. Maybe even to love' (367). Significantly, the serial killer, suffering his punishment in the state of 'punitive coma,' is the person whom she will care for.

36 That the interpretation of Chesterton's stories turns the mirror on the interpreter is best attested by the work of Jorge Luis Borges. His rewriting of Chesterton's stories (for example, 'The Theme of the Traitor and the Hero' [1970c] is based on Chesterton's 'The Sign of the Broken Sword' [1981a]), his use of the mirror motif combined with the mode of association by contrast, and the connection of the detective's investigation with a metaphysical quest, all demonstrate his deep understanding of the game Chesterton plays with the reader. In rewriting this game, however, Borges uses it for his own purposes, since his allegories are secular and aesthetic ones, yielding what Merivale calls 'self-reflexive postmodern artist-parables' (1997b, 165).

37 Hannah Charney (1987) has compared the transferential exchange involved in telling detective stories to jokes; she argues, however, that this association makes them anti-Oedipal. She fails to perceive that the joke teller's recognition of a third party – actual or as an internalized sanction – situates joke telling in a triangular situation, which, as Skura argues, is 'the kind of adult relationship epitomized in the oedipal triangle' (1981, 181).

2 Abduction: Interpreting Signs for Narrative Ends

1 Strictly speaking, no perfect crime could, in these terms, be the basis of a detective story. Not only does the genre insist on the revelation of who the criminal is, but, more importantly, the perfect crime, in this sense, is not narratively interesting. Hence, usually even the cleverest criminals fail to control every aspect of their crimes, making it possible for the detectives to trace these crimes back to them. Or, as the serial killer of Philip Kerr's *A Philosophical Investigation* expresses it: 'it is ironic that while [perfect murders] continue to remain in a state of perfection – that is, they are unsolved –

the artistry must go unsung. It is only when they fall some way short of perfection that they may be celebrated at all' (1995, 273). A common explanation for such oversights is the pride criminals take in their crime 'texts,' making them secretly wish that someone would recognize them as the 'authors.' For example, in the whodunit, the *nom de plume* of 'the wandering maniac,' to whose authorship the community often assigns the deed, is ambiguous from the criminals' perspective, because, on the one hand, it provides proof of their success, but, on the other hand, it shows that others do not appreciate the unusual cleverness and aesthetic ingenuity of the crime. Thus, only detectives are their true opponents. In those rather rare instances in which no one in the fictional world discovers the identity of the perpetrator, the *reader* does, as in Richard Hull's *The Murder of My Aunt* (1934) or in Maj Sjöwall and Per Wahlöö's police procedural *The Locked Room* (1973).

2 Holmes frequently expounds on this principle with statements such as: 'You know my method. It is founded upon the observance of trifles' ('The Boscombe Valley Mystery' 1985a, 80); 'Indeed, I have found that it is usually in unimportant matters that there is a field for observation ...'; and 'Never trust to general impressions, my boy, but concentrate yourself upon details' ('The Case of Identity' 1985a, 51, 57).

3 This strategy of copycatting is a motif familiar from Poe's 'The Purloined Letter,' where Dupin imitates Minister D—'s tactics in stealing back the Queen's letter, as well as from Chesterton's 'The Sign of the Broken Sword' (1981a), where the English troops hang their treacherous leader, General St Claire, and make it seem as if the enemy had done it.

4 Such absences are examples of the zero signifier. 'In various systems of signs,' says Sebeok, 'a sign vehicle can sometimes – when contextual conditions are appropriate – signify by its very absence, occur, that is, in *zero* form' (1994, 18). The most famous example of the significance of absence is, of course, from Doyle's 'The Adventure of Silver Blaze' (1985b), in which a valuable horse has been stolen from a stable in spite of the presence of a watchdog. 'Is there any other point to which you would wish to draw my attention?' [Holmes] 'To the curious incident of the dog in the night-time.' 'The dog did nothing in the night-time.' [Holmes] 'That was the curious incident' (250). Holmes selects from his stock of experience a rule that might account for his observation, postulating a conjecture on that basis. By drawing on the rule according to which 'dogs do not bark at people they know well,' he concludes that the horse thief must be someone closely associated with the stables.

5 Choosing my own examples is, of course, directly linked up with the focus

on the narrative aspect of abduction. Yet in doing so, I am also playing with detective fiction as an academic reader: part of this game is finding one's own examples of abduction. Instead of contributing to the already-existing stock of equestrian examples, I want to point to the existence of other motifs besides the horse as having an interesting history within the detective story. In such books as Dashiell Hammett's *The Glass Key* (1980b) and Agatha Christie's *Dead Man's Folly* (1956b) and *Evil under the Sun* (1941), for example, the hat plays, although not in the same manner in each story, a central role in solving the crime. The significance of this motif derives from the fact that the hat covers the head, the locus of scheming and machinations. As the criminal in Kerr's *A Philosophical Investigation* points out, 'it's because the head ... is where all the trouble started' (1995, 9).

6 The game with the author and the detective is not incompatible with the game against them. One might even claim that the game with the author makes the reader a better hand at playing against him or her by making the reader aware of the author's and the detective's competence and the kinds of 'tricks' this competence allows them to perform. For example, our familiarity with the importance of contextual and coreferential selections may help us to disambiguate clues more quickly than the detective does. Moreover, if one is chiefly concerned with aesthetic appreciation, as Robert Champigny (1977) is in his game against detective-story authors, then clearly such appreciation necessitates an understanding of how the inferential process works, because the coherence, plausibility, elegance, and inventiveness of this process are what is appraised aesthetically.

7 Ryan explains that this synthesizing capacity is significant, for readers cannot store in memory complete semantic representations of plot, but 'schematic blueprints,' which they then complete as needed by bridging informational gaps through reasoning and knowledge of the world (1991, 202).

8 The description of such moments of insight is a generic convention. The following two excerpts convey the stereotypical form in which these moments are rendered, emphasizing the simultaneous perception of the whole and the network the parts form in that whole: '[Poirot] was in a daze – a glorious daze where isolated facts spun wildly round before settling neatly into their appointed places. It was like a kaleidoscope – shoe buckles, size nine stockings, a damaged face, the low tastes in literature of Alfred the page boy, the activities of Mr Amberiotis, and the part played by the late Mr. Morley, all rose up and whirled and settled themselves down into a coherent pattern. For the first time, Hercule Poirot was looking at the case *the right way up*' (Christie, *One, Two, Buckle My Shoe*, 1940, 186; italics in the

original). Or, 'In the morning [Wexford] awoke clear-headed and calm. Immediately he remembered what it was Wendy had said to him. It had been when she told him Veronica was to play in a tennis singles final. The significance was in what it reminded him of, and now he remembered that too and as he did so everything began to fall gently and smoothly into place, so that he felt like one recalling and using the combination of a safe until the door slowly swings open' (Rendell, *An Unkindness of Ravens*, 1990a, 386). In classical detective stories these moments function to challenge the reader: do we, too, see the pattern?

9 Holmes claims that 'observation with me is second nature' (*A Study in Scarlet* 1987, 16). To receive intimations of revealing details, the investigators need to open up to the scene of the crime and the encounters with the suspects so as to let the scene and the persons accost or 'speak' to them in some indirect way. Observation already entails an unconscious perception and discrimination among aspects of the world. This attitude derives strong intimations of truth from observation, without necessarily at first being able to specify the specific circumstances that suggested those intimations (Sebeok and Sebeok 1983, 18–19; Ginzburg 1983, 110).

10 G.K. Chesterton's 'The Blue Cross' (1981a) nicely illustrates the significance of the 'middle term,' that is, the selection of the fact to be explained. Valentin, a detective pursuing the great criminal Flambeau, catches him thanks to the intervention of Father Brown; Valentin, however, has not understood any of the events in which he has been engaged: 'He [Valentin] had come to the end of his chase; yet somehow he had missed the middle of it. When he failed (which was seldom), he had usually grasped the clue, but nevertheless missed the criminal. Here he had grasped the criminal, but he could not grasp the clue' [the excluded middle term] (19).

11 Holmes himself explains this reasoning process in the following fashion: 'In solving a problem of this sort, the grand thing is to be able to reason backwards ... There are few people ... who, if you told them a result, would be able to evolve from their own inner consciousness what the steps were which led up to that result. This power is what I mean when I talk of reasoning backwards, or analytically' (*A Study in Scarlet* 1987, 104).

12 In the same volume, Ginzburg, too, concentrates on imprints, symptoms, and clues in explaining the similarities between the abductive practices of the art historian Morelli, the psychoanalyst Freud, and the detective Holmes. It depends on the semiotician how he or she classifies these signs. Sebeok, for example, holds symptoms to be an independent species of signs, saying that clues are the 'detectival' synonyms of symptoms, while imprints are examples of indexical signs (1994, 47, 71). He reminds the reader, how-

ever, that for Peirce, imprints, symptoms, and clues are all examples of indexical signs (48–50). By definition, 'a sign is said to be indexic insofar as its signifier is contiguous with its signified, or is a sample of it' (31). The classification of signs is not the issue here; what is more important is that, while the detection process is going on, detectives seem to seize on the indexical *aspect* of any sign in trying to uncover the criminal. This is because they treat these signs as referring back to some previous point in time, e.g., the committing of the crime. And within the 'text' of the crime, the various signs function as indices of the criminal's presence at the scene as well as of his or her mental makeup, intentions, and goals (i.e., as indices of his or her individuality), all of which function as causal factors underlying the crime. Hence in Hammett's *The Glass Key*, Ned Beaumont treats the fact that the body of Taylor Henry is without a hat and a walking stick as indexical signs (clues) of someone's having taken them away from the scene of the crime. Conjecturing what happened to these items (although not finding definite proof), he charges Senator Henry with the murder of his own son. After the crime is solved, Beaumont seems to read these signs as *symbols* of corruption, for the pact the Senator made with Paul Madvig, Beaumont's best friend, over the body of Taylor Henry, causes Beaumont to reject Madvig for good (1980b, ch. 10).

13 Sebeok points out that a key attribute of indexical signs is the operation of *renvoi*, or referral: Friday's footprint in the sand 'directs Robinson Crusoe back to some day, presumably prior to Friday, in the past. The index, as it were, inverts causality. In Friday's case, the vector of the index points to a bygone day in that a *signans*, the imprint of some foot in the sand, temporally rebounds to a *signatum*, the highly probable presence of some other creature on the island' (1994, 71). Ginzburg adds that in moving from the part to the whole, from the effect to its cause, the decipherer of tracks invariably produces a narrative sequence – at its simplest, 'someone passed this way.' He even wagers that hunters may have been the first storytellers, because they knew how to read a coherent sequence of events from the silent, even almost imperceptible signs left by their prey (1983, 89). Sebeok reminds us that underlying this reading operation is 'the medieval and modern comparison between the world – metaphorically, the Book of Nature – and the book, both assumed to lie open ready to be read once one knows how to interpret indexical signs' (1994, 72).

14 John Dickson Carr's 'The Footprint in the Sky' provides a good example of an attempt to 'lie with imprints.' In this story, footprints in snow, made by size four shoes, go from a house to an adjacent house and back where a burglary with assault has been committed. Everyone suspects Dorothy, who

not only wears this size but also has quarrelled with the victim. Colonel March, however, is able to show that the culprit – who wears size ten – used Dorothy's shoes as *gloves*: 'And in this unusual but highly practical pair of gloves ... Harry Ventnor simply walked across to the other cottage on his hands' (1992, 74). Were it not for a smudged print of the criminal's shoe on a hedge, the wrong person would have been convicted: 'Carrying himself on his hands, his feet were curved up and back over the arch of his body to balance him; he blundered, and smeared that disembodied footprint on the side of the hedge' (74). Colonel March reads this sign also as a symbol of the criminal's aesthetic sensibility in manipulating signs to his advantage: 'To be quite frank, I am delighted with the device. It is crime upside down; it is leaving a footprint in the sky' (74).

15 By placing the events in an English village, the narrator of George's book deliberately evokes traditional whodunit connotations. In the whodunit context, villagers tend to be very good at distinguishing pregnancy from obesity; that they have failed to do so in this case serves the narrator's purpose of underlining the hideousness of incest and the indifference of these villagers, making them close their eyes to what they do not want to see.

16 Lynley fulfils his function as a detective by drawing conclusions about the broad outline of the events and the identity of the murderer before the final confrontation. Having the criminal recount his or her narrative is an old detective-story convention. It has to do, on the one hand, with the manner in which the limits of the detective's knowledge and capabilities are conceived, and, on the other, with the degree to which a narrator lets other voices besides that of the detective be heard. The confession gives the criminal the opportunity to explain the events from his or her own perspective.

17 One of the most impressive examples is Dennis Potter's television series, *The Singing Detective*, in which Marlow, suffering from neurosis and psoriasis, works through his childhood trauma with the help of a psychiatrist. There are thus two detectives, Marlow and a meta-detective, working side by side.

18 Conjecture, as Ginzburg (1983, 110) demonstrates, has always entailed the notion of expertise characterized by an intimate closeness of understanding, interpretation, and application. It also makes use of the kinds of knowledge which tend to be unspoken and whose rules do not easily lend themselves to being formally articulated. One does not learn this model simply by applying rules, so not everyone is capable of reading the hidden reality behind surface manifestations.

19 The theme of incest in all its variations is surely one of the most topical in current detective stories. Examples abound: Keith Oatley's *The Case of Emily*

V. (1993), Ruth Rendell's *An Unkindness of Ravens* (1985), and Barbara Wilson's *Sisters of the Road* (1986), to name but a few. The feminist detective story has used this theme in order to reflect on the misuse of power within the family, but it has wider relevance in the genre, especially thanks to the similarity of the detective-story plot with the plot of Sophocles' *Oedipus Rex*.

20   When the reader is playing against the author and the detective, it seems that our chances of success depend on our skills in making undercoded abductions, precisely because they involve contextual and coreferential selections. The author tries to lead us astray by making us view the whole case or individual clues against an erroneous background. Often authors reinforce these wrong choices by having the detective make the same mistake. Calculating that the reader-player often neglects to mistrust the conjectures by the detective, they turn our incautious trust in this figure against us.

21   Only some clues are objects. Detectives can read anything as clues: gestures, living environs, habits, apparel, diction, and so on.

22   MacWhirter's name is decidedly unusual, so that it seems an odd choice for the murderer to make. The narrator makes the murderer's random choice of a name from a hotel register the ironic twist of the story: had he used his own name, his suit would not have fallen into the hands of MacWhirter, who infers this man's wicked scheme from it. And what is the murderer's own name? It is Nevile (Devil) Strange. The author's naming of this character is a daring act on her part, for readers who are well acquainted with the moral system underlying Christie's work can guess the identity of the perpetrator from the very first mention of this character. I explore this aspect in more detail in chapter 6.

23   Notice that this formulation includes the possibility that we may come up with a more ingenious interpretation of the clues than the author, thus gaining an aesthetic upper hand over our opponent. Champigny's *What Will Have Happened* (1977) demonstrates how a reader-player can take authors to task over weaknesses and incoherencies in conjecture and the assumptions on which the crime plot rests (see, e.g., 112–16 on the use of nursery rhymes). He occasionally suggests how a narrative could have been improved (e.g., Christie's *Murder at the Vicarage*, 40).

24   Rabinowitz analyses *The Maltese Falcon* in order to show how the barter school notion of truth, evoked throughout the narrative, finally gives way to Fort Knoxism, 'deconstruct[ing] the patient deconstruction of foundationalism that forms the very basis of the novel's epistemological project' (1994, 173).

3 Fitting the Solution to the Mystery

1 Poe's sympathies were with German Idealism and Idealist aesthetics, which saw art as an autonomous and self-sufficient enterprise that could be discussed only in terms of its formal properties. In his writings on composition Poe stressed the determinations of proportion, claiming that prose fiction ought to emulate the precision, consistency, and rigid consequence of mathematical problems (Steele 1981–2, 561). Constructing the plot backwards was offered as the major means to this end. The ending reverberates back onto the whole narrative, and in its light the reader can perceive the pattern of interlocking elements, appreciating its artful fabrication. The backward construction has been studied in detail by Porter (1981, ch. 2).

2 Although Dexter sets his books in a police context, they are not, strictly speaking, procedurals, for police work as such receives little attention, while Morse's reasoning is the main point of interest.

3 Of course, the detective's name contains a self-reflexive joke, for it is synonymous with the Morse code.

4 This tension derives partly from the fact that Morse likes to drink alcohol, often in large quantities, while he thinks, thus stimulating his imagination and opening the door to strange notions. In this sense, his drinking is reminiscent of Sherlock Holmes's use of cocaine. While Holmes uses drugs to sharpen his ratiocination, Morse needs alcohol to feed the creative side of his mind, with the state of intoxication facilitating his listening for the voice of the crime text: '[Morse] wasn't quite sure whether his own oft-repeated insistence that he could always think more lucidly after an extra ration of alcohol was wholly true. He certainly *believed* it to be true, though; and quite certainly many a breakthrough in previous investigations had been made under such circumstances ... Yet for Morse (and he quite simply accepted the fact) the world *did* seem a much warmer, more manageable place after a few pints of beer; and quite certainly he knew that (for himself, at any rate) it was on such occasions that the imaginative processes usually *started*. It may have been something to do with the very *liquidity* of alcohol, for he had often seen these processes in terms of just such a metaphor. It was as if he were lulled and sitting idly on the sea-front, and watching, almost entranced, as some great Master of the Tides drew in the foam-fringed curtains of the waters towards his feet and then pulled them back in slow retreat to the creative sea' (*The Secret of Annexe 3*, 1991d, 96–7).

5 This term is from Bremond and Pavel (1995, 190).

6 They originate in Alexander Zholkovski's (1984) discussion of ten different *elementary expressive devices* through which a theme, existing apart from and

prior to any particular text, is articulated in a specific work of art. Bremond modifies considerably Zholkovski's approach, however, by reversing its direction, going from text to theme, as happens during reading. Thereby he emphasizes the reader's role of discovery and recognition instead of the author's. For Bremond's thorough assessment of Zholkovski's study, *Themes and Texts: Toward a Poetics of Expressiveness*, see his review 'Et le thème s'est fait texte ...: À propos d'un Essai d'Alexander Zholkovsky' (1986).

7 The operations Bremond describes are basic in two senses. They are basic in providing only very general instructions to the themer of how to order and combine themes. But by being general, it seems that they are necessarily inscribed in *any* interpretational system as the conventional backbone directing every act of theming. Theming is impossible without the positioning of certain textual elements which illustrate a given theme, and this choice inevitably entails the suppression of a host of other feasible thematic clues suggested by the text. After all, the suppression of a theme is not only tied to the degree of textual support a theme gets but also to the themer's thematizing attention, which cannot follow up every lead. As the very process of theming represents the themer's attempt to grasp what a text is about and how exactly it is about the theme or cluster of themes we take it to represent, such operations as composition and decomposition as well as generalization and specification provide the basic means with which this 'what' and 'how' of a theme may be stated and demonstrated.

8 'Yet [Morse] sensed that those next few minutes, after Ashenden [the tour leader] had finished speaking with Kemp, might well have been the crucial ones in that concatenation of events which had finally led to murder; and he questioned Ashenden further' (428).

9 The classic example of a detective's failure to read the case correctly is, of course, E.C. Bentley's *Trent's Last Case* (1929).

10 The source for this quotation is given as Bryan Magee's *Aspects of Wagner*. The author's game with the reader is complicated by the epigraphs Dexter frequently uses at the beginning of each chapter. They are analogous with the events of the chapter, providing the reader with bookish commentary on them. Jim Collins suggests that in the classical detective story such 'privileging of the library is itself an essential step in the move to encircle the diegesis with a wall of books, thereby creating a "reality" which is primarily discursive' (1989, 52). Certainly Dexter creates an intertextual sheathing, as it were, directing the reader's attention to the narrator's playful handling of generic conventions and intertextual material. This aspect needs its own study.

11 Morse explains the cleverness of the deception: 'Now the deception practised by Kemp was a very clever one. If he was going to be late on parade ...

every pressure would be on the other two group leaders, Sheila Williams and Cedric Downes, to keep the tourists adequately amused by each of them shouldering an extra responsibility' (470). As regards the alibi, he says: 'For [Downes] is suddenly, miraculously, aware that he has got wonderful – no! – a *perfect* alibi; an alibi which has been given to him *by the very person he has just killed*. O lovely irony! Kemp had told Ashenden, and Ashenden had then told everyone else, that he [Kemp] would not be back from London until 3 p.m. And that meant that Downes could not *possibly* have killed Kemp before that time ...' (471).

12 Morse realizes that the witness has misheard 'Babbington' (Kemp's academic publisher) as 'Paddington.' Kemp missed the train because he was held up by his editor.

13 An agent's deliberate decision not to act represents what Ryan (1991, 132–4) calls a *passive move*. In these instances, 'the nondoer's goal is to let events follow their course even though he or she is in a position to prevent this development' (132). Passive moves are based on the non-doer's evaluation of the current state of things and her projection of two possibilities: first, the feasible state without the non-doer taking the available move, and, second, the state resulting from that move. On the basis of this evaluation, she deems non-action more fitting for her goals than action.

14 The agent's realization of plans may involve enlisting the help of others by delegating the execution of either the whole plan or some portions of it to someone else. Such a transfer of control involves an element of risk, for the helpers, having a will of their own, may either take over completely or confess to the cooperation (Ryan 1991, 140–1); accomplices are often the weak link.

15 There is a potential weakness in the author's design of this crime story, because the Strattons, in promising to help the Aldriches, do not know what they are supposed to do. From the Aldriches' perspective, it would, of course, be foolish to reveal beforehand that they expect the accomplices to dispose of a body. The author sidesteps this problem by indicating that Mr Stratton, who, very conveniently, is a mortician by vocation, accepts the moral justification of the killing, and is, therefore, willing to help.

16 This claim is verified by Anthony Berkeley's *The Poisoned Chocolates Case* (1929) in which the police and six private detectives read the same crime, each coming up with a different solution.

17 Many of Morse's abductions as well as Holmes's reading of the dusty hat further demonstrate that there is no necessary relationship between the object and the conclusions drawn from it. It is typical of whodunits to pile a host of undercoded abductions on a clue and present them as if they were the inevitable, even obligatory, results of hypothesizing. Such abductions

often produce a lot of excessive information that is in no way significant in explaining why or how a given crime took place. There is thus an important distinction between hypotheses that are directly relevant for the explanation of the crime and those that function purely as pseudo-analytical conversations and feats of ratiocination. These latter exercises are predominantly generic 'romps,' with the detective's analytic *forte* demonstrating his or her (and the author's) mental dexterity in all that *can* be read off the evidence. The logical reasoning of a classical detective is thus injected with a strong sense of the ridiculous, even of the absurd. Such 'romps' reveal also the detective's 'thematic personality.'

18 Generally speaking, the notion of tellability refers to the quality that makes situations and events reportable, or worthy of being told (Prince 1987, 81). As Detective Inspector Lennart Kollberg goes out to enjoy a walk in the rain, the narrator of *The Laughing Policeman* by Maj Sjöwall and Per Wahlöö drily states that '[a]t the same time eight murders and one attempted murder were committed in Stockholm' (1971, 5). Thereby the narrator points to the factor which makes this particular story tellable, a massacre being an extraordinary event that drastically departs from the ordinary – at least in Sweden. Narratives usually motivate their existence somehow, showing what reasons account for their being worth telling. As regards subject matter or the substance of narrative, the detective-story genre grounds its tellability in a number of stable concerns such as (moral) transgression, death, the desire to know, and (the difficulty of the) mystery. It is possible to distinguish between the narrative appeal of universal human concerns (death, sexuality, curiosity) and the narrative interest based on cultural trends and topical issues (the corrupting influence of money and power on the police force, the status of women in law enforcement, etc.) (see Ryan 1991, 154).

19 Morse's love of coincidences is a repeated motif throughout Dexter's work.

20 Another comparison, this time from Chesterton's work, throws further light on Dexter's practice. In 'The Honour of Israel Gow,' Father Brown startles his companions by connecting the disparate clues pointing to some unidentified, unlawful state of things. The priest points out to others that 'only you said that nobody could connect snuff and diamonds and clockwork and candles. I give you that connexion off-hand. The real truth, I am very sure, lies deeper' (1981a, 81). Dexter's practice is that of finding the connections among disparate clues, for, unlike Chesterton, he is not interested in any 'deeper truths.' Again, this shows us that authors play different games through their detectives' thematizations.

21 A motif as central to the hard-boiled tradition as is the body-in-the-library motif to the soft-boiled.

22 This parallelism is explicitly spelled out by Zen's musings: 'His visit to

Andrea Dorfin the night before had merely served to confirm his sense that everything was slipping away from him. The old man's parting words had echoed his own realisation that the fate of Rosetta Zulian, like that of Ivan Durridge, and for that matter his own father, would quite likely never be known' (127).

23 Zen himself is acutely aware of the principle of narrative diversification that accompanies, for example, his projection of how things could have been: 'Do you ever feel that? That every time you come to a crossroads in your life, there's a ghostly double which splits off and goes the other way, the route you didn't take. I know exactly what he's like, my married version. I might as well be him. I could easily be. It just so happens that I'm not' (92). This principle explains his 'voluntary exile' (16), for his reason is that '[t]hose ghostly doubles I was talking about are thicker on the ground here than anywhere else' (93).

24 I am using Ryan's (1991, 135–6) representation of the structure of plans. It is made up of a series of steps, consisting of three components: (1) a non-accidental event, which can be a deliberate action, a sudden reaction, or an event of mental perception; (2) a set of preconditions for the accomplishment of this event; (3) a set of postconditions capturing the results of the planned event. One of the postconditions represents the (sub)goal of the planner, while the others may correspond to the anticipated side-effects of the event. In a plan, the units are linked by an enabling relation. This means that a postcondition of a plan-unit coincides with the precondition of another step. The matching element is the goal of the first step of the plan. Ryan defines a sequence of events as constituting a plan for a goal 'if the goal is the postcondition of the last step, all steps are linked together by enabling relations, and the planner (or main agent) is in a position to take the action that will start the chain of causes and effects' (135).

25 In describing Zen's vision of this new goal, the narrator evokes a military image, thereby strengthening Zen's similarity to his ancestors: 'The ideal which inspired him was nothing as abstract as Justice or Truth. His dream was personal, and attainable. Having scored a great coup by solving the Durridge case where everyone else had failed, he would apply for a permanent transfer and return in triumph to his native city. He would bring his mother back from her exile in Rome; back to her friends and the way of life she had been forced to give up. Once the Durridge case came to court, Cristiana Morosini would have the perfect excuse for divorcing her disgraced husband. And a year or so later, she and Zen could marry without exciting any adverse comment' (282).

26 Dal Maschio explains that the deal between him and the Croats was 'about

establishing credibility and goodwill with a potential ally and trading-partner in the federal and regional Europe of the future' (309), but the ultimate motive is betrayed by his statement that Croatia may one day be under the Venetian flag, where it rightfully belongs (308). Italy's secret police have hushed up the Durridge case, because their chiefs sold him illegal guns.

27 In their final encounter, Ada Zulian tells Zen what she thinks is the truth about Rosetta's fate (300–3). There is a rumour that the Germans, mistaking Rosetta for her Jewish friend, Rosa Coin, carted Rosetta off to a concentration camp where she died. Ada Zulian refuses to believe this story; instead, she thinks that Andrea Dorfin, a man whom Rosetta had befriended, is implicated in her daughter's disappearance. Zen understands this story to mean that Dorfin, a pedophile, has abused and then killed Rosetta. Towards the end, Zen learns the truth from Dorfin and Rosa Coin, whom he meets accidentally (317–24). A homosexual with a lover, Dorfin had no interest in Rosetta other than friendship. Rosetta, pestered by her mother's pretensions of being better than everyone else, sought the company of both Dorfin and Rosa Coin. After hearing that Rosa and her family were to be deported to Germany, Rosetta hanged herself in Dorfin's kitchen. To save Rosa's life, Dorfin dressed Rosetta up as Rosa, telling the authorities that Rosa had committed suicide in order to escape the camp. He then kept Rosa hidden in his attic until the end of the war. To ensure the success of this plan, he never tells the truth to Ada Zulian.

28 The nature of this connection remains unspecified, but the reader may surmise that it has to do with Zen's association of Dal Maschio's political views with those of the Fascists. Dal Maschio's rise to power would represent a return to bigotry and might lead to new armed conflicts, which, in turn, would cause further breaking up of families and disappearances.

29 Ryan assigns such embedded narratives, consisting, for example, of aspirations and plans, to the virtual level of narrative, which describes what characters hope (or fear) reality to be like.

30 This piece of information cannot but reverberate back to earlier information that Zen's ex-girlfriend, Tania, is pregnant, making the reader wonder whether Zen is this child's father.

4 The Reading of Guilt

1 Take the whodunit as an example of such simplification. It deals almost exclusively with murder, committed in an unusual manner or circumstances. Its convention of making the least likely, or, conversely, the most likely suspect the culprit dictates plot construction and which characters can

occupy this role. The cast of characters consists of well-known stereotypes (the English rose, the army colonel, the domineering wife, the gentrified land-owner) belonging to a restricted social stratum. The main motives for murder – greed, self-protection, revenge – structure interpersonal relations according to set patterns.

2 Booth emphasizes that speaking of ethos does not necessarily entail moral judgment. Playing the piano, for example, is ethical in his sense without having any particular moral value. Yet, as he points out, any discussion of ethos easily leads to moral evaluation: '[e]thical critics need not begin with the intent to evaluate, but their descriptions will always entail appraisals of the value of what is described: there are no neutral ethical terms, and a fully responsible ethical criticism will make explicit those appraisals that are implicit whenever a reader or listener reports on stories about human beings in action' (8–9).

3 Predictability guides conjecture, suggesting that, in fitting actions to agents, detectives use the idea of a continuum moving from the notion of harmony in an ethos (a good person commits good acts), through mixture (a person with virtues and vices commits good and bad acts), to discord (a good person commits an uncharacteristic bad act or vice versa). Obviously, the degree of predictability lessens as one goes from the pole where ethos is in balance to the one where it is not.

4 Experience plays a major role in conjectures about the criminal's ethos. Kerr's *March Violets* (1993a) handily demonstrates this role. Investigating the theft of diamonds, followed by arson and murder, Bernhard Gunther reasons that '[p]laying van der Lubbe and torching the place doesn't sound like the sort of thing a professional thief would do, but neither does murder' (21). He seeks confirmation for his hypothesis that someone other than a professional 'nutcracker' has ransacked the safe: '"Was your Kurt the type of puzzler to leave a nut he'd cracked open?" Bock folded the fifty and shook his head. "Nobody was ever tidier round a job than Kurt Mutschmann." I nodded. "That's what I thought"' (160).

5 All these examples are gynocentric, if not feminist. Feminist critics of the genre claim that female, and in particular, feminist, detective-story writers show this sustained interest in human relationships, especially in female character and friendship (Reddy 1990; Munt 1994).

6 From a narrative perspective, Chatman points out, traits are narrative adjectives, which brings out nicely the reciprocal determination of character and action in our thinking (1978, 125). As not all traits have relevance for a character's actions, some simply enable, for example, the fleshing out of a lifelike person.

7 Barthes argues that readers use the proper name to unify the relatively stable qualities and the complex or even contradictory traits they attribute to a given character (1974, 67–8). In detective narratives, however, the proper name does not necessarily have this unifying function, because the character we have all along taken to be 'Jones' may actually be exposed as 'Smith,' the criminal of the story. Generic conventions affect the reader's approach to character construction: in detective stories it would appear that a character's ethos must fit the kinds of actions, attitudes, and beliefs that are thought to accompany his or her particular role in the interactional fabric. The criminal's mistake often derives from the inability to keep these components in harmony. The emphasis on a character's propensity to act in a certain way as part of ethos underlines predictability in the construction of character in this genre.

8 Occasionally, the type-matches-the-crime line of thinking is explicitly foregrounded, as in Kerr's *March Violets* (1993a): 'Over the years, I've come to belong to the school of detection that favors good, old-fashioned, circumstantial evidence of the kind that says a fellow did it because he was the type who'd do that sort of thing anyway' (99).

9 Like, for example, the criminals in G.K. Chesterton's 'The Man in the Passage' (1981b); Christie's *Three Act Tragedy* (1964b); Dashiell Hammett's *The Dain Curse* (1980a); and Ngaio Marsh's *Light Thickens* (1983).

10 Like, for example, the criminals in Anthony Berkeley's *The Poisoned Chocolates Case* (1951); A.J. Holt's *Watch Me* (1995); P.D. James's *Unnatural Causes* (1989b); and L.R. Wright's *Sleep While I Sing* (1988). For an extensive analysis of the murderer-as-artist as based on Romantic notions, see Black's *The Aesthetics of Murder* (1991).

11 An explicit example of the synthetic dimension in constructing ethos is Kerr's *March Violets* (1993a). Set in 1930s Berlin, it describes the frantic opportunism of many Germans in their efforts to get as much as they can out of the changed political climate by endorsing Nazi politics and policies. The term 'March Violet' refers to the ethos of such an immoral opportunist, who, in order to get the best possible position, claims that he or she has always been a supporter or even a member of the National Socialist Party. The book invites us to use our observations of *many* characters in order to construct the *stereotypical ethos* uniting them all.

12 Chatman (1983) concurs with Phelan's view that 'there may be genuinely "themeless" narratives,' although 'one could say minimally that any narrative, whatever else it does, demonstrates that "life is or could be like that"' (177). He suggests that '[f]rom the perspective of a general text theory, narratives with strongly marked themes or theses may be said to function as

exempla for open-issue texts or assertion texts that happen not to be stated as such' (178).

13 Both the detective story and the crime novel make use of the ethos of the 'murderee,' i.e., the person who falls victim to the murderer on account of his or her personal characteristics. *A Grave Talent* illustrates this notion well. The strangled children are relegated to the role of victim simply because of the ulterior motives of the psychopathic killer. However, Vaun Adams's ethos may be said to encompass her being a victim because of certain deeds she has committed in the past to which the killer is now responding. Good examples of the murderee's ethos are the narrators of Francis Iles's *Before the Fact* (1980) and Ruth Rendell's *Heartstones* (1991a), the latter being a variation of the situation in Richard Hull's *The Murder of My Aunt* (1979).

14 The hypothesis brings into view the major and minor premises of the practical syllogism. The major premise concerns the agent's desire statement, his or her goal of action, and his or her belief about what constitutes the given goal, whereas the minor premise addresses the specific means for reaching this goal (Nussbaum 1978, 176). When related to our example, the major premise depicts the murderer's belief that seeing the painter suffer is the primary goal that satisfies his desire.

15 Sometimes the specific means will need further deliberative work, and the agent has to break up the plan into a series of subplans until he or she identifies means that lie within reach.

16 An important specification must be made here. The culprit's actions in *A Grave Talent* are rational within the system of his desires, and he would be capable of justifying his actions with reference to this system. It appears that detective stories depict at least two major approaches to this question. In both instances the rationale given is intimately tied up with values. First, the rationale of a criminal act may be based on the very rationale that generally governs the actions of agents in a specific society. For example, to hanker after money, wealth, and prestige is perfectly rational in both soft- and hard-boiled detective fiction. The criminal either wants too much of these things or chooses to attain them through unacceptable means. Second, the criminal may follow an alternative rationale originating either from a psychic disorder or from an alternative view of life.

17 The narrator's way of stretching out the solving of the crime is worth mentioning. Once the police realize that Adams is not the culprit and develop a theory about the type of person to look for, the easiest thing to do would be, of course, to ask Adams who fits the bill. The artist, however, sinks into a catatonic state after the murder attempt, and her former psychiatrist has to be engaged to bring her out of it. In the meantime, the police delve into her

past and solve the question of the perpetrator's identity by themselves. The motivating factor for this narrative strategy is the elaboration of character. The investigators collect each and every bit of information they can about both the victim and the culprit, further dramatizing the process of drawing up a character's ethos. Moreover, the catatonic state and its unusual cure are, I think, meant to enrich our sense of the very 'core' of Adams's character as an artist. The reader's response to such strategies as these is a question to which I return later.

18 The narrator's creation of the mimetic dimension of ethos often relies on emphasizing its complexity. This strategy seems typical of quest-through-character detective stories, where lifelikeness depends on the demonstration of the variety of a character's traits and the difficulty of fitting them into a coherent whole. Kate Martinelli's musings in *A Grave Talent* illustrate this strategy well: 'Such was the outline of the life of Vaun Adams, built up from the stack of papers, nearly a foot thick, that sat on Kate's desk at home. ... And yet, when Kate should have felt that she knew this woman better than her own sister ... she simply could not connect these segments into a whole; she simply could not match the avalanche of words to the woman in the brown corduroy trousers who had served her a sandwich ... Kate's mind could not make the most tenuous of links between the woman and the girl she had been' (140–1).

19 I consider only Vaun Adams in this role, because the murdered children are given no identity in the book, functioning solely as the murderer's means to his primary goal.

20 Two excerpts describing the murderer's ethos usefully illustrate this claim. The first is a psychiatrist's assessment of him: 'The mind of someone like Andy Lewis is not finally comprehensible to a normal, sane human being. You can trace patterns, even analyze the labyrinth enough to plot its development, but motives and sequences are very slippery things, even at the best of times' (209). The second is an art therapist's evaluation: 'As a therapist I am required to deny the possibility of such a thing as innate evil. There are reasons why people become twisted. As a human being, however, I recognize its presence. This man Lewis must be stopped' (259).

21 Often the choice of means figures among the main moral conflicts of a detective narrative. In these cases, the general (moral) principles of criminal investigation clash with what seems most effective – if somehow morally unacceptable – in a particular crime case. From a 'technical' perspective, the 'end justifies the means' type of thinking seems warranted, especially if it promises to further the investigation or bring in results hard to obtain in any other way. After all, the purpose is usually (ostensibly) good: to catch the

criminal and protect the community. The methods criminals use often further complicate the choice of strategy. If detectives are, for example, fighting against a powerful criminal organization or trying to capture a serial killer, lawful means of crime solving may seem ineffectual, adding to the pressure to bend a few rules. The criminals' use of illegal and violent means may compel detectives to answer in kind. Also, the social context may, by refusing to back up investigators, force them to use shady strategies. Questions of self-protection and personal survival may complicate the moral assessment of the investigative performance.

22 This piece of information is kept back from the reader until midway through the book, when we are told that Martinelli refuses to tell her colleagues about her sexual orientation out of fear of discrimination and insult. As in many other feminist detective narratives, it is maintained that women's position in the police force is difficult. Any 'additional' differences besides being women only increase their predicament. (On this topic, see, for example, Reddy [1990]; Munt [1994]; and Irons, ed., *Feminism in Women's Detective Fiction* [1995].) The narrator's strategy may have to do with the reader's possible prejudice. Making the reader first observe a character who is ethically sound and then revealing her lesbianism may be the narrator's way of emphasizing that one cannot appraise ethos on the basis of sexual orientation.

23 Booth differentiates between *nonce beliefs* and *fixed values* as the means of identifying an implied author's ethical values and norms. Fixed values are based on the 'facts' of a given narrative, including the way the fictional world works, its norms of causation, the kind of behaviour that can be expected in it, and so on. Nonce beliefs are facts the reader embraces only for the duration of the story, whereas fixed values are those beliefs the narrative depends on for its effects and which are by implication applicable to the real world. As fixed values reveal the implied author's notion of what human life is and how it should be lived, grasping them is necessary if the reader is to join the authorial audience (1988, 142–4).

24 Nussbaum adds that this scrutiny fosters the ethical discussion of literature in the spirit of what she calls 'the Aristotelian procedure' (1990, 27–8), which tells us to be respectful of difference, but also persistent in looking for consistent and shareable answers to the 'how to live' question she, as well as Booth, sees as subtending ethical inquiry. She describes this process in the following way: 'It is built into the procedure itself that we will not simply stop with an enumeration of differences and with the verdict that we cannot fairly compare, cannot rationally decide. It instructs us to do what we can to compare and to choose as best we can, in the knowledge that no comparison

is, perhaps, altogether above somebody's reproach, since we must translate each of the alternatives into our own evolving terms and hold them up against the resources of our own imaginations, our own incomplete sense of life' (28).

25 As King's book in its sustained focus on ethos belongs to a smallish subgenre, one might maintain that, on the whole, Booth is correct. Yet the generic question of guilt always implicitly involves the reader in an appraisal of ethos, even if this assessment may not be complex. Moreover, when characters are mere stereotypes, their very stereotypicality builds a world which functions according to certain ethical guidelines. I explore this idea in the chapter 6 discussion on Agatha Christie.

26 Defending the pleasures of popular fiction as relaxing entertainment, Nussbaum reproaches Booth's sweepingly negative attitude. Yet the terms in which she herself speaks of the subject border on the distasteful. She invites us to imagine a situation in which two people are seeking relaxation. The one hires a prostitute and indulges in casual sex, while the other buys a Dick Francis detective story and lies on the couch all evening reading. Nussbaum's point is that the person hiring the prostitute is engaged in a transaction that exploits and debases both a person and an intimate activity, while the one reading Dick Francis is not harming anyone. 'Surely she is not exploiting the writer: indeed, she is treating Francis exactly as he would wish [lying on the couch or in bed with him?], in a not undignified business transaction' (1990, 240). Discussed in terms of economic exchange, and associated, although through negation, with sex, the 'complete numbing distraction' (240) provided by popular literature acquires a suspect hue that does not entirely escape the connection with some (mental, emotional?) form of prostitution.

27 Again, Booth uses the detective story to drive home his point: 'Authors of murder mysteries often testify to immense labor designed to deceive us: weeks and months spent building a puzzle that we will never spend longer than a few hours on, as we follow, more or less energetically while the knots are tied and untied. It is as if they were our servants, hired to entertain us for an hour, with no expectation that we would ever invite them to come live with us and be our loves' (186).

28 The suggested attitude comes close to Nussbaum's (1995) conception of an ethically responsible approach to the reading experience. Agreeing with Booth that readers are also responsible to authors for the quality of their reading, she suggests that adopting the perspective of what she calls the *judicious spectator* enables the reader to exercise critical judgment in dialogue with other readers. The judicious spectator is first and foremost a spectator

in that she is not personally involved in the events, although she cares about the participants as a concerned friend (72–7).

29 Although Booth insists on this plethora of kinds, he seems, nevertheless, to strive for the construction of a universal scale, respectful of the sense of an appropriate mean, that can be applied to any kind whatsoever. If we follow this line of thinking, then popular literature will always be evaluated as being ethically less beneficial than so-called serious literature, as it either falls short of the chosen mean (by being, for example, too easy or too shallow) or overruns it (by being, for instance, excessively explicit, graphic, or lewd). (It can, of course, do both simultaneously, as books by Mickey · Spillane demonstrate, for example.) And even if we apply these criteria only within one genre, there remains implicit the notion that the given genre is ultimately to be compared with our (evolving) sense of what constitutes the literary canon, because for Booth the canon continues to provide the store of ethically most commendable book-friends.

30 Cawelti (1976, 11–12) mentions two particularly effective types of stereotype vitalization. The first is to combine opposing stereotypical traits in order to create a paradoxical, memorable character. The inner duality of many a fictional detective relies on this strategy (for example, Sherlock Holmes's rationality and romanticism). The second mode is the addition of significant touches of human complexity or frailty to a stereotypical character, without, however, disrupting the formulaic mould. An example is Raymond Chandler's Philip Marlowe.

31 Of other examples using the artist-as-victim figure one can mention Chandler's *The Long Goodbye* (1971b); Christie's *Five Little Pigs* (1959b); P.D. James's *Unnatural Causes* (1989b); and Sayers's *Five Red Herrings* (1975). King's book differs from them in letting the artist survive the attempts on her life.

32 Frequently such authors encounter the problem of representing the fictional artist's works, for it is difficult to produce convincing illustrations. Very few authors are capable of producing examples as good as the excerpts from Sebastian Knight's fictional novels in Vladimir Nabokov's *The Real Life of Sebastian Knight* (1992). King skilfully solves this dilemma by choosing another art form than fiction and by having various characters, including art critics, describe Adams's paintings.

33 If Booth represents the traditional disdain of literary critics towards formulaic fiction, such a critic as John Fiske stands at the opposite end with his enthusiastic, uncritical defence of various forms of popular fiction and culture. His *Understanding Popular Culture* (1989) is interesting in that he attempts to formulate criteria attuned to the specifics of pop culture, yet his

ardent desire to prove its various merits leads to embarrassing over interpretations (for an example of such overinterpretation, see ch. 5 on analysing
popular texts).

5 Putting Together an Ethical View of Life

1 There is a connection to New Critical understanding of theme here. Monroe
C. Beardsley, for example, defines theme as a concept, an abstracted quality
or relation, singled out for the reader's contemplation. As a concept of a
high degree of generality, theme provides the link between the literary work
and other coded human experiences of both literature and real-life issues.
By forging this link, theme enables the reader to relate the one to the other
(1958, 403–9). Because themes are bounded off and moulded by literary
structures and forms, Nussbaum argues, they bring a 'greater precision' to
literature's formulation of ethical issues than do conventional philosophical
texts, effecting that 'heightened awareness' which enables the reader to
understand these dilemmas more profoundly (1990, 47). This position
equates aesthetic value, especially such features as complexity and openness, with philosophical value, underscoring Nussbaum's striving to establish only 'certain literary texts' (23) as moral philosophy. Therefore, her
criteria best suit the masterworks of the Western literary canon (45–6) from
which she takes her examples. The equation of certain literary texts with
moral philosophy is, however, the most contested part of her argument. For
this study, it is not particularly important, as mainstream detective fiction
would in any case never be considered for this role. For a good argument
against Nussbaum's position, see Lamarque and Olsen (1994, 386–97).
2 That the portrayal of the 'worst crime imaginable' is profoundly affected by
generic conventions becomes evident once one thinks of such extreme
crimes as genocide, the representation of which seems to lie beyond the
scope of the detective-story genre. This restriction derives from the fact that
the genre depicts crime through *individuals*: crime is something that happens between individual, identifiable persons. The two major subgenres
handle this individualistic emphasis differently, however. The whodunit
assigns guilt and responsibility to a single person, while the hard-boiled
detective narrative often treats individuals as representatives of various
larger social issues. This strategy is demonstrated particularly well by the
first two books of Kerr's historiographical hard-boiled trilogy, *Berlin Noir*
(1993). Set in the Berlin of the 1930s, *March Violets* (1993a) and *The Pale
Criminal* (1993b) deal with a theft and a blackmail case, respectively,
through the investigation of which emerges the political situation of Nazi

Germany with its persecution of Jews, gypsies, and homosexuals. In *March Violets*, the private detective Bernie Gunther, captured by Obergruppen-führer Heydrich, is even sent to the concentration camp in Dachau to obtain information about stolen incriminating documents from the thief who is hiding there (ch. 18). The systematic maltreatment and killing of the Jews in the camp forms the background for Gunther's attempt to accomplish the task that will ensure his own survival. In both books, the crime cases dealing with the fates of individuals function as synecdochic signs of the much larger malaise infecting German society.

3 Early criticism of the genre emphasized what E.M. Wrong (1946) called 'the immanence of justice' or what Joseph Wood Krutch (1946) characterized as 'justice triumphant' as forming the moral centre of the whodunit (see also Sayers 1988b and Nicolson 1946). Yet even then it was noted that legal procedures and scenes of punishment are usually omitted, for they might sway the reader's sympathy to the side of the criminal, destroying the formal pleasure of artful plot construction. Nancy Wingate's examination of whodunit endings shows that the revelation of the criminal's identity is the main issue. Being exposed as the culprit equals punishment: knowing who is the social misfit is enough (1979).

4 Consider, for example, Nussbaum's many questions concerning focalization (1990, 32) as helping the reader to assess a work's view of life. In the case of the whodunit, they are of no particular help unless the reader knows that focalization is the narrator's stock means of directing our perception and understanding of the crime depicted. The manipulative use of focalization serves an important end in the thrust-and-parry between narrator and reader, having, as I hope to show, considerable ethical weight.

5 Think, for example, of Sayers's (1988b) rule against love interests in the whodunit, which all the Queens of Crime – Agatha Christie, Ngaio Marsh, Margery Allingham, and Sayers herself – were, time and again, happy to break. Yet its significance in Sayers's work differs from that, for example, in Christie's: Sayers used it to probe the limits of the genre, whereas Christie needed love interest to confirm the restitution of order at the end. For an analysis of Sayers's use of this rule, see Wald's 'Strong Poison: Love and the Novelistic in Dorothy Sayers' (1990).

6 It is no accident that my description here reproduces the main points of Nussbaum's portrayal of Aristotelian ethical deliberation (1978, 210–19; 1986, ch. 10), because she sees literature as supplying an example of, and an exercise in, moral reasoning. She lays much emphasis on the illustration of how characters work out a moral choice, because this process is demonstrated from a subjective point of view. She links this feature with the practi-

cal situation which moral agents face in everyday life when they cannot
decide on the basis of abstract, general rules, but have to take into consideration the specific circumstances.

7 Particularly clear-cut instances are, of course, those in which the ending
reveals the detective to be the criminal, as in Israel Zangwill's *The Big-Bow
Mystery* (1923) and Edgar Wallace's *The Crimson Circle* (1994). Another typical way of distancing is the placing of the detective in a situation of moral
conflict, the resolving of which reveals morally questionable features in the
protagonist, as, for example, in H.R.F. Keating's *The Good Detective* (1996).

8 The reader's appraising of an author's view of life suggests that we might
find much to criticize in that view. The reader can then adopt a 'postmor-
tem' approach familiar from ideological critique. We work with the notion
of ideology as an explanatory and legitimating system presenting itself as
coherent and complete. In reading, we try to identify the strategies used in a
text which make the text's ideological tenets seem coherently consistent. We
also look for various textual gaps and discrepancies revealing what the
ideology evoked cannot adequately account for. In so doing, we play
against the author and the text, analysing how the textualized ideology tries
to construct us as social subjects willing to accept a particular view of how
things stand and what is good (see Belsey 1980, ch. 5).

9 This strategy has the reader view the fictional world from the perspective of
the author-reader game, for what is portrayed as being there in the fictional
world – down to the existence of certain objects functioning as clues – is
dictated by the manipulative handling of the narrative material. *Wolf to the
Slaughter* underlines this game aspect, for example, through the quotations
from Romantic poetry framing each of the book's three parts. Consider the
Omar Khayyám verse quoted as an epigraph: "'Tis all a Chequer-board of
Nights and Days / Where Destiny with Men for pieces plays: / Hither and
thither moves, and mates, and slays, / and one by one back in the closet
lays." Irwin (1994) reminds us that the various games – the characters being
moved on the narrator's game board – taking place in the fictional world
are all allusions to the game between the narrator and the reader.

10 In the Wexford series, Rendell always uses an extradiegetic-heterodiegetic
narrator (a third-person narrator), that is, a narrator in the first degree who
is absent from the story this narrator tells. In order to respect the
narratological distinction between the narrator and the implied author, I
here use the term 'narrator' when I talk about the narrating instance in
Rendell's books; when I talk about the implied author, I use either the term
'author' or the name 'Rendell,' without, however, referring to the flesh-and-
blood author.

11 As usual, Burden's disapproval is strong; three facts about the alleged victim suggest to him her 'thorough immorality': she always has large sums of money with her; her house is extremely untidy; and she is sexually free (43).

12 That the equation between beauty and goodness does not hold is another inversion typical of Rendell, yet this negated equation is culturally so common that it has relatively little, if any, shock value. The Rendell series reader learns to become wary of any female who resembles the model for Leonardo da Vinci's *La Giaconda* or women in paintings by Mantegna, Botticelli, or Fra Angelico, for this likeness frequently functions as a sign of moral depravity.

13 Wexford acknowledges his own complicity in the young policeman's fate, thinking he has not insisted strongly enough that this man drop the sweetheart on the grounds that her father's brushes with the law make her bad company for a policeman. Yet Wexford cannot but congratulate himself on not having time to introduce this young man, whose moral armour proved so fragile, to his own daughter: 'He only thanked God that it had all come to light in time. Another day and he'd have asked Drayton if he'd care to make one of a group of young people Sheila was organising to the theatre in Chichester. Another day ...' (181).

14 Straightforward clues are often of a narrowly technical nature, concerning, for example, information about time and place. The ambiguous clues offer two (or more) interpretations of the same thing, with the narrator attempting to make the reader settle on the wrong version. Wrong clues (red herrings) open up purely erroneous avenues of conjecture.

15 That this play stays within well-demarcated bounds is not surprising, for breaking this moral mould would require a thorough revision, even destruction, of the generic conventions themselves, as the example of the metaphysical detective narrative demonstrates. (See Holquist 1983; Spanos 1972; and Tani 1984 for forceful arguments supporting this view.)

16 The basic schema Barthes presents of the constitution of myth is, briefly, the following: a sign of a semiotic system (e.g., linguistic or pictorial) is taken up by a second-order (mythical) system, whereby this sign becomes a signifier in the new system in which it is implanted. While the sign in its first-order system expressed the meaning arising from the conjunction of the signifier and signified, in this second-order system it functions as the form to which new concepts are assigned through signification (1973, 121–4).

17 Stephen Knight (1980) and Dennis Porter (1981) argue that the 'mythological' mode of signification underlying the whodunit's view of life hides its functioning, immersing the reader in 'fixed forms of social seeing' (Porter, 116) and blinding us to the biases of the ideological notions at work. '"Myth,"' writes Porter, expressing the crux of Barthes's argument, 'implies

a form of unreflective thought that permits political reality and its socioeco-nomic base to be dehistoricized. Through "myth" a value system becomes omnipresent and determinative and, if acknowledged at all, is looked upon as part of the permanent and necessary order of things' (119). Therefore, Knight adds, '[c]ultural productions [such as the detective story] appear to deal with real problems but are in fact both conceived and resolved in terms of the ideology of the culture group dominant in the society' (4). Following traditional ideological critiques, they argue that one has to take up the posi-tion of the *aberrant* reader, who, by reading against the grain, surgically opens up the text in order to uncover its ideological underpinnings (the term is Eco's 1979, 8, 22).

18 The ending provides proof for this awareness. The fitting of most narrative details into a neat pattern has the inevitable effect of making the solution seem at least somewhat, and sometimes blatantly, ridiculous. The detec-tive's pretence of (scientific) logical rationality (instead of narrative rational-ity) spotlights the often strained and incredible quality of the solution, thereby calling on the reader to consider the tenets of the explanation. Once we start thinking about them, we usually notice fissures, even contradic-tions, that we have to take at face value for the explanation to work. In *Wolf to the Slaughter*, for example, the reader may wonder at the total suppression of the extenuating circumstances of the killing, or at the character contradic-tion on which the solution depends: the culprit is spunky enough to run a household and a shop and stand her ground with a threatening sadist, but once the killing is done, she is simply a frightened, but calculating, Giaconda. Or the reader may think about the class division on which the solution builds: the culprit comes from the working class, and the detec-tive's explanation implies her 'genetic deficiency.' We may ponder the fact that the convention of innocent-looking beauty as a mask of guilt folds the solution back into the traditional scapegoating of women.

19 We find the *folie à deux* motif in, for example, Rendell's *Kissing the Gunner's Daughter* (1991b); *Shake Hands Forever* (1994); *Some Lie and Some Die* (1974); and *An Unkindness of Ravens* (1990a).

20 What Rendell writes in the introduction to *Ruth Rendell's Anthology of the Murderous Mind* (Rendell, ed., 1996) further elucidates her attitude. She emphasizes that murder as such is not interesting; instead, the 'impetus to murder, the passions and terrors which bring it to pass and the varieties of feeling surrounding the act that make of a sordid or revolting event compul-sive fascination' (vii), is what draws us to varieties of crime fiction. The focus on the murderous mind reveals 'the dark side of human nature that is in us all, even the most innocent and blameless,' and with the help of fic-

tional criminals we may acquire a glimpse of 'what lies beneath the surface of our own controlled and purified consciousness' (x). Claiming that the purpose of crime fiction is to gain an understanding of the motives for murder, Rendell nevertheless posits the 'murderous mind' as a profound enigma, because the explanations we can reach remain just 'inklings' (xi) of what goes on in such a mind.

21 Žižek also points out that the blind spots characteristic of each attitude derive from these assumptions, for the ironist reduces reality itself to fiction, while the cynic naïvely believes in ultimate reality outside the cobweb of symbolic fictions (1996, 208).

22 This notion acquired consensus early on among detective-fiction critics. W.H. Auden, for example, notes that 'whatever he may say, I think Mr. Chandler is interested in writing, not detective stories, but serious studies of a criminal milieu, the Great Wrong Place, and his powerful but extremely depressing books should be read and judged, not as escape literature, but as works of art' (1988, 19). Edmund Wilson, a professed detective-story hater, admits to a liking for Chandler's books, because 'of a malaise conveyed to the reader, the horror of a hidden conspiracy that is continually turning up in the most varied and unlikely forms' (1988, 38).

23 Steven Marcus (1974) describes this task in the context of Dashiell Hammett's novels. He notes that they generate a feeling of ambiguity by making the reader wonder whose side Hammett's detectives are on, or whether there is, for them, a side apart from their own. The reading experience is, Marcus argues, one of moral complexity and uncertainty that entails, simultaneously, a description and a critique of the hard-boiled hero and his role.

24 The term is Ruehlman's (1984, 64).

25 The use of a first-person narrator reminds us of the distinction between narrator and implied author made within the semiotic model of communication (Booth 1983 and Chatman 1978). Booth understands the implied author as the flesh-and-blood author's 'second self,' the governing textual consciousness of the whole work and the source of the norms embodied in it. Chatman underlines the semiotic nature of the implied author, seeing it as a construct which the reader infers and assembles from all the components of the text. Whichever version one prefers, this distinction works to highlight the fact that the reader's task is to evaluate the narrator's mode of narration. As the text may contain clues indicating that the implied author disagrees with the first-person narrator (for example, the narrator may turn out to be unreliable), this narrator may ultimately be treated critically.

26 Archer's response to this contradiction is typical: self-irony and occasional

self-loathing (e.g., 42–4, 48). Hard-boiled novels abound with similar examples of self-flagellation, the purpose of which is to suggest the investigator's basic moral integrity. By admitting he does wrong, the detective indicates that he knows what is right; the justification ostensibly derives from the imperatives of the situation, but he may also have a secret agenda of his own.

27 Whodunit detectives also follow a professional code, but whereas that mode stresses reason, hard-boiled professionalism emphasizes reason *and* action as necessary components of this code.

28 'Lit from below by the yellow flaring light, [Puddler's] face was barely human. It was low-browed and prognathous like a Neanderthal man's, heavy and forlorn, without thought. It wasn't fair to blame him for what he did. He was a savage accidentally dropped in the steel-and-concrete jungle, a trained beast of burden, a fighting machine. But I blamed him. I had to. I had to take what he'd handed me or find a way to hand it back to him' (127).

29 Part of Hammett's contribution is the creation of two memorable figures – the Continental Op and Sam Spade – who are motivated by nothing other than professionalism, the obsessive ambition to do the job as it should be done. But even in these instances the reader is first made to search for other, more 'sentimental' motives, only in order to arrive at the conclusion that the detective is nothing other than his role.

30 As has been noted, the hard-boiled narrative makes use of quest romance motifs (Grella 1988b and Jameson 1983). The dream connects with these narrative patterns, for a central convention of quest-romance is the hero's perilous journey through the labyrinthine, evil underworld (Frye 1973, 189). It suggests that knightly ideals supply one familiar model for both the protagonist and the reader for structuring the investigator's task and values, although this comparison may be made in order to reject these ideals as ineffective, or inappropriate in the context of the hard-boiled world.

31 This existential slant is exemplified well by the millionaire's daughter, Miranda, who is, like her namesake in Shakespeare's *The Tempest*, honest, resilient, and self-reflective. She has the resources to develop into a morally upright person, for, in spite of all her posturing, her principles are sound. But only after she confronts fate is her moral decency established. In existential philosophy, only death enables the final assessment of a character and a life.

32 Judging by the whole Archer series, it seems that traditional heroism is among the values that are to be rejected as inappropriate to the twentieth-century world. Macdonald's criticism seems to target the simplification of

issues which traditional heroism often entails. In his books, crimes mainly stem from psychological complexities (especially those arising from family relations) for which there are no hard-and-fast solutions and explanations. Traditional heroism is rejected because it involves ideals that are impossible to attain: it either engages people in quests doomed to fail or makes them give up even trying.

33 *One Lonely Night* (1951, 149). The Spillanian hard-boiled narrative illustrates D.A. Miller's (1988, 2–10) analysis of the detective-story genre as grounded in the notion of policing as insulated from the middle class world. A writer like Spillane confines the actions of the police and the private eye mainly to a delinquent milieu, representing this milieu as an enclosed space that only the police and the criminals inhabit. Such a closure constitutes an 'inside' as well as an 'outside': outside and surrounding the world of criminality lies middle-class private life, whose 'alternative' character depends on its being kept free from the police. Likewise, Hammett and Chandler restrict the actions of the private eye to the realms of the criminal underworld, the poor, and the rich. If members of the middle class are criminals in these books, they are invariably professionals, often doctors or lawyers. What makes Macdonald such an interesting writer is his examination of the middle class as the locus and source of crimes.

34 In *The Moving Target* Archer's main task is to ensure that the millionaire stays alive; however, the millionaire is murdered while the detective lies unconscious nearby. This typical turn of events is found in other hard-boiled narratives as well – for example, in Chandler's *Farewell, My Lovely* ([1976b], the murder of Lindsay Marriott) and *The Lady in the Lake* ([1976d], the murder of Mildred Haviland).

35 In describing narrative motivation in these terms, I am suggesting that the hard-boiled novel has interesting links with, although it is certainly *not* identical with, the narrative and thematic patterns Kenneth Bruffee (1983) analyses as *elegiac romance*. Briefly put, the elegiac romance is a story about the narrator's obsession with a dead, 'heroic' friend which the narrator tries to overcome through writing (or telling) the friend's biography. In the course of ostensibly telling the hero's life, the narrator actually tells the story of his own, re-evaluating both his hero and himself. This exercise frees him from his obsessive attachment and from its concomitant state of arrested emotional development. In chronological order, the sequence of events of an elegiac romance runs roughly as follows: in the fictional past, a young or a middle-aged person, usually male, has encountered another person (also male) and transformed him into a heroic figure by projecting onto him his own private wish-fulfilling fantasies. The friend has indifferently accepted

the heroic role, but has done little to return the esteem. Eventually, the 'heroic' friend dies, and, crushed by the loss, the hero-worshipper starts, in the dramatized fictional present, to memorialize the hero by writing his biography. The plot thus moves between the past and the present moment. While seemingly about the other person, the narrative is actually about an 'I' who gains personal fulfilment through the act of narration (47–51). Examples of the elegiac romance include F. Scott Fitzgerald's *The Great Gatsby* (1950), Joseph Conrad's *Heart of Darkness* (1899) and *Lord Jim* (1900), and Henry James's 'The Aspern Papers' (1888). The most obvious links between this mode and the detective-story genre are seen in such metaphysical detective stories as Vladimir Nabokov's *The Real Life of Sebastian Knight* (1992) and Paul Auster's *The Locked Room* (1988). But there are other links as well. Cawelti mentions the relevance of Fitzgerald's work to the hard-boiled narrative (1976, 180–1). Chandler's *Farewell, My Lovely* and Macdonald's *Black Money* (1996) are variations of *The Great Gatsby*. (Chandler's *The Big Sleep* [1976a] and *The Long Goodbye* [1971b] would also seem to be related to the elegiac mode.) Even Mickey Spillane's *I, the Jury* (1947) might fit this pattern, for it tells the story of Mike Hammer's obsession with his dead best friend. Žižek suggests further affinities by drawing attention to Robert Penn Warren's elegiac romance, *All the King's Men* (1948), as a *noir* work with all the crucial ingredients of the hard-boiled universe: the corrupted and charismatic paternal figure, the ambiguous attitude of the journalist-detective, the theme of fidelity and betrayal, the link between social depravity and the 'ontological' corruption of the universe, and so on (1992, 24ff).

36 A version of the despised 'had-I-but-known' formula involving an incompetent female 'detective,' Daphne du Maurier's *Rebecca* (1992) is a good illustration of self-recovery as narrative motivation. It is a fascinating close relative of the elegiac romance, particularly interesting and unusual in its focus on female relationships. It tells of the obsessive fixation of the nameless narrator with her husband's dead first wife, Rebecca, her failed attempts to emulate the dead woman, and her gradual realization of the destructiveness of this model. That the narrator has never met the 'heroic' model alive emphasizes that Rebecca is the projection of her own psychic pressures. The narrative is her effort to become finally free of the false ideal she set for herself in the past.

37 Archer's cynicism, for example, is shown when the female kidnapper tells him her story, saying that love motivated the crime. Archer is quick to dismiss her with this remark: 'I won't buy love's young dream from you, Betty. He was a boy, and you're an old woman, as experience goes. I think you sucked him in. You needed a finger man, and he looked easy' (166).

38 Spillane's books are strewn with passages in which the narrator describes moments of loss of control: for example, 'I went crazy for a second. Stark, raving mad. My head was a throbbing thing that laughed and screamed for me to go on, bringing the sounds out of my mouth before I could stop it. When the madness went away I was panting like a dog, my breath coming in short, hot gasps' (*Vengeance Is Mine* [1950], 139–40.) The narrator's formative powers are limited, as these bouts of rage are expressed with the help of trite animal imagery. This raving madness of Hammer-like figures has meaning to it, because the all-consuming emotion arises in response to the wickedness of the opponent. A.J. Holt's revenge narrative *Watch Me* (1995) develops the Spillanian investigator's attitude further by showing how the end-justifies-the-means strategy ultimately leads to a situation in which the investigator no longer thinks of the moral justification of transgressive deeds, for killing has become satisfying in itself.

39 As not all hard-boiled detective stories employ first-person narration, however, does the foregoing analysis apply to stories using a third-person narrator? Dashiell Hammett's *The Glass Key* (1980b) provides an example for considering how a third-person (an extra- and heterodiegetic) narrator varies the situation familiar from Macdonald's novel. The novel is famous for its omission of direct narratorial commentary and interpretation, as the narrator neutrally reports what the protagonist, Ned Beaumont, sees and does, presenting, in addition, various sources of strictly factual information such as newspaper accounts, letters, and so on. This separation of the narrator and the investigator does not, however, affect the author-reader game, for the reader's task is still to evaluate the moral code directing Beaumont's decisions and actions, relating this examination to the analysis of the narrator's strategies and assessing the combination. Again, the dichotomy of art and life governs the reader's movement between the corruption of the fictional world and the overt stylization of the narrator, which might be described as strikingly minimalist. The reticence of the narrator is, of course, what makes the task challenging in this novel. But can we still talk about the narrative thrust in terms of self-realization? I think we can, if we realize that this description has all along drawn on the rhetorical analysis of narrative, embracing the narrator, the audience, and the story told. Steady focalization through the protagonist keeps the individual's experience at the forefront, whereas the externalized, objective approach, emphasizing Beaumont's inscrutability, directs the reader's attention to the narrator and the motivation for this reticence. Let it be noted, however, that elegiac romance, according to Bruffee's definition, insists on a first-person (an intradiegetic-homodiegetic) narrator.

6 The Anatomy of Good and Evil in Agatha Christie

1 Christie also wrote numerous plays, the best known of which is *The Mouse-trap*. Many are based on her novels and short stories (see the bibliography in Barnard [1980]). The theatre motif shows in her titles such as *Curtain, Three Act Tragedy, Taken at the Flood, Sad Cypress,* and *By the Pricking of My Thumbs* (the last three allude to Shakespeare). Some books begin with a 'cast of characters' list; others have (would-be) actors/actresses and playwrights as characters (e.g., *Appointment with Death, They Do It with Mirrors*); there are dozens of references to Shakespeare, especially to *Othello* and *Macbeth* (see Bargainnier 1980, 168). The narrator also underlines the theatricality of her world by continually comparing the actions of her characters to play-acting. In chapter 18 of Christie's *Peril at End House* (1966c), for example, the narrator emphasizes theatricality with such brief reminders as the following: 'with Poirot coming and going as a kind of fantastic clown, making a periodic appearance in a circus'; 'his pose of baffled despair was admirable'; 'the amount of subterfuge involved must have been colossal' (154); 'the farce you do not play it as well as I do'; 'Ah, what a comedy!' (155); 'keeping a secret is an art that requires many lies magnificently told, and a great aptitude for playing the comedy and enjoying it' (158), and so forth.

2 The revelation of the victim as someone unexpected is very typical in the work of Chesterton. See, for example, 'The Secret Garden,' 'The Man with Two Beards,' and 'The Sign of the Broken Sword' (1981a).

3 The detectives' skills thus include the ability to evaluate what the actual *positional constellations* between the suspects are. The helplessness of the police and the suspects in the face of crime suggests that it takes special astuteness to decipher such patterns. Therefore, the two polar opposites – the criminals and the detectives – seem to be the figures most perceptive of, and sensitive to, the moral system of the community.

4 Note that in the kind of analysis employed by Lacan (1988), the triangle describes, first and foremost, the three orders (the real, the imaginary, and the symbolic) structuring the subject's life. Irwin (1994) relates this pattern to the structure of self-consciousness: the reflecting I, the reflected I, and the subject's awareness of this mutual mirroring relationship. As the whodunit largely externalizes that which the metaphysical detective narrative internalizes, I mainly discuss the geometrical patterns as distributed among the different set players within the interactive field.

5 Quadrangles result from doubling, for, as we saw in chapter 1, doubling tends to involve first splitting and then doubling. The detective's antagonistic relation to the criminal presents this pattern in its rudimentary form, for

the criminal duplicates externally the internal division in the detective's self, but with the master/slave polarity of that division characteristically reversed so that 'doubling tends to be a structure of four halves problematically balanced across the inner/outer limit of the self rather than a structure of two separate, opposing wholes' (Irwin, 5).

6 My corpus consists of the following thirty-four novels, including books in the Hercule Poirot and Miss Jane Marple series, and books outside them, as well: *The ABC Murders; After the Funeral; Appointment with Death; The Body in the Library; Cards on the Table; A Caribbean Mystery; Cat among the Pigeons; The Clocks; Crooked House; Curtain: Poirot's Last Case; Dead Man's Folly; Death on the Nile; Evil under the Sun; Five Little Pigs; 4:50 from Paddington; Hallowe'en Party; The Labours of Hercules; The Mirror Crack'd from Side to Side; Mrs McGinty's Dead; Murder at the Vicarage; A Murder Is Announced; Murder on the Links; The Murder of Roger Ackroyd; The Mysterious Affair at Styles; One, Two, Buckle My Shoe; Peril at End House; A Pocket Full of Rye; Sad Cypress; The Sittaford Mystery; Taken at the Flood; They Do It with Mirrors; Three Act Tragedy;* and *Towards Zero.* The bibliography indicates the editions used.

7 Christie typically places her characters in front of a mirror in moments of turmoil. The mirror image serves to underline a feeling of strangeness, of an inner otherness, making people wonder who they are, as, for example, in *Taken at the Flood* (1948): 'She stood in her bedroom, looking curiously at her face in the mirror. It was, she thought, the face of a stranger ...' (83).

8 This association is by no means an isolated phenomenon in Christie's *oeuvre.* In 'The Cretan Bull' (*The Labours of Hercules*), for example, she plays explicitly with the idea of the intended victim as a kind of Minotaur, a man whose 'magnificient physique' resembles that of a bull (143) and who is supposedly going mad, thanks to heredity. This bull-man is also placed in a labyrinth – a locked room – to prevent him from committing further bloody deeds (in the past weeks he has presumably cut the throats of animals, smearing himself with blood). Strange sights torment him: 'Last night, for instance – I wasn't a man any longer. I was first of all a bull – a mad bull – racing about in blazing sunlight – tasting dust and blood in my mouth' (151). The victim is aware that there is a reversal taking place in which his human side is being eclipsed by his animal side: 'It isn't *I* who do these things – it's someone else who comes into me – who takes possession of me – who turns me from a man into a raving monster who wants blood and who can't drink water' (152).

9 As Žižek points out, this means that fictional detectives must be capable of folding the criminal's deception back upon itself: in forcing the lie to articu-

late the truth, they use deception in order to produce its inverted form, arriving at the truth through the mirror image of the lie (1991, 57).

10 The figure of the wrong suspect (i.e., a false lead) is not necessarily simultaneously a scapegoat as well. The community must readily believe in the scapegoat's guilt and/or the real criminal must frame this person as a scapegoat. When Christie uses scapegoats, they are typically the victim's relatives or other close associates, a fact which gives a certain *legitimacy* to their resentment of the victim's blocking actions. She employs this figure to build up relations of reflection in which the criminal and the scapegoat are often similar as regards motive, but different in terms of the justification of their claims.

11 Numerous books show Christie's fondness for this situation: *Dead Man's Folly*; *Death on the Nile*; *Murder on the Links*; *Elephants Can Remember*; *Hallowe'en Party*; *The Mysterious Affair at Styles*; *One, Two, Buckle My Shoe*; *Taken at the Flood*; and *They Do It with Mirrors*, to name a few.

12 The other major variation builds around the metamorphosis pattern. A couple sees the chance for one of them to take the place of a third, wealthier person, who is often, but not always, dead to begin with. Together they sustain the deception about identity, until they are threatened either with exposure (*Dead Man's Folly*, *The Clocks*) or with the various complications of their own crumbling union (*Mrs McGinty's Dead*, *Taken at the Flood*), compelling either one or both to resort to crime.

13 By playing on the inner/outer relationship, Christie uses a typical generic motif, but transposes it from the physical into the interpersonal realm. The familiar motifs expressing this physical problematics are the locked room, the hidden object, and the labyrinth mysteries, each of which seems to violate the normal possibilities of solid bodies or objects passing into or out of finite spaces (see Irwin, 180–1). Irwin shows that the metaphysical detective story uses the physical inner/outer oscillation in order to examine the mystery of consciousness, especially the mutually constitutive opposition created between aspects of the mind. He fails to consider the interpersonal uses of the inner/outer relationship, however, portraying a bond between two persons in which a third party is left out. By confusing the fictional community and the reader as to who is actually paired with whom, Christie employs this interpersonal configuration in order to underline the wickedness of her culprits, who manipulate marital relationships to their own ends. This transposition is familiar from the metaphysical detective story as well: consider the protagonist-narrators of Nabokov's *The Real Life of Sebastian Knight* and Auster's *The Locked Room*, who fantasize that, by wooing a brother's

girlfriend (*The Real Life of Sebastian Knight*) or by not only marrying a friend's wife but also making love to his mother (*The Locked Room*), they become 'insiders' to whatever the brother or friend shared with this person. Their ultimate aim is to merge with the brother or friend: to move permanently from the outside of another person's mind to the inside of that mind.

14 Christie's choice of this name may be a self-reflexive joke, underlining the whodunit author's own similarity with the criminal.

15 By drawing this configuration on the basis of the relationships obtaining among female characters, I am emphasizing the change Christie introduces to Poe's legacy. While Poe's analytic detective stories express male fears of femininity (see Irwin, chs 24 and 25), it appears that in Christie's narratives women characters function as embodiments of both the basest evil (e.g., *Appointment with Death*) and the highest good. This feature suggests that Christie holds women responsible for the upkeep and transmission of social order: they are its most sinister threats, but also its true salvation.

16 The royal terminology I am using here derives from three sources. First, Christie herself uses royal imagery in order to focus on social relations; the terms 'king' and 'queen' reflect notions about what proper social order is like. Second, in Poe's 'The Purloined Letter' the crime concerns the royal couple; finally, Irwin imports the royal terminology from this short story into his own analysis.

17 In making this association, I am not assuming that Christie herself made it or expected her readers to make it, although, as the wife of an archaeologist, she would have been familiar with such things as alchemy and labyrinths.

18 Speaking of the king and queen figures in terms of the sun and the moon derives from the alchemical tradition, which represents alchemy as the marriage of the red king and the white queen (Irwin, 47).

19 Revenge presents a situation in which the victim functions as a *distorting mirror* for the criminal. In such books as *Crooked House*, *Five Little Pigs*, and *Towards Zero*, the criminal murders (or attempts to murder) the victim, because the latter has seriously wounded the criminal's sense of self by explicitly pointing to some fundamental flaw in him or her. Murder is the obliteration of such a distorting mirror.

20 Irwin explains that the preoccupation with these distinctions comes to the metaphysical detective story mainly through the riddle or puzzle element 'whose problematic form encrypts the mystery of human identity and whose solution enacts, through the hero's exercise of reason, the difference between the rational and the irrational' (228). In unravelling the puzzling crime by following the thread from one clue to another, the detective moves gradually towards the centre of the labyrinthine enigma until the culminat-

ing encounter with the monstrous criminal. This process of unravelling and the recurring motifs of the ape, the locked room, and the labyrinth are allusions to the myths of Theseus and Oedipus, dealing with the personal and communal significance of self-knowledge. The incest motif that subsumes these myths shows how the hero's self-knowledge is linked to the recognition and acknowledgment of him by his father, on the one hand, and how the striving for the absoluteness of self-knowledge may lead to a suicidal dissolution of self, on the other. The incest taboo functions to institute the notion of kinship, the sense of a clear network of relationships within which the self is located. It constitutes the cultural means of signifying the difference between the human and the inhuman by implying that humans who commit incest are behaving like animals. The taboo refers also to the damaging and destructive effects of self-love, conceived of as the inability to break out of the family circle in choosing a love-object. This feature sets the humans apart from the gods, who, knowing their own uniqueness, recognize only their close relations as possible breeding partners. Although humans have godlike minds, they cannot achieve the same level of self-recognition and self-absorption as the gods can (see Irwin, ch. 23).

21 Both strategies can, of course, be used by one and the same character.

22 The prime example of non-rivalrous modelling (or *external mediation*) is the world of Don Quixote, where the knight imitates Amadis of Gaul, while Sancho Panza imitates the knight. The model is inaccessible to the imitator, because the imitator believes that the model is, in one way or another, out of reach. Therefore, he openly venerates the model, subordinating his endeavours to those of the model (Girard 1966, 1–10).

23 To keep any doubts from arising concerning the role of hierarchy and the envy it calls forth, Christie has her characters occasionally engage in wholesale blaming of the criminal, proclaiming that the responsibility for getting carried away by the pull of envy is solely his or hers. In *The Sittaford Mystery*, a character explains the murderer's actions in the following fashion: 'I told you that Burnaby was a jealous man. Friends indeed! For more than twenty years Trevelyan has done everything a bit better than Burnaby. He ski-ed better, and he climbed better and he shot better and he did crossword puzzles better. Burnaby wasn't a big enough man to stand it. Trevelyan was rich and he was poor. It's been going on a long time. I can tell you it's a difficult thing to go on really liking a man who can do everything just a little better than you can. Burnaby was a narrow-minded, small-natured man. He let it get on his nerves' (200.)

24 The delusional fantasy of Christie's criminals is the belief that, once they have committed the crime and installed themselves in the position they

hanker after, rivalry simply stops. The added irony is that, by assuming the position (and sometimes the identity) of the models, the murderers themselves become the very thing they resented and hated. This is, of course, the irony Borges underlines in 'Ibn-Hakkan-al-Bokhari, Dead in His Labyrinth.'

25 In *Appointment with Death*, Mrs Boynton, the victim-master, revels in advance in the prospect of exposing the slave-imitator, now Lady Westholme, to the world in a spectacularly humiliating fashion: by turning the mirror on a ladylike façade to make it reveal a former servant girl, 'criminal' in her aspirations to prestige. The power game of blackmail shows that Mrs Boynton needs the victim's fawning and cringing to sustain her sense of superiority, as it convinces her that the position after which the victim hankers is hers by right. Quite fittingly, Mrs Boynton is a former prison wardress and the criminal, Lady Westholme, her former prisoner.

26 Christie often underlines a substantial moral difference between the criminal and the victim. In *Three Act Tragedy*, for example, Sir Charles Cartwright kills Sir Bartholomew Strange because the latter would thwart his plan to commit bigamy. Revealingly, the aristocratic victim is doubled by an aristocratic criminal, Sir Charles, who impersonates the victim's *butler* as the means to his ends. The chosen role betrays, of course, the criminal's moral character as constituted by the perversion of 'true' aristocracy. It is also revealed that Cartwright is a knighted commoner whose original name is Charles Mugg (i.e,. a fool), which further emphasizes his status as the authentic title-holder's wicked and lowly double. Other distinctions involve, for example, the person's ability to love others and evoke love in return (*Peril at End House*), but in some instances there is no moral quality whatsoever setting the victim apart from the criminal (e.g., *Appointment with Death*).

27 This difference shows most clearly against the present-day canon of metaphysical detective stories. When Christie began writing in the 1920s, the whodunit was just taking shape as a distinct subgenre. Her only direct access to what was later to emerge as the metaphysical variant were Poe and Chesterton; her work exhibits, however, occasional flashes of the metaphysical, especially in terms of the nature of the solution. For example, *The ABC Murders* (1957a; first published in 1936) and *The Murder of Roger Ackroyd* (1957b; first published in 1926) invite the reader to examine the various self-reflexive textual strategies generating the mystery. Borges published his first metaphysical detective story, 'The Garden of Forking Paths,' in 1941.

28 Psychotic pathology coheres with suberb reasoning, as the example of many a master criminal demonstrates (e.g., Professor Moriarty in Conan Doyle's

short stories). One weighty objection to insanity as an explanation in Christie's world (and elsewhere in the soft-boiled tradition) is that, by definition, it poses no moral questions, for the insane are considered by law incapable of making moral distinctions.

29 Christie uses the imagery familiar from descriptions of the criminal's self-concept to depict the detective's sense of self. For example, in 'The Cretan Bull' (*The Labours of Hercules*), the narrator records the following incident: '"I know who you are, you know." "Ah, that, it is no secret!" Poirot waved a royal hand. He was not *incognito*, the gesture seemed to say. He was travelling as Himself.' (144). The fact that Poirot is here travelling as himself reminds us, of course, that he frequently travels as someone else; also, he indulges in role playing if it furthers his cause.

30 There is some comedy here, as this ending contains an intertextual allusion to Chesterton's short story 'The Blue Cross,' which concludes with the detective Valentin's and the thief Flambeau's joint bow of veneration in front of Father Brown: 'Flambeau was an artist and a sportsman. He stepped back and swept Valentin a great bow. "Do not bow to me, *mon ami*," said Valentin, with silver clearness. "Let us both bow to our master." And they both stood an instant uncovered, while the little Essex priest blinked about for his umbrella' (1981a, 23).

31 Obviously, this ending of the Poirot series borrows from Conan Doyle's failed attempt to close off the Sherlock Holmes series by having Holmes and Professor Moriarty kill each other at the Reichenbach Falls.

32 It is unlikely that this criminal could be convicted on an 'accessory before the fact' charge, for he never himself aids his victims in any way in their crimes. His method is purely verbal.

33 The author emphasizes the role of envy and jealousy (which for Girard have the same root) in a key scene immediately before the suspicious death of a guest at Styles. The criminal has taken advantage of the entangled love triangles involving a scientist and his ailing wife with the result that almost every guest wishes the death of some other guest. In this tension-filled atmosphere, Hastings tries to solve a crossword puzzle by reading out the clues to others. They serve as clues to crimes in the author's world more generally: 'even love or third party risk' (paramour), 'the chaps between the hills are unkind' (tor-men-tor), 'And Echo whate'er is asked her answers ...' (Death), and '"Jealousy is a green-eyed monster," this person said' (Iago) (123). While the first clue singles out love triangles as the cause of crime, the other three allude to the tormenting emotions leading to death. Envy and jealousy make the message of death reverberate within perpetrators, pushing them towards murderous action.

34 Christie has Poirot explain the initiating moment of what he thinks of as the arousal of the culprit's envious desire: 'One of the most significant things was a remark about him having been laughed at at school for nearly being sick when seeing a dead rabbit. There, I think, was an incident that may have left a deep impression on him. He disliked blood and violence and his prestige suffered in consequence. Subconsciously, I should say, he has waited to redeem himself by being bold and ruthless' (171). By calling forth a deep sense of inferiority, derision makes the others' bold reaction seem the model to be imitated.

35 Vertical transcendence is the ideal; yet, as it makes people equal before God, but not among themselves, it easily gives way to rivalry and crime, as happened with Cain and Abel.

36 In his consideration of the detective story from a rereading perspective, Champigny (1977) demonstrates throughout his book how a reader may beat the author by reflecting on the author's use of narrative and generic conventions. In reading Christie's *Murder at the Vicarage*, for example, Champigny notes that he recognized what he calls the return pattern: the most likely person is first singled out as the primary suspect; then this hypothesis is rejected; but the ending establishes the correctness of the first hypothesis. He also spotted Christie's repeated use of accomplices. The familiarity of these patterns made him hope that they were false clues. A more attractive prospect was the vicar's wife, thanks to her status and the fact that, the vicar being the narrator, she is 'narratively close to home' (40). What disappointed Champigny was not the solution, 'but its preparation insofar as it chose to make another pattern less appropriate, a pattern that, on the basis of my reading experience, would have been fresher and, in view of the chosen narrator, more ironical' (40).

37 The subtler the author's game with the reader, the more self-reflexive clues there are pointing to creative literary play. Thereby both author and reader become rereaders and rewriters.

7 Symbolic Exchanges with Death: Raymond Chandler

1 Irwin maintains that, thanks to its quest-romance structure, the hard-boiled detective story belongs to a different genre than the analytic (metaphysical) detective story (1994, 1). Yet he concedes that, in Hammett's *The Dain Curse* and Chandler's *The Big Sleep*, 'there are Oedipal resonances suggesting some understanding of Poe's original story.' He goes on to remark that, admiring these writers, Borges nevertheless thought that their detective stories bore 'only a minimal relationship to the central structures and liter-

ary/epistemological seriousness of the genre Poe founded' (431). The hard-boiled link with the Poe-Borges legacy may not, however, be as tenuous as Irwin claims. Even if, as Borges notes, Poe 'never invoked the help of the sedentary French gentleman Auguste Dupin ... to determine the precise crime of "The Man of the Crowd"' (quoted in Irwin, 2), this is exactly what many hard-boiled authors attempt to do. Merivale convincingly argues for the common lineage of the mainstream 'gumshoe detective story' and the metaphysical 'Gumshoe Gothic' to be traced back to Poe's tale, drawing attention to the motifs of the gumshoe detective reading clues during his sinister pursuit of the Man of the Crowd 'through the "mean streets" of a labyrinthine modern city' (1997b, 170). In effect, both variants make use of the notion of the narrative line as forming a labyrinth through which, or, rather, in which, the narrator and reader make their way, throwing us back on the Poe-esque locked-room mystery. Does not Lönnrot's pursuit of Red Scharlach in 'Death and the Compass' (1970a) and the nameless narrator's journey to the deadly encounter with Stephen Albert in 'The Garden of Forking Paths' (1970b) resemble the hard-boiled gumshoe's approach to his quarry?

2 The motif of the missing person is typical of the hard-boiled narrative more generally. In Chandler's work, *The Big Sleep* (1976a); *Farewell, My Lovely* (1976b); *The Lady in the Lake* (1976d); *The Little Sister* (1971a), and *The Long Goodbye* (1971b) are straightforward missing-person cases, while *The High Window* (1976c) is a missing-object case, but one which metonymically alludes to a man's fate. In *Playback* (1977), Marlowe follows a woman to prevent her from becoming a missing person. All of Chandler's novels form my corpus in this chapter.

3 Brooks reads Conan Doyle's story 'The Musgrave Ritual' as an allegory of plot, for it demonstrates narrative as the acting out of the implications of metaphor, that is, the central question initiating the plot (1984, 23–8). Chandlerian plot construction is conventional in this sense: the incomprehensible metaphor, represented by the enigmatic fate of the missing person, must be unpacked as metonymy, literally by tracing the movements of this person. In its unpacking, the original metaphor is enacted both spatially (Marlowe's repetition of the missing person's movements) and temporally (as the reader follows Marlowe's efforts to put together an explanation). The plotting of the solution leads to a place (the place where the body of the missing person is found), which opens up temporal constructions (the story of perverted human relationships), redirecting attention to Marlowe's search for his self.

4 The motif of the missing person unites the hard-boiled detective story with

the metaphysical one. The metaphysical detective story, however, differs from its mainstream relative in underlining the *actual* conflation of the generic roles. This reduction into solipsist unity takes place not only within the fictional world of the metaphysical version, but also at its *narrative* level, especially when it uses the elegiac-romance structure (Bruffee 1983, Merivale 1999). In presenting a situation in which '*I'm* telling you a story about *him* which is *really* a story about *Me*' (in Merivale's [1999, 107, my italics] useful short definition of the narrative structure), the metaphysical variant spotlights the fluidity of identities among characters and narrators.

5 An association made by Cawelti (1976, 180–1).

6 'I'm sorry for her ... Could be I'm fond of her too in a remote sort of way. Someday she'll need me and I'll be the only guy around not holding a chisel. Likely enough then I'll flunk out' (18).

7 Marlowe speaks only once with Sylvia Lennox, and this telephone call ends in disagreement about what is best for Terry Lennox: '"The guy was down and out, starving, dirty, without a bean. You could have found him if it had been worth your time. He didn't want anything from you then and he probably doesn't want anything from you now." "That," she said coolly, "is something you couldn't possibly know anything about. Good night." And she hung up' (11).

8 This is the traditional Aristotelian notion of friendship (see Nussbaum 1986, 355, 364). It seems likely that Chandler has had some such male-oriented concept in mind, because, compared to the hardships the detective endures and his persistence in digging out the truth about the Lennox case, the narrative supplies the reader with surprisingly little information about the actual friendship between these men. This sparseness appears to function as a clue to the gendering of the reader's role, for it seems to require a *male* reader to fill out the elliptical description with his understanding of what the best of friendships is. Hence the female reader's position can be described as being on the outside looking in.

9 There could never be meaningful bonding either between men and women or between women in Chandler's books. The description of such bondings is one of the major changes the feminist detective story (e.g., Paretsky, Grafton, Wilson) has introduced.

10 These traits are largely shared by Roger Wade as well. He characterizes himself, for example, by saying that '[a]ll writers are punks and I am one of the punkiest ... I'm an egotistical son of a bitch, a literary prostitute or pimp ... and an all-around heel' (142).

11 Marlowe explains that he thought Lennox 'a nice guy because [he] had a nice nature' (310). His belief in Lennox's innocence can be explained in the

light of the so-called *virtue ethics* (on the basis of information supplied on page 77), which holds that one's actions are grounded in one's character, understood as a compilation of particular virtues and vices. One cannot perform acts that are out of character: a basically good person is incapable of committing heinous acts. Marlowe repeatedly says that he cannot envisage this friend as the *kind* of person who could beat his wife's head to a bloody pulp (31, 56, 133, 188, 201). Hence, although Lennox's life is not morally admirable, as many of his actions are self-destructive and his marriage unwise and unhealthy, Marlowe nevertheless seems to hold that neither adversity (wartime experiences) nor wrong choices have indelibly marred this man whose virtue may, paradoxically, be best proven by his weakness and self-loathing. Given the corruption of Chandler's world, self-destructive behaviour may actually be read as a sign of moral suffering in the face of worldly evil.

12 In his farewell letter, Lennox asks Marlowe to re-enact their last morning together. After having performed this sentimental rite, Marlowe feels profoundly dissatisfied: 'It didn't seem quite enough to do for five thousand dollars' (69). This sense keeps steadily growing, marring his memory of the friendship: 'In the safe would be my portrait of Madison. I could go down and play with that, and with the five crisp hundred dollar bills that still smelled of coffee. I could do that, but I didn't want to. Something inside me had gone sour. None of it really belonged to me. What was it supposed to buy? How much loyalty can a dead man use?' (179.)

13 In effect, choosing the Other becomes a way of choosing oneself: 'It is to believe in oneself thanks to the Other' (Girard 1966, 37). Marlowe's engagement in clearing his friend's name resembles the narrator's experience in Auster's metaphysical detective story, *The Locked Room*: 'the more fully I disappeared into my ambitions for Fanshawe, the more sharply I came into focus for myself' (1988, 57). But whereas Auster's narrator 'disappears' into another *concrete* person, Marlowe doggedly pursues an *abstraction*, a difference which has ethical significance.

14 Lennox's position as the scapegoat reveals the far-reaching corruption of Chandler's world, for he is a mock image of the scapegoat. Moreover, society, as represented by the police and the system of justice, is ready to accept Lennox in this role of scapegoat, for, given the prominent position of the victim's father, it wants to protect the father's privilege and privacy. The official system is not interested in the truth, but in a pat solution that helps it to bury the case.

15 Lennox refers in passing to his scarred face in Marlowe's hearing (18), but Marlowe learns its cause from Lennox's gangster friends. Marlowe errone-

ously thinks that this act is the sign of heroic potential buried beneath the trauma of Lennox's wartime captivity at the hands of the Germans. Again, Marlowe is mistaken, as Lennox's explanation in the end makes clear: 'I was in the Commandos, bud. They don't take you if you're just a piece of fluff. I got badly hurt and it wasn't any fun with those Nazi doctors. It did something to me' (311). When he begins his quest, Marlowe is blind to this morally marring 'something.'

16 It is interesting that Eileen Wade finds the fact of Lennox's capture untransposable into the themes of youth and heroism according to which she spins her tale. But capture implies rough treatment, even torture, which may be distasteful if one wants a 'sanitized' vision of a 'beautiful' death in the snow.

17 Lennox concedes that he has no stable sense of self: 'An act is all there is. There isn't anything else. In here – ' he tapped his chest with the lighter – 'there isn't anything. I've had it, Marlowe. I had it long ago' (311).

18 Smith draws attention to the fact that Marlowe's defence of his technique – 'I wanted to clear an innocent man' – is double-edged, because forcing Eileen Wade to confess and commit suicide clears the innocent Lennox from suspicion in his wife's murder, but it also clears Marlowe of any responsibility for the writer's death (605). The situation is morally even more complex, because this 'clearing of an innocent man' is meant to camouflage the similarity between Marlowe and Eileen Wade.

19 As is typical of twentieth-century detective stories in general, all include a murder, although not necessarily in quite as elegiac terms as Chandler's work does. All his titles refer to death. *The Big Sleep* evokes the state of being dead; *Farewell, My Lovely* and *The Long Goodbye* refer to death-in-life, the process of dying, and mourning; *The High Window* and *The Lady in the Lake* allude metonymically to the event of murder; *The Little Sister* reveals the identity of a vicarious murderer; whereas *Playback*, by referring to the repetition of a traumatic event involving death, implies the possibility of playing the situation back for the second time, in a different manner.

20 Žižek (1992, 151) uses the term 'the living dead' to describe the hard-boiled investigator's position of being 'in-between-two-deaths' (the Lacanian *l'entre-deux-morts*). The investigation alerts the various criminals entangled in a case to the threat of exposure; in order to avert it, they pronounce a death sentence on the detective. Although alive, the detective is thus already marked as dead. The criminals aim at killing the detective before, or at least at the very moment, he uncovers the truth. Hence, truth means for the detective potential death.

21 Whereas descriptions of the losing of consciousness are marked by their

briefness, reflecting the surprise and swiftness of this event, the narrator usually outlines the regaining of consciousness in detail and with mock-ironic detachment.

22 In *Red Harvest*, the Continental Op spends an evening with Dinah Brand, drinking and taking laudanum. He passes out and, in waking up, finds that he is holding an icepick which has been stabbed through Brand's breast. Only the fact that the lights are out suggests that he isn't the murderer, for he cannot envisage first killing the woman, then turning off the light and returning to lie next to her.

23 Here my argument differs from Žižek's analysis of the narrative situation in the hard-boiled detective story. In the whodunit, he argues, the separation of the chronicler (a Watson figure or an omniscient narrator) from the detective ensures that the detective functions as the subject supposed to know (*le sujet supposé savoir*), that is, as someone who guarantees that the crime will have a communally sharable meaning. This position results from transference, stemming from the community's agreement on the detective's function. Žižek claims this setup to be structurally impossible in first-person narration, for one can occupy this position only if there is another person for whom one has this epistemological function (1991, 62–3). Žižek, however, forgets the reader, a fact which we already encountered in his analysis of the whodunit. It is both possible and plausible to argue, and this is the line I take, that first-person narration may be constructed in such a way that the narrator becomes the subject supposed to know in the *reader's* eyes.

24 Occasionally, the labyrinth motif is overtly sexualized, as in *Farewell, My Lovely*. Knight draws attention to Lindsay Marriott's death in Purissima Canyon, the name of which 'sounds like a dreamlike and notionally hygienic orifice that turns malign; the detail of the scene confirms this tenuous implication. Marriott's car is forced through a thorny, narrow gap and he is left dead inside; Marlowe is battered but escapes from this emblematic *vagina dentata*' (1980, 157).

25 It is possible to distinguish two different strategies the detective adopts in dealing with male victims. The first tactic is based on repetition, with Marlowe assuming the position the double has occupied earlier. The second strategy shows Marlowe witnessing the feared encounter by proxy. The first strategy is well illustrated by *The Big Sleep*. The detective's understanding of the murderer's primitive reactions helps him to protect his own life and arrange the repetition of the original scene of suffering which confirms her guilt. *Farewell, My Lovely* depicts an example of the 'proxy' strategy. In this book Marlowe helps Moose Malloy find his missing lover; he even arranges their encounter. Given the circumstances, he can guess it will end in

Malloy's death, which gives him the opportunity to observe how the double fares.

26 In the narrator's eyes death seems to have universal redeeming power. In *The Little Sister*, Marlowe witnesses the death of Orrin Quest, a particularly unpleasant character, describing the event in the following fashion: 'Something happened to his face and behind his face, the indefinable thing that happens in that always baffling and inscrutable moment, the smoothing out, the going back over the years of innocence. The face now had a vague inner amusement, an almost roguish lift at the corners of the mouth. All of which was very silly, because I knew damn well, if I ever knew anything at all, that Orrin P. Quest had not been that kind of boy' (1971a, 170–1). This redeeming power extends also to female criminals; the narrator finds the deaths of Velma Valento (*Farewell, My Lovely*) and Dolores Gonzales (*The Little Sister*) admirable in that the former kills herself in order to spare her husband's feelings, while the latter does not try to escape the punishment-revenge her ex-husband metes out to her. In both instances, however, the women have to atone for their deeds by dying, before the narrator is willing to show them respect.

27 The feminine-coded otherness of death as something beyond signification shows in the fact that of the total of thirty-three depictions of death in the author's seven novels, Marlowe observes directly only three female corpses (Jessie Florian's in *Farewell, My Lovely*; Crystal Kingsley's and Mildred Haviland's in *The Lady in the Lake*). These descriptions are among the most brutal in the author's work. For example, only a female corpse is characterized as having a face looking like '[a] blotch of gray dough, a nightmare with human hair on it' (*The Lady in the Lake*, 1976d, 40).

28 Jean Baudrillard argues in his genealogy of death in *Symbolic Exchange and Death* (1993) that the idea of such an exchange has its roots in an archaic conception of life and death familiar from the symbolic order of so-called primitive societies. Marlowe's identification with a male double is reminiscent of the primitive's regard for his shadowy double as a partner with whom he has a personal and concrete relationship. This is a non-alienated reciprocity in which both parties can interact with one another. The primitive can approach the double and trade with him as with some original, living person. Baudrillard maintains that the primitive's symbolic exchange with death alters 'natural,' aleatory, and irreversible death into death that is given and received, and, thanks to its being reversible in such an exchange, death becomes soluble in it. In other words, this barter makes the opposition between life and death disappear so that death no longer poses itself as the end to life (131–2; 140–2).

29 One of the euphemistic expressions the narrator uses for death is 'big sleep.'
30 One such fissure is worth noting. In *The Long Goodbye* the narrator describes how, on Lennox's request, he re-enacts his last morning with the friend: 'I did what he asked me, sentimental or not. I poured two cups and added some bourbon to his and set it down on the side of the table where he had sat the morning I took him to the plane. I lit a cigarette for him and set it in an ash tray beside the cup. I watched the steam rise from the coffee and the thin thread of smoke rise from the cigarette. Outside in the tecoma a bird was gussing around, talking to himself in low chirps, with an occasional brief flutter of wings' (69). As he believes Lennox to be dead, the detective can try to achieve contact with him only indirectly, through this breakfast ritual; yet there is no feeling of communication, and the singing of the bird underlines the fact that life goes on.
31 The emphasis on the death of friendship, the death of ideals, and the eventual triumph of death itself distinguishes the hard-boiled narrative from the whodunit.
32 In suggesting Gatsby's basic decency, Nick is, of course, implying that he himself 'turned out alright' as well. Given the elegiac context, the narrator's self-satisfaction is inevitable; Fitzgerald is just subtler than Chandler in making this suggestion. *Playback* marks a turn of direction in the author's work. It ends in a phone call by Linda Loring to Marlowe, asking him to marry her. As Marlowe believes he will never meet her again, this call from Paris – a place equivalent to the shady Hades he has been evoking throughout the series – amounts to a tangible message from someone to whom he has fondly and sadly said goodbye (see *The Long Goodbye* [300] and *Playback* [1977, 76]). This time, the one occupying the place of the double has remained faithful and chaste ('I've been faithful to you. I don't know why. The world is full of men. But I've been faithful to you' [*Playback*, 167]), suggesting that the narrator will be willing to risk the sexual encounter with a woman.
33 Examples of the elegiac romance, these narratives shape this reciprocal relationship as one between a 'knight' (the quarry) and a 'squire' (the metaphysical detective). They depict two ultimately diverging quests, for the knight figure, who first functions as the narrator's idealized hero, is himself involved in a quest of his own. For a while, the protagonist-narrator idealizes this quest, trying to appropriate it into his life. The relationship between the two men is clearly based on imitation and emulation of one by the other. Bruffee's description of the squire's obsession with the knight is revealing, for he maintains that the squire has 'fallen in love with [his] master's madness and his role,' claiming that he 'live[s] into the other' (40). This depic-

tion fits well Girard's characterization of internal mimetic modelling, where the object of desire begins to wane, while desire is increasingly directed at the model himself: the desiring subject wants to assimilate and become his model; he wants to steal from the model his very being of perfect knight (1966, 53–6). The narrator eventually realizes the fundamental falseness of the knight's quest, which leads him to reject it in favour of the narrator's own, much more modest and basically non-heroic, life project (Bruffee, 28–41). In Girardian terms, such narratives are *novelistic* (*romanesque*) works instead of *romantic* (*romantique*) ones, for they reveal the presence and significance of the model and present the imitator's strategy of freeing himself from the strait-jacket of enslaving mimetic desire (1966, 17–18).

34 Nabokov's treatment of the mirror mechanism differs from Auster's. In *The Real Life of Sebastian Knight* (1992) Nabokov underlines the mutuality of life a separate self shares with other selves, a mutuality which makes the interchangeability of one for the other possible. Even if this awareness of interpersonal communion is largely unconscious and available only in brief epiphanic glimpses, the knowledge of its existence makes the burden of the loneliness of selfhood bearable for the narrator of this book. The narrator of Auster's *The Locked Room* comes to a related realization, but through another route: 'We exist for ourselves, perhaps, and at times we even have a glimmer of who we are, but in the end we can never be sure, and as our lives go on, we become more and more opaque to ourselves, more and more aware of our own incoherence. No one can cross the boundary into another – for the simple reason that no one can gain access to himself' (1988, 80–1). The self is always incoherent, as the motif of the locked room demonstrates by playing on the paradoxical oscillation between inside and outside. The self is inside, locked within one's body; yet even if it is located within one's body, one cannot penetrate it. Even when one thinks one ventures inside the recesses of one's self, one soon finds that what one takes to be the inside is only another manifestation of the barriers keeping one outside: one cannot know oneself.

Works Cited

Detective Stories

This bibliography includes both the detective stories analysed in detail and those that are briefly alluded to as examples of a given theme. The first date cited is that of the edition used.

Auster, Paul. 1988. *The Locked Room*. New York: Penguin. Original edn 1986.

Bentley, E.C. 1976. *Trent's Last Case*. New York: Garland. Original edn 1929.

Berkeley, Anthony. 1951. *The Poisoned Chocolates Case*. New York: Pocket. Original edn 1929.

Borges, Jorge Luis. 1970a. 'Death and the Compass.' In Donald A. Yates and James E. Irby, eds and trans., *Labyrinths: Selected Stories and Other Writings*. London: Penguin. Story originally pub. 1942.

– 1970b. 'The Garden of Forking Paths.' In Donald A. Yates and James E. Irby, eds and trans., *Labyrinths: Selected Stories and Other Writings*. London: Penguin. Story originally pub. 1941.

– 1970c. 'The Theme of the Traitor and the Hero.' In Donald A. Yates and James E. Irby, eds and trans., *Labyrinths: Selected Stories and Other Writings*. London: Penguin.

– 1978. 'Ibn Hakkan al-Bokhari, Dead in His Labyrinth.' In Norman Thomas di Giovanni, ed. and trans., *The Aleph and Other Stories, 1933–1969*. New York: Dutton. Story originally pub. 1951.

Carr, Caleb. 1994. *The Alienist*. New York: Bantam.

Carr, John Dickson. 1992. 'A Footprint in the Sky.' In Peter Haining, ed., *The Television Detectives' Omnibus: Great Tales of Crime and Detection*. London: Artus. Story originally pub. as 'A Clue in the Snow,' 1940.

Chandler, Raymond. 1971a. *The Little Sister*. New York: Ballantine. Original edn 1949.

– 1971b. *The Long Goodbye*. New York: Ballantine. Original edn 1953.

– 1976a. *The Big Sleep*. New York: Vintage. Original edn 1939.

– 1976b. *Farewell, My Lovely*. New York: Vintage. Original edn 1940.

– 1976c. *The High Window*. New York: Vintage. Original edn 1942.

– 1976d. *The Lady in the Lake*. New York: Vintage. Original edn 1943.

– 1977. *Playback*. New York: Ballantine. Original edn 1958.

Chesterton, G.K. 1981a. *The Innocence of Father Brown*. In *The Penguin Complete Father Brown*. London: Penguin. Original edn 1910.

– 1981b. *The Wisdom of Father Brown*. In *The Penguin Complete Father Brown*. London: Penguin. Original edn 1913.

– 1981c. *The Secret of Father Brown*. In *The Penguin Complete Father Brown*. London: Penguin. Original edn 1927.

Christie, Agatha. 1937. *Death on the Nile*. London: Collins.

– 1940. *One, Two, Buckle My Shoe*. London: Collins.

– 1941. *Evil under the Sun*. New York: Pocket.

– 1944. *Towards Zero*. London: Collins.

– 1950. *A Murder Is Announced*. New York: Pocket.

– 1951. *Cards on the Table*. London: Pan. Original edn 1936.

– 1954. *The Mysterious Affair at Styles*. London: Pan. Original edn 1920.

– 1955. *Mrs McGinty's Dead*. London: Fontana. Original edn 1952.

– 1956a. *After the Funeral*. London: Fontana. Original edn 1953.

– 1956b. *Dead Man's Folly*. London: Fontana.

– 1956c. *The Sittaford Mystery*. London: Pan. Original edn 1931.

– 1957a. *The ABC Murders*. London: Fontana. Original edn 1936.

– 1957b. *The Murder of Roger Ackroyd*. London: Fontana. Original edn 1926.

– 1958. *A Pocket Full of Rye*. London: Fontana. Original edn 1953.

– 1959a. *Crooked House*. London: Fontana. Original edn 1949.

– 1959b. *Five Little Pigs*. London: Fontana. Original edn 1943.

– 1961a. *The Labours of Hercules*. London: Fontana. Original edn 1947.

– 1961b. *Murder at the Vicarage*. London: Fontana. Original edn 1930.

– 1961c. *Taken at the Flood*. London: Fontana. Original edn 1948.

– 1962a. *The Body in the Library*. London: Fontana. Original edn 1942.

– 1962b. *Cat among the Pigeons*. London: Fontana. Original edn 1959.

– 1963. *And Then There Were None*. New York: Dell. Original edn 1939.

– 1964a. *Appointment with Death*. New York: Dell. Original edn 1938.

– 1964b. *Three Act Tragedy*. London: Pan. Original edn 1935.

– 1965. *The Mirror Crack'd from Side to Side*. London: Fontana. Original edn 1962.

– 1966a. *A Caribbean Mystery*. London: Fontana. Original edn 1964.
– 1966b. *The Clocks*. London: Fontana. Original edn 1963.
– 1966c. *Peril at End House*. London: Pan. Original edn 1932.
– 1970. *Hallowe'en Party*. London: Fontana. Original edn 1969.
– 1971. *They Do It with Mirrors*. London: Pan. Original edn 1952.
– 1973. *Elephants Can Remember*. New York: Dell. Original edn 1972.
– 1974. *4:50 from Paddington*. London: Pan. Original edn 1957.
– 1977. *Curtain: Poirot's Last Case*. London: Fontana. Original edn 1975.
– 1978. *Murder on the Links*. London: Triad. Original edn 1923.
– 1984. *Sad Cypress*. New York: Berkeley. Original edn 1940.
Cornwell, Patricia. 1993. *Cruel and Unusual*. London: Warner.
Dexter, Colin. 1991a. *The Dead of Jericho*. In *The First Inspector Morse Omnibus*. London: Pan. Original edn 1977.
– 1991b. *Last Seen Wearing*. In *The Second Inspector Morse Omnibus*. London: Pan. Original edn 1978.
– 1991c. *The Riddle of the Third Mile*. In *The Second Inspector Morse Omnibus*. London: Pan. Original edn 1983.
– 1991d. *The Secret of Annexe 3*. In *The Second Inspector Morse Omnibus*. London: Pan. Original edn 1986.
– 1991e. *Service of All the Dead*. In *The First Inspector Morse Omnibus*. London: Pan. Original edn 1979.
– 1991f. *The Silent World of Nicholas Quinn*. In *The First Inspector Morse Omnibus*. London: Pan. Original edn 1981.
– 1994a. *The Jewel That Was Ours*. In *The Third Inspector Morse Omnibus*. London: Pan. Original edn 1991.
– 1994b. *Last Bus to Woodstock*. In *The Third Inspector Morse Omnibus*. London: Pan. Original edn 1975.
– 1994c. *The Wench Is Dead*. In *The Third Inspector Morse Omnibus*. London: Pan. Original edn 1989.
– 1996. *Death Is Now My Neighbour*. London: Macmillan.
Dibdin, Michael. 1988. *Ratking*. London: Macmillan.
– 1994. *Dead Lagoon*. London: Macmillan.
– 1996. *Così Fan Tutti*. London: Faber and Faber.
Doyle, Arthur Conan. 1985a. *The Adventures of Sherlock Holmes*. In *Sherlock Holmes: The Complete Illustrated Short Stories*. London: Chancellor Press. Original edn 1891–2.
– 1985b. *The Memoirs of Sherlock Holmes*. In *Sherlock Holmes: The Complete Illustrated Short Stories*. London: Chancellor Press. Original edn 1892–3.
– 1987. *A Study in Scarlet*. In *Sherlock Holmes: The Complete Illustrated Novels*. London: Chancellor Press. Original edn 1887.

du Maurier, Daphne. 1992. *Rebecca*. London: Fontana. Original edn 1938.

George, Elizabeth. 1989. *A Great Deliverance*. New York: Bantam.

Hammett, Dashiell. 1980a. *The Dain Curse*. In *Dashiell Hammett: Five Complete Novels*. New York: Avenel. Original edn 1929.

– 1980b. *The Glass Key*. In *Dashiell Hammett: Five Complete Novels*. Original edn 1933.

– 1980c. *The Maltese Falcon*. In *Dashiell Hammett: Five Complete Novels*. Original edn 1930.

– 1980d. *Red Harvest*. In *Dashiell Hammett: Five Complete Novels*. Original edn 1929.

Holt, A.J. 1995. *Watch Me*. London: Headline.

Hull, Richard. 1979. *The Murder of My Aunt*. New York: International. Original edn 1934.

Iles, Francis. 1980. *Before the Fact*. New York: Perennial Library. Original edn 1932.

James, P.D. 1989a. *A Taste for Death*. London: Penguin. Original edn 1986.

– 1989b. *Unnatural Causes*. London: Penguin. Original edn 1967.

Keating, H.R.F. 1996. *The Good Detective*. London: Pan. Original edn 1995.

Kerr, Philip. 1993a. *March Violets*. In *Berlin Noir*. London: Penguin. Original edn 1989.

– 1993b. *The Pale Criminal*. In *Berlin Noir*. London: Penguin. Original edn 1990.

– 1995. *A Philosophical Investigation*. Toronto: Seal. Original edn 1992.

King, Laurie. 1993. *A Grave Talent*. New York: Bantam.

le Carré, John. 1980. *A Murder of Quality*. New York: Bantam. Original edn 1963.

Macdonald, Ross. 1986. *The Moving Target*. London: Allison & Busby. Original edn 1949.

– 1996. *Black Money*. New York: Vintage. Original edn 1965.

Marsh, Ngaio. 1983. *Light Thickens*. London: Fontana.

Nabokov, Vladimir. 1992. *The Real Life of Sebastian Knight*. New York: Vintage. Original edn 1941.

Oatley, Keith. 1993. *The Case of Emily V*. London: Martin Secker and Warburg.

Paretsky, Sara. 1990. *Burn Marks*. New York: Dell.

Poe, E.A. 1994a. 'The Murders in the Rue Morgue.' In *Selected Tales*. London: Penguin. Story originally pub. 1841.

– 1994b. 'The Purloined Letter.' In *Selected Tales*. London: Penguin. Story originally pub. 1844.

Rendell, Ruth. 1967. *Wolf to the Slaughter*. London: Arrow.

– 1974. *Some Lie and Some Die*. London: Arrow. Original edn 1973.

– 1979. *From Doon with Death*. London: Arrow. Original edn 1964.

– 1989. *A Guilty Thing Surprised*. In *The Second Wexford Omnibus*. London: Arrow. Original edn 1970.

- 1990a. *An Unkindness of Ravens*. In *The Ruth Rendell Mysteries*. London: Arrow. Original edn 1985.
- 1990b. *The Veiled One*. In *The Ruth Rendell Mysteries*. London: Arrow. Original edn 1988.
- 1991a. *Heartstones*. London: Arrow. Original edn 1987.
- 1991b. *Kissing the Gunner's Daughter*. London: Arrow.
- 1994. *Shake Hands Forever*. London: Arrow. Original edn 1975.
Ross, Veronica. 1996. *The Anastasia Connection*. Stratford, Ont.: Mercury.
Sanders, Lawrence. 1973. *The First Deadly Sin*. New York: Putnam.
Sayers, Dorothy L. 1975. *Five Red Herrings*. London: New English Library. Original edn 1931.
- 1986. *Gaudy Night*. New York: Harper & Row. Original edn 1935.
Sjöwall, Maj, and Per Wahlöö. 1971. *The Laughing Policeman*. Trans. Alan Blair. London: Gollancz.
- 1973. *The Locked Room*. Trans. Paul Britten Austin. Harmondsworth: Penguin.
Spillane, Mickey. 1951. *One Lonely Night*. New York: Signet.
- 1950. *Vengeance Is Mine*. New York: Signet.
- 1953. *Kiss Me, Deadly*. New York: Signet.
Tey, Josephine. 1996. *The Daughter of Time*. London: Victor Gollancz. Original edn 1951.
Wallace, Edgar. 1994. *Punainen ympyrä (The Crimson Circle)*. Helsinki: WSOY. Original edn 1922.
Walters, Minette. 1996. *The Dark Room*. London: Pan. Original edn 1995.
Wilson, Barbara. 1988. *Sisters of the Road*. Seattle: Seal.
Wright, L.R. 1988. *Sleep While I Sing*. London: Fontana. Original edn 1986.
Zangwill, Israel. 1923. *The Big-Bow Mystery*. New York: Macmillan. Original edn 1892.

Reference Works

Abrams, M.H. 1953. *The Mirror and the Lamp: Romantic Theory and the Critical Tradition*. New York: Oxford UP.
Amossy, Ruth. 1984. 'Stereotypes and Representation in Fiction.' *Poetics Today*. 5.4: 689–700.
Auden, W.H. 1988. 'The Guilty Vicarage.' In his *The Dyer's Hand and Other Essays*. London: Faber 1948. Reprinted in Winks, ed., *Detective Fiction* 15–24. (Page references are to the reprint edition.)
Bargainnier, Earl F. 1980. *The Gentle Art of Murder: The Detective Fiction of Agatha Christie*. Bowling Green: Bowling Green State UP.
Barnard, Robert. 1980. *A Talent to Deceive: An Appreciation of Agatha Christie*. New York: Dodd.

Barthes, Roland. 1973. *Mythologies*. Trans. Annette Lavers. London: Paladin.
– 1974. *S/Z: An Essay in Method*. Trans. Richard Howard. New York: Noonday Press.
Baudrillard, Jean. 1993. *Symbolic Exchange and Death*. Trans. Iain Hamilton Grant. London: Sage Publications.
Beardsley, Monroe C. 1958. *Aesthetics: Problems in the Philosophy of Criticism*. New York: Harcourt.
Beekman, E.M. 1973. 'Raymond Chandler and an American Genre.' *The Massachusetts Review* (Winter): 149–73.
Belsey, Catherine. 1980. *Critical Practice*. London: Routledge.
Bennett, Donna. 1979. 'The Detective Story: Towards a Definition of Genre.' *PTL: A Journal for Descriptive Poetics and the Theory of Literature* 4: 233–66.
Black, Joel. 1990. *The Aesthetics of Murder: A Study in Romantic Literature and Contemporary Culture*. Baltimore and London: Johns Hopkins UP.
Bonfantini, Massimo A., and Giampaolo Proni. 1983. 'To Guess or Not to Guess?' In Eco and Sebeok, eds, *The Sign of Three*, 119–34.
Booth, Wayne C. 1983. *The Rhetoric of Fiction*. 2nd. enlarged ed. Chicago: U of Chicago P.
– 1988. *The Company We Keep: An Ethics of Fiction*. Berkeley: U of California P.
Bremond, Claude. 1986. 'Et le thème s'est fait texte ...: À propos d'un Essai d'Alexander Zholkovsky.' *Canadian Review of Comparative Literature* (Dec.): 600–17.
– 1988. 'En lisant un fable.' *Communications* 47: *Variations sur le thème*: 41–62.
Bremond, Claude, Joshua Landy, and Thomas Pavel, eds. 1995. *Thematics: New Approaches*, New York: State U of New York P.
Bremond, Claude, and Thomas Pavel. 1995. 'The End of an Anathema.' In Bremond, Landy, and Pavel, eds, *Thematics: New Approaches*, 181–92.
Brinker, Menachem. 1993. 'Theme and Interpretation.' In Sollers, ed., *The Return of Thematic Criticism*, 21–37.
Brooks, Peter. 1984. *Reading for the Plot: Design and Intention in Narrative*. Cambridge, Mass.: Harvard UP.
– 1993. *Body Work: Objects of Desire in Modern Narrative*. Cambridge, Mass.: Harvard UP.
– 1994. *Psychoanalysis and Storytelling*. London: Basil Blackwell.
Bruffee, Kenneth. 1983. *Elegiac Romance: Cultural Change and Loss of the Hero in Modern Fiction*. Ithaca: Cornell UP.
Calinescu, Matei. 1993. *Rereading*. New Haven: Yale UP.
Caillois, Roger. 1983. 'The Detective Novel as a Game.' In *Puissance du roman*. Buenos Aires: Sur 1941. Reprinted in Most and Stowe, eds, *The Poetics of Murder*, 1–12. (Page references are to the reprint edition.)

– 1984. *The Mystery Novel. (Le roman policier.)* Trans. Roberto Yahni and A.W. Sadler. Bronxville, N.Y.: Laughing Buddha.

Cawelti, John G. 1976. *Adventure, Mystery, and Romance: Formula Stories as Art and Popular Culture.* Chicago: U of Chicago P.

Champigny, Robert. 1977. *What Will Have Happened: A Philosophical and Technical Essay on Mystery Stories.* Bloomington: Indiana UP.

Chandler, Raymond. 1946. 'The Simple Art of Murder: An Essay.' *Atlantic Monthly* (Dec. 1944). Reprinted with author's revisions in Haycraft, ed., *The Art of the Mystery Story,* 222–37. (Page references are to reprint edition.)

Charney, Hannah. 1981. *The Detective Novel of Manners: Hedonism, Morality, and the Life of Reason.* London: Associated UP.

Chatman, Seymour. 1978. *Story and Discourse: Narrative Structure in Fiction and Film.* Ithaca, N.Y.: Cornell UP.

– 1983. 'On the Notion of Theme in Narrative.' In John Fisher, ed., *Essays on Aesthetics: Perspectives on the Work of Monroe C. Beardsley,* 161–79. Philadelphia: Temple UP.

Chesterton, G.K. 1946. 'A Defence of Detective Stories.' In his *The Defendant.* New York: Dodd, Mead 1902. Reprinted in Haycraft, ed., *The Art of the Mystery Story,* 3–6. (Page references are to the reprint edition.)

Christianson, Scott R. 1990. 'A Heap of Broken Images: Hard-Boiled Detective Fiction and the Discourse(s) of Modernity.' In Walker and Frazer, eds, *The Cunning Craft,* 135–48.

Collins, Jim. 1989. *Uncommon Cultures: Popular Culture and Post-Modernism.* New York: Routledge.

The Concise Oxford Dictionary of Current English. 1976. Oxford: Clarendon.

Dayton, Tim. 1993. '"The Annihilated Content of the Wish": Class and Gender in Mickey Spillane's *I, The Jury.*' *Clues* 14.1: 87–104.

Derrida, Jacques. 1988. 'The Purveyor of Truth.' Trans. Alan Bass. In Muller and Richardson, eds, *The Purloined Poe,* 173–212.

Dettmar, Kevin J.H. 1990. 'From Interpretation to "Intrepidation": Joyce's "The Sisters" as a Precursor of the Postmodern Mystery.' In Walker and Frazer, eds, *The Cunning Craft,* 149–65.

Doležel, Lubomír. 1995. 'A Semantics for Thematics: The Case of the Double.' In Bremond, Landy, and Pavel, eds, *Thematics: New Approaches,* 89–102.

Eco, Umberto. 1976. *A Theory of Semiotics.* Bloomington: Indiana UP.

– 1979. *The Role of the Reader: Explorations in the Semiotics of Texts.* Bloomington: Indiana UP.

– 1983. 'Horns, Hooves, Insteps.' In Eco and Sebeok, eds, *The Sign of Three,* 198–220.

– 1984. *Semiotics and the Philosophy of Language.* London: Macmillan.

– 1985. *Postscript to the Name of the Rose*. Trans. William Weaver. New York: Harcourt.

– 1990. *The Limits of Interpretation*. Bloomington: Indiana UP.

Eco, Umberto, and Thomas A. Sebeok, eds. 1983. *The Sign of Three: Dupin, Holmes, Peirce*. Bloomington: Indiana UP.

Fiske, John. 1989. *Understanding Popular Culture*. Boston: Unwin Hyman.

Fitzgerald, F. Scott. 1950. *The Great Gatsby*. London: Penguin. Original edn 1926.

Frank, Joseph. 1963. 'Spatial Form in Modern Literature.' In his *The Widening Gyre: Crisis and Mastery in Modern Literature*. New Brunswick: Rutgers UP.

– 1991. *The Idea of Spatial Form*. New Brunswick: Rutgers UP.

Freeman, R. Austin. 1946. 'The Art of the Detective Story.' In Haycraft, ed., *The Art of the Mystery Story*, 7–17. Originally pub. 1924.

Freud, Sigmund. 1961a. 'The Dissolution of the Oedipus Complex.' In James Strachey, ed., *The Standard Edition of the Complete Psychological Works of Sigmund Freud*. Vol. 19. London: Hogarth. Original edn 1924.

– 1961b. 'The Ego and the Id.' In Strachey, ed., *Standard Edition of the Complete Psychological Works*, Vol. 19. London: Hogarth. Original edn 1923.

Frye, Northrop. 1973. *The Anatomy of Criticism*. Princeton: Princeton UP. Original edn 1957.

Gallop, Jane. 1988. 'The American Other.' In her *Reading Lacan*, 1985. Ithaca, N.Y.: Cornell UP. Reprinted in Muller and Richardson, eds, *The Purloined Poe*, 268–82. (Page references are to the reprint edition.)

Genette, Gerard. 1980. *Narrative Discourse*. Trans. Jane E. Levin. Oxford: Basil Blackwell.

Ginzburg, Carlo. 1983. 'Morelli, Freud, and Sherlock Holmes: Clues and Scientific Method.' In Eco and Sebeok, eds, *The Sign of Three*, 81–118.

Girard, René. 1966. *Deceit, Desire, and the Novel: Self and Other in Literary Structure*. Trans. Yvonne Freccero. Baltimore: Johns Hopkins UP.

– 1991. *A Theater of Envy: William Shakespeare*. New York: Oxford UP.

Gregory, Sinda. 1985. *Private Investigations: The Novels of Dashiell Hammett*. Carbondale and Edwardsville: Southern Illinois UP.

Grella, George. 1988a. 'Murder and Manners: The Formal Detective Novel.' In *Novel: A Forum on Fiction* 4.3 (1970): 30–48. Reprinted in Winks, ed., *Detective Fiction*, 84–102. (Page references are to the reprint edition.)

– 1988b. 'Murder and Mean Streets: The Hard-Boiled Detective Novel.' *Contempora* I (1970): 6–15. Reprinted in Winks, ed., *Detective Fiction*, 103–20. (Page references are to the reprint edition.)

Grossvogel, David I. 1979. 'Agatha Christie: Containment of the Unknown.' In his *Mystery and Its Fictions: From Oedipus to Agatha Christie*, 39–52. Baltimore: Johns Hopkins UP.

Haycraft, Howard. 1974. *Murder for Pleasure: The Life and Times of the Detective Story*. 2nd enlarged ed. New York: Biblio and Tannen. Original edn 1941.

Haycraft, Howard, ed. 1946. *The Art of the Mystery Story: A Collection of Critical Essays*. New York: Simon and Schuster.

Heissenbüttel, Helmut. 1983. 'Rules of the Game of the Crime Novel.' Trans. Glenn W. Most and William W. Stowe. In Most and Stowe, eds, *The Poetics of Murder*, 79–92.

Hodgson, John A. 1992. 'The Recoil of "The Speckled Band": Detective Story and Detective Discourse.' *Poetics Today* 13.2: 309–24.

Holquist, Michael. 1983. 'The Whodunit and Other Questions: Metaphysical Detective Stories in Post-War Fiction.' *New Literary History* 3.1. (1971): 135–56. Reprinted in Most and Stowe, eds, *The Poetics of Murder*, 149–74. (Page references are to the reprint edition.)

The Holy Bible. Authorized King James's Version. 1959. London: Collins.

Hoy, David Couzens. 1978. *The Critical Circle: Literature, History, and Philosophical Hermeneutics*. Berkeley: U of California P.

Hühn, Peter. 1987. 'The Detective as Reader: Narrativity and Reading Concepts in Detective Fiction.' *Modern Fiction Studies* 33.3: 451–66.

Hunter, Lynette. 1979. *G.K. Chesterton: Explorations in Allegory*. London: Macmillan.

Irons, Glenwood, ed. 1995. *Feminism in Women's Detective Fiction*. Toronto: U of Toronto P.

Irwin, John T. 1994. *The Mystery to a Solution: Poe, Borges, and the Analytic Detective Story*. Baltimore and London: Johns Hopkins UP.

Jameson, F.R. 1983. 'On Raymond Chandler.' *Southern Review* 6 (1970): 624–50. Reprinted in Most and Stowe, eds, *The Poetics of Murder*, 122–48. (Page reference are to the reprint edition.)

Johnson, Barbara. 1988. 'The Frame of Reference: Poe, Lacan, Derrida.' *Yale French Studies* 55–6 (1977): 457–505. Reprinted in Muller and Richardson, eds, *The Purloined Poe*, 213–51. (Page references are to the reprint edition.)

Kermode, Frank. 1967. *The Sense of An Ending: Studies in the Theory of Fiction*. New York: Oxford UP.

– 1983. 'Novel and Narrative.' In John Halperin, ed., *The Theory of the Novel: New Essays*. New York: Oxford UP 1974. Reprinted in Most and Stowe, eds, *The Poetics of Murder*, 175–96. (Page references are to the reprint edition.)

Knight, Stephen. 1980. *Form and Ideology in Crime Fiction*. London: Macmillan.

Knox, Ronald A. 1946. 'A Detective Story Decalogue.' Introduction to *The Best English Detective Stories*. London: Faber 1928. Reprinted in Haycraft, ed., *The Art of the Mystery Story*, 194–6. (Page references are to the reprint edition.)

Knuuttila, Simo. 1989. 'Selitykset.' ('Explanations.') In Knuuttila's edition of Aristotle's *Nikomakhoksen etiikka*. (*Nicomachean Ethics*). Helsinki: Gaudeamus.

Krutch, Joseph Wood. 1946. 'Only a Detective Story.' *Nation* (25 Nov. 1944.) Reprinted in Haycraft, ed., *The Art of the Mystery Story*, 178–85. (Page references are to the reprint edition.)

Lacan, Jacques. 1988. 'Seminar on "The Purloined Letter."' *French Freud: Structural Studies in Psychoanalysis*. In *Yale French Studies* 48 (1972). Trans. Jeffrey Mehlman. Reprinted in Muller and Richardson, eds, *The Purloined Poe*, 28–54. (Page references are to the reprint edition.)

Lamarque, Peter, and Stein Haugom Olsen. 1994. *Truth, Fiction, and Literature: A Philosophical Perspective*. London: Clarendon.

Lid, R.W. 1969. 'Philip Marlowe Speaking.' *The Kenyon Review* 31.2: 153–78.

Livingston, Paisley. 1992. *Models of Desire: René Girard and the Psychology of Mimesis*. Baltimore: Johns Hopkins UP.

Lovitt, Carl R. 1990. 'Controlling Discourse in Detective Fiction, or Caring Very Much Who Killed Roger Ackroyd.' In Walker and Frazer, eds, *The Cunning Craft*, 68–85.

Maida, Patricia D., and Nicholas B. Spornick. 1982. *Murder She Wrote: A Study of Agatha Christie's Detective Fiction*. Bowling Green: Bowling Green State UP.

Marcus, Steven. 1974. 'Introduction.' *The Continental Op*, by Dashiell Hammett, 7–23. New York: Random House.

Margolies, Edward. 1982. *Which Way Did He Go? The Private Eye in Dashiell Hammett, Raymond Chandler, Chester Himes, and Ross Macdonald*. New York: Holmes and Meier.

Mason, Michael. 1977. 'Marlowe, Men and Women.' In Miriam Gross, ed., *The World of Raymond Chandler*, 90–101. London: Weidenfeld and Nicolson.

Merivale, Patricia. 1968. 'The Flaunting of Artifice in Vladimir Nabokov, and Jorge Luis Borges.' In L.S. Dembo, ed., *Nabokov: The Man and His Work*, 290–324. Madison: U of Wisconsin P.

– 1997. 'The Austerized Version.' *Contemporary Literature* 38.1: 182–93.

– 1999. 'Gumshoe Gothics: "The Man of the Crowd" and His Followers.' In Raymond A. Prier and Gerald Gillespie, eds, *Narrative Ironies*. Text: Studies in Comparative Literature 5, 163–79. Rodopi: Amsterdam. Reprinted in Merivale and Sweeny, eds, *Detecting Texts*, 101–16. (Page references are to the reprint edition.)

– 1999. 'The Game's Afoot: On the Trail of the Metaphysical Detective Story.' In Merivale and Sweeney, eds, *Detecting Texts*, 1–24.

Merivale, Patricia, and Susan Elizabeth Sweeney, eds. 1999. *Detecting Texts: The Metaphysical Detective Story from Poe to Postmodernism*. Philadelphia: U of Pennsylvania P.

Miller, D.A. 1988. *The Novel and the Police*. Berkeley: U of California P.

Miller, J. Hillis. 1992. *Ariadne's Thread: Story Lines*. New Haven: Yale UP.

Morrison, Karl F. 1988. *I Am You: The Hermeneutics of Empathy in Western Literature, Art, and Theology*. Princeton: Princeton UP.

Most, Glenn W. 1983. 'The Hippocratic Smile: John le Carré and the Traditions of the Detective Novel.' In Most and Stowe, eds, *The Poetics of Murder*, 341–65.

Most, Glenn W., and William W. Stowe, eds. 1983. *The Poetics of Murder. Detective Fiction and Literary Theory*. New York: Harcourt Brace Jovanovich.

Muller, John P., and William J. Richardson, eds, 1988. *The Purloined Poe: Lacan, Derrida, and Psychoanalytic Reading*. Baltimore: Johns Hopkins UP.

Munt, Sally R. 1994. *Murder by the Book? Feminism and the Crime Novel*. London: Routledge.

Nicolson, Marjorie. 1946. 'The Professor and the Detective.' *Atlantic Monthly* (Apr. 1929). Reprinted in Haycraft, ed., *The Art of the Mystery Story*, 110–27. (Page references are to the reprint edition.)

Nussbaum, Martha Craven. 1978. *Aristotle's* De Motu Animalium. Princeton: Princeton UP.

– 1986. *The Fragility of Goodness: Luck and Ethics in Greek Tragedy and Philosophy*. Cambridge: Cambridge UP.

– 1990. *Love's Knowledge: Essays on Philosophy and Literature*. Oxford: Oxford UP.

– 1995. *Poetic Justice: The Literary Imagination and Public Life*. Boston: Beacon.

Palmer, Jerry. 1978. *Thrillers: Genesis and Structure of a Popular Genre*. London: Edward Arnold.

Parker, Robert B. 1984. *The Private Eye in Hammett and Chandler*. Northridge: Lord John.

Pederson-Krag, Geraldine. 1983. 'Detective Stories and the Primal Scene.' *Psychoanalytic Quarterly* 18 (1949): 207–14. Reprinted in Most and Stowe, eds, *The Poetics of Murder*, 13–20. (Page references are to the reprint edition.)

Phelan, James. 1989. *Reading People, Reading Plots: Character, Progression, and the Interpretation of Narrative*. Chicago: U of Chicago P.

Porter, Dennis. 1981. *The Pursuit of Crime: Art and Ideology in Detective Fiction*. New Haven and London: Yale UP.

– 1988. 'Detection and Ethics: The Case of P.D. James.' In Rader and Zettler, eds, *The Sleuth and the Scholar*, 11–18.

Priestman, Martin. 1990. *Detective Fiction and Literature: The Figure on the Carpet*. London: Macmillan.

Prince, Gerald. 1980. 'Notes on the Text as Reader.' In Susan R. Suleiman and Inge Crossman, eds, *The Reader in the Text: Essays on Audience and Interpretation*, 225–40. Princeton: Princeton UP.

– 1987. *A Dictionary of Narratology*. Lincoln: U of Nebraska P.

– 1992. *Narrative as Theme: Studies in French Fiction*. Lincoln and London: U of Nebraska P.

Pyrhönen, Heta. 1994. *Murder from an Academic Angle: An Introduction to the Study of the Detective Narrative.* Columbia, S.C.: Camden House.

Rabinowitz, Peter J. 1980. 'Rats behind the Wainscoting: Politics, Convention, and Chandler's *The Big Sleep.*' *Texas Studies in Literature and Language* 22.2: 224–45.

– 1987. *Before Reading: Narrative Conventions and the Politics of Interpretation.* Ithaca: Cornell UP.

– 1994. '"How Did You Know He Licked His Lips?": Second Person Knowledge and First Person Power in *The Maltese Falcon.*' In James Phelan and Peter J. Rabinowitz, eds, *Understanding Narrative,* 157–77. Columbus: Ohio State UP.

Rader, Barbara A., and Howard G. Zettler, eds. 1988. *The Sleuth and the Scholar: Origins, Evolutions, and Current Trends in Detective Fiction.* New York: Greenwood Press.

Reddy, Maureen T. 1990. 'The Feminist Counter-Tradition in Crime: Cross, Grafton, Paretsky, and Wilson.' In Walker and Frazer, eds, *The Cunning Craft,* 174–87.

Rendell, Ruth, ed. 1996. *Ruth Rendell's Anthology of the Murderous Mind.* Introduction by Ruth Rendell. Reprint of *The Reason Why: An Anthology of the Murderous Mind,* 1995. London: Vintage.

Roberts, Thomas J. 1990. *An Aesthetics of Junk Fiction.* Athens and London: U of Georgia Press.

Ruehlman, William. 1984. *Saint with a Gun: The Unlawful American Private Eye.* New York: New York UP.

Ryan, Marie-Laure. 1991. *Possible Worlds, Artificial Intelligence, and Narrative Theory.* Bloomington: Indiana UP.

– 1993. 'In Search of the Narrative Theme.' In Sollers, ed., *The Return of Thematic Criticism,* 169–90.

Rycroft, Charles. 1968. 'The Analysis of a Detective Story.' In his *Imagination and Reality: Psycho-Analytical Essays, 1951–1961.* London: Hogarth Press. Originally pub. 1957.

Sayers, Dorothy L. 1988a. 'Aristotle on Detective Fiction.' In her *Unpopular Opinions.* London: Victor Gollancz 1946. Reprinted in Winks, ed., *Detective Fiction,* 25–34. (Page references are to the reprint edition.)

– 1988b. 'The Omnibus of Crime.' Introduction to her *The Omnibus of Crime.* New York: Payson and Clarke 1929. Reprinted in Winks, ed., *Detective Fiction,* 53–83. (Page references are to the reprint edition.)

Schaeffer, Jean-Marie. 1989. 'Literary Genres and Textual Genericity.' In Ralph Cohen, ed., *The Future of Literary Theory,* 167–87. London: Routledge.

Sebeok, Thomas A. 1994. *Signs: An Introduction to Semiotics.* Toronto: U of Toronto P.

Sebeok, Thomas A., and Jean Umiker-Sebeok. 1983. '"You Know My Method": A Juxtaposition of Charles S. Peirce and Sherlock Holmes.' In Eco and Sebeok, eds, *The Sign of Three*, 11–54.

Shcheglov, Yuri, and Alexander Zholkovski. 1987. *Poetics of Expressiveness: A Theory and Applications*. Amsterdam: John Benjamins.

Shklovsky, Victor. 1990. 'Sherlock Holmes and the Mystery Story.' Trans. B. Sher. In Shklovsky's *Theory of Prose*. Elmwood Park, Ill.: Dalkey Archive Press, 101–16. Originally pub. 1929.

Skura, Meredith Anne. 1981. *The Literary Use of the Psychoanalytic Process*. New Haven: Yale UP.

Slotkin, Richard. 1988. 'The Hard-Boiled Detective Story: From the Open Range to the Mean Streets.' In Rader and Zettler, eds, *The Sleuth and the Scholar*, 91–100.

Smith, Johanna. 1989. 'Raymond Chandler and the Business of Literature.' *Texas Studies in Language and Literature* 31.4: 592–610.

Sollers, Werner, ed., 1993. *The Return of Thematic Criticism*. Cambridge, Mass.: Harvard UP.

Spanos, William. 1972. 'The Detective and the Boundary: Some Notes on the Postmodern Literary Imagination.' *Boundary* 2 1.1: 147–68.

Speir, Jerry. 1981. *Raymond Chandler*. New York: Ungar.

Spence, Donald P. 1987. 'Narrative Recursion.' In Shlomith Rimmon-Kenan, ed., *Discourse in Psychoanalysis and Literature*. London: Methuen.

Steele, Timothy. 1981–2. 'The Structure of the Detective Story: Classical or Modern?' *Modern Fiction Studies* 27.4: 555–70.

Stowe, William. 1983. 'From Semiotics to Hermeneutics: Modes of Detection in Doyle and Chandler.' In Most and Stowe, eds, *The Poetics of Murder*, 366–83.

Sweeney, S.E. 1990. 'Locked Rooms: Detective Fiction, Narrative Theory, and Self-Reflexivity.' In Walker and Frazer, eds, *The Cunning Craft*, 1–14.

Tani, Stefano. 1984. *The Doomed Detective: The Contribution of the Detective Novel to Postmodern American and Italian Fiction*. Carbondale and Edwardsville: Southern Illinois UP.

Todorov, Tzvetan. 1977. 'The Typology of Detective Fiction.' Trans. R. Howard. In Todorov's *The Poetics of Prose*, 42–52. Oxford: Basil Blackwell.

Truzzi, Marcello. 1983. 'Sherlock Holmes: Applied Social Psychologist.' In Eco and Sebeok, eds, *The Sign of Three*, 55–80.

Van Dine, S.S. 1946. 'Twenty Rules for Writing Detective Stories.' *The American Magazine* (Sept. 1928). Reprinted in Haycraft, ed., *The Art of the Mystery Story*, 189–93. (Page reference are to the reprint edition.)

Wagoner, Mary S. 1986. *Agatha Christie*. Boston: Twayne.

Wald, Gayle F. 1990. 'Strong Poison: Love and the Novelistic in Dorothy Sayers.' In Walker and Frazer, eds, *The Cunning Craft*, 98–108.

Walker, Ronald G., and June M. Frazer, eds., 1990. *The Cunning Craft: Original Essays on Detective Fiction and Literary Theory.* Macomb: Western Illinois UP.

Wilson, Edmund. 1988. 'Who Cares Who Killed Roger Ackroyd?' In his *Classics and Commercials: A Literary Chronicle of the Forties*, 257–65. New York: Vintage 1950. Reprinted in Winks, ed., *Detective Fiction*, 35–40. (Page references are to the reprint edition.)

Wimmers, Inge Crosman. 1988. 'Thématique et poétique de la lecture romanesque.' *Communications* 47: *Variations sur le thème*, 63–78.

Wingate, Nancy. 1979. 'Getting Away with Murder: An Analysis.' *Journal of Popular Culture* 12.4: 581–603.

Winks, Robin W., ed. 1988. *Detective Fiction: A Collection of Critical Essays.* Rev. ed. Woodstock: Foul Play Press.

Woods, Robin. 1990. '"His Appearance Is against Him": The Emergence of the Detective.' In Walker and Frazer, eds, *The Cunning Craft*, 15–24.

Wrong, E.M. 1946. 'Crime and Detection.' In his *Crime and Detection*. London: Oxford UP 1926. Reprinted in Haycraft, ed., *The Art of the Mystery Story: A Collection of Critical Essays*, 18–32. (Page references are to the reprint edition.)

Zholkovski, Alexander. 1984. *Themes and Texts: Toward a Poetics of Expressiveness.* Ithaca: Cornell UP.

Žižek, Slavoj. 1991. *Looking Awry: An Introduction to Jacques Lacan through Popular Culture.* Cambridge, Mass.: MIT.

– 1992. *Enjoy Your Symptom! Jacques Lacan in Hollywood and Out.* London: Routledge.

– 1996. *The Indivisible Remainder: An Essay on Schelling and Related Matters.* London: Verso.

Index